DATE DUE

Decision Support and Idea Processing Systems

Lawrence F. Young
University of Cincinnati

wcb
Wm. C. Brown Publishers
Dubuque, Iowa

To my wife, Diane, who, more than anyone,
enlarged my view of what is possible . . . and to
the dividends: Greg, Lisa, Jamie, . . . Adi and
Rone, . . . and. . . .

Cover design by Ben Neff

Copyright © 1989 by Wm. C. Brown Publishers. All rights reserved

Library of Congress Catalog Card Number: 87–72309

ISBN 0–697–00742–01

No part of this publication may be reproduced, stored in a retrieval
system, or transmitted, in any form or by any means, electronic,
mechanical, photocopying, recording, or otherwise, without the prior
written permission of the publisher.

Printed in the United States of America by Wm. C. Brown Publishers
2460 Kerper Boulevard, Dubuque, IA 52001

10 9 8 7 6 5 4 3 2 1

Contents

Preface

This text has three main purposes: (1) to summarize main stream concepts and practices that have come to be called Decision Support Systems (DSS), (2) to enlarge upon DSS by describing the foundations, concepts, and early practices of a newer form of computer support system called Idea Processing, intended to aid qualitative thinking and the development of ideas, and (3) to provide a basis for the unification of these two types of computer support systems. Another purpose of this text is to present the basic foundations of knowledge-based (expert) systems sufficiently to clarify their differences and similarities to both varieties of support systems, to present the growing role of knowledge-based systems as enhancements to support systems, and to put into perspective their potential benefits as well as their limitations.

The main task of unifying the more traditional forms of DSS and the newer modes of idea processing support may be somewhat akin to attempting to bridge what C. P. Snow called the "Two Culture Gap" (between scientists and nonscientists). But in this context the gap is between those who have renounced what they consider to be fuzzy-minded, undisciplined, soft thinking, and have pledged their full allegiance to mathematical and analytical methods; and those who abjure what they characterize as bloodless, spiritless logical analysis and have instead adhered to creative, intuitive, and freewheeling verbal modes of innovating and elaborating upon ideas. It is an underlying premise of this text that computer-based support in organizations can, should, and in fact is beginning to, encompass both mathematical-analytical and intuitive-qualitative decision process approaches, and to span the gap between them.

This text is intended for several audiences. A primary use should be as a text in an introductory graduate course in Decision Support Systems given within an MBA program, especially for those with a concentration in Management Information Systems (MIS). I have used most of the material presented in such a course given many times over the last several years. Students in this type of course should have a general business education background at an undergraduate level, and a minimum "technical" education which includes an introductory course in computer programming and in the fundamentals of Management Information Systems. In this kind of DSS course it is generally most effective to supplement text readings, lectures, and discussions with "hands on" projects which require either or both the on paper design of a DSS (or idea processing) interface and the actual use of DSS/idea processing software to develop particular applications. For a software package usage type of student project, it will usually be necessary to refer to a specific software instruction manual to supplement this text. The text attempts to concentrate throughout on generic support capabilities rather than on specific "how-to-use" mechanics, and it is therefore software independent. However, its use in understanding concepts and general functional capabilities should facilitate learning the specific protocols of a particular software language.

Similarly, the text is appropriate for use in an undergraduate course or special topics/independent study in Decision Support Systems for advanced (third or fourth year) students with the requisite educational background stated previously.

Secondary audiences and uses may include the following:

1. General business practitioners engaged in management or in staff support of managers, including MIS personnel; Information Center supporting staffs; DSS development, education, and consulting groups; and knowledge engineering groups. All of these may find useful guidelines for the implementation and management of support systems as well as an introduction to knowledge-based systems and their use in the context of support systems.

2. Computer Sciences or Information Studies students may find useful material on the design and use of interactive user-controlled systems, and on the relation of knowledge-based systems to support systems. The text could be used as a main or supplementary text in courses outside a business school under the aegis of these academic departments.

3. Instructors in cognitive psychology or sociology courses dealing with the interacting effects of human-computer systems on human behavior, creative capabilities, problem solving strategies, and the representation of human knowledge, may find this to be a suitable supplementary text.

4. Software developers and researchers interested in expanding the repertoire of computer tools and in understanding and enhancing the effectiveness of such tools in the support of human decision processes should also find useful material in this text.

5. The intellectually curious independent reader who is technologically literate and open-minded enough to allow that not all computer-related applications are inherently antihuman may find material of interest.

Although intended to be read as a whole by its primary audience, the structure of the text facilitates a selective or "weighted concentration" reading strategy. Chapter 1 is a general introduction to computer support system concepts. It is followed by part 1, chapters 2 through 7, which comprise the basics of DSS, exclusive of idea processing support. Chapter 3 in part 1 covers basic topics on models, modeling, and model processing not usually found in other DSS texts. For those already familiar with these topics from studies or experience in operations research, this chapter may be skipped or rapidly reviewed without harm to the continuity of the text. For those who will be going through chapter 3 (a longer than average chapter) in its entirety, it may be convenient to cover it in two separate parts, with the first part covering the main topics from the beginning of the chapter through *The Importance of Modeling to DSS* and *Types of Models,* and the second part covering the remainder of the chapter starting with the topic of *The Major Modes of Model Processing.*

Those with no immediate interest in idea processing can concentrate on the traditional analytical aspects of support found in part 1 (although it is hoped that they will venture into parts 2 and 3 for at least a cursory reading). Part 2 concerns idea processing support for qualitative thinking, and consists of chapters 8, 9, and 10. Part 3 (chapters 11, 12, and 13) addresses common issues in both types of support, such as their relation to and use of the knowledge-based (expert) systems approach, economic justification, potential misuse, and ultimate integration into a common support system environment.

The exhibits found throughout the text are intended to illustrate general concepts while the examples are aimed at illustrating how these concepts are applied. Exhibits and examples are placed within the text adjacent to the related topics being discussed rather than at the end of chapters or in an appendix. This positioning is intended to more clearly indicate which topics relate to the exhibits and examples. Wherever a longer example appears, the reader may wish to skip over it on first reading in order not to break the continuity of the text, and to subsequently return to it for a more careful reading.

I wish to thank those who reviewed the text and made many helpful suggestions. These include: Willard Laird, Montgomery College–Takoma, University of Maryland; James R. King, Jr., Baylor University; Ronald Kizior, Loyola University of Chicago; Jacques Ajenstat, University of Quebec at Montreal; Paul H. Cheney, University of Georgia; Jane Fedorowicz, Boston University; Steve Kimbrough, University of Pennsylvania; and Cary Hughes, North Texas State University.

Appreciation is extended to the graduate MBA students at Drexel University who took my class in Decision Support Systems (C613) and thereby helped in the development and debugging of the material in this text. Of these, particular thanks is due to Kathleen Tague, who researched and wrote an excellent paper relating DSS to expert systems which was useful in developing some of the material on expert systems found in chapter 11.

Thanks are also due to all the organizers and members of the Working Group on Decision Support Systems (WG 8.3) of the International Federation for Information Processing (IFIP) for serving as a sounding board for some of the ideas in this text on idea processing, for providing me with the intellectual stimulation of their own ideas, and for the good conversation and collegiality they provided in several meetings at various locations around the world. I wish to especially cite my fellow task group members: John Hawgood, PA Computers and Telecommunications, London; Cyril Brookes, University of New South Wales, Australia; Michel Klein, Centre HEC-ISA, France; Ron Lee, University of Texas, USA; Leif Methlie, Norges Handelshogskole, Norway; Oleg Larichev, Institute for Systems Studies, USSR; and Anna Vari, State Office for Technical Development, Hungary; from all of whom I learned much and drew encouragement to complete this project.

I also gratefully acknowledge the support of my recent past institution, Drexel University, and to my colleagues there.

Lawrence F. Young,
Director of Information Systems Programs
College of Business Administration
University of Cincinnati
Cincinnati, Ohio

Introduction: Computer Systems as Mind Levers

True wisdom lies in grasping the tool one needs.[1]
Arthur C. Clark, The Frank Nelson Doubleday Lectures, 1972–73, in
Technology and the Frontiers of Knowledge. New York: Double & Company,
Inc.

Decision Support and Idea Processing Systems: Levers for the Human Mind

The types of computer programs that have come to be called *decision support systems* (*DSS*) were only a few years ago considered to be avant-garde. They are now fairly well established and widely used in many organizations. Such systems provide the means for interactive, user-controlled, human-computer dialogues to help decision makers cope with semistructured (somewhat fuzzy) decision processes. An illustrative segment of a user-system dialogue within one type of DSS application is given in example 1.1.

The two fundamental hallmarks of the DSS approach are:

1. *Support* rather than replacement (automation) of human cognitive processes.
2. An attempt to *follow* and *facilitate* the natural human process rather than to force-fit it into a designer's notion of the best process.

The foundation premise of DSS is that proper implementation of these two thematic principles in semi-structured decision processes will, in time, result in an increase (improvement, not optimization) in *effectiveness* in reaching ultimate objectives rather than mere processing *efficiency*. We will discuss at greater length later in this and subsequent chapters the problem characteristics, application, development and implications of DSS.

EXAMPLE 1.1
AN ILLUSTRATION OF A DSS DIALOGUE

Note: In the following illustrated dialogue between a human decision maker and a computer, the *italicized* text indicates the decision maker's internal thoughts while the CAPITALIZED plain text represents the decision maker's actual keyboard entries that are input to the computer. The computer output responses are shown in **boldface**.

I know the main aspects of the situation I'm now concerned with, but I'm not sure about my goals or all the relevant effects. I'll start by stating major definitions and my judgments.

REVENUE = MY UNIT SALES * MY UNIT PRICE
MY UNIT SALES = 20,000,000 + (MY MARKETING BUDGET * SALES UNITS GAINED PER MARKETING $ SPENT) + PRICE EFFECT
PROFIT = REVENUE − COSTS
COSTS = MY MARKETING BUDGET + OTHER COSTS
MARKET SHARE = [MY UNIT SALES/(COMPETITORS UNIT SALES + MY UNIT SALES] * 100.
PERCENT PROFIT = (PROFIT/REVENUE) * 100.

Now let me think, what is the effect of my raising or lowering our unit price? Suppose I estimate it to be. . . .

PRICE EFFECT = −2,000,000 * (MY UNIT PRICE − $1.00)

Now I'll estimate. . . .

COMPETITORS UNIT SALES = 500,000,000
OTHER COSTS = $60,000,000

Now suppose I try out what happens if. . . .

MY MARKETING BUDGET = $20,000,000
MY UNIT PRICE = $4.00
SALES UNITS GAINED PER MARKETING $ SPENT = 1.4

Now let's see what the computer calculates the results to be.

REVENUE = $168,000,000
MY UNIT SALES = 42,000,000
PROFIT = $88,000,000
COSTS = $80,000,000
MARKET SHARE = 7.75%
PERCENT PROFIT RETURN ON REVENUE = 52.4%

Not bad at all! Now let's see what happens to my market share and percent profit if the effectiveness of our marketing effort drops drastically so that. . . .

SALES UNITS GAINED PER MARKETING $ SPENT = 0.3
MARKET SHARE = ?
PERCENT PROFIT RETURN ON REVENUE = ?

MARKET SHARE = 3.85%
PERCENT PROFIT RETURN ON REVENUE = 0%

We only break even then. OK, what happens if we charge $2.00 per unit instead of $4.00. Keeping everything else equal, what does my marketing effectiveness ratio have to be then in order to break even?

MY UNIT PRICE = $2.00
TARGET FOR PERCENT PROFIT RETURN ON REVENUE = 0%
SALES UNITS GAINED PER MARKETING $ SPENT = ?

SALES UNITS GAINED PER MARKETING $ SPENT = 1.1

(Note: This conversation could continue as long as the decision maker wishes to try out additional assumptions and decisions and assess the outcomes of interest.)

More recent developments indicate an emerging new form of supporting decision makers in ways that significantly differ from the approaches that have been labeled DSS. Called *idea processing* (*IP*), these emerging new computer systems and research efforts also are concerned with providing interactive aid in semi-structured processes. But unlike DSS, idea processing systems deal with verbally described ideas and unformatted text information as the building blocks of conceptual models. A brief illustration of a dialogue segment of one kind of idea processing application is given in example 1.2.

DSS utilizes mathematical model "what if" types of analysis, numerical data base manipulation, and quantitative or spacial graphic representations. Idea processing, in contrast, is concerned with the support of qualitative *word model* analysis, manipulation and idea development.

We will further contrast DSS and idea processing and discuss the nature and applications of IP in greater detail in part 2 of this book.

DSS and idea processing are two sides of the same coin. They are united in terms of common technical features such as interactive, user-controlled processing by means of a nonprocedural "user friendly" conversational language and other facilitative interface design features. But more importantly, these specific common design features are based on the same two fundamental principles: (1) support rather than replacement, and (2) following a natural human process. DSS and IP are both means to *leverage* the human mind in coping with fuzzy, or semistructured problems. (The exact meaning of semistructured in this context will be discussed in the latter part of this chapter.)

As illustrated in examples 1.1 and 1.2 and noted above, DSS deals largely with numerical data while idea processing deals with text as data. Furthermore, the nature of both the computer processing steps and the human thought processes involved are different in DSS and idea processing applications. Their commonality as mind levers stems from their use of support-facilitative design features in contrast to automation, whether automation implies machine executed calculation and simple rule-driven data processing or more complex forms of artificial intelligence (AI). The distinctions between support and automation will be discussed in greater detail later in this chapter.

There is another connection (perhaps a literal connection) between DSS and idea processing. After sufficient experience in coping with complex semistructured verbal models and learning about relationships between elements of the problem, insights are often gained. These insights sometimes evolve into a reformulation of the initially qualitative problem into a semistructured mathematical model and analytical process. There is therefore a potential logical linkage and transference between the applications of idea processing and DSS. Ultimately, there may also be an operational computer software linkage in the form of new support systems that will aid in converting verbal descriptive models into mathematical models. The integration of analytical forms of DSS and idea processing is discussed in chapter 13. This potential integration

EXAMPLE 1.2
AN ILLUSTRATED IDEA PROCESSING DIALOGUE

Note: The following user-computer dialogue utilizes type styles as in example 1.1 and also italicizes the user input words or phrases that are standard commands or control entries to this illustrative outline processing type of support system.

I just read about more small businesses using microcomputers. It must be very confusing for them to get started and select systems. There may be an opportunity there for a new approach. I'll keep a record as my ideas develop.

*SMALL BUSINESS CONFUSED ABOUT COMPUTERS

*HIGH COST OF CONSULTANTS

*BIGGEST MISTAKE: THEY BUY HARDWARE FIRST, THEN SOFTWARE

*BASIC NEEDS DEPEND ON FEW PARAMETERS

*CONTRADICTION TO BE RESOLVED: LOW COST-PROFITABLE, COMPETENT CONSULTING

Now maybe I can organize these thoughts a bit. Which are the major points? Which are subtopics?

MAJOR KEY WORDS
SMALL BUSINESS AND COMPUTERS
CONSULTING

OUTLINE

(Note: Prior entries which do not contain any of the key words just entered will be considered to be subtopics. Subtopics are placed under major topics if they contain common word stems, otherwise they are placed arbitrarily under the first major topic.)

*SMALL BUSINESS CONFUSED ABOUT COMPUTERS

    **BIGGEST MISTAKE: THEY BUY HARDWARE FIRST, THEN SOFTWARE

    **BASIC NEEDS DEPEND ON FEW PARAMETERS

*CONTRADICTION TO BE RESOLVED: LOW COST-PROFITABLE, COMPETENT CONSULTING

    **HIGH COST OF CONSULTANTS

Let's see, I think the point about basic needs belongs under the last major category.

(Note: User selects this entry and moves it by means of a computer pointing device called a mouse. The mouse enables the user to highlight the selected entry and to indicate the new desired entry point for the line.)

---

is another reason for unifying the discussion of these two forms of mind leveraging, with DSS comprising the quantitative side of the coin and IP the qualitative side.

These two forms of support may also be related to different general mental approaches that have been associated with the two hemispheres of the human brain. Much remains to be discovered about the brain, and the current physiological description of left versus right brain functioning may turn out to be incorrect or incomplete. But there is a useful distinction that can be made between the analytical, specific, and linear approaches that have been associated with the left side of the brain and the less prescriptive, more holistic, and intuitive functions associated with the right brain hemisphere (Restak 1979).

*SMALL BUSINESS CONFUSED ABOUT COMPUTERS

    **BIGGEST MISTAKE: THEY BUY HARDWARE FIRST, THEN SOFTWARE

*CONTRADICTION TO BE RESOLVED: LOW COST-PROFITABLE, COMPETENT CONSULTING

    **HIGH COST OF CONSULTANTS

    **BASIC NEEDS DEPEND ON FEW PARAMETERS

Now I see a few points need to be added.

    *THE NEED TO ANALYZE REQUIREMENTS
    *THE COMMON BASIC APPLICATIONS
    *THE KEY-LEVERAGING EXPERTISE
    *USING THE COMPUTER TO SELECT COMPUTER SYSTEMS

(Note: User indicates via the mouse where these points should be inserted. The computer automatically reformats and displays the complete new outline.)

*SMALL BUSINESS CONFUSED ABOUT COMPUTERS

    **BIGGEST MISTAKE: THEY BUY HARDWARE FIRST, THEN SOFTWARE

    **THE NEED TO ANALYZE REQUIREMENTS

    **THE COMMON BASIC APPLICATIONS

*CONTRADICTION TO BE RESOLVED: LOW COST-PROFITABLE, COMPETENT CONSULTING

    **HIGH COST OF CONSULTANTS

    **THE KEY = LEVERAGING EXPERTISE

    **BASIC NEEDS DEPEND ON FEW PARAMETERS

    **USING THE COMPUTER TO SELECT COMPUTER SYSTEMS

I think I remember a document I have stored about small business needs. I'll try to retrieve it and start filling in the text here.

<u>RETRIEVE SMALL BUSINESS NEEDS; INSERT</u>

(Note: The system retrieves the document and inserts it under "**THE COMMON BASIC APPLICATIOINS" as indicated by the user's mouse selection of that point. The user may go on to enter new text under other topics, modify prior entries, and reorganize the developing document by merely relocating the headings. Any text associated with headings automatically is relocated.)

The computer can be characterized, at least in its physical functioning as well as in its applications to date, as being essentially a "left-brained" step-by-step literal-minded device used to support people who generally follow left-brained modes of thinking and analysis. DSS, its goal to support unstructured (or semistructured) decision making notwithstanding, has still been an essentially left-brained approach in that it mainly aids the linear, prescriptive, analytically normative approaches to model building and information acquisition (Robey and Taggart 1982). Some forms of idea processing may provide a greater potential for providing support to those who think in right-brained, less specific ways and have hitherto been left out as potential computer users. As modes of support move closer to the right-brained forms of holistic and metaphorical thinking associated with human creativity, vast new potential for the computer as an effective mind lever may emerge (Young 1983).

With the definition and advancement of DSS in the 1970s and the addition of idea processing in the 1980s, both of which have been and continue to be spurred by the rapid spread of microcomputers and user friendly software, our perception of the computer and its real meaning in our lives and organizations has had to be revised. As we will discuss in the next section, this is not the first such revision nor is it likely to be the last.

The Computer: Changing Images and Realities

The post–World War II initial human-computer encounter can be likened to meeting an extraterrestial celebrity in the middle of its welcoming cocktail party reception. Excited ripples spread through the crowd from the first few contacts. Accuracy in reporting first impressions deteriorates rapidly with distance from the source. Even at the center of contact the immediate image corresponds only roughly with reality. Indeed, the real nature of the creature is not yet manifest in the circumstances of this first encounter.

Within one human generation since its arrival, most of us have had some contact with the computer and its three generations of offspring. However, those who are technologically untrained are still encumbered with entirely unreal images of the computer. Others, with only a little knowledge, have extrapolated far beyond their direct experience.

As has been noted elsewhere,* a little knowledge can be dangerous and technological illiteracy often leads to either phobia or blind reverence of technology. The computer has stimulated both extreme reactions of fear and adulation.

But careful, level-headed professional observers, sticking only to the "facts," have also been unable to keep *understanding* on a par with the changing character of computer technology and application.

Understanding where computers could lead us and how to manage and control the journey requires more than being in possession of the facts. As new uses of the computer are unveiled, new ways to explain its true nature to ourselves are needed.

Often, new dimensions in the human-computer relationship could best be characterized by metaphors. Earlier metaphors of *brain, super clerk, idiot savant,* and *monitor* have more recently been joined by *expert* and *mind lever.*

Hellman (1976) notes that a common fear is that technology will bring surveillance and manipulation to the point of perfection . . . and that depersonalization and loss of privacy are both associated with the growing use of the computer. Despite the fact that 1984 did not materialize according to Orwell's vision, these themes cannot and should not merely be attributed to ignorance and are of the deepest concern to many knowledgeable technologists. But, Hellman points out, blind fear of technology is self-defeating and largely caused by psychological projection. We displace our fears of ourselves and fellow human beings onto machines and technology. Understanding technology is prerequisite to controlling its use.

The image of *brain,* however poorly current computers resemble a real human brain, grew out of the initial association (late 1940s and 1950s) of computers with complex mathematical calculations in the physical sciences (such as nuclear physics). Also contributing to this image were publicized early artificial intelligence (AI) "tricks" such as programming a computer to play chess (Shannon 1950, 1956) and, somewhat later, Weizenbaum's ELIZA program, which "conversed" in the style of a psychiatrist (Weizenbaum 1966).

In contrast, the tag of *super clerk* became appropriate when, in the 1950s and 1960s, large businesses began to realize the great potential of computers to replace both manual labor and a variety of specialized data processing machines with this single general purpose device. Stripping off its guise as mild-mannered scientist, the computer revealed its new identity as super clerk. As super clerk, the computer could rapidly and accurately process great volumes of transaction documents* such as payroll checks (the first application, in 1954, for a commercially installed computer) and sales orders without so much as a ten minute coffee break. Its payoff now seemed to be that of a tireless efficiency engine. The computer was capable not only of reducing costs but, more importantly in an era of rapid economic growth, it was able to handle workloads that could not otherwise be completed in time by entire armies of yet unborn, unrecruited clerks.

In the latter 1960s and 1970s, the costs of storing large amounts of computer readable data were seen to be decreasing significantly and the speed of retrieving specific chunks of it directly were, at the same time, increasing. The new image arising from these factors is that of the *idiot savant,* an entity without wit, wisdom, or conscious awareness of its own functioning. Despite its apparent witlessness, it was able to perform amazing feats of recalling exactly the item called for from a repository of previously ingested volumes and associating it with related data records. New applications based on this retrieval capability of computers came to the fore and the "data base system " concept was born (Luke 1975).

As the progression of clerical automation and data storage-retrieval applications became linked to each other in organizational systems, a new image presented itself to managers. The computer could provide the mechanism to *control* organizational processes by monitoring them as it converted the details being processed into categorized summaries of information. Summary control reports, initially seen as a secondary by-product of transaction processing, became the central focus of a new wave of systems development. The concept of management information systems (MIS) came into vogue. Although MIS was then and is now generally defined broadly to encompass using computers to aid managers with information for all forms of decision making related to

---

*Aron (1969) states that "for several years, computer applications were just bigger and better accounting machine applications" and "were essentially all transaction-oriented; that is, they performed the same set of operations on each transaction in the input stream."

both planning and control (Davis1974; Ahituv and Neumann 1986), applications in the 1970s generally focused on control reporting (McCosh and Scott Morton 1978).* The metaphor of *monitor* emphasizes this role of the computer as the main performance feedback agent in an organizational control loop.

In the 1970s and1980s, the new metaphor of *expert* has joined the panoply of images of the computer. Systems have been developed that not only store and retrieve data, but also represent logical relationships in a network of linked statements characterized as a knowledge base. Furthermore, they do not merely retrieve previously stored conclusions. They are programmed with a set of "if-then" (or "if-then maybe") inference rules that can be applied to the knowledge base to *generate* rather than merely retrieve conclusions or assessments (Barr and Feigenbaum 1981).* An early application was medical diagnosis (MYCIN) (Shortliffe 1976). Because the relationships and inference rules were derived from the mental processes and knowledge of one or more specialists in a given field such as expert medical diagnosticians or tax experts, such systems have been called expert systems.

The notion of the computer as *mind lever* is also relatively new and emphasizes some of the salient characteristics of those applications that have come to be called decision support systems (DSS). DSS applications were first identified in the early 1970s as "management decision systems" (Scott Morton 1971) and rapidly spread in the 1980s through new packages and microcomputers. The hallmark of such systems is that they are intended to *interact with* and *enhance* the special mental capabilities of the user, thereby *facilitating* learning, creativity, and the development of decisions rather than merely replacing or simulating an entire human function. This mind lever role of the computer is the subject of this book and represents applications that are growing rapidly under the heading of decision support systems and the emerging extension to DSS called idea processing support.

As disparate as the images of brain, super clerk, idiot savant, monitor and most versions of expert are from one another, they have one dimension in common that distinguishes them from that of the mind lever. The former metaphors all highlight the *automation* of tasks otherwise performed by people. As noted, the contrasting essence of the mind lever is its concentration on *support* instead of *replacement* of key mental processes.

---

*McCosh and Scott Morton (1978) observed that "almost all MIS activity so far has taken place in the 'structured' half of the matrix—specifically, in the operational control area."

*Barr and Feigenbaum (1981) describe expert systems as follows: "Typically, the user interacts with an expert system in a 'consultation dialogue,' just as he would interact with a human who had some type of expertise—explaining his problem, performing suggested tests, and asking questions about proposed solutions. . . . Furthermore, much research in this area of AI has focused on endowing these systems with the ability to *explain* their reasoning, both to make the consultation more acceptable to the user and to help the human expert find errors in the system's reasoning when they occur."

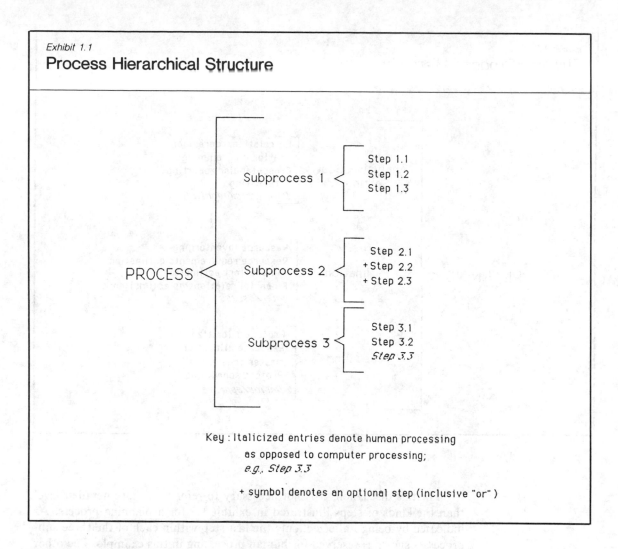

Exhibit 1.1

Process Hierarchical Structure

PROCESS
- Subprocess 1
  - Step 1.1
  - Step 1.2
  - Step 1.3
- Subprocess 2
  - Step 2.1
  - + Step 2.2
  - + Step 2.3
- Subprocess 3
  - Step 3.1
  - Step 3.2
  - *Step 3.3*

Key : Italicized entries denote human processing
as opposed to computer processing;
e.g., Step 3.3

+ symbol denotes an optional step (inclusive "or")

Process Automation Versus Support

To facilitate the discussion of automation and support, it is first necessary to envisage a *process* as consisting of a set of *subprocesses,* which in turn are made up of *steps,* as illustrated in exhibit 1.1. This hierarchical structure can be carried forward so that steps can be broken up into their component parts, and so on, until a functional module can no longer be subdivided into components without losing all functionality. Loss of functionality is manifested by the lack of ability to produce any useful output.

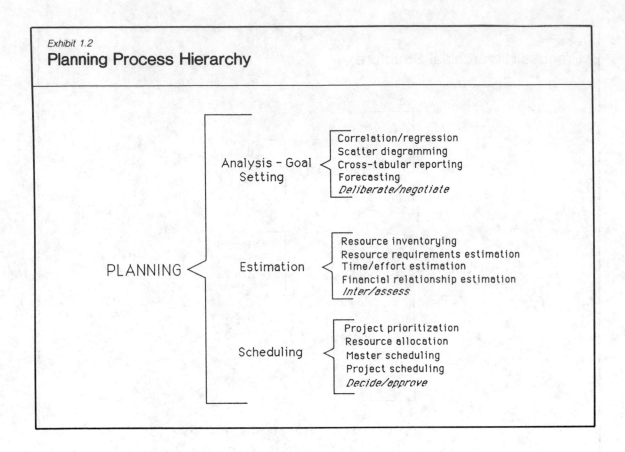

Exhibit 1.2
Planning Process Hierarchy

PLANNING

Analysis – Goal Setting
- Correlation/regression
- Scatter diagramming
- Cross-tabular reporting
- Forecasting
- *Deliberate/negotiate*

Estimation
- Resource inventorying
- Resource requirements estimation
- Time/effort estimation
- Financial relationship estimation
- *Inter/assess*

Scheduling
- Project prioritization
- Resource allocation
- Master scheduling
- Project scheduling
- *Decide/approve*

For this discussion, it is not necessary to refer to a more detailed level than the kinds of steps illustrated in exhibit 1.2 for a planning process. As indicated by being italicized, only the last step within each of the three subprocesses shown is reserved for human processing in this example. The other steps can be carried out by a computer.

The steps in this example represent an entire program or routine which could be further subdivided into software modules. The smallest functional module of a computer program (a function or subroutine) would comprise a more detailed level than that of the steps shown in this example. In the discussion which follows, the terms *process, subprocess,* and *step* will be used as generally described above.

Computer-based automation and support differ significantly from each other in:

1. Concept;
2. The nature of their respective potential payoffs;
3. Their relevant systems development methodologies;
4. The relevant organizational structures, management practices, and required abilities of their staff specialists;
5. Their respective effects on job design and work satisfaction; and
6. Their organizational and cultural effects.

The Automation Concept

In concept, automation is the *conversion* of human processes which produce definable, useful outputs into computer processes. After automation, all steps (other than source data acquisition and assessment and use of information in final decision making) that are needed to transform process inputs into process outputs are carried out by the computer alone.

Total automation includes even the acquisition of input by automatic sensors in the environment in which relevant events occur. Furthermore, in total automation, information outputs also are tied to actuators (robots or other electromechanical devices) which carry out operations dictated by the end product computer information outputs.

In most instances of automation of information processing, human beings remain involved in using computer process outputs through such steps as *inferring* or *deciding* and others shown in exhibit 1.2 in the example of a planning process.

Automation has generally been associated with mechanical, clerical, manual processes. For manual or mechanical processes, the data processing logic and data flow between detailed processing modules (below the level of a *step*) is well understood and can be unambiguously documented. This enables conversion of the logic of processing into a computer program to take place directly as a technically well-defined task.

Complex mental processes such as medical diagnosis and other forms of decision making, in contrast, have not been understood as well . If, however, after research is carried out, a detailed structured process can be defined which does capture human logic—or differs but *produces the same results*—then a computer can be programmed to automate that process.

Artificial intelligence research is making gains in this direction. As it does, the automation of more mental processes may become as feasible as the automation of the simpler clerical mental and manual processes.

Thus the term automation can apply to widely diverse processes, as long as the focus is on replacing human processing with computer processing.

The Support Concept

Computer-based support need not document in advance the step by step processing required because it does not have to create computer programs to carry out each step of the complete process in order to provide benefits. Major portions of the process (not limited to supplying inputs) can continue to be carried out by a human being because:

1. These process steps are insufficiently understood,
2. Because human processing offers certain explicit advantages, or
3. Simply because the user prefers to do them.

A support system automates *something,* but only selected generic steps within a larger process. Overall control of the process and often the execution of major steps required to complete the process are left to the human being. Process control exercised by the user can include some or all of the following:

1. Deciding *during processing* on the inclusion or exclusion of particular automated steps within a process.
2. Determining the overall strategy of processing for the *current processing* occasion by:
   a) Following one sequence of steps or another (subprocess branching control),
   b) Causing the repetition of a subprocess (major iteration control).
3. Setting and resetting (*during* the overall process) of subprocess or step parameters which determine the nature of the function and its outputs.

A key distinction between support and automation is the timing of human control and the allocation of human control between different people. As can be seen in the previous descriptions of user control, emphasis in support is on *live* control decisions made interactively during the process.

In automation, human control decisions are made by the program designer prior to the beginning of processing. (A partial exception may be the setting of parameters such as the number of records to be processed on a particular occasion. This may be done by a user even in an automated system, but would be carried out at the outset of the entire process for all steps in which parameters are required rather than individually as each step occurs and interim results are presented to the user.)

In contrast, a support process provides for human control *as it is going on* by interspersing user control with the display of results in progress. While a designer must provide the system's capability to *ever* perform particular steps, *on the spot* processing decisions regarding inclusion, sequence, and iteration can be made by the user *interactively.*

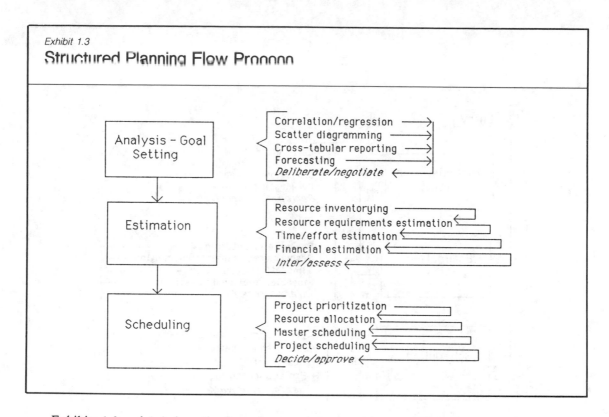

Exhibit 1.3
Structured Planning Flow Prooooo

Analysis – Goal Setting
- Correlation/regression ⟶
- Scatter diagramming ⟶
- Cross-tabular reporting ⟶
- Forecasting ⟶
- *Deliberate/negotiate* ⟵

Estimation
- Resource inventorying
- Resource requirements estimation
- Time/effort estimation
- Financial estimation
- *Inter/assess* ⟵

Scheduling
- Project prioritization
- Resource allocation
- Master scheduling
- Project scheduling
- *Decide/approve* ⟵

Exhibits 1.3 and 1.4 show the flow of processing control in two different versions of the planning process example first presented in exhibit 1.2. In the more structured process shown in exhibit 1.3, the subprocess of analysis–goal setting includes four independently processed computer steps each of which sends its output to the human last step of *deliberate/negotiate*. The estimation subprocess is then carried out by the sequential execution of four computer steps and a final human step in which each step produces output which becomes input to the succeeding step. Upon completion of estimation, the third and last subprocess of scheduling is carried out in sequential steps similar to the preceding subprocess. Control over process flow is predetermined and designed as an automated information process in which the user can only control whether and how the subprocess computer outputs are used.

Exhibit 1.4 shows the planning process in a different, semistructured version. In this case, the user controls the point of entry in the process as well as repetition of entire subprocesses or selected steps as often as desired under varying parameters and initial conditions. In addition, each of the computer steps is optional and could be omitted entirely, at the user's option. This

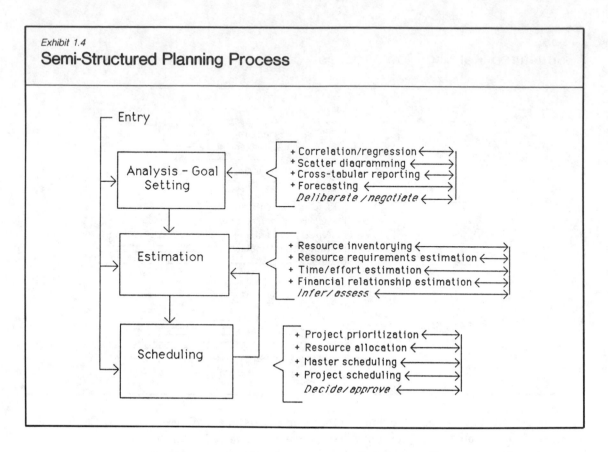

Exhibit 1.4
Semi-Structured Planning Process

Entry

Analysis - Goal Setting
+ Correlation/regression
+ Scatter diagramming
+ Cross-tabular reporting
+ Forecasting
Deliberate / negotiate

Estimation
+ Resource inventorying
+ Resource requirements estimation
+ Time/effort estimation
+ Financial relationship estimation
Infer / assess

Scheduling
+ Project prioritization
+ Resource allocation
+ Master scheduling
+ Project scheduling
Decide / approve

semistructured process flow supports the user with computer execution of the user's bidding. Because the process flow can vary widely from one planning process cycle to the next and the variation is not fixed in the design of a self-controlled computer system, the *process* is not said to be automated even though individual *steps* are executed by a computer.

Motivating Goals Behind Automation vs Support

Automation has as its primary goals any of the following:

1. The attainment of operating efficiencies in the form of reduced processing costs and/or increased output volumes;
2. The reduction or elimination of processing-induced output errors by means of standardized mechanized processing;
3. Enhanced operating reliability by the elimination of human processing delays and nonperformance;
4. The ability to meet *real time* or rigorous timing requirements unattainable by other means;
5. The elimination of human exposure to processing-related hazards.

Support may aim at and provide most of the above goals (1 through 4), but generally only as secondary benefits that can augment more fundamental payoffs of the support approach. These other payoffs stem from the enhancement of individual and organizational learning through more flexible modes of analysis. The ultimate *effectiveness* of management decision making is the expected result of supporting analysis and learning. Efficiency in the performance of standard operations is sufficient to justify automation, but for processes that can benefit from the support approach time and cost efficiencies may merely be utilized to make more thorough analysis affordable.

It can be said that:

1. The benefits of automation are generally gained by improving the *means* with which prescribed, structured work operations are carried out; while
2. Support benefits depend on the *results* of *management* tasks which precede, specify and modify structured work operations.

Support addresses the less structured decision making and analysis activities of managers and specialists who must identify, plan, and direct work operations. Support can only try to enhance rather than replace those tasks that are quintessentially managerial because such tasks are mainly *cognitive* in nature. A cognitive process requires active *awareness* and *judgment* as means of determining the nature of the process itself as it is carried out. Cognition is thus an essential part of any subsystem we designate to be *self-organizing*, that is, a subsystem which autonomously sets goals and determines its own methods for reaching them.

The elements of awareness and judgment are currently only definable to the extent that we can define their meaning as human attributes.*

One can automate *doing;* one can support *thinking*.

As long as a process involves the need or desire to retain human autonomy in organizing and controlling the nature of the processing itself during processing, computer support may be appropriate while automation is not.

If, for example, a manager wishes to have a report produced according to his/her specifications, the process of producing that report can be automated. If, however, a manager wishes or needs to have a staff specialist exercise judgment and professional expertise in selecting and controlling the means of analysis and the presentation of results, then computer support can be applied by the analyst but automation cannot remove the analyst from the picture.

---

*Whether or not future computer technology will be capable of self-aware, cognitive processes involving judgment is a matter of speculation. The meaning of these terms and of intelligence in general have been of interest to researchers in artificial intelligence (AI) and are discussed in Douglas Hofstadter's book *Godel, Escher, Bach, an eternal golden braid* (1979), and elsewhere.

In either case, using the term "support" in a more general sense, we can say that the report supports the managerial user regardless of how it was produced. But the *process* which produces the report is a different matter, and is either an automated or supported process depending on the role (or absence of role) for a human interacting with a computer system.

It is important to understand that the distinction between automation and support is not a matter of whether the inputs and outputs of a process are supplied and used by clerks as opposed to managers. We often associate automation with clerical or transactional processing which produces detailed operational documents seldom or never handled by managers. Highly summarized control reports, on the other hand, are produced for the direct use of managers. But as we have seen in the above example, the terms automation and support refer to the nature and extent of human involvement and control of information production processes rather than who is the user of process outputs.

It is thus processing requirements and the state of computer technology that determines for us whether an automation approach can be considered at all.

But subsequent analysis or judgment can be applied to determine whether or not the form of computer processing (either automation or support) is worthwhile or desirable.

Structured Versus Semi-structured Processes

Process Structure

The ability to automate any process, whether it involves decision making, general problem solving methods, numerical calculation, or other forms of data processing, depends on our state of knowledge of the step by step operations needed to carry out the process.

We may not know how to specify the necessary processing steps simply because we as individuals, or all of us collectively, have not yet learned enough to be able to do so. An alternative reason may be that such a specified set of operations is inherently unknowable for some processes that are too chaotic, volatile, random, complex, or otherwise indeterminate. In either case, whether the limitation lies in us or in the process itself, we cannot sufficiently specify operations in order to automate some processes.

The ability to specify a process step by step, as well as identify the number and characteristics of each step's inputs and outputs, is what we mean by *structure*. A process may be described as *unstructured* either because of its inherent nature or because of the state of knowledge of the person dealing with the situation. This can result in ambiguous use of language since it is often not the process itself which is unstructured, but human discernment of process details. If a particular person lacks sufficient knowledge to specify structure, another may be able to do so if that person were consulted. Thus some processes that could be treated as structured will not be, simply because of unawareness of one's lack of knowledge or the unavailability of expert advise.

Few processes (if any), that we can identify at all, are literally unstructured. Total lack of structure would imply that not even one useful subprocess could be specified even though other subprocesses and the master processing logic which linked all subprocesses into a unified process could not be specified. Nearly all identifiable processes therefore fall into the categories of structured and semistructured, although the latter category covers a wide range with respect to how much structure can be specified.*

Until the DSS approach became manifest, most of us tended to think of computer applications as being synonymous with automation. As we have discussed earlier in this chapter, support systems not only do not require automation of all subprocesses, they require that some remain unautomated. Human interactive control and the carrying out of some internal, unspecified, mental steps is a necessary part of those processes we designate to be supported rather than automated.

Support systems are, by definition, applicable to semistructured processes. DSS is concerned with those semistructured processes related to decision making.

Structure in Decision Making

The same characteristics described above as determining the degree of structure for any process apply also to the process of decision making. Examining the nature of a particular decision making process and situation, we can find both structured and semistructured cases. To perform such an examination and assessment we must first have a generic descriptive model of decision making processes and decisions.

A descriptive model of a decision making process was proposed by Simon (1960) and a more static model of an individual decision has been provided by decision theory.

Simon's process model consists of breaking a decision process into three major subprocesses. These consist of:

1. Intelligence: the stage in which the environment is scanned for problems and/or opportunities that will require decisions to be made and implemented.
2. Design: the stage in which possible courses of action which will comprise an alternative strategy are invented or otherwise generated or identified, developed, analyzed, and assessed for feasibility.
3. Choice: the stage in which one of the alternative strategies is selected (decided upon) and subsequently implemented.

*Many early writers on DSS have described it as applying to "unstructured" decision processes. For the definitional reason given above, the author considers this to be imprecise and prefers the adjective "semistructured" as the more accurate designation of supported processes.

EXAMPLE 1.3

A CASE OF A STRUCTURED DECISION MAKING PROCESS

A rule-driven production foreman's problem.

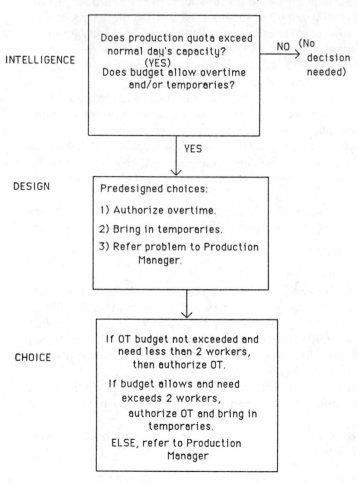

INTELLIGENCE — Does production quota exceed normal day's capacity? (YES) Does budget allow overtime and/or temporaries? — NO → (No decision needed)

YES

DESIGN — Predesigned choices:
1) Authorize overtime.
2) Bring in temporaries.
3) Refer problem to Production Manager.

CHOICE — If OT budget not exceeded and need less than 2 workers, then authorize OT.

If budget allows and need exceeds 2 workers, authorize OT and bring in temporaries.

ELSE, refer to Production Manager

Cases can be found in which each of these stages are highly structured and others in which some or all stages are semistructured.

An example in which all three stages are structured is given in example 1.3 while example 1.4 represents a semistructured decision process.

It should be noted that the choice stage often may be semistructured even when the prior stages of problem identification and design and generation of alternative strategies are highly structured. This situation can be better understood by reference to the decision theory model of a decision situation.

EXAMPLE 1.4

A CASE OF A SEMISTRUCTURED DECISION MAKING PROCESS

A motion picture producer's problem.

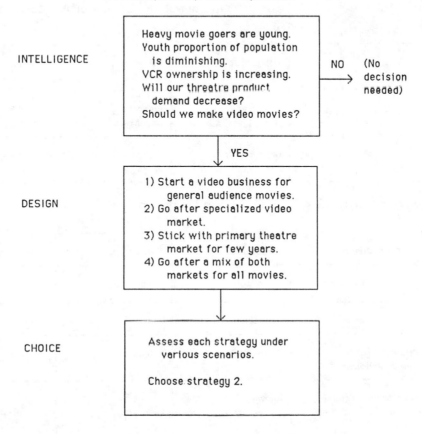

INTELLIGENCE

Heavy movie goers are young.
Youth proportion of population
  is diminishing.
VCR ownership is increasing.
Will our threatre product
  demand decrease?
Should we make video movies?

NO → (No decision needed)

YES

DESIGN

1) Start a video business for
     general audience movies.
2) Go after specialized video
     market.
3) Stick with primary theatre
     market for few years.
4) Go after a mix of both
     markets for all movies.

CHOICE

Assess each strategy under
    various scenarios.

Choose strategy 2.

Decision theory envisions any decision problem as consisting of the elements of:

1. Alternative strategies, defined as courses of action or a particular combination of "settings" of the variables under the control of the decision maker.
2. A combination of conditions (particular "settings") of the relevant variables which are not controllable by the decision maker (traditionally called "states of nature" although the conditions could be man-made by persons other than the decision maker).

Exhibit 1.5

a) The Decision Theory Model of a Decision Problem

Strategies	"States of Nature" (Uncontrollable Conditions)		
	N_1	N_2	N_3
S_1	outcome$_{1,1}$ payoff$_{1,1}$	outcome$_{1,2}$ payoff$_{1,2}$	outcome$_{1,3}$ payoff$_{1,3}$
S_2	outcome$_{2,1}$ payoff$_{2,1}$	outcome$_{2,2}$ payoff$_{2,2}$	outcome$_{2,3}$ payoff$_{2,3}$
S_3	outcome$_{3,1}$ payoff$_{3,1}$	outcome$_{3,2}$ payoff$_{3,2}$	outcome$_{3,3}$ payoff$_{3,3}$

b) Degree of Structure in a Decision Problem

Components of a decision problem	Structured	Semistructured	Unstructured
Outcomes, payoffs	Identifiable	(some	unknown
Strategies	Definable	known, or	unknown
"States of Nature" (relevant uncontrollable conditions)	Known	estimated;	unknown
Relationships between Strategies, States of Nature and Outcomes, payoffs	Known	some unknown.)	unknown

3. Interactions between each strategy and each state of nature that result in outcomes of importance to the decision maker and which can be measured in some form of payoff units (often money).
4. A criterion or analysis rule by which a decision maker can assess the situation and select a particular strategy.

These decision problem elements are envisioned as forming a matrix as illustrated in exhibit 1.5.

With reference to this model we often find problems that are easily definable in terms of the outcome or payoff of interest to the decision maker, in which the strategies are easily identifiable by a simple generating rule, in which the uncontrollable or given conditions are perfectly known, and in which the payoff can be straightforwardly calculated as a function of each strategy-state of nature combination. Yet even in this kind of situation the selection of a given strategy (Simon's last stage of choice) may not be well structured because of the sheer magnitude of the number of possible strategies. An example of such a problem is the classical traveling salesperson problem, represented in example 1.5.

In such otherwise structured problems, the availability of mathematical processing techniques (algorithms such as the simplex method of linear programming (LP)) may come to our rescue. The effect of such algorithms is that the power of mathematics (mathematical proofs, theorems, and the algorithms deduced from them) enables us to eliminate the explicit assessment of many possible strategies because they cannot possibly be optimal choices. Such algorithms provide structure to the choice stage, if they exist. For the traveling salesperson problem shown in example 1.5, there is no general *optimization* algorithm. But as a practical matter, several versions of another type of structured algorithm called a *heuristic* algorithm have been devised to find a solution to most instances of the traveling salesperson problem.

A heuristic algorithm is a kind of mathematical rule-of-thumb that will not be guaranteed by mathematical proof to find the single optimal strategy, but will nearly always result in a much better outcome than a decision maker would discover through unaided trial and error. Such algorithms usually have similar processing steps to those of optimization algorithms and for that reason we place them both in the same category of structured ways to deal with the choice stage of decision making. That is, both optimization and heuristic algorithms follow sequential steps to generate an initial strategy, then find some way of moving from it to a better strategy, and of then performing a test to determine whether to search further or to stop. The essential difference is that heuristics lack the mathematical authority based on a proof that they must result in an optimal choice. Several heuristic algorithms can and have been programmed for computer execution of a wide variety of applications such as the traveling salesperson problem. Optimization algorithms exist for other structured problems such as the product mix (oil refinery output, minimum cost diet) problem. The simplex optimization algorithm of linear programming (LP) applies to many of these kinds of problems.

Further complications in decision making often arise from the lack of certainty about which set of uncontrolled variables comprising a state of nature will actually be in operation at the time a strategy will be implemented. But analytical methods to deal with uncertainty and risk exist in statistical decision theory to both assign probabilities and to take them into account in strategy choice algorithms. Thus a stochastic (probabilistic) decision model does not necessarily imply that the decision process is lacking in structure.

EXAMPLE 1.5

THE TRAVELING SALESPERSON PROBLEM

A structured situation....
   Only one "state of nature" (the map), outcomes, payoffs
   are known, relationship to strategies known.

But........too many strategies, and no optimization algorithm

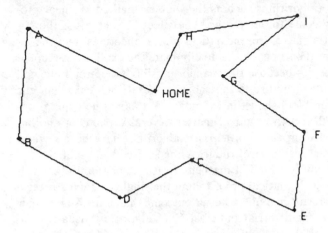

PROBLEM
Start from home base and visit each city once, making
a complete circuit and returning to home base...while
minimizing total travel distance (the outcome) and
total travel cost (the payoff). Assume cost is proportional
to distance.
The number of possible circuits (T) can be computed as:
(consider the same sequence clockwise or
counterclockwise as counting only once, e.g., A-B-C-D
         is the same as D-C-B-A
   T = (N-1) !/2
             where N is the number of cities
   For example:

N	T
10	181,440
20	60, 822,550,204,416,000

The Decision Theory Focus of Operations Research Versus The Decision Process Focus of DSS

It can be observed that the decision theory model (shown in exhibit 1.5) is focused mainly upon the choice stage of Simon's model. It takes as its starting point an already identified decision problem (the result of Simon's intelligence stage) and a list or an automatic means of generating strategies (such a list or strategy generating method is the result of Simon's design stage). This decision theory framework is our major reference for attempting to formulate and solve decisions as structured choice processes. While many analysts have been concerned with all aspects of decision making, the main thrust of the discipline of operations research/management science (OR/MS; the two names generally are used interchangeably) has been modeling systems to be used in the choice stage.

The newer approach of decision support systems has attempted to go further in enhancing the earlier stages (intelligence and design) of the decision process described by Simon when those stages can not be carried out by simple, self-evident, or trivial methods.

In addition to semi-structured aspects of the intelligence and design stages, there are problems in which decision theory (and the optimization or heuristic algorithms derived from it) is insufficient because of gaps in our knowledge and ability to structure the choice stage.

With regard to all three phases of the Simon model, more semistructured decision processes are found at higher organizational levels than at the lowest levels of management. The strategic level (top executive management) should ideally contain *no* structured decision making processes because of the very nature of the strategic mission. Structured processes and problems should normally be delegated downward or automated. They do not require the attention of a top executive *because* they are structured. One primary way to distinguish between the need for higher versus lower level attention is the degree of need for a *self-organizing* approach to coping with a problem.

The tactical (middle) management level probably is involved with many more semi-structured problems than structured ones. The proportions are reversed at the lowest operational level of supervisory management, where managers more often serve to control conformance to preestablished standards and less often have to organize themselves and others to cope with new or unique processes.

Given these distributions and concentration of types of decision processes, it follows that the traditional optimization focus of OR/MS generally finds more applications at lower levels of management while DSS is more often applicable at higher levels.

However, as will be discussed in the next chapter and later chapters, optimization techniques may be suitable for a structured portion of a problem within a wider, semistructured decision process. Also OR/MS knowledge is often needed to guide and facilitate the DSS approach and to prevent its misapplication when more direct methods are available. For all of these reasons, OR/MS is a key source discipline for the effective development and application of DSS.

Relationship between Decision Making and Idea Processing

The notion of processing ideas in an organizational environment can be described as a multiphase process with phases that parallel the decision process described above. Intelligence corresponds to the recognition or awareness of the existence of a notion having some relevance to the thinker or the organization. Design in idea processing is the stage in which the thinker relates the initial notion to other concepts and places it into some logical and pragmatic context. Choice in idea processing is the stage in which the thinker imposes closure by accepting or rejecting the validity of the idea for its utility for achieving some goal or for clarifying a broader knowledge model.

Moreover, ideas and aspects of decisions, problems, and strategies are often different labels for the identical conceptual entity. One can have and develop an idea which is actually a decision problem definition or a strategy. One also makes decisions in the process of developing an idea. The operational difference is usually the difference between the qualitative nature of most idea processing and the quantitative methods associated with at least a class of decision making problems. This difference is not absolute because much policy formation and decision making deals entirely with verbal statements and arguments.

We even have the equivalent of mathematical optimization procedures and arithmetic operations for sufficiently structured aspects of idea processing. These structured idea processing operations are found in certain formalized rules of symbolic logic (such as syllogisms and predicate calculus). Since we can identify structured operations that apply to ideas as well as many instances in which these structured operations can not be seen to explicitly apply, we can apply the same observations regarding the degree of structure in decision making to the area of idea processing. There is need for the support of semistructured aspects of idea processing as well as the potential to automate more structured idea processes through artificial intelligence approaches.

It is probably not a controversial observation, however, that most verbal idea processing in organizations is still informal, semistructured, and unsupported by computer-based systems. It is the thesis of this book that this latter condition is changing and idea processing systems of at least as much variety as the earlier analytical forms of DSS will be developed and will penetrate to a wide number of organizational users and independent individuals.

Review Questions, Exercises, and Discussion Topics

Review Questions

1. What are the main differences in the functions of (*a*) support, and (*b*) automation?
2. What are the similarities and differences between analytical decision support systems and idea processing systems?
3. What actual kinds of computer applications lie behind the image of the computer as a *super clerk?* As a *brain?* As an *idiot savant?* As a *monitor?* As an *expert?* As a *mind lever?*
4. Describe the nature of human control in a computer-based support process and contrast it with the kind of human control that may be found in an automation process?
5. What are the motivating goals for (*a*) automation, and (*b*) support?
6. What is meant by a *cognitive* process? How do managerial tasks involve cognition? How does the cognitive requirement of human tasks relate to the feasibility of (*a*) automation, and (*b*) support?
7. What are the major differences between any process that could properly be called *structured* and an *unstructured* process?
8. Identify and describe the main stages of a decision process as described by Simon.
9. What, according to decision theory, are the main elements of any decision problem? Relate and contrast the decision theory model to Simon's descriptive model.
10. What is an *optimization algorithm* and how does it relate to the decision theory model of a decision problem?
11. Can all structured decision problems be solved with an optimization algorithm? What are the similarities and differences between an *optimization* algorithm and a *heuristic* algorithm?
12. Are all decision problems involving uncertainty necessarily unstructured or semistructured?
13. Where in a typical organizational hierarchy are more semistructured decision processes found? Why?
14. How does idea processing relate to decision processes?

Exercises

1. With respect to Simon's model of a decision process, (*a*) describe a case of structured decision making (as in example 1.3), and (*b*) describe a case of semistructured decision making (as in example 1.4).
2. Identify and assess the potential benefits of automating the process you described in your response to question 1, part (*a*) above. Why might you not automate the process or parts of the process?
3. Which parts of the process you described in response to question 1, part (*b*) could be automated and which might be supported? State why.

Discussion Topics

1. What practical implications does the image of the computer have with respect to:
   (*a*) who enters computer-related careers, (*b*) how organizations use computers, (*c*) public policy and social effects, and (*d*) general and specialized education? Is the image changing now? In what ways and for whom?
2. If automation of cognitive processes ultimately became feasible with advances in artificial intelligence, would the automation of management in a business organization be desirable (in general, for selected jobs)? What benefits and dangers may be involved?
3. Is the concept of using computers in a supporting mind lever role a generally appealing one; does it have any negative associations; to you personally, to others? What kinds of people in what kinds of jobs might find computer support appealing, unappealing?
4. What might be done to enable the average manager to better distinguish between decision processes that can be structured and those that can not? Is this a significant question? Why (or why not)?
5. Discuss the proposition: *Ideas come from some deep well-spring of creativity within the human psyche and computers cannot and should not have anything to do with this inherently mystical human process.*

References

Ahituv, N., Neumann, S. 1986. *Principle of Information Systems for Management.* 2d ed. Dubuque, Ia.: Wm. C. Brown.

Aron, J. D. 1969. "Information Systems in Perspective." *Computing Surveys* (December) 4.

Barr, A., Feigenbaum, E. A. 1981. *The Handbook of Artificial Intelligence.* Los Altos, Calif.: HeurisTech Press and William Kauffmann, Inc. 1:9.

Campbell, J. 1982. *Grammatical Man—Information, Entropy, Language, and Life.* New York: Simon and Schuster.

Davis, G. B. 1974. *Management Information Systems—Conceptual foundations, structure, and development.* New York: McGraw-Hill.

Hellman H 1976 *Technophobia Getting Out of the Technology Trap,* New York: M. Evans & Company.

Hofstadter, D. 1979. *Godel, Escher, Bach, an eternal golden braid.* New York: Basic Books.

Luke, J. 1975. "Data Base Systems: Putting Management Back in the Picture." *CSC Report* 9:1, Computer Sciences Corporation.

McCosh, A. M., Scott Morton, M. S. 1978. *Management Decision Support Systems.* New York: Halsted Press, John Wiley & Sons.

Restak, R. M. 1979. *The Brain, The Last Frontier.* New York: Doubleday and Company.

Robey, D., Taggart, W. 1982. "Human Information Processing in Information and Decision Support Systems." *MIS Quarterly* 6 (June) 2:61–73.

Scott Morton, M. S. 1971. *Management Decision Systems: Computer Based Support for Decision Making.* Division of Research, Harvard University, Cambridge, Mass.

Shannon, C. E. 1950. Programming a Computer for Playing Chess", *Philosophical Magazine* 41 (Series 7):256–75.

———. 1956. "A Chess-Playing Machine." in *The World of Mathematics.* Edited by J. R. Newman. New York: Simon and Schuster. 4:2124–33.

Simon, H. A. 1960. *The New Science of Management.* New York: Harper and Row.

Shortliffe, E. H. 1976. *Computer-based Medical Consultations: MYCIN.* New York: North-Holland.

Weizenbaum, J. 1966. "ELIZA—A Computer Program for the Study of Natural Language Communication between Man and Machine." *CACM* 9:36–45.

Young, L. F. 1983. "Computer Support for Creative Decision-Making: Right-Brained DSS." in *Processes and Tools for Decision Support.* Edited by H. G. Sol, New York: North-Holland Publishing Company. 47–64, ©IFIP.

Decision Support System Basics

Part 1

DSS Components, Development, Software
Selection, and Management

Functional Components of a Decision Support System

2

Things being thus ordered, he would defer the execution of his designs no longer, being spurred on the more vehemently by the want which he esteemed his delays wrought in the world, according to the wrongs that he resolved to right, the harms he meant to redress, the excesses he would amend, the abuses that he would better, and the debts he would satisfy.
Chapter II, *Don Quixote of the Mancha.* by Miguel de Cervantes, translated by T. Shelton, New York: P. F. Collier & Son Corporation, 1937.

This chapter will describe the major generic functions of both packaged software and customized programs which are most commonly used as DSS application tools. DSS software tools are found in current practice both with separate, stand-alone capabilities as well as in the form of more-or-less integrated packages. The advantages and limitations of independent and variously integrated types of software will be discussed. The discussion will attempt to be descriptive in broad strokes sufficient to serve as a preliminary introduction for those unfamiliar with DSS software and its range of application. While it is clear that there is no substitute for actual usage to become familiar with the capabilities of any software, a prior briefing on what the software *enables you to do* (rather than precisely *how it is used*), should help as an orientation for first-time users. This focus on generic functionality for DSS applications will thus omit details of the multitude of specific language features of the wide variety of software vendors' offerings. Operational details such as these can best be obtained from vendors' manuals or other more specialized publications (See *DSS–85, A Guide to Products and Services*).

In summary then, this chapter will expand upon the conceptual foundations (initial definitions, concepts and brief descriptions) of DSS given in chapter 1, in order to answer two fundamental questions:

1. What can one currently do with DSS software tools?
2. To what extent can DSS functional components be tied together with each other and with other information system components?

This chapter will answer the first question more thoroughly and establish a foundation for further discussion in later chapters on the *integration* issue contained in the second question. In dealing with DSS software, we will also focus mainly on generic packages rather than user designed and custom-programmed specific DSS applications. While at an earlier time few such packages were available and most DSS software had to be "homegrown" in third generation programming languages such as FORTRAN, BASIC, and APL, more recent trends are to obtain generalized DSS packages of both microcomputer and mainframe varieties and use these as generators for specific user applications. Issues related to the design and selection of each these (software make and buy) approaches will be discussed further in chapter 6 (DSS Development and Software Selection).

Technical Tools versus Functional Software Components of DSS

Basic *technical tools* of DSS consist of computing equipment such as microcomputers and mainframes; output equipment such as CRT display devices and printers; information media such as graphic displays, audio signals, and printed reports; user input vehicles such as a keyboard, touchscreen, and a handheld "mouse" device to control the selection of items displayed on a CRT screen display; and communications between these components via direct cable connections or telecommunications. These basic technical tools are illustrated in exhibit 2.1. The aspects of these tools that most effect the nature of the communications interface between the support system and the user will be discussed in chapter 4.

The *functional software components* are the computer programs that enable a user to activate and manipulate these otherwise passive tools in order to perform the desired information processing tasks (see Kein and Philippakis 1985). These functional software components can be designed by their developers to vary widely in their functional scope. They can be very general and broad in their functionality or more specific to a limited set of tasks within a single managerial functional area such as finance, marketing, or production. In order to provide a context to aid in understanding the variety and application of this kind of software, this chapter will present an overview of the user-DSS-environment system and describe categories of functional software components that determine the character of the DSS. These modes of categorizing DSS software components include:

1. Two major functional classifications—status access and analysis;
2. Functional subcategories of these two major components;
3. Nonprocedural DSS generators versus programming languages; and
4. Integrated DSS components and linkages to other information systems versus stand-alone software components.

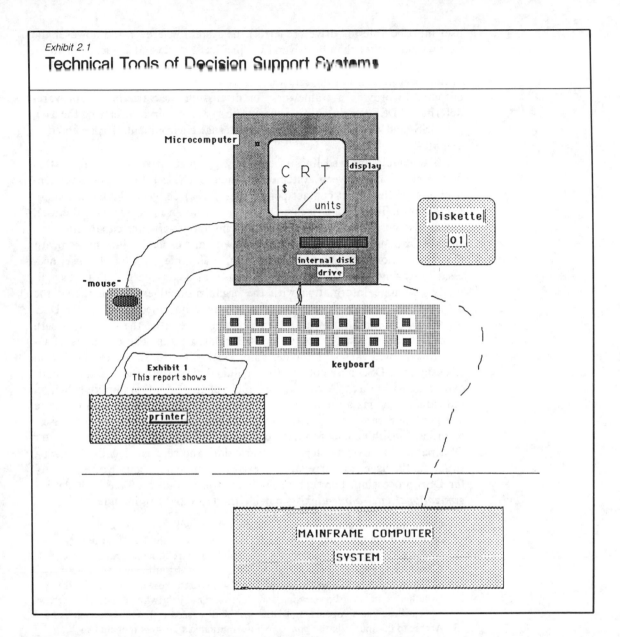

Exhibit 2.1

Technical Tools of Decision Support Systems

The User-DSS-Environment (U-D-E) System

Given the availability of a basic set of technical hardware tools (such as those in exhibit 2.1) which provide a relatively constant technical environment; the character, power, and scope of a DSS can vary widely and is determined mainly by its functional software. While the nonsoftware technical tools can be thought of as the steering mechanisms of a vehicle, the software itself determines where and how the user can drive. It is fundamental to the DSS concept that the user must be able to "drive" (control) the system wherever and however the user wishes, rather than be driven by it in a fixed mode and sequence of steps. But within this broad dictum, the design of DSS software determines the limits of the repertoire, if not the selection, of user-initiated operations and types of outputs. To provide a framework for discussing the varieties of software-determined DSS functionality, a schematic systems overview relating the user, the DSS, and the organizational and external environments is presented in exhibit 2.2.

The double-arrowed lines in exhibit 2.2 represent two-way information flow connections between system components. These information flow connections are the direct contact points (*interfaces*) between the main components shown. The DSS is seen as not only having an interface with the user, but as also possessing the potential (depending on software capabilities and communications linkage) to communicate with and exchange information with the organization and even with the external environment without the user necessarily serving as an intermediary. The user also can and generally does directly exchange information with the organizational environment and the external environment without using the DSS as an intermediary. Thus the DSS is only one potential link with the environmental realities the user copes with in formulating and carrying out decision-related tasks. The character of U-D-E linkage will vary with the design of DSS software. In one extreme form of design, the DSS may not be *directly* linked at all with the organization or external environment. A common example of this situation obtains when an individual user has a microcomputer without any communication linkage to a larger (mainframe) computer, or to mainframe computer accessed data bases, or to local machine encoded data base storage, but has only microcomputer DSS packages and can enter and retrieve data and requests locally. In such a situation, the user or a surrogate serves as the immediate source of input data for DSS processing. For such an individual user, the interface with the *organizational environment* exists outside the DSS and can include:

1. Other organizational members in communication with the user via direct contacts or via communications media not linked with the DSS and not computer-based (such as telephone, manually prepared memos, reports, etc.);
2. Computer-supported communications with other users utilizing electronic mail and/or word processing software which is not integrated with DSS software (whether or not word processing and electronic mail software should themselves be considered as components of DSS will be discussed in the next section); and
3. Access to computer-based *non-DSS* information systems components such as transaction processing and regular summary reporting systems which are also not integrated with DSS software.

An interface can be seen to exist in exhibit 2.2 between the organizational environment and the external world, indicating that information is exchanged directly between them (as well as potentially flowing through the user and the

Exhibit 2.2

The User-DSS-Environment System Overview

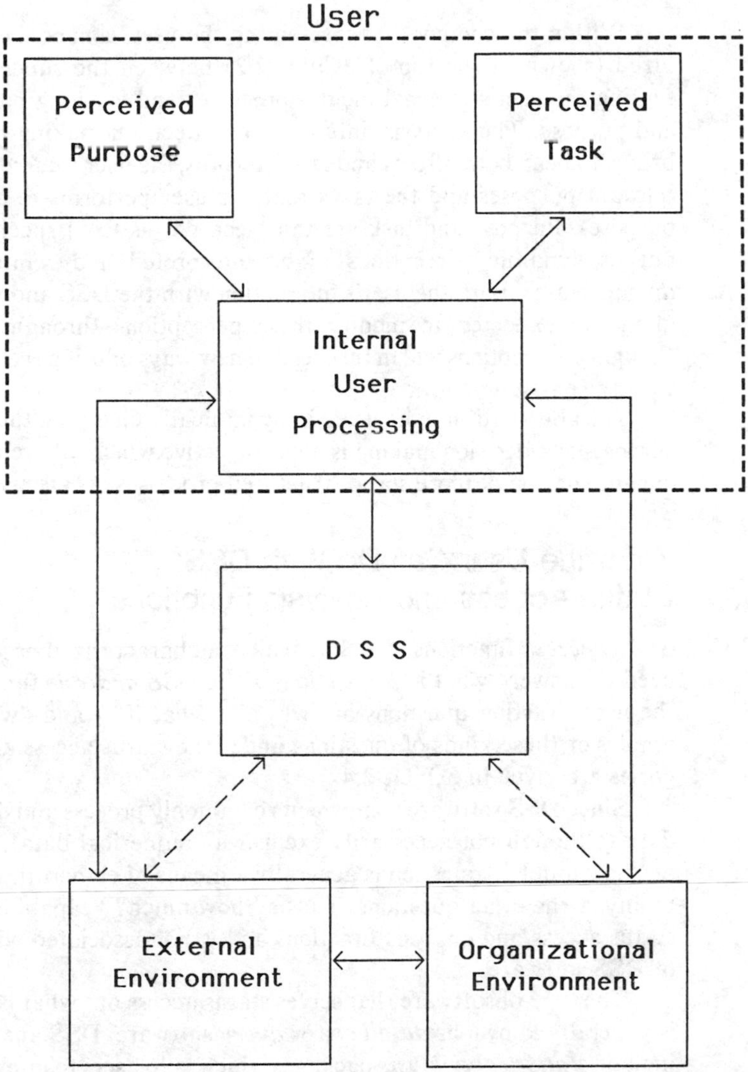

```
                              User
  ┌ ─ ─ ─ ─ ─ ─ ─ ─ ─ ─ ─ ─ ─ ─ ─ ─ ─ ─ ─ ─ ┐
  │  ┌──────────────┐        ┌──────────────┐ │
  │  │  Perceived   │        │  Perceived   │ │
  │  │   Purpose    │        │    Task      │ │
  │  └──────────────┘        └──────────────┘ │
  │           ┌──────────────┐                │
  │           │   Internal   │                │
  │           │     User     │                │
  │           │  Processing  │                │
  │           └──────────────┘                │
  └ ─ ─ ─ ─ ─ ─ ─ ─ ─ ─ ─ ─ ─ ─ ─ ─ ─ ─ ─ ─ ┘
              ┌──────────────┐
              │    D S S     │
              └──────────────┘
  ┌──────────────┐        ┌──────────────┐
  │   External   │        │Organizational│
  │ Environment  │◄──────►│ Environment  │
  └──────────────┘        └──────────────┘
```

DSS). This direct organizational-external environment link can be provided by other formal components of a computer-based information system (such as the transaction-processing and control-reporting MIS components) as well as informal communications. Examples of the types of content of the various intercomponent information flows within the U-D-E system are given in exhibit 2.3.

Within the component representing the user, connections are also recognized (shown at the top of exhibit 2.2) between the subcomponents representing the user's internal mental processes and evolving perceptions of task and purpose. The analysis, inference, and decision-making processing a user brings to bear both affects and is affected by the user's current perceptions of relevant purposes and the tasks that the user performs to accomplish those purposes. Purpose and task are thus seen not as fixed specified assignments but as dynamic perceptions to be interpreted and reinterpreted by the manager-user. Both the user's interaction with the DSS and with the environment are expected to modify these perceptions through learning. These changing perceptions will in turn lead to new ways of using the DSS and dealing with the environment.

The ability to support users in dynamically changing their perspective of purpose-task-decision making is a key objective which differentiates DSS from the automation of more static structured processes, as discussed in chapter 1.

What the User Can Do With DSS: Status Access and Analysis Functions

Status access functions of DSS have been characterized as serving the user's need to answer "what is?" questions while DSS *analysis* functions respond to the user's further questions of "why?," "what if?," and "what's best?" Examples of these kinds of questions under the status access and analysis categories are given in exhibit 2.4.

Since DSS software components commonly process and display numerical data (although not necessarily exclusively numerical data), the quantitative or "how much?" question is generally a means of elaborating on the response to any of the other questions. Thus a "how much?" capability is part of both status access and analysis functions and is not associated with only one kind of DSS software.

The type of software that serves status access or "what is?" user inquiries is generally known as *data base* or *query* software. DSS analysis components include *statistical analysis* packages which help users to infer answers to some "why?" questions by finding associations between different variables. While

Exhibit 2.3
User DSS-Environment Information Flows

From:	To: User	DSS	Organizational Environment	External Environment
User	Inferences	Commands, input data, control Input	Reports, decisions, recommendations, inquiries, responses	Inquiries, promotional info, professional exchanges, purchses
DSS	Retrieved numerical data, computation results, messages, graphics, prompts, completed analysis, instructional guides, memory aids, retrieved text	—	Data base updates, data base requests, completed plans, messages, inquiries, responses to inquiries	Inquiries, responses to inquiries
Organizational Environment	Reports, decisions, inquiries, messages, responses to inquiries, recommendations	Data base updates, data base requests, completed plans, completed analysis, messages, inquiries	—	Promotional/ advertising info, purchasing info, product/ service info requests, legal/tax reports
External Environment	Professional info, inquiries, vendor responses/ promotion/ advertising	External data base responses, input for strategic data bases on markets/ competitors, messages	Marketing research, economic data/ analysis, product info requests, buying info	—

Exhibit 2.4
Examples of Status Access and Analysis Questions

Status Access Questions

What Is

- the total amount of our dollar sales last year to the Acme company?
- our current inventory of finished assemblies of our Model A at our Chicago warehouse?
- the number of employees we have with over fifteen years of service?
- what is the average amount of our spring unit sales to all industrial customers in the Northeast over the last five years?

Analysis Questions

What If

- we lower our price by 10 percent and increase advertising by 20 percent, . . . how much will we sell? . . . at what profit?
- we buy out the Acme Supply Company for a 2 to 1 exchange of stock, . . . what will be the effect on the new company's earnings per share? . . . on cash flow?

Why

- are our sales declining for our lower price lines, . . . is there a relationship to demographic family size trends? . . . to competitive advertising expenditures? . . . to metropolitan area employment rates?
- do young men prefer our brand of beer, . . . to what extent does preference depend on heartiness?. . . lightness?. . . on dryness?

What's best

- between entering the market with our new product now or under the conditions expected next year?
- between investing in company X versus company Y?

it is true that statistical analysis can only assess the degree of statistical association between variables and not actual causality, it enables the user to make logical inferences upon a better analytical basis. An important subcategory of DSS analysis software is modeling packages which support the user primarily in exploring "what if?" questions and to a lesser extent "what's best?" questions. Modeling software includes the microcomputer software known as *spreadsheet packages* as well as mainframe software generally known as *modeling languages.* (Models and the support of user modeling is discussed at length in chapter 3 and the variations of microcomputer versus mainframe software is discussed in chapter 5.)

Graphics packages are another type of functional software which mainly deal with the mode of presentation of information derived from either status access or analysis functions. Like numerical data, graphics such as bar charts, pie charts, scatter diagrams, or trend lines are essentially vehicles for representing "how much?" patterns of information. Graphics software components can therefore be categorized as primarily serving the DSS-user interface function as well as to enhance communication of results to others rather than as DSS status access or analysis functional components per se.

Some may consider word processing and electronic mail software to be components of DSS. Others prefer to classify electronic mail as *communications support,* rather than DSS, and word processing as a form of *office automation* and not DSS. It is our position that the *manner* in which software is used in each instance is the key determinant of whether or not an application should or should not be considered to be a DSS. Using the criterion of whether usage is essentially support or automation as discussed in chapter 1, within limits, a given software package can be considered to be (like technical tools) a passive tool that can take on a meaningful characterization only in the context of its application in each particular set of circumstances. However, although the manner of usage of these software packages is controlled by the user, some kinds of software are generally designed for, and more often used as decision support tools. Thus while there is no hard boundary between DSS software and communications or automation software, there are at least fuzzy boundaries and software tools can generally be placed in relative positions with regard to those boundaries. Exhibit 2.5 attempts to place the various types of software mentioned above in conceptually relative positions with respect to their design and usage as functional tools for decision support versus automation and communication.

Case Example of the Status Access DSS Function

The following case illustrates the main capabilities of a typical DSS status access component.

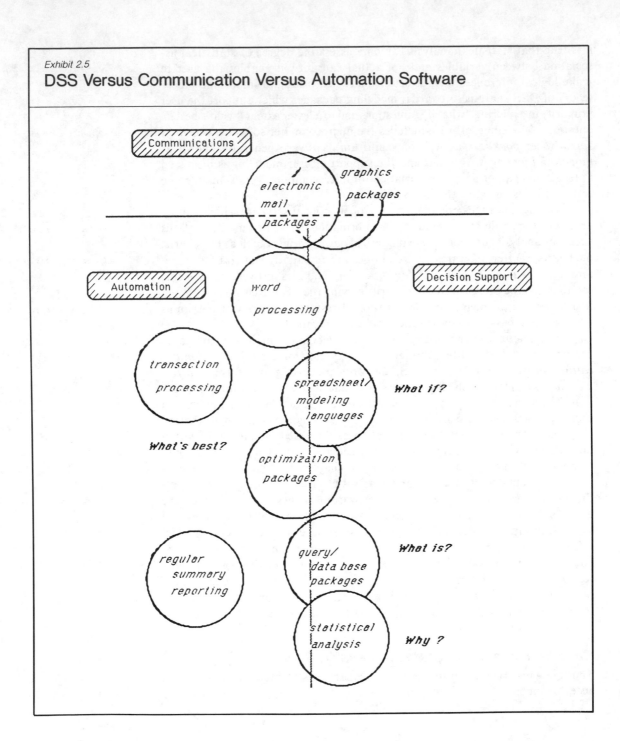

Exhibit 2.5

DSS Versus Communication Versus Automation Software

Communications

electronic
mail
packages

graphics
packages

Automation

word
processing

Decision Support

transaction
processing

spreadsheet/
modeling
languages

What if?

What's best?

optimization
packages

regular
summary
reporting

query/
data base
packages

What is?

statistical
analysis

Why ?

EXAMPLE 2.1

WHAT IS GOING ON OUT THERE?

Problem Background:
The DRD Technology Group, Inc.*

(*"The DRD Technology Group, Inc" is a fictitious composite of real firms.)

The DRD Technology Group, Inc, is a large multi-divisional decentralized corporation. The company had a wide variety of information systems of all types running both within each division as well as regular periodic corporate consolidated financial reporting systems produced by a central information systems department. The central information systems department also maintained many general packages for the use of anyone in the company through terminals connected to a time-sharing mainframe computer. Recently a corporate staff group was organized and charged with doing a strategic analysis for the corporation as a whole and supporting strategic planning for all divisions. The group performed a number of technological assessments and long term trend analyses in various areas of advanced electronic equipment and chemical technology, mainly utilizing secondary sources and special reports of consulting services. The group then found itself called upon by top management to reexamine the entire business from nontraditional points of view. It became important to examine the position of the company with respect to all its product offerings on the basis of markets that cut across established organizational lines. In attempting to meet these requests, the group found the existing computer-based information systems to be inadequate.

The Strategic Data Base System

An information systems/management science analyst worked with the strategic corporate staff group to determine their needs for a computer-based DSS. It was agreed that a new data base was required in order to enable the corporation to flexibly analyze product-market segments and to enable the corporation to determine their position in markets that were not necessarily congruent with existing divisional structures.

For example, a current planning question required the corporation to assess their position and profit potential in health care markets. Nearly all of the company's divisions marketed products to various segments of the health care market but no regular sales or financial reporting systems were structured in a manner that made it possible to automatically aggregate activities and performance of the corporation as a whole in health care. It was felt that a newly designed data base could be constructed for the health care market and it could serve as a prototype for a more extensive strategic data base system to cover a wider variety of product-market segments that may become of interest to the corporation. The data base would be accessible through a "user friendly" query package running on the mainframe time-sharing system that the staff planning specialists could use without spending more than a few hours of initial learning time. The query package claimed to enable the users to request any type of report that could be generated from the contents of the data base by typing inquiries in "natural language," that is, in normal English without having to adhere to a special vocabulary of command words and format rules. The data base itself would contain both information that could be captured from existing systems as well as new information from external sources to fill current gaps in reliably and consistently measuring competitive sales and market trends. The purpose of the new data base system would not be to produce additional standard regular reports, but to enable the staff users to perform ad hoc examinations of what was happening in the health care market as a basis for entertaining alternative business strategies and determine the need for developing more detailed analyses.

The general kinds of questions the staff analysts initially wanted to pursue included:

1. How financially important is health care to us as a corporation?

2. To which segments of the health care market do we sell?

3. How much do we sell in each market segment?

EXAMPLE 2.1 continued

4. Who are the chief competitors in each market segment?

5. What is our share (as a corporation) in each market segment?

6. What changes are occurring in these market segments?

The Health Care Strategic Data Base

According to the needs described in the previous section, the data base was designed and built around the entity of a *product-market segment,* which was defined as the combination of a particular kind of product (such as medical recording film) and a particular market segment (such as hospitals). The data base accommodated a number of product-market segments and contained a number of characteristics of each product-market segment. These characteristics, including the specific identity of each product and each market segment, comprised the data elements that made up the data base. A *data dictionary* was developed to convey the contents of the data base. It was structured as follows:

Health Care Data Dictionary

Entity: Product-Market Segment
Data Elements for this entity:

PRODUCT-MARKET: A compound element consisting of the name of the product and the name of the market segment

PRODUCT NAME: The alphabetic generic name of the product

MARKET NAME: The alphabetic name of the market segment

OUR PRODUCT: A compound element consisting of identity of the identity of our division selling this product and its sales in physical units and dollars

DIVISION: The name of our division producing this product

CURRENTEARNINGS: The current dollar earnings (in $000) of this product in this market segment

LASTEARNINGS: Last year's dollar earnings(in $000) of this product in this segment

SALES: A compound data element consisting of the items below

    CURRENTUNITSALES: The quantity of our sales to this segment in physical units for the most recent year

    LASTUNITSALES: The quantity of our sales to this segment in physical units for the previous year

    CURRENT$SALES: The dollar value of our sales to this segment for the most recent year

    LAST$SALES: The dollar value of our sales to this segment for the previous year

MARKET SIZE: A compound element consisting of items below

    POPULATION: The number of potential customers (buying units) for this product (from all suppliers) in this segment

    PENETRATION: The number of buying units currently purchasing to any extent from any supplier expressed as a percentage of population

    CONCENTRATION: The percentage of buying units currently purchasing to any extent from any supplier which accounts for 50 percent of all sales dollar values in this segment

    CURRENT VALUE: The current year's dollar value of all sales of this product in this segment

    CURRENT UNITS: The current year's number of units sold of this product in this segment

COMPETITORS: A compound element consisting of the items below

    LARGEST THREE COMPETITORS: A compound element consisting of the items below

NAMES (Note: Competitors need not be in order of their size)

NAME1: The alphabetic name of one of the 3 largest competitors

NAME2: The name of another of the 3 largest competitors

NAME3: The name of another of the 3 largest competitors

SALES: (Note: All competitor's sales data reflects product sales only in the particular market segment identified by the market name above)

CURRENT UNITS1: The current unit sales of the "NAME1" competitor

CURRENT UNITS2: The current unit sales of the "NAME2" competitor

CURRENT UNITS3: The current unit sales of the "NAME3" competitor

CURRENT $FOR1: The current dollar sales of the "NAME1" competitor

CURRENT $FOR2: The current dollar sales of the "NAME2" competitor

CURRENT $FOR3: The current dollar sales of the "NAME3" competitor

LAST UNITS1: Last year's unit sales of the "NAME1" competitor

LAST UNITS2: Last year's unit sales of the "NAME2" competitor

LAST UNITS3: Last year's unit sales of the "NAME3" competitor

LAST $FOR1: Last year's dollar sales of the "NAME1" competitor

LAST $FOR2: Last year's dollar sales of the "NAME2" competitor

LAST $FOR3: Last year's dollar sales of the "NAME3" competitor

OTHER PRODUCT STATUS:

STATUSFOR1: The strength of the strongest other product sold by this competitor in this market segment (eg., "strong," "moderate," "weak," or "none")

STATUSFOR2: The strength of the strongest other product sold by this competitor in this market segment

STATUSFOR3: The strength of the strongest other product sold by this competitor in this market segment

The initial extent of the data base included twenty products and four major market segments. Many, but not all, products were sold in all four market segments so that the number of product-market combinations was somewhat less than eighty (20×4). The four major market segments included:

1. Hospitals
2. Private offices/clinics
3. Blood banks
4. Biomedical research institutions

Products included a variety of medical diagnostic equipment and instruments, imaging films and supplies, pharmaceuticals, and surgical supplies.

Sample Queries

Utilizing the data base described above and the "natural language" software package, a number of initial queries were made and used in an initial assessment of what was happening in health care and the extent of the corporation's stake in this field as a totality and in each of its major segments. The following dialogue illustrates how this capability was used.

Note: In the following dialogue, CAPITALIZED text represents the decision maker's actual keyboard entries that are input to the computer. The computer output responses are shown in **boldface.**

EXAMPLE 2.1 *continued*

THE DRD TECHNOLOGY GROUP, INC.

MARKET SEGMENTS	CURRENT $ MM	SALES %	MARKET SHARE (%)	EARNINGS $ MM	%
1. HOSPITALS	622.0	73.2	15.5	53.1	74.9
2. PRIVATE OFFICES/ CLINICS	170.0	20.0	14.0	14.2	20.0
3. BLOOD BANKS	8.0	0.9	9.0	0.7	1.0
4. BIOMEDICAL RESEARCH	50.0	5.9	40.0	2.9	4.1
ALL	850.0	100.0	21.0	70.9	100.0

WHICH PRODUCTS ARE SOLD AT ALL IN EACH MARKET?

(Note: The phrase ''sold at all'' is interpreted as meaning that sales are greater than zero. In a less natural, less ''intelligent'' system, the user would have to directly make a statement such as
LIST MARKET SEGMENTS BY PRODUCTS WITH OUR$SALES GT 0 . . . in which GT stands for ''greater than.'')

	MARKET SEGMENTS			
OUR PRODUCTS	HOSPITALS	PRIVATE OFFICES/ CLINICS	BLOOD BANKS	BIOMEDICAL RESEARCH
1. MEDICAL X-RAY FILM	X	X	———	———
2. NARCOTIC ANALGESIC	X	X	———	———
3. BLOOD SEPARATOR CENTRIFUGES	X	———	X	X
4. .... etc. through product 20.				

WHAT ARE OUR CURRENT TOTAL DOLLAR SALES IN ALL SEGMENTS OF HEALTH CARE?

(Note: In a more structured command language form, rather than in natural language, this query might appear as follows, with the italicized portion being a reserved command term and the phrase following being a standard name of a data element.

TOTAL OUR PRODUCT CURRENT$SALES

It can be seen that the natural language package must have the capability of interpreting the sentence and extracting the part of it that is equivalent to the command and the part that defines the elements to be processed. These language aspects of a DSS interface will be discussed in chapter 4.)

The response to this simply stated query is a single quantity, but one of great importance and not ever before produced by any regular reporting system.

OUR CURRENT TOTAL DOLLAR SALES IN ALL SEGMENTS OF HEALTH CARE

$850,000,000.

DISPLAY OUR CURRENT TOTAL DOLLAR SALES, MARKET SHARE, AND EARNINGS BY MARKET SEGMENT AND IN TOTAL FOR ALL SEGMENTS. ALSO SHOW SEGMENT DOLLAR SALES AND EARNINGS AS A PERCENT OF THEIR TOTALS.

OUR MARKET SHARE NOT DEFINED OR FOUND IN DATA BASE.

PLEASE DEFINE IT OR REPHRASE OUR MARKET SHARE =

(OUR PRODUCT CURRENT$SALES / MARKET SIZE CURRENT VALUE) * 100

A wide variety of additional queries were made, and indeed are still being made on occasion by planners and analysts. Without displaying responses, these include the following examples:

1. What are our current sales, market share, and earnings in the private office/clinic segment for each product, and what percent of our total sales and earnings does each product account for?

2. Compute percentage gain in sales units for our products in each segment for the last two years and list percentage gain and sales units by product and market segment. ("Percentage gain" would have to have been previously defined or designed into the system's vocabulary or defined at the time of the query in response to the system's prompting.)

3. Which of our products in which market segment gained the largest increase in market share over the last two years? Which lost the most market share?

4. Which of our competitor's products in which market segment gained the largest increase in market share over the last two years? Which lost the most market share?

5. Are there any product-market segments in which our current market share exceeds 5 percent and in which penetration is less than 20 percent? What is our strongest competitor's market share, product status?

It can seen from the user queries given in example 2.1 that the query package used has a number of basic processing capabilities. Basic processing capabilities which are common to most query systems, including some not illustrated explicitly in example 2.1, include the following:

1. The ability to retrieve and display a specific set of data elements for a particular entity in the data base.
2. The ability to list these data elements for all entries in the data base or for a subset that meet one or more selection criteria.
3. The ability to compute and display totals and to calculate percentages.
4. The ability to calculate and display new information that can be defined as an arithmetic function of data elements that exist in the data base.
5. The ability to sort listings into ascending or descending order on one or more data items.
6. The ability to display basic standard statistics that can be derived from items in the data base, such as the arithmetic mean, minimum value, maximum value, and variance.

Graphic Display Functions

The status access function of a DSS may be enhanced by the added communication power of graphics. The answer to a "what is ?" question could be derived from a data base query system such as described in example 2.1 with essentially tabular displays, or the query system may pass its results to a graphics software component which, under user control, could present outputs such as bar charts, trend lines, etc. Some simple examples of graphics output alternatives for some of the displays in example 2.1 are given in example 2.2.

A graphics component could also comprise an output alternative for the results of a "what if ?" mathematical model component. In addition, graphics systems exist as stand-alone software offering a separate capability in which the user directly enters input data to be converted into graphic form.

Communications among a group of stakeholders as well as internal "communication" within a single decision maker or analyst can be a critical factor in evolving a strategy for a semistructured decision problem. In this respect, the improved clarity and interpretability of pictorial graphic outputs may have a more central role than that of a mere alternative medium of presentation of final results. The *language* of graphic communication may be the primary vehicle for analysis and the development of a decision strategy. If this is the case, then graphics communication and analysis becomes a true DSS function rather than only a DSS interface or a convenient means of automating the production of presentation exhibits. As yet, the possibility for the use of graphic *input* of user assumptions about patterns and relationships is little explored.

EXAMPLE 2.2

GRAPHIC QUERY OUTPUTS

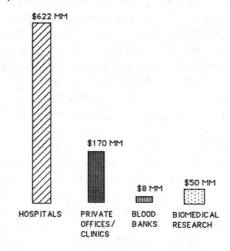

Query : Pie chart our dollar market share in biomedical research.

Response :

40%

Query : Bar chart our current dollar sales by market segment.

Response :

$622 MM

$170 MM

$8 MM $50 MM

HOSPITALS   PRIVATE   BLOOD   BIOMEDICAL
            OFFICES/   BANKS   RESEARCH
            CLINICS

Using a light-pen, mouse, or touch screen device, nonmathematician users could draw or point to a picture of a relationship rather than enter a set of numbers or specify an equation. Graphic information may then comprise a two-way vehicle for the user-DSS interface.

On the other hand, graphic outputs should not be considered superior in all cases to numerical or alphanumerical tabular displays (DeSanctis 1984; Miller 1969). Each form has its advantages. Numerical outputs are generally preferable when the user needs to make a limited number of quantitative comparisons between information elements or variables (such as comparing this year's outcomes to last year's, or actual to planned outcomes, or our results to those of our main competitor). Graphics are generally most effective when it is useful for the user(s) to scan an entire pattern which represents many variables. The relationship between interactive graphics and the problem of visual pattern recognition has been explored by Chien (1978). Chien states:

". . . the increasing use of intelligent terminals has led me to believe that interactive graphics will become a significant tool in both pattern recognition and practical applications" (preface, 1978). . . . "It is particularly useful when one is faced with a large data base of which analytical and statistical characteristics must be calculated dynamically and in real time. In the event of minimum prior knowledge regarding the data base, man-machine interplay via some graphical medium often becomes a necessity." (p. 2, 1978)

Analysis Functions: "Why?" and "What If?"
—Exploring "Why?"

In the context of example 2.1, examining *what* is happening using the status access capability of a data base query system might well lead the user into formulating some notions about *why* these things are happening. The information provided by responses to queries, when combined with knowledge the user has acquired through other sources, may be considered by an experienced user to provide a sufficient basis for making inferences on what underlying causes are at work. These inferences can then provide the basis for user decisions. In some cases, however, a manager or a staff analyst serving a manager may want to apply a more formal statistical analytical approach to testing or exploring for underlying relationships. An interactive statistical analysis capability enhances the ease with which such analyses can be carried out. Also, even when formal analytical rigor may not be needed or desired, statistical methods can often play a useful supporting role. Statistical methods can do this by combining the "what is" retrieval capability of a query system with the power of statistical methods to search out and highlight significant associations to the user. It is often possible to substitute a few statistical analyses for a great many more exploratory data base queries.

For example, a user may want to know if his company's proportion of product sales in general (for all products in all market segments) are related to a number of different factors. These may include market population, market penetration, market concentration of sales, and the sales of the largest competitor. The user could make unique queries, respectively asking to display sales against each of these factors, thus making four queries and getting four tabular responses. As an alternative, a single request could be made for a multiple regression in which the company's relative sales is the dependent variable and the other four factors are independent variables. In other more complex cases with more extensive data bases, hundreds of exploratory queries could be avoided by a more efficient statistical analysis strategy. In the current example, the single regression run would be made against the (up to) eighty "observations" or cases provided by twenty products in each of the four market segments in which they are sold. Given the availability of interactive statistical software (such as the interactive SPSS package), a user regression run request might be made via a terminal entry such as the following:

(Note: CAPITALIZED entries are made by the user, system prompts are **Boldface.**)

PROCEDURE REGRESSION;

Dependent Variable OUR PRODUCT CURRENT$SALES /MARKET SIZE CURRENT VALUE

Independent Variables MARKET SIZE POPULATION , PENETRATION, CONCENTRATION, LARGEST THREE COMPETITORS SALES CURRENT$FOR1;

RUN ALL STATISTICS.

The "statistics" provided along with the response commonly include significance levels (such as 0.01, 0.05, etc.) which indicate the level of risk that the degree of association found for each independent variable is due only to sampling error and is thus not a reliable or real association. These indicators of significance can aid the knowledgeable user in making inferences based on the results. The query system, in contrast, simply presents data without such indicators of significance. It should further be noted that a commonly used feature of statistical packages is the ability to produce cross-tabular results which are essentially the same in content (although not necessarily in format) as those query system displays which summarize data by one variable within another category, such as sales by product within region. However, the statistical TABLE response will commonly include measures of significance, similar in purpose to those provided with a regression analysis. A cross-tabulation request might appear as follows:

PROCEDURE TABLE;

Row Variable OUR PRODUCT CURRENT$SALES/MARKET SIZE CURRENT VALUE

Column Variable MARKET SIZE POPULATION;

RUN ALL STATISTICS.

While statistical analysis methods and the technical interpretation of statistical outputs are not within the scope of this text, it is relevant to note how statistical results relate to the management concern of inferring "why." For example, it might be found through statistical analysis that our company's relative product sales (market share) are generally positively correlated with the penetration of a market by all products. Such an association, if it is statistically significant, simply states that we tend to have higher market shares for our product in those instances in which higher proportions of potential customers are actually doing some purchasing of anybody's (ours or any of our competitors) product. This statistical association could be interpreted to imply that we are concentrating our competitive selling efforts in the same places our competitors are selling. This might indicate that we (and our competitors) are overlooking other largely untapped market segments. These "why" implications are not presented by the statistical analysis itself in so many words. They are built upon the association highlighted by statistical analysis through the additional knowledge, experience, and reasoning ability of the user-analyst. Of course it may already be clear to the user that these relatively untapped markets are untapped because it is too hard and too costly and unprofitable to attempt to sell more in them. That may have been known in formulating marketing strategy and thus the statistical association found may only indicate that the company is doing what it set out to do. In this case, and in some other cases of apparent statistical association, the association is preordained by policy or other known structural constraints, and does not represent a newly found association that helps to reshape strategy through new insights.

The ease and convenience of use of an interactive statistical analysis capability could enhance the thoroughness and efficiency of learning what is happening and why it is happening *if* this capability is used by a knowledgeable statistical analyst who understands both statistical methods and the business phenomenon to which they are being applied. A managerial user unfamiliar with statistics should seek the help of such an intermediary rather than use this kind of DSS capability directly.

In addition to the use of statistical analysis as a basis for making general inferences leading to managerial decisions, the analysis is often used to make more specific quantitative inferences which combine interest in knowing "how much" along with a concern with "why." For example, a statistical analysis may help to infer not only that our market share tends to increase in higher penetration markets, but that it tends to increase by 1 percent in market share for every 2 percent change in penetration. If such a quantitative relationship is statistically reliable and makes sense to an experienced user, it might serve as the basis for a forecasting or planning model which can serve the user as a "what if?" or "what's best?" tool for further analysis before making any final decisions. In this case, it is important for a user to recognize that a statistical model used for the analysis of past or current associations between variables should not automatically be accepted as a forecasting or causal model that is intended to represent future relationships without critical examination. Rather than statistical findings alone, the user's knowledge or the knowledge of an expert consultant on the phenomenon being managed must provide the main authority for a future related planning model. This caveat should be kept in mind by managers regardless of how technically sophisticated the analysis may be. In this sense, statistical software, like other DSS tools, can only support rather than replace the user's judgment in complex semistructured situations.

Another approach to user support in answering "why?" questions is beginning to be developed through the expert systems approach of building specialized knowledge into the system itself (Blanning 1984; Methlie and Sprague 1985. Such rule-based computer languages as Prolog and Lisp may be used to express the logical reasoning of an expert in order to help a less expert user understand the "why?" of a given situation. Also, some DSS software is now being offered which provides for including such expert-based knowledge within the same system that offers a query and modeling capability. These knowledge-based approaches, however, are not yet highly developed for general management situations. The integration of expertise modules within support systems is discussed further in chapter 11.

"What If?" Analysis Using Modeling Software

A brief example of a "what if?" type of analysis was shown in example 1.1 in chapter 1. In that example, the model consisted of several definitional statements (statements that are true by definition or convention) and two causal relationships (statements linking outcomes to their causes) that could have been derived from the user's experience or from a combination of the user's experience and prior statistical analysis. (The distinction between *definitional* and *causal* and other types of model statements are discussed further in chapter 3.) The definitional statements include such statements as:

    a. PROFIT = REVENUE − COSTS
    b. REVENUE = MY UNIT SALES * MY UNIT PRICE
    c. PERCENT PROFIT = (PROFIT/REVENUE) * 100

The only causal relationships represented in this model are:

    1. MY UNIT SALES = 20,000,000 + (MY MARKETING BUDGET * SALES UNITS GAINED PER MARKETING $ SPENT) + PRICE EFFECT
    2. PRICE EFFECT = 2,000,000 * (MY UNIT PRICE − $1.00)

Other statements in the model simply enable the user to supply values for particular variables, such as MY UNIT PRICE = $4.00.

The "what if?" capability of modeling software refers primarily to the ease with which the user can change any of the values of any of the variables in the model in order to immediately see the effects on other outcomes of interest to the user. For example, in this simple model the user may want to vary the total amount spent on selling, advertising and promotion (MY MARKETING BUDGET), as well as the product's selling price (MY UNIT PRICE), and such parameters as 20,000,000 in statement 1 or 2,000,000 in statement 2. Varying these values and other values as input to the model, the model processing software component immediately recomputes the entire model and enables the user to immediately see the effects on dependent outcomes of interest such as revenue, profit, and market share.

DSS modeling software (Bodily 1985; McLeod 1985; Wagner 1981) provides users with a facility for:

    1. Stating the model relationships without concern as to the sequence of the statements.

2. Processing the model and displaying the calculated results of all or any selected set of variables included in the model.
3. Easily changing any of the values of model variables or the functional relationships themselves in order to test out various conditions the user may wish to explore.

The situations in which this type of DSS "what if" analysis is more appropriate than using other kinds of modeling approaches (such as optimization) with different kinds of software is discussed in chapter 3.

The special nature of the language of DSS modeling software is distinguished from a programming language such as FORTRAN or APL by referring to such DSS software as a *modeling language*. A modeling language is *nonprocedural* (see Leavenworth [1977] on nonprocedural processing in general) in that it enables a model builder to express a model in any order that seems natural and to control the use of the model (initiating processing, varying inputs, modifying the model, selecting outputs and formats for display) without having to express the step by step program processing needed or to adhere to the syntactical rules and statement precedence required to use a procedural programming language such as those mentioned previously. The essential difference is that a modeling language separates the need to express the model itself, the real task of the model builder/user, from expressing the logic needed to process the model, by building this ancillary task into the modeling language software. While this nonprocedurality characteristic is more or less common to all DSS modeling (as well as other types of DSS software), there are many specific differences of language style and specific operations between modeling language software packages. Two main categories of modeling software are:

1. Mainframe modeling languages such as IFPS, System W, and Express.
2. Microcomputer spreadsheet modeling packages such as LOTUS 1–2–3, Multiplan, Context MBA, and Visicalc.

The mainframe type of modeling languages are similar in conversational style to the example discussed above (example 1.1). They utilize equation-like and general action initiating command statements as the vehicle for enabling the user to express a model and control its processing. The spreadsheet packages (LeBlond and Cobb 1983) use a very different kind of framework for expressing a model, that of the two-dimensional spreadsheet with rows referring to different variables, columns referring to different time periods or any other type of user-defined categorization such as different company divisions or geographic regions. A spreadsheet variation of the model discussed above is illustrated in example 2.3. User entries in each cell are either specific data values or functional relationships. This is shown in the portion of example 2.3 labeled MODEL FORMULAS. As each formula and constant data value is

EXAMPLE 2.3
SPREADSHEET VERSION OF EXAMPLE 1.1

MODEL FORMULAS

	1	2	3
1			
2		QUARTER1	QUARTER2
3			
4	REVENUE	=MYUNITSALES*MYUNITPRICE	=MYUNITSALES*MYUNITPRICE
5	MYUNITSALES	=5000000+(MYMARKETINGBUDGET*ADDEDSALESPERMKTDOLLAR)+PRICEEFFE(	=5000000+(MYMARKETINGBUDGI
6	MYUNITPRICE	4	4
7	MYMARKETINGBUDGET	5000000	5000000
8	ADDEDSALESPERMKTDOLLAR	1.4	1.4
9	COSTS	=MYMARKETINGBUDGET+OTHERCOSTS	=MYMARKETINGBUDGET+OTHERC
10	OTHERCOSTS	15000000	15000000
11	PROFIT	=REVENUE-COSTS	=REVENUE-COSTS
12	PERCENTPROFIT	=(PROFIT/REVENUE)*100	=(PROFIT/REVENUE)*100
13	PRICEEFFECT	=-500000*(MYUNITPRICE-1)	=-500000*(MYUNITPRICE-1)
14	COMPETINGSALES	17500000	17500000
15	MARKETSHARE	=(MYUNITSALES/(MYUNITSALES+COMPETINGSALES))*100	=(MYUNITSALES/(MYUNITSALES

	4	5	6
1			
2	QUARTER3	QUARTER4	TOTALYEAR
3			
4	=MYUNITSALES*MYUNITPRICE	=MYUNITSALES*MYUNITPRICE	=SUM(RC[-4]:RC[-1])
5	=5000000+(MYMARKETINGBU	=5000000+(MYMARKETINGBUDGI	=SUM(RC[-4]:RC[-1])
6	4	4	
7	5000000	5000000	=SUM(RC[-4]:RC[-1])
8	1.4	1.4	
9	=MYMARKETINGBUDGET+OTHE	=MYMARKETINGBUDGET+OTHERC	=SUM(RC[-4]:RC[-1])
10	15000000	15000000	=SUM(RC[-4]:RC[-1])
11	=REVENUE-COSTS	=REVENUE-COSTS	=SUM(RC[-4]:RC[-1])
12	=(PROFIT/REVENUE)*100	=(PROFIT/REVENUE)*100	=(PROFIT/REVENUE)*100
13	=-500000*(MYUNITPRICE-1)	=-500000*(MYUNITPRICE-1)	
14	17500000	17500000	=SUM(RC[-4]:RC[-1])
15	=(MYUNITSALES/(MYUNITSAI	=(MYUNITSALES/(MYUNITSALES	=(MYUNITSALES/(MYUNITSALES+COMPETINGSALES))*100

NUMERICAL RESULTS

	1	2	3	4	5	6
1						
2		QUARTER1	QUARTER2	QUARTER3	QUARTER4	TOTALYEAR
3						
4	REVENUE	42,000,000	42,000,000	42,000,000	42,000,000	168,000,000.00
5	MYUNITSALES	10,500,000	10,500,000	10,500,000	10,500,000	42,000,000.00
6	MYUNITPRICE	4	4	4	4	
7	MYMARKETINGBUDGET	5,000,000	5,000,000	5,000,000	5,000,000	20,000,000.00
8	ADDEDSALESPERMKTDOLLAR	1.4	1.4	1.4	1.4	
9	COSTS	20,000,000	20,000,000	20,000,000	20,000,000	80,000,000.00
10	OTHERCOSTS	15,000,000	15,000,000	15,000,000	15,000,000	60,000,000.00
11	PROFIT	22,000,000	22,000,000	22,000,000	22,000,000	88,000,000.00
12	PERCENTPROFIT	52.38	52.38	52.38	52.38	52.38
13	PRICEEFFECT	-1,500,000	-1,500,000	-1,500,000	-1,500,000	
14	COMPETINGSALES	17,500,000	17,500,000	17,500,000	17,500,000	70,000,000.00
15	MARKETSHARE	37.5	37.5	37.5	37.5	37.5

entered into the spreadsheet, all other cells are calculated and recalculated. When all the required data and relationships have been entered, the user can see total results such as those shown in example 2.3 as NUMERICAL RE-SULTS. For subsequent "what if" trial scenarios such as those desired by the user referred to in example 1.1, the spreadsheet is modified as desired and totally recalculated. This could be illustrated as NUMERICAL RESULTS for SECOND TRIAL ESTIMATES and NUMERICAL RESULTS for THIRD TRIAL ESTIMATES in the same manner as example 2.3. The same kind of user analysis and thinking process can thus be supported either by the "command statement" type of dialogue shown in example 1.1, or the comparable use of spreadsheet scenarios illustrated in example 2.3.

Because spreadsheet software and mainframe modeling languages are quite different in their appearance and were developed independently for initially different users (mainframe users versus microcomputer users), at an early stage it was less common to recognize that their functions as DSS modeling software were actually the same in nature if not in the scope and size of their application problems. In recent practice it has become more common for the same user to use these packages in concert with one another by moving data between the two types of modeling software. In such situations, it is usual (but not uniformly necessary) to use the more powerful mainframe languages for larger corporate models and the micro-based spreadsheet modeling software for individual analysis of a more localized nature.

The varying interface characteristics and the main differences between mainframe and microcomputer modeling software will be discussed more fully in chapters 4 and 5.

"What's Best?" Software

To answer "what's best?" questions when this is possible for certain aspects of a larger problem, optimization procedures such as those of linear programming have been incorporated within some mainframe DSS modeling languages (for example, the IFPS system has an optimization add-on called IFPOS). These capabilities seem to be seldom used and are primarily Operations Research tools for structured decisions rather than DSS tools. However, they can be used effectively in conjunction with DSS functions in certain situations. Ways in which such "what's best" decision strategy generating tools can be used in conjunction with the decision testing kind of DSS "what if?" tools are discussed in chapter 3.

DSS Generators, Specific DSS, and Programming Tools

In the early period of DSS application development (1960s and early 1970s), the lack of availability of generic software for either ad hoc query "what is?" functions or modeling and model processing "what if?" functions made it necessary for organizations to write their own programs (or to contract them out) for interactive DSS types of applications. In that era, basic DSS software tools were nearly all application programmers' tools such as FORTRAN and APL programming languages used for processing in an interactive terminal-based time-sharing computing environment. The completed programs, if they were well-designed, enabled a nonprogrammer user to interact directly and easily with the system by providing input data and selecting processing and output options. However, any changes the user required in the model itself or in the processing and output options already built into the computer program, required the user to request such changes through a programmer. The need for both this human "toolsmith" intermediary and the need for modifying computer programs represented a limitation in reaction time to user learning and user-system interaction.

The appearance of generic modeling and query software for both mainframe and microcomputers represented the removal of a major cost, convenience, and flexibility barrier to the initial development and evolutionary modification of DSS applications. The generic mainframe modeling languages were referred to as "DSS generators," since they provided a nonprogramming means of developing a DSS model for a particular application such as creating and analyzing a financial plan, a marketing plan, or a production plan. The modeling language representation of a particular modeling application was referred to as a "specific DSS." The same terminology contrasting a "DSS generator" with a "specific DSS" was not usually applied to the distinction between nonprocedural generic query languages (Leavenworth 1977) and custom programmed multioption report writers, but it would seem to be equally applicable.

Of course, the generic DSS generator, whether in the form of a modeling language or that of a query language, is itself a computer program written in a procedural language such as FORTRAN. But the base procedural language is invisible to the user, while the query or model the user expresses and may modify *is* visible, accessible, and understandable to a nonprogramming user. Thus we can consider three levels of languages, (1) programming languages appropriate for interactive applications, (2) DSS generators, and (3) DSS specific application representations. Each of these play a role in providing DSS capability, but, depending on the existence or absence of DSS generators, different requirements are placed on users and supporting toolsmiths or intermediaries. The varying roles of these different levels of software tools and human agents are illustrated in exhibit 2.6.

It is clear that, on the whole, the advent of nonprocedural user friendly DSS generic software radically lowered, if it didn't entirely remove, a barrier to user learning and user-system interaction. Users could think more directly in terms of how they viewed their problem and the nature of the analysis and output they wanted, without having to specify, either directly or through intermediaries, the detailed computer process needed to produce the desired results. However, while it is true that the ease of use and nonprocedural nature

Exhibit 2.6
Varying Roles of Software Tools and Human Agents

.... Software Tools		.... Human Agents		
Specific DSS Software	*Base Programming Language*	*User*	*Toolsmith*	*Intermediary*

CONDITION (1): No DSS Generator Available

Directly controls and limits user interaction with the system.	Language to specify the specific DSS.	Supplies inputs, selects options provided in the specific DSS.	Writes specific DSS in the base programming language.	Toolsmith also serves to modify specific DSS.

CONDITION (2): A DSS Generator Is Available

Created and modified in DSS generator language.	Used to create the DSS generator.	Can do all as above, Plus can create and modify specific DSS without toolsmith or other intermediary if knows DSS generator language.	Programs, maintains, the DSS generator	Helps only as needed for complex cases.

of most DSS generator packages stand in sharp contrast with third generation programming languages, it is also true that in practice these have been relative, not absolute, improvements. Ease of use varies significantly between different packages purporting to be nonprogrammers' tools. For any given package, ease of use will also vary from person to person, depending on individual differences and backgrounds. For a person with a given set of knowledge, skills, and thinking style, the scope of operational capabilities built into a system is generally inversely related to ease of use. The more powerful the system (the more it can do), the more the user has to learn. However, the ease with which the user can learn these system features and capabilities will strongly depend on whether the user's past experience can be transferred to this situation.

Ease of use depends not only on the degree of learning required to know *how* to cause the system to do something, but also depends on what the user must understand about the meaning of a given operation, function, or mode of analysis. For example, you can learn the expressions or statements necessary to cause the system to carry out a multiple regression analysis, but for effective use you must also already know or learn what such an analysis actually is, and how to interpret and apply the results. If you have never before heard of multiple regression and many other kinds of system capabilities, you cannot know whether or not they will be useful to you until you first acquire some definitions in already familiar terms. In order to make a system easy to learn and use, the boundaries between systems intended to support specialists of different kinds versus systems intended to support management generalists should be taken into account by both system designers and users. This is difficult to accomplish in a manner that will always properly match users to systems, because these boundaries cannot be precisely discerned and they are likely to shift over time.

The nonprocedural nature of DSS packages also varies from one package to another, with some language features still being required to follow rules for usage precedence even though they are largely free of the rigid, pervasive, step by step, logical sequence constraints of programming languages. At one extreme, some packages may be only marginally easier to use without significant training of nonprogramming users and the acquisition of new thinking patterns much like those needed for effective computer programming. At an opposite extreme, some languages are nearly free of syntactical rules and purport to be "natural" in that one can "speak" (actually *type* in most cases) to the computer in much the same way one might address another person. While such *natural languages* would appear to represent the ultimate in ease of use, users often find that "speaking" to a largely literal-minded computer program requires a new kind of communications skill. While the computer system may approach human flexibility regarding syntax, it is still far from possessing human ability for appropriate semantic interpretation in the presence of ambiguity.

Degrees of Integration between DSS Components

The concept of integration of computer applications has been an information resource management concern predating DSS. In traditional computer applications, the question of integration centered on the extent to which the output of one application, such as sales order processing, could be directly used without transformation as input to other applications, such as sales analysis and reporting, and accounts receivable. When different applications were developed independently without first considering the information flows required throughout an entire system, it often became necessary to subsequently add processing steps in order to change record formats, code structures, and other data representation features so that applications could be linked to one another without the intervention of manual data conversion operations. In other cases, lack of a prior systems view of data flow between applications could not be remedied by the interspersion of new file conversion modules. In such cases it was often necessary to rewrite portions of existing programs or to entirely replace programs. Experience taught systems planners about the twin penalties of inefficient processing and redevelopment costs for the failure to initially design integrated systems.

In the end-user computing environments appropriate to DSS, integration includes, but goes beyond the question of data transfer between different modes of processing. In user-controlled DSS processing, the actual sequence of processing steps performed within any given usage session can be expected to vary from one session to another. If, for example, a user has just made a query resulting in the display of numerical data in a tabular format, on one occasion the user may go on to make several new queries and then end the session. On another occasion, the user may make a query, examine the tabular response and then want to see it in graphic form. After seeing the graphic display, the user may have a new idea about a related spreadsheet model and want to change a particular relationship or an assigned input value, see selected model results numerically, and then want to graph these same results. The ease with which the user can procede from step to step depends now on two aspects of integration:

1. How directly and effortlessly data produced or selected within one processing step can be made available to a subsequent processing step.
2. How directly and effortlessly the user can move from one kind of processing (such as modeling or query language processing) into another kind (such as graphics or statistical processing).

An unintegrated set of DSS tools enables the user to work within only one kind of processing at a time, so that moving from, for example, a query package to a spreadsheet package, requires that the user execute the required procedure to end the query session and subsequently initiate the use of the spreadsheet package. This would often require physical procedures such as changing disks, issuing special keyboard commands to end one session and start another, as well as switching one's mental framework from the different language protocols and style of one package to that of another. If there is no compatibility or predesigned integration of the different packages, any output information obtained from the use of one package would have to be manually reentered by the user. This situation of complete lack of integration is schematically shown in the upper portion of exhibit 2.7.

Partially, or quasi-integrated DSS tools could take a number of forms, a common one represented by the lower portion of exhibit 2.7. In this case, the transfer of data from one DSS software component to another can be accomplished without manual reentry of data. A software component is included

Exhibit 2.7

Unintegrated and Quasi-Integrated DSS Components

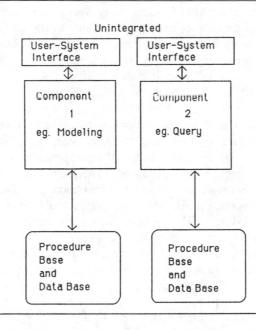

Unintegrated

| User-System Interface | User-System Interface |

Component 1 eg. Modeling

Component 2 eg. Query

Procedure Base and Data Base

Procedure Base and Data Base

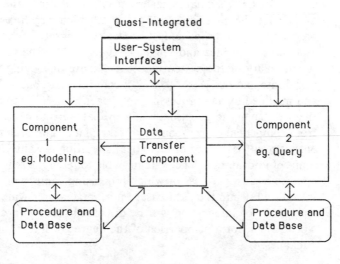

Quasi-Integrated

User-System Interface

Component 1 eg. Modeling

Data Transfer Component

Component 2 eg. Query

Procedure and Data Base

Procedure and Data Base

which handles the transfer of data including any necessary reformatting required. Also, the user need not go through a full sign-off procedure or have to physically remove one software component from accessibility to the computer before initiating and using another. Instead there is a common user-system interface that controls the conversation within each component as well as the termination of one component and initiation of another. While this removes much of the burden from the user it still does not represent complete system integration. As shown in the diagram, each DSS processing component includes, or is linked to its own data base and set of procedures. The internal design of these varies from one component to another so that the user still must initiate specific steps to move from one component to another that break the smooth flow of functional processes that parallel the user's analytical process. Systems such as these have typically been "patched together" by adding a common interface and data transfer component to preexisting, independently designed packages. The style of the user languages therefore vary so that the user still must switch from one mental language framework to another. These factors decrease the degree of integration and user friendliness ideally desired. The ideal system would be one in which the user need think only of the analysis and content of the problem being worked on, and not at all about how to "drive" the system. "Driving" would be natural and automatic, and, in a perfectly integrated system, would not require users to be aware of having to exit from a turnpike and turn onto a dirt road, each of which require different driving skills and practices.

The ideally integrated DSS (one which has probably not yet been entirely achieved by any available generic package) is illustrated in exhibit 2.8.

Unlike the quasi-integrated system which may link two or three or more preexisting DSS components, this ideally integrated system is designed so that a common interface and language style enables the user to control the full functionality of the system without a sense of moving from one processing world into another. Also, there is a common data base which can be accessed and modified by any processing component via the common interface without the user having to go through any special steps to cause the transfer of data from component to component to take place. The user need only state what output result is desired or analytical operation is wanted with respect to what items of information. The system is able to fetch the required information and operate on it regardless of which processing component originally may have introduced it into the data base. Interface features which provide one degree or another of integration will be discussed further in chapter 4. (See Info-world, 1984, for a comparison of the degree of integration between different packages.)

Exhibit 2.8

Integration of DSS Software Components

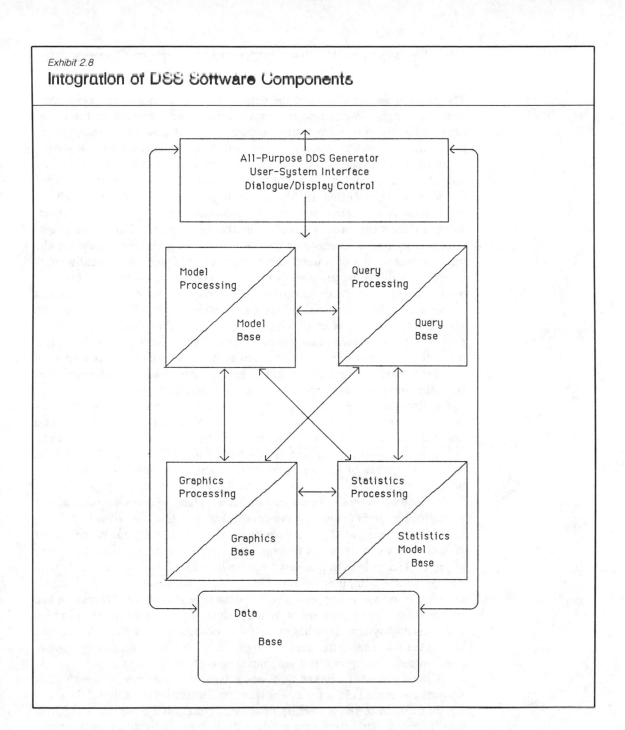

DSS Linkages with Other Information System Components and Organizational Support

The previous section discussed the degree of integration between DSS components. Integration can also be examined from the viewpoint of the entire organizational information system, including the administrative transaction-based reporting applications, repeatedly used Operations Research model-based applications, and special research applications which monitor and report on the external environment. It was mentioned earlier in this chapter (and illustrated in exhibit 2.2) that a DSS may or may not be directly linked with the organizational or external environment and able to exchange data with them. When a DSS is not directly linked with other organizational information systems it cannot gain access to or provide data to these systems except via the manual intervention of a user. Early stages of DSS use are generally characterized by this stand-alone mode of usage. As usage develops, DSS becomes more widespread in the organization, and starts to be formally considered as a basic corporate capability that must be taken into account in the MIS master plan. Users often find it increasingly necessary to gain access to data that is part of corporate information systems (Young 1984). For example, initially a marketing user may enter only a limited amount of his own recent sales data in order to perform an analysis. Later, having learned what can be extracted from that limited data supply, the user wants to make comparative analyses to data from other regions as well as historical trend analyses. This data has already been captured through the sales order processing and reporting system and retained in a mainframe data base. At this point the user will request access to the mainframe system rather than go through the wasteful and time consuming process of reentering data into a microcomputer from printed reports.

In addition to greater needs for data access, planning processes often evolve which require users to analyze and develop plans on their individual DSS that later must be integrated into a departmental or corporate plan. When a mass of such needs and demands become manifest, a communications linkage is added to DSS tools so that microcomputer-based DSS can communicate with the mainframe computer (Major 1984). Most commonly, the initial micro-mainframe linkage is to enable selected data to be *downloaded* (accessed and transmitted) at the users request from a mainframe administrative transaction and reporting system data base into a microcomputer disk file. This is done so that the microcomputer user can apply local DSS tools such as microcomputer spreadsheet, query, and graphics languages to the data.

Ultimately, a fully linked DSS would be able to communicate with other systems components in a variety of ways, as illustrated in exhibit 2.9.

In addition to the capability to select, extract, and download data from corporate or other mainframe resident data bases, individuals working in a DSS mode will be able to communicate with others who are also using DSS

Exhibit 2.9

DSS Linkages to Other Information System Components

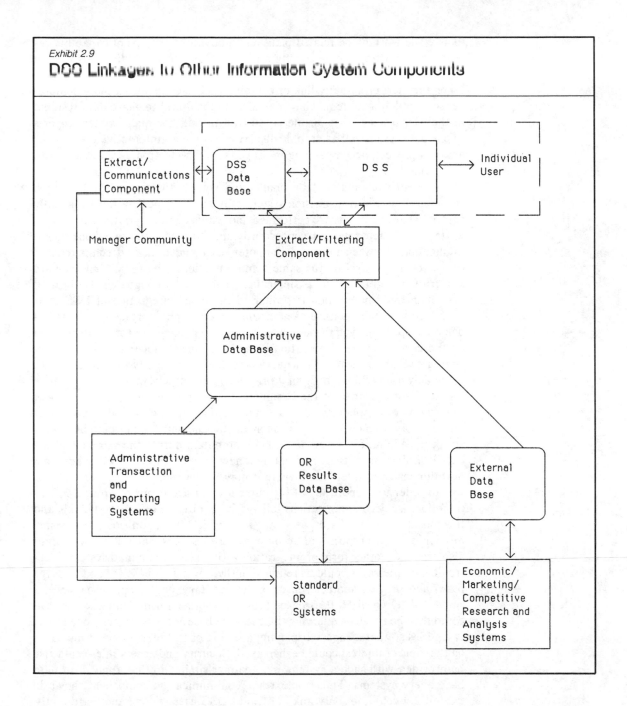

tools while working on related plans and analyses. This type of capability re-positions DSS from being strictly a means of supporting individuals into an *organizational support* tool. A group of users may find it useful to view each other's models or actually link or combine their models into a more compre-hensive modeling system. They may also find it useful to share data residing in their local data bases, or merely to transmit ad hoc query system reports to one another as well as graphic displays. In such an interactive planning or analysis process, accompanying messages sent via electronic mail would also be useful.

Currently, computer data, image, and voice transmission can occur via common lines and transmission systems. But users generally must manually control what operations are performed and which computer outputs are trans-mitted, while separately or concurrently speaking over the telephone. Com-munications between user and computer, user and user, and computer and computer may travel on the same communications "highway," but they are not truly integrated into a single user-controlled dialogue. This form of "common line" integration is similar to the quasi-integration of DSS tools described in the previous section, in which a common interface may exist but one must speak or type through it in different languages and styles depending on the current mode of operation being performed. Voice control of micro-computer DSS systems such as query languages is currently available, but not yet widely used (*Personal Computing* 1984). Ultimately, more comprehensive forms of voice control of the computer system and the complete *functional* integration of telephone voice transmission along with data and image trans-mission may become a reality. In such an environment, users would be able to speak to each other as well as to their computers during the same telephone call in similar ways, thereby creating a new level of immediacy and adding a new dimension to interaction where it may be desired.

In order to support any of the current or future forms of group DSS in-teraction, a telecommunications linkage is required between individuals and their local DSS data bases, as shown in exhibit 2.9. In addition to the trans-mission of DSS outputs and accompanying messages, such a linkage might also provide another form of integration with an electronic mail system. Elec-tronic mail messages could be retained in their own data base (or text message base) and provide another source of commentary, or "soft information," as suggested by Cyril H. P. Brookes (1983). Another form of interactive DSS could then be based on querying this message base according to precoded topic categories so that a report displaying a listing or full text of recent messages on the topic of interest could be displayed. Security and access rules could also be provided with such a system, in a manner similar to that applied for data base query systems. Thus, the extract/communication component shown in exhibit 2.9 could not only link individual DSS users to one another directly, but also link them indirectly through the repository of their stored messages. Such a facility could further enhance communications and accessibility to the common pool of organizational knowledge, adding yet another dimension to decision support. A similar capability may become feasible with the development of new uses of artificial intelligence to analyze and query the contents of unformatted word processing documents and relate these to DSS analyses. Such a capability could change the present word processing aspect of office automation into another dimension of DSS (Blanning 1983).

A third form of feedback that could also be provided by an extract/communications component would link individual DSS data bases to the operations research system. Standard, periodically run OR models may require inputs that are the result of analyses performed by particular managers. These inputs may be estimated with the use of DSS tools and retained in the user's local data base for subsequent extraction and direct transmission into the OR modeling systems that require them. This closes the loop between structured OR models and semistructured DSS analysis, enabling OR outputs to be taken into account by individual DSS users who in turn can add their judgments and other information sources to produce new estimates that are subsequently used by OR models. In addition to data linkages, DSS models may themselves evolve through user learning and ultimately become sufficiently developed and stable so that they can be transferred to the OR model base and accepted as repeatedly useful OR tools.

A similar phenomenon to the potential evolution of semistructured DSS models into structured OR systems has been observed to exist with respect to the ad hoc query aspect of DSS. Users find that they evolve certain queries that they find repeatedly useful to apply on a regular basis. Such queries should then be incorporated into the regular reporting system and produced automatically rather than only upon the user's request. An ability to cause the system to automatically extract such queries from the DSS and transfer them to the mainframe would be a useful addition to a completely integrated DSS-information system.*

Conclusion

This chapter has described the functional components of DSS in order to survey the scope of what users can actually do with DSS software. Because an important aspect of DSS is its ease of use as an end-user capability, *what* can be done is inseparable from *how easily* it can be done. Both the nature of the user-DSS interface and the nature of the integration of these tools determine ease of use and these subjects have also been introduced in this chapter. The leverage DSS provides users over their organizational tasks is also constrained

---

*Because of the faster processing offered by compiled languages, such a transfer may also imply that the query should be translated into a compiled programming language such as COBOL rather that continually interpreted by a query language processor on each processing occasion in order to avoid inefficient use of the mainframe CPU.

by the extent of communications linkages provided between DSS users and between each user and other components of the complete information system. This subject has also been introduced. Subsequent chapters will elaborate on many of the issues introduced here regarding the nature of the user-DSS interface and the differences and relationships between mainframe and microcomputer DSS functions. In addition to query languages, graphics, and statistical DSS capabilities, the important aspect of microcomputer spreadsheet and mainframe modeling languages was introduced in this chapter. DSS modeling can be a controversial subject in that it provides both a potentially powerful capability while also increasing the potential for misuse by inexperienced and inadequately trained users. The next chapter is devoted to the subject of models and end-user modeling. (The potential misuse of modeling and other types of support systems is discussed in chapter 12.)

Review Questions, Exercises, and Discussion Topics

Review Questions

1. If one were to walk into a business office and see a set of hardware on a desktop which includes a microcomputer, a printer, a keyboard, and a "mouse," can one conclude that the person working at that desk has a DSS ? Why, or why not?
2. What is the nature of the relationships between: (*a*) the user's perceptions of task, (*b*) purpose, and (*c*) the decision analysis that is carried out with the support of DSS hardware and software tools? To what extent do these relationships remain stable and unchanging or do they evolve? On what factors do the answers to the prior questions depend?
3. A query or data base software package offers which of the following functions to users?
   a) A "what if?" analysis.
   b) A "what's best?" analysis.
   c) A "what is?" status access function.
4. How does a statistical analysis capability help users to infer answers to "why?" questions? What are the limitations of this kind of tool?
5. How can statistical analysis be used for a similar purpose as a query system? What advantage might the statistical analysis have over the query system in this regard?
6. What is meant by the "how much?" type of question? Which DSS tool(s) can be used, and in what ways, to address this question?
7. What are the three main kinds of functions provided by modeling software?
8. How does the use of a DSS modeling language differ from the use of FORTRAN for creating a DSS modeling application?
9. Do spreadsheet packages and mainframe modeling languages have the same or different purposes? In what way(s) do they differ?
10. How does the use of a "DSS generator" enhance the basic purposes of a DSS capability?

11. How is the ease of use of a DSS software package related to the scope and power of its functionality?

12. What is the difference in training users how to operate a system in a mechanical sense versus how to use it for a meaningful problem analysis? Give an example of each kind of know-how that a user would need.

13. Consider that a perfectly natural language query system was available. How would a dialogue with such a system be similar to a dialogue between a manager and a clerical assistant? In what ways would the manager-query DSS dialogue differ from the manager-assistant dialogue?

14. What are the two main aspects of integration within a multifunction DSS? Which of these is similar to the main focus of integration within traditional information systems?

15. In an early stage DSS, users generally enter their own data and store any data they want to retain on a locally retained storage medium such as a microcomputer floppy or hard disk. Describe what usually occurs in later stages to make this arrangement inadequate.

16. What might be desirable to share between different DSS users? How might such sharing take place? What technical capabilities would be required to support such sharing?

17. Describe how the use (and possibly misuse) of a DSS query system over a period of time might be related to the efficient use of a regular reporting systems component of an MIS.

18. How might a "text message base" derived from an electronic mail system be used in conjunction with other DSS capabilities?

19. How might a systems linkage between a regular operations research model-based system and a DSS modeling capability provide any benefits to both the DSS user and for the OR model-based system?

Exercises

1. Assume you are developing a data base query system to be used on a microcomputer by high school guidance counselors in advising students in selecting a college to attend.
   a) What items should the data base contain?
   b) List several sample queries in *natural language* that might be asked in a typical session.
   c) Give an example of a sensible query in this problem context that the query system could not respond to properly. State why.

2. For the system in the previous question, what kind(s) of regular report needs might become obviously useful after some experience with using the query capability? Describe the contents of such reports and the regular time cycle for processing them?

3. Describe an application of a spreadsheet package which:
   a) is essentially automation of a structured process rather than really decision support;
   b) does utilize a DSS "what if" type of analysis in a semistructured decision problem.

4. Assume you are the marketing manager of a large domestic airline. Your regular monthly sales reporting system indicates a decline in certain markets over the last three months but does not tell you why this has occurred. Assuming the availability of an extensive data base and complete DSS software, what kinds of analyses would you consider making to help you to better understand the situation and what (if anything) to do about it?

5. In the previous problem, assume that all recent past memos and manager to manager messages sent via electronic mail have been categorized and retained in a text message base. Describe how you might query such a soft information base in the context of the situation described above. Give example queries and responses in a sample dialogue.

6. A medium-size manufacturing company makes original and replacement automobile parts sold to both manufacturers and to replacement part distributors. The manager responsible for production and inventory has his/her own microcomputer DSS, including his/her own data bases, spreadsheet planning models, and query and spreadsheet software. The marketing manager has obtained similar hardware and software tools and uses them for his/her own area sales planning and analysis. Describe specific applications and ways these facilities might be coordinated and integrated with one another. What benefits might derive from such integration? What problems might be encountered in an effort to integrate these facilities? How could these problems be (or have been) mitigated or avoided?

Discussion Topics

1. Discuss the ways in which an electronic mail capability may be considered to play a decision support role and those in which it does not?

2. Discuss the proposition that "ease of use" also provides "ease of misuse."

3. How does the main focus and concept of office automation differ from that of DSS? Which technical tools would both word processing and DSS utilize? How might word processing documents be usefully integrated with DSS outputs?

4. Discuss what the evolution of stand-alone DSS capabilities into a need for more integrated systems implies about the role of MIS and general management in planning and organizing for DSS.

5. Discuss the implications of the advent of nonprocedural DSS generator software for the education of future managers. Give reasons why they should or should not continue to be required to learn a procedural programming language.

References

Blanning, R. W. 1983. "What Is Happening in DSS?." *INTERFACES* 13(October)5:76.

Blanning, R. W. 1984. "Management Applications of Expert Systems." *Information and Management* 7 (December).

Bodily, S. E. 1985. *Modern Decision Making, A Guide To Modeling With Decision Support Software.* New York: McGraw-Hill.

Brookes, C. H. P. 1983. "Text Processing as a Tool for DSS Design." In *Processes and Tools for Decision Support* edited by H. G. Sol, New York: North-Holland.

Chien, Yi-tzuu 1978. *Interactive Pattern Recognition.* New York: Marcel Dekker, Inc. and Basel.

DeSanctis, G. 1984. "Computer Graphics As Decision Aids: Directions for Research." *Decision Sciences* 15 (Fall):463–87.

DSS-85. "A Guide to (Software) Products and Services." (Vendors' listing and brief package descriptions) The Institute for Advancement of Decision Support Systems, Providence, RI 02903, (April).

InfoWorld. 1984. "Integration Wars . . . Framework vs. Symphony." 6 (October 29)44:51–59.

Kein, Robert T., Philippakis A. S. 1985. "Decision Support Systems in Practice: Profile of Management and Professional Work Stations." *Transactions,* DSS–85, (The Institute for Advancement of Decision Support Systems, 290 Westminster Street, Providence, RI 02903), San Francisco, (April 1–4):77–79.

Leavenworth, B. M. 1977. "Non-procedural Data Processing." *The Computer Journal* 20 (February)1:5–9.

LeBlond, Geoffrey T., Cobb, Douglas F. 1983. *Using 1–2–3.* Indianapolis: Que Corporation.

McLeod, Raymond, Jr. 1985. *Decision Support Software for the IBM Personal Computer.* SRA.

Major, Mike 1984. "DSS Outlook: Micros, Links, AI, Integration." *Software News* 4 (December)12:26–28.

Methlie, L., Sprague, R. (Editors) 1985. *Knowledge Representation for Decision Support Systems.* New York: North-Holland.

Miller, I. M. 1969. "Computer Graphics for Decision-Making." *Harvard Business Review* November–December:121–32.

Personal Computing. 1984. Interview: "TI's Mike McMahan Discusses Speech Technology." January:237–41.

Wagner, G. R. 1981. "Decision Support Systems: The Real Substance" *INTERFACES* 11 (April)2:77–86.

Young, Lawrence F. 1984. "A Corporate Strategy for Decision Support Systems." *Journal of Information Systems Management* 1 (Winter)1:58–62.

Models and End-User Modeling for DSS

3

The reader may object that anything so simple . . . is hardly likely to be true description of anything so complicated. . . . In reply appeal must be made to a working rule known as Occam's Razor whereby the simplest possible descriptions are to be used until they are proved to be inadequate.
Lewis Fry Richardson, "Mathematics of War and Foreign Politics," p. 1247 in Volume Two of *The World of Mathematics*. New York: Simon and Schuster, 1956.

For readers with training or experience in operations research, the descriptions of models and model processing in this chapter will already be familiar. Such readers may want to skip over the first part of the chapter and review the latter section on *The Major Modes of Model Processing*. This latter section aims at clarifying certain distinctions between DSS model usage and more traditional OR model usage. This material may benefit OR specialists who are called upon to guide and train managers in the effective use of model-based methods. Other readers unfamiliar with modeling methods should find this chapter useful as an introduction to basic uses and methods of modeling. The aims are to enable managers who are not mathematicians to become more comfortable, self-sufficient, and effective in using model-based DSS. The discussion in this chapter is independent of particular software packages but makes reference to some general features found in many DSS modeling packages.

The Importance of Modeling to DSS

As seen in the previous chapter, model-based support is a basic form of decision support, whether it consists of utilizing a modeling component within an integrated DSS software system or a stand-alone system for developing and using models. In order to utilize such supporting software effectively, the user needs some understanding of the fundamental concepts of models and modeling. A minimum level of understanding should enable a user to know when the guidance of a specialist is needed before going ahead in mechanically applying easy to use modeling software. The existence of user-friendly modeling software makes it easy to create bad models and to misuse good models as well as to gain benefits from proper usage.

This chapter will not offer a simple path for nonspecialists to become as proficient at model building as experienced management scientists. No such "royal road" to modeling expertise is available. However, a large number of significant management decision situations do not require more than elementary knowledge of model building or the use of models built by others. This chapter will attempt to:

1. Summarize the fundamentals nonspecialists need to know in order to handle many problems on their own with the aid of user-friendly DSS software tools; and
2. Provide guidelines to help nonspecialists to distinguish between problems they can usefully handle themselves and those that require greater expertise or that may not be suitable candidates for the DSS approach at all.

To accomplish these aims, the chapter will discuss:

1. The nature and purposes of mathematical models, and which purposes are most closely related to the DSS approach.
2. Basic types of models and model processing, and which are best served by DSS versus other approaches.
3. Strategies and methods of model building and usage, and which are most appropriate for DSS versus more traditional approaches.

The Nature and Purposes of Models

A mathematical model is a symbolic statement, or a set of such statements, which expresses some beliefs or truths about an aspect of reality. Like language in general, mathematical models attempt to compress the richness, complexity, and variety of a portion of reality into a more concise, abstract, limited representation. But in contrast to ordinary language, mathematics provides greater power and efficiency in focusing upon particular selected, clearly defined aspects of a situation. Only those aspects are selected that are outstanding or most relevant to the modeler's current purpose. Ambiguous detail or other aspects of less interest are omitted from the stark statements made in the language of mathematics.

The language of mathematical models is appropriate to one way we deal with understanding a complex environment. This way is the *reductive* process which is the heart of the scientific method. In the reductive process complex observations of reality are simplified by filtering them through a series of steps in which we *analyze, relate, generalize,* and ultimately *formulate action strategies.* Analysis entails breaking apart a whole into its parts; relating involves seeing how parts are associated with other parts; generalizing involves perceiving how such associations may apply to larger categories of phenomena.

An alternative, and possibly parallel way of dealing with complex reality is a holistic form of perception in which no apparent explicit observation of separated elements takes place. (As mentioned in chapter 1, this type of holistic perception has been associated with the functions of the right brain hemisphere.) In this mode, somehow, the mind and body takes in full undifferentiated patterns and achieves some form of understanding. Often, the basis for this understanding and the process used to arrive at it cannot be articulated to one's self or to another. It appears that this holistic (sometimes called *intuitive*) approach cannot be articulated precisely because it does not utilize the reductive approach of explicit language or symbolic modeling. This unconscious, holistic mode of knowing and thinking has apparently been used effectively by many senior managers and others. There is no conclusive evidence that either the reductive, scientific, rational approach or the holistic, intuitive way of knowing is superior to the other. The same person may manifest each approach on different occasions and perhaps both human capabilities are necessary for understanding.

However, the explicit, rule-controlled, abstract language of mathematical modeling has provided a proven powerful tool for analyzing, understanding, and coping with complexity. Progress in idea processing support, which will be discussed in part 2 of this book, may provide a path to leverage more holistic forms of thinking. But the discussion in this chapter is limited to the purposes and the power of mathematical modeling.

The power of a mathematical model derives from its ability to:

1. Abstract and unambiguously represent only that portion of reality selected for analysis; and
2. Utilize the well-defined operations of mathematics to derive additional knowledge which is implied by, but lies hidden within, the original statements of the model.

A simple example may illustrate some differences between using ordinary language and using mathematics to describe a particular phenomenon. Consider the phenomenon of an object hurtling through some specific physical space. This phenomenon varies in character according to the precise identity and nature of the object, its location, its surroundings, its past history, and the precise conditions of those things which lie ahead in its path or will enter its path. A verbal description of this situation will, however lengthy, select only a portion of the full reality to convey. Moreover, the verbal description may be imprecise and still be useful. Indeed, it may be the intention of the description's author to merely convey an impression for the reader's vicarious experience or as a means of evoking a memory.

A mathematical model of this situation, in contrast, will separate the phenomenon into precisely defined elements that each leave as few gaps as possible to be filled in by evoked impressions. If major aspects of reality are left out, it should be the intention of the model builder that they are *not* to be filled in by impressionistic memory. The model not only limits the part of reality selected, but may purposely make individual statements which are, by themselves, literally false descriptions of the reality being modeled. Such separately simple fictions are useful if they can be combined to form sufficiently true approximations for the purpose at hand. For instance, in this example, the object can be assumed to be a perfect point mass, without size or shape, hurtling through an airless vacuum in a totally empty world. This is, of course, not true, but it enables us to use some well understood laws of motion which are true under these idealized circumstances. We can then try to add other statements in the model that may describe how an object with more realistic characteristics would deviate in its behavior from the idealized object. This strategy of decomposing, or analyzing, a complex phenomenon into simpler, better understood or understandable components is fundamental to modeling.

But decomposition, or factoring a system into its elements, is not sufficient. A selection must be made among all the possible elements and a recombination of the selected elemental statements made in order to adequately represent those aspects of the phenomenon that are essential to the model builder's immediate purpose.

As we have defined the DSS approach, DSS modeling attempts to deal with situations of interest to a decision maker in which the decision problem is of a *semistructured* nature and thus cannot be authoritatively and completely stated in the form of a final, valid model. Since modeling imposes structure, the lack of completely understood structure implies that a DSS model can only be considered a temporary, trial, and imperfect view of the relevant variables and their relationship to one another. A DSS model should be expected to be changed and improved as it is used and the model builder learns from usage, new data, and knowledge derived from experience external to the model.

All scientific laws, under the empirical methods of science, are also subject to eventual change and elaboration. But the emphasis in more structured scientific approaches to modeling is on the careful gathering of data, hypothesis testing, and the calibration of accurate relationships before declaring one has a valid model that can be generally applied to a class of phenomena. DSS models aim at supporting managers and policy makers, not scientists. Managerial decision makers must cope with complex current realities as best they can, typically under the pressure of time. In contrast to the emphasis on objectivity in matters of science, many managerial models are understood to be unavoidably and unabashedly subjective, at least in part. As such, they are changeable at will. They aim primarily at being an accurate and consistent reflection of the decision maker's best state of knowledge and belief, within time, money, and information limitations. They need not be, and typically cannot be, confined only to statements that can be independently verified by independent observers. These different orientations and purposes between science and management are reflected in the methods of model building for DSS.

Aside from differences between scientific and managerial modeling, all mathematical models, as discussed above, attempt to:

1. Describe phenomena in concise, consistent, unambiguous ways that will foster understanding; and
2. Provide a vehicle for analysis that can yield additional information that is implicit, but not explicitly stated, in the description.

In addition, a managerial decision maker dealing with semistructured decision problems can also aim at one or more of the following benefits from the use of models within a DSS:

1. To more fully understand the implications of one's own judgments, and to modify judgments where they appear to be inconsistent with one another or with what is known:
2. To aid in effective advocacy by means of more thorough analysis and testing of alternative assumptions and strategy alternatives;
3. To identify decision problem variables to which critical outcomes appear to be most sensitive, so that further efforts at information gathering and analysis can be more effectively directed;
4. To increase the speed and efficiency of analysis so that more alternatives can be examined, thereby increasing the likelihood of identifying a better strategy; and
5. To more efficiently and consistently generate, integrate, and judgmentally modify forecasts of outcomes needed for planning.

Example 3.1 and example 3.2 summarize two cases of the use of modeling in business situations derived from my experience. The cases differ from one another markedly with respect to the nature and complexity of the respective model development methods and systems needed for their use. These contrasting cases illustrate some of the points made in this section with regard to the benefits to be derived from the use of models in decision situations that were only partially structured and contained significant need for the role of informed judgment.

EXAMPLE 3.1
A COMPLEX ADVERTISING MEDIA PLANNING SYSTEM

In large advertising agencies, media planners have the task of constructing a strategy and specific schedule for the use of media vehicles in carrying the advertising messages for their clients' products and services. For large advertisers such as automobile manufacturers, makers of soft drinks, headache remedies, etc., the national media budget can be several millions of dollars and the effectiveness of the advertising determines the extent to which many more millions of dollars in sales are realized. The content and style of the advertising message must be orchestrated with the choice of both the class of media used (TV, magazines, newspapers, radio, etc.) and the specific vehicles within a class. The timing of usage of these vehicles, their respective audience sizes, and advertising costs, must all be taken into account in order to accomplish the advertising objectives. These objectives are generally expressed in terms of identifying one or more targeted consumer population groups (identified by their demographic or buying or lifestyle characteristics) and the "ideal" frequency of their exposure to the advertising message. Constraints such as the available media budget and the scheduling and availability of the media vehicles must also be taken into account.

Prior to the 1960s and the use of computers, the quantitative base of information available to and used by media planners was limited to highly aggregated data on the average audience size, its demographic composition and the cost of individual media vehicles. Using such data, it was possible to manually, or with the use of office calculators, estimate a few more key outcomes of a combination of vehicles in a schedule such as *net reach,* that is, the percentage of the targeted population that would be exposed at least once to the entire advertising schedule. It was also a simple matter to add up the average audience figures for each individual usage of each vehicle used in the schedule in order to arrive at the *gross exposure opportunities* provided by the schedule. Then, dividing gross exposures by the number of people reached (as indicated by the net reach estimate), the average exposures per person

reached was determined. In a simple example, consider a schedule that included ten uses of magazine A, which for an average issue had an audience of 100,000 adult men, and five uses of magazine B, which has an average audience of 200,000 adult men. The gross exposure opportunities among adult men for this schedule would simply be ($10 \times 100,000$) + ($5 \times 200,000$) or 2 million exposure opportunities among adult men. If it were estimated that this schedule reached a net total of 200,000 different men (because of duplicated multiple exposure of many of the same men) then each man reached was exposed ten times on average (2 million divided by 200,000).

It was realized that comparing alternative schedules only on the basis of such averages and their relative costs, masked a large portion of the real outcomes and could lead to choosing less effective schedules. Knowledge of the complete *distribution* of exposure frequencies among a targeted group was desired, but represented a complex problem for ordinary statistical estimation and noncomputerized methods. After the acquisition of staff operations research (OR) specialists and computers in the early 1960s, the media planning problem was one of the first tackled by several large advertising agencies. (A more complete description of the media modeling systems developed by major agencies in this period can be found in Young [1970].) One system developed by me for the Interpublic Group of Companies to aid in this problem consisted of two large scale computerized models called SCANS and FAST. Large agencies are still concerned with this problem and methods to perform similar types of analysis are currently generally available through external time sharing services or through in-house time-sharing facilities.

SCANS (SChedule ANalysis by Simulation) was a system that was capable of producing detailed frequency distributions of exposure for up to five target groups and ten alternative schedules on a single computer run. Its output was tabular and graphic and showed the number and proportion of each group that would be exposed once, twice, three times, and so on, up to the maximum exposure frequency possible. It used a data base of a simulated but statistically representative sample of 3,892 adults and 1,500 teenagers. These sample records contained individual characteristics and exposure probabilities to each of hundreds of media vehicles. An elaborate set of model-based computer programs was developed to create the data base, check its consistency against several external surveys, and update it. United States Census data and several syndicated surveys provided basic inputs to the portion of the system that created the data base. A special form of a method called *goal programming* was utilized to provide a best fit of the exposure probabilities outcomes to known data. (It was learned by the developers of SCANS that a competing system had used a method of estimating exposure probabilities that was much simpler and straight-forwardly based on using survey statistics measuring four week exposure frequency. They had assumed that those who reported reading three out of the last four issues had an exposure probability of 0.75, those reading two of the last four had an exposure probability of 0.5, etc. The interesting thing about this direct approach was that it was demonstrably wrong and resulted in estimates that could not even reproduce the known data it started from when the probabilities were used in expressions for the binomial distribution. This illustrates that even analysts with master's degrees can err and when systems methods are confidential and unpublishable because of their use as competitive weapons, managers should insist on some other form of external verification.)

FAST (Frequency Aimed Selection Technique) was a special model that used the linear programming simplex algorithm to generate a media schedule that would come closest to delivering the desired number of exposures to the specified target groups. The model was generated by using the SCANS data base of individuals as if they were observations to a statistical regression best fit problem. This resulted in deriving parameters for the so-called *normal equations* of regression which were then entered, along with other constraints such as budget and media availabilities, into a goal programming model embedded in FAST. FAST could then be used to generate an "optimal" schedule, that is, one

that would minimize the proportion of the target population likely to receive much lower or higher exposures than the specified ideal number of exposures. SCANS could then be used to simulate this optimal schedule, as a means of verifying it and determining the entire distribution of exposures, and also simultaneously simulate several deviating alternative schedules. The non-optimal alternatives were generally created by using the optimal schedule as a starting point and then judgmentally taking into account factors that were not included in the FAST model (such as, the client's partiality for a particular magazine which the model "didn't like"). The SCANS run could then provide a means of comparison of outcomes and their sensitivity to certain variations as a better basis for a final choice.

The users of these systems included planners for several different advertising accounts. Many of these users initially used FAST before using SCANS in the manner described above. After a number of planning cycles, most of these users decreased their usage of FAST and often used SCANS exclusively. When this usage pattern was noticed and users were asked why they often bypassed usage of FAST, they responded that they already had learned what they needed to know from prior usage of FAST. Their earliest experiences showed and convinced them that the schedules derived from FAST were significantly different from the kinds of schedules they had used in the past to achieve similar objectives. Their old intuitions were seen to be inadequate, but they had learned new principles of scheduling from FAST that they could now apply without again using the system. Thus the FAST model, to some extent, had put itself out of business through its successful application.

SCANS usage however, showed no sign of slackening over a period of several years. It continued to be used because it enabled media planners to try out many variations of plans, to consider more target groups, to document their analyses and thereby more readily convince their clients of the effectiveness of their proposed plans, and to accomplish this at low cost and with fast turn-around. It even resulted in some cases in lowering the cost of an effective schedule, thereby freeing funds

EXAMPLE 3.1 continued

for other kinds of marketing communication or research proposed by the agency. This went a long way in reinforcing the confidence of the client in the agency's professionalism.

In this case, a significant portion of the decision problem was structured, but affordable methods of obtaining the required data and innovative methods of performing the required analyses had to be developed. Less structured aspects of the decision situation remained, such as the specification of "ideal" exposure frequency, the relative importance of different target groups, and the intangible impacts of different advertising vehicles. For these aspects of the problem the systems developed enabled planners to continue to apply their judgment or externally learned knowledge. Usage of the systems also resulted in learning new "intuitions" and increasing the planners' effectiveness in advocating their proposed plans.

But this was an elaborate system to develop and maintain and required OR specialists and computer programmers to play key development roles. It was clearly not an undertaking for one unaided manager using a DSS generator package to *develop* and *maintain* this system. However, after an initial orientation, the system could be, and usually was, used by individual planners interacting with the models without the aid of intermediaries.

In example 3.2, a much less elaborate modeling effort was utilized than that described in example 3.1.

In the cases illustrated in examples 3.1 and 3.2, it is clear that specialized knowledge was required to create the models and the systems to implement them, although once developed they resulted in systems that could be flexibly applied by users interacting with them directly, without continuous need for technical intermediaries.

In many other cases, however, user-friendly DSS software should increasingly be applicable to both the development and use of models by decision makers who are not themselves modeling specialists, working alone without human modeling experts at their side. Such capability is attainable through formal management education (as in an MBA program) as well as through short workshops and in-house professional education. It also seems likely that user-modeling capability will be extended by building more modeling expertise and guidance into DSS generators themselves. This seems to be a promising juncture of the expert system approach and general model-based DSS generator usage. The remainder of this chapter discusses some of the basics of models, modeling, and principles applicable to end-user DSS modeling that may provide a foundation for both approaches of more knowledgeable users as well as more "intelligent" DSS generator software to aid them. The examples and illustrations given for end-user DSS modeling all refer to situations in which the manager-user is likely to have sufficient *realm* knowledge based on experience to know what aspects of reality should be covered by the model. They are also situations which do not require more than simple algebraic relationships to sufficiently represent reality.

EXAMPLE 3.2

A QUICK AND DIRTY MULTI-MILLION DOLLAR FORECAST

At the start of each new television season in early September new programs are introduced and there is a large stake in advertising dollars riding on which of the three major networks will have the largest share of the watching audience in prime evening time periods. Because the audience size of any particular half-hour show is affected by the size of the previous show's audience, the stakes go beyond any one show or advertiser and are of general concern to the networks, to advertising agencies, and to large TV advertisers. By definition, *share of audience* is the percentage of the total viewing households in a given period that watch each station. There are three major networks: NBC, CBS, and ABC. In each locality a station may be affiliated with one of these networks or may carry independent programming. Thus the shares of each network plus total independent viewing adds up to 100 percent of the viewing audience of TV during any time slot. These shares may change significantly over time, especially when new shows are introduced, reflecting some switching of viewing as members of the audience try out a new show or view the same show in the ensuing week.

In this case, the chief media research analyst of a major agency was interested in monitoring the audience share statistics that became available each week at the beginning of the season in order to forecast how the shares would finally break down. The analyst was aware of one theory of switching which assumes that about constant proportions of a given audience population group watching any one show will switch from that show to another particular show or remain loyal from week to week. These pair-wise flows of audience in and out between shows result in changes in total shares from week to week until all of the in and out switching ultimately equalizes and an equilibrium of shares is reached. It is also recognized that many factors could upset this balance and could change the switching proportions at any time, thereby invalidating the theory of constant switching proportions between shows.

The media analyst enlisted the aid of an OR specialist and asked how the share data from early weeks' results could be used in a switching model that could forecast later weeks' audience share results. It was of particular concern to try and obtain a forecast as early as possible. But the earlier the forecast had to be made, the fewer the weeks of share data available. This was directly related to the ability to use a switching model to make a forecast at all, unless the model itself were simplified. But the final dilemma was that if the model were oversimplified it would be unlikely to represent the real switching phenomenon well enough to provide any reliable forecast.

The media analyst and the OR specialist worked together to formulate the switching model that follows.

Definition of symbols used:

S_{Ni} NBC's audience share in the i'th week

S_{Ci} CBS's audience share in the i'th week

S_{xi} All other's audience share in the i'th week

p_{NC} The probability of switching from the NBC show to the CBS show

p_{NN} The probability of viewing NBC next period after viewing NBC this period.

p_{Nx} The probability of viewing ABC or any independent (nonnetwork) show next period after viewing NBC this period.

p_{CN}, p_{CC}, p_{Cx}, p_{xN}, p_{xC}, p_{xx} are similarly defined switching probabilities for CBS and for the "all other" (x) category denoting ABC and independent shows lumped together.

The relationships comprising the model used are as follows:

(The first five equations represent definitional relationships.)

1. $S_{N2} + S_{C2} + S_{x2} = 100.0$
2. $S_{N3} + S_{C3} + S_{x3} = 100.0$
3. $p_{NN} + p_{NC} + p_{Nx} = 1.0$
4. $p_{CN} + p_{CC} + p_{Cx} = 1.0$
5. $p_{xN} + p_{xC} + p_{xx} = 1.0$

(The next two equations relate shares in week two to shares in the prior week.)

EXAMPLE 3.2 *continued*

6. $S_{N2} = p_{NN}S_{N1} + p_{CN}S_{C1} + p_{xN}S_{x1}$

7. $S_{C2} = p_{NC}S_{N1} + p_{CC}S_{C1} + p_{xC}S_{x1}$

(The next two equations relate shares in week three to shares in the prior week)

8. $S_{N3} = p_{NN}S_{N2} + p_{CN}S_{C2} + p_{xN}S_{x1}$

9. $S_{C3} + p_{NC}S_{N2} + p_{CC}S_{C2} + p_{xC}S_{x2}$

The above model was used at the conclusion of the third week of the season, when actual share data for S_{N2}, S_{C2}, S_{N3}, and S_{C3} was available. These nine equations enabled calculation of the nine unknown switching probabilities: p_{NN}, p_{NC}, p_{Nx}, p_{CN}, p_{CC}, p_{Cx}, p_{xN}, p_{xC}, p_{xx}. These probabilities then enabled us to estimate the future shares in each week with equations of the form:

i) $S_{Ni+1} = p_{NN}S_{Ni} + p_{CN}S_{Ci} + p_{xN}S_{xi}$

ii) $S_{Ci+1} = p_{NC}S_{Ni} + p_{CC}S_{Ci} + p_{xC}S_{xi}$

(It can be noted that using the "x" category to lump together ABC and all independent stations causes the model to deviate somewhat from reality but has the advantage of simplifying the model and thereby reducing the number of switching probabilities that must be estimated. This, in turn, enables an estimate to be made with less data and, consequently, a week earlier. This approach could be carried a step further to eliminate another network from explicit consideration but the model would then become too unrepresentative of the real situation to be useful.)

In addition, since by definition equilibrium is reached when the shares in each week remain the same as in the prior week, at equilibrium—

$$S_{Ni+1} = S_{Ni} \text{ and } S_{Ci+1} = S_{Ci} \text{ and } S_{xi+1} = S_{xi}$$

—and these future equilibrium share values could also be calculated.

The model was first used at the end of the third week to estimate the fourth week shares which were then compared to the actual reported shares at the end of the fourth week. These varied somewhat. Future forecasts were then made two different ways. One forecast was made with the fourth additional week of actual shares used in the model in place of the first week of data to produce a new estimate of probabilities and the future shares based on them. In addition, the original two weeks of data and derived probabilities were used

unchanged to project shares into future weeks. The results were judgmentally weighted and combined to arrive at the next forecast.

The results of this exercise were that each week's forecast was reasonably close to the actual shares until the sixth week when there was a marked deviation of forecast from actual. It was believed that this was largely due to a blitz of special promotion that upset any constant switching probability structure that may have existed. It was concluded that a stable set of switching probabilities assumed by the theory underlying this model of a Markov process was only a potentially useful starting point to approximate results if all other conditions remained constant. The modeling system could be modified to facilitate judgmental adjustments based on what was known to be happening to influence the switching probabilities. It should also be made clear that this entire approach was an attempt to avoid the much higher costs involved in obtaining switching data more directly through the use of a panel of viewers who recorded and reported their viewing over time.

This case, like example 3.1, illustrates the learning benefit of modeling. Unlike the prior case, however, it required a relatively simple and straight-forward model development effort that was carried out with a minimum of two persons' time and very little machine calculation. It provided both some immediate insights and the basis of a next version of a model-based forecasting system that could be developed to include both the theoretical starting point of the switching model with the continually refined judgment of an astute experienced observer. However, neither this case, nor the prior one, could have been carried out without some specialized knowledge of modeling. But not very much additional knowledge was needed by the media analyst in this case in order to have eliminated the need for the guidance provided by the OR specialist. While by no means a sophisticated mathematician, this user had been an undergraduate mathematics major. He was very experienced at making pragmatic forecasts and estimates that consistently proved to be accurate. His methods were not mathematically elegant and they would not have been acceptable for publication in a learned journal. Their only virtue was that these methods, in combination with his well-honed judgment, worked well enough for this man to become known as "The Guru of Madison Avenue."

Types of Models

The Treatment of Time

There are many ways of classifying models. One of the basic modes of classification refers to the way the model treats *time*. One may take only a single snapshot or highly aggregated view of the phenomena of interest in which everything occurs in a single interval, whether long or short in duration. In such a case, the model does not represent changes occurring over several periods of time, because the passage of time is not explicitly represented in the model at all. Such models are called *static* models whereas those models that do represent the passage of time explicitly are categorized under the heading of *dynamic* models. The following brief examples of portions of each of these types of models illustrate this difference:

An Example of Static Model Statements
REVENUE = GROSS SALES − RETURNS
GROSS PROFIT = REVENUE − FIXED COSTS − VARIABLE COSTS
TAXES = GROSS PROFIT × TAX RATE
NET PROFIT = GROSS PROFIT − TAXES

An Example of Dynamic Model Statements
$REVENUE_t = GROSS SALES_t − RETURNS_{t-1}$
$GROSS PROFIT_t = REVENUE_t − FIXED COSTS_t − VARIABLE COSTS_t$
$YEAR'S GROSS = \Sigma_{t=1,T}(GROSS PROFIT_t)$
TAXES = YEAR'S GROSS × TAX RATE
NET PROFIT = YEAR'S GROSS − TAXES

In the case of the static model, the entire model may refer to a single particular time interval, such as the year 1987, or may be intended as a general model without reference to any particular time period. In either case, information about the intended time domain of the static model is external to the model itself and time plays no explicit role in using the model for analysis or evaluation. In contrast, the dynamic model can be used to evaluate outcomes such as NET PROFIT and TAXES for the entire period or domain of the model only by considering the value of other variables in individual time periods and then aggregating these results over all time periods. Which of these types of models is appropriate in a given situation depends on both the information needs of the user and the nature of the situation being modeled. The user may want to learn more about intermediate outcomes and patterns over time as well as aggregated outcomes and thus opt for a dynamic model. The same results may be obtainable in some cases through the repeated usage of a static model with each separate run referring to a different time period, but this can be more cumbersome than a single use of a dynamic model. In other cases, a dynamic model is required not because the user necessarily wants to see period by period interim results, but because that is the only way (or the easiest way) to model the situation and to obtain the final aggregate results desired. For example, a model may require an estimate of annual sales revenue that cannot be reasonably obtained directly by a method that simply extends the last few years' actual sales into the future. The sales may result from only a few large projects that are the result of highly individual circumstances and thus follow no particular pattern in the aggregate. However, the user may best be able to identify specific projects, assess their likelihood of occurrence, their associated expenditures, and the revenues they will produce, by separately considering each month of the year. The aggregate results in this case are more reliably attainable by modeling each month explicitly.

The Treatment of Uncertainty

Every business planning situation is concerned with the future and therefore must consider some degree of uncertainty about both associative and causal relationships and specific quantitative outcomes. The only relationships that can be considered to be known with certainty are those that are true by definition such as:

$$\text{NET PROFIT} = \text{GROSS PROFIT} - \text{TAXES}$$

In contrast, consider a model that postulated the relationship between sales and those factors that had a significant causal impact on sales, such as:

$$\text{SALES} = \text{MINIMUM} + \text{ADVERTISING EFFECT} + \text{PRICE} \\ \text{EFFECT} + \text{COMPETITOR EFFECT} + \text{ECONOMY EFFECT}$$

The model builder is likely to have some degree of uncertainty about the extent and the nature of the effects of these impact factors on sales. Different kinds of effects may be represented by different mathematical expressions using different parameters and tried out to test their reasonableness. As experience is gained and more historical data is captured and analyzed, the modeler may modify these relationships. Uncertainty may thereby be reduced as experience and learning takes place.

But a statement such as that relating NET PROFIT to GROSS PROFIT and TAXES can be accepted with certainty not just because of our confidence in the enduring character of death and taxes, but because this statement merely represents a traditional accounting definition of what is meant by the expression NET PROFIT. If a model contains nothing but such specific dictionary-type definitions, all the relationships in the model could be accepted with certainty. This is true of all the statements, as far as they went, given in the examples of both static and dynamic cases in the previous section. However, the *relationships* may be certain by definition at the same time that some *variables* contained within the statement will take on future values that are not known with certainty. In the examples in the previous section this is true for variables such as GROSS SALES, RETURNS, FIXED COSTS, VARIABLE COSTS, and TAX RATE, whether or not they are subscripted with respect to time. Any of these could reasonably be expected to change to different values over some range of possibilities with different degrees of likelihood.

Just as with respect to the treatment of time, models can be classified with regard to whether or not they represent this kind of uncertainty explicitly or not. Those that do not explicitly represent uncertain or probabilistic variables are called determinisitic models while those that do are called *stochastic* (or *probabilistic* or, sometimes, depending on the methodology of evaluation, *Monte Carlo simulation*) models. In the previous section's examples, uncertainty was not explicitly treated, although the user of such models should be well aware that some of the variables cannot have values known in advance with certainty. This modeling approach assumes that the user will enter values considered to be the most likely ones and the user will not want to use the model to analytically assess the degree of risk or statistical confidence intervals associated with outcomes given by the model. The user could, however, run the model repeatedly, each time entering a different assumed value for variables that are not mathematically dependent on other variables. In this manner, the model that does not explicitly deal with uncertainty could still be used to explore a wide range of possibilities and their associated outcomes. (This would be similar to the tactic of using a static model repeatedly through independent runs in order to see results over successive or different time periods, instead of directly incorporating time into a dynamic model.) The inexplicit approach to dealing with uncertainty by trying out particular alternative settings of variables may be unwieldy and is likely to be incomplete compared to explicitly representing uncertainty.

A means of explicitly representing probabilistic assumptions is to use a model in which some variables are allowed to take on a range of values according to a statistical distribution of values. In many DSS modeling packages this is usually done most succinctly by stating the nature or shape of the distribution (such as normal, triangular, binomial, etc.) by its name or formula, and by specifying the parameters of the distribution (such as its mean and variance, or range, etc., depending on which distribution is used). Then the model can be evaluated by using a method known as Monte Carlo technique, in which a number of random samplings of values are selected from the distribution specified. In software which includes Monte Carlo technique, (sometimes identified as a *risk analysis* method) this is done by using statements such as:

VARIABLE COSTS = NORRAND (500, 100)

(This example is taken from the IFPS system, in which NORRAND is a special function meaning a normally distributed random variable, which in this case comes from a distribution with parameters of a mean of 500 and a standard deviation of 100 units, with "units" being defined in any way the user desires.)

When the complete model, within which this statement is incorporated, is to be evaluated, instead of the user giving a command such as SOLVE, the user enters the following type of command:

MONTE CARLO 400

(This causes 400, or some other number entered by the user, sample values to be randomly selected, one at a time, from the normal distribution of VARIABLE COSTS with parameters as given in the model. Other variables, such as GROSS PROFIT, with values that are calculated based on the value of VARIABLE COSTS and other variables, are calculated and recalculated for each of the 400 random values selected for VARIABLE COSTS. If more than one stochastic variable is used in the model, a sample value is taken from each distribution defined and the model is evaluated 400 times, once for each Monte Carlo trial.)

The results are then presented not just as a single-valued outcome, but as a set of different values for each outcome variable taken at intervals over a full range. A probability is also stated that the actual outcome will be equal to or greater than each value level presented. For example, the results will show that GROSS PROFITS will be $600,000 or more with a 90 percent probability, $800,000 or more with an 80 percent probability, $1,112,000 or more with a 70 percent probability, etc.

Modeling of this type requires some specialized knowledge in order to select the most relevant distribution, specify its parameters, and to properly interpret the results of using a model containing such probabilistic relationships. For this reason, Monte Carlo capabilities built into DSS generators have reportedly been seldom used by nonspecialists (probably the best policy if consulting help is unavailable). It would seem that this capability in unaided nonspecialist hands is most vulnerable to misuse. This is an area in which new DSS model generator software may become more usable by integrating a statistics expert system module within the DSS. Such a statistics expert module could interact with the user in a dialogue similar to that between a client and a human expert to determine if a stochastic approach is suitable, to diagnose the appropriate statistical distribution to apply, to advise on the number of random sampling trials needed, and to guide the nonspecialist user in interpreting the results.

The Major Modes of Model Processing

In a model which attempts to describe a given decision situation, whether it is a static or dynamic model, deterministic or stochastic, the model contains variables that can be categorized under three major headings:

1. Outcome variables, which measure the key objectives and other results of interest to decision makers;

2. Controllable impact variables, which measure those factors which decision makers decide about (and therefore control) and which are expected to have significant impacts on the outcome variables; and
3. Uncontrollable impact variables, which measure those factors which are expected to have significant impacts on outcomes and thus have to be taken into account even though they are not controlled or decided upon by the decision makers in this situation.

The model itself merely describes the linkage between all these variables. It is an essentially *passive* reflection of how the model builder views the decision problem and does nothing more than concisely state mathematically what is already known. This in itself may be very useful in that it makes knowledge and beliefs explicit, and thereby enables them to be critically examined and modified. But to go further in using the model to assess or choose a course of action, a method of processing must be applied to the descriptive model. Such model processing methods fall into two major categories:

1. Those methods that automatically result in the generation of decision strategies, that is, that find the optimal or best-that-can-be-found settings of the controllable (decision) variables; and,
2. Those methods that compute the outcome variables, given both controllable and uncontrollable impact variables as user-supplied trial inputs or as calculated results of given relationships.

The former model processing approach will be referred to as decision strategy generation and the latter as decision strategy testing in the ensuing discussion.

(Note: The subscript $_t$ denotes a particular time period, numbered consecutively from 1 through the maximum number, T, of periods considered, with $_{t-1}$ indicating a variable's value one time period earlier than time period$_t$. The Greek letter Σ indicates a summation over time periods.)

Decision Strategy Generation

For decision models with certain kinds of mathematical structure, mathematical processing methods have been developed which result in a solution for values of the controllable variables (such as PRODUCTION QUANTITY, NUMBER OF MACHINES) that guarantees the optimization of a specified outcome (such as minimum COST). Such processing methods are generally iterative procedures called optimization algorithms, which upon each iteration (repetitive processing cycle) produce a solution which improves upon the previous one. These iterations are carried out, converging upon the best solution, until the testing of a specified mathematical rule dictates that the best solution has been reached and the iterations should halt. A general flowchart of this processing is shown in exhibit 3.1. An example of such an optimization algorithm is the simplex algorithm of linear programming (Gass 1958). Another useful set of optimization processing procedures for many structured time-sequenced problems is derived from Bellman's dynamic programming principles (Bellman 1957).

A variation of the algorithmic approach is the use of heuristic processing methods which also attempt to iteratively converge upon a solution, but which do not necessarily result in a mathematically optimal result. While an optimization algorithm relies on a mathematical proof or optimality rule, for some otherwise structured problems no such mathematically proven rule is available. (An example of such a case is the traveling salesperson problem, shown in example 1.5 in chapter 1.) This approach relies on a heuristic algorithm (a "rule of thumb" or logically derived solution procedure) that, although not guaranteed to produce an absolutely optimal result, will nearly always at least produce a very good solution that would be hard for a decision maker to improve upon using unaided "cut and try" solutions. Standard computer programs exist for the traveling salesperson problem and generally produce good results within affordable amounts of computer time for problems of up to about fifty cities. The same general processing flow shown in exhibit 3.1 applies to heuristic algorithms as well as to optimization algorithms, although the detailed processing logic of solution generation and testing in each iteration differs in the two approaches. For example, in testing a given solution in each iteration, an optimization algorithm may rely on a stopping rule such as all values within a vector of values being equal to zero. The mathematical proof underlying the algorithm guarantees that when that condition exists, the optimal solution has been found. In contrast, the stopping rule for a heuristic algorithm may depend on simply cutting off processing at some affordable number of iterations (N, the count of iterations, reaches some preset maximum number) or stopping when the improvement in the current solution compared to the previous one is smaller than some specified percentage.

While both optimization and heuristic model processing methods are important and useful OR tools, they are essentially applicable to highly structured decision situations or only to highly structured components of a larger semistructured decision problem. A major limitation of this approach is that it requires being more mathematically specific about the decision maker's objectives than is either natural or appropriate for many real situations. For decision generating algorithms, objectives are treated in one of the following ways:

1. A single variable (such as COSTS or NET PROFIT) is identified as the objective, and is mathematically related to the controllable variables in a function referred to as the objective function. This algorithm then is aimed at minimizing (as in the case of COSTS) or maximizing (as in the case of NET PROFIT) the objective function.

Exhibit 3.1

Optimization or Heuristic Model Processing

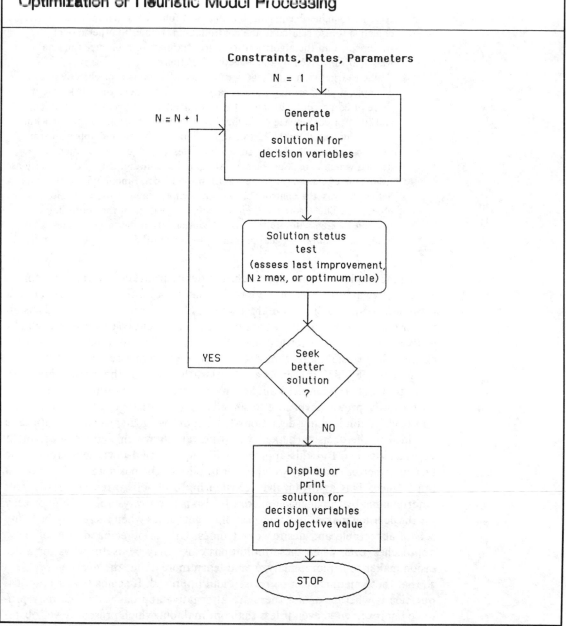

Constraints, Rates, Parameters

N = 1

Generate
trial
solution N for
decision variables

N = N + 1

Solution status
test
(assess last improvement,
N ≥ max, or optimum rule)

Seek
better
solution
?

YES

NO

Display or
print
solution for
decision variables
and objective value

STOP

2. Multiple objectives may be included, but must be expressed in comparable units of measure and given explicit weights of importance relative to one another so that they can be combined in a total weighted measure that can serve as a single objective in the objective function. Each individual objective is also related to the controllable variables in other model statements and the algorithm seeks to maximize or minimize the total weighted sum given by the objective function.

3. Explicit target values may be set for each of a number of objectives. For example, a planner may state as target values for next year: (a) market share of 25 percent, (b) sales of $50 million, (c) net profit of $5 million, and (d) a price increase of no more than 5 percent for major product lines.

   As indicated by the last goal, if desired, an allowable upper and/or lower bound may be set for some objectives. An objective function is defined which expresses the sum, weighted or unweighted, of the deviations from each of the target values. Within the model, functional relationships define the way the controllable variables affect each of the multiple objectives. The algorithm then solves for the values of the controllable variables which will minimize the deviations from the target values. This approach is known as goal programming or multiobjective programming (Zeleny 1974).

In the single objective approach, the decision maker is forced to express one objective at a time when there really may be several that are interrelated. If the second approach of a weighted sum of objectives is followed, the decision maker must be explicit about the relative independent contributions each objective variable makes toward a total situation. This may be inappropriate because the decision maker may really only be able to assess the outcomes as a complete set which is seen as a totality rather than as the incremental sum of its parts. (For example, a higher market share may not always be traded off for lower profits according to some constant exchange rate.) In the third approach of minimizing deviations from multiple goals, a wider latitude is provided to the decision maker in setting targets which together describe a desired situation. But this approach still requires that deviations from these targets either be explicitly weighted or implicitly all considered to be of equal importance. This again involves considering trade-offs often not easily predeterminable by the decision maker. It also is not always appropriate or easy for the decision maker to define a set of target values when there may be many sets of acceptable and desirable outcomes. On the other hand, any of these approaches, even when these limitations exist, may be useful ways for a decision maker to explore, analyze, and learn more about the decision problem so that these methods can be revised and improved. It seems that a practical question is whether or not there are alternative approaches which may produce improvements, even if less than optimal, but which present fewer obstacles for end-users in setting up and using them, than these specialized tools of operations research.

The solution generation methods discussed above have not generally been classified as DSS tools and have not yet been well integrated or widely used within the framework of larger DSS model generator systems. One reason for this is that they are most appropriate for more structured decision problems with more prescribed solution processes. Another reason is that these methods are tools primarily for OR staff specialists rather than for use by unaided general managers. There also may be managerial resistance to their use not only because the methods are arcane and unfamiliar to many managers, but because the approach is unnatural and unsuitable to the way these managers think.

However, decision generating algorithms can often potentially play a useful role for structured components of larger semistructured problems. In such an approach, no attempt is made to force the entire problem into an optimization type of model processing, but optimization is used in a supporting role on a relatively independent aspect of the situation. This allows managers to start from a base derived from the model and then concentrate their analysis and judgment on the rest of the problem. This was the way in which the FAST model (a decision generator) was used in conjunction with SCANS (a decision testing system) in the media planning case illustration presented in example 3.1. The increased usage of optimization and heuristic algorithms also seems to be a potential area for the development and use of expert systems modules within DSS model generators. Such an approach could attempt to build some of the guidance needed by managers into the interactive software rather than relying on the availability and use of scarce OR specialists.

Decision Strategy Testing

In cases of systems that are too complex and insufficiently understood to describe their behavior in the aggregate by a limited number of mathematical statements, the methods of optimization or heuristic modeling are not feasible. Often a complex process could, however, be represented by a network of individually simpler and sufficiently understood subprocesses. In such cases it has been found useful to analyze the full system by simulating the behavior of its component parts and linking each of the parts to one another. This is done by keeping track of individual outputs that become inputs to other components in the networked system and thus determine their behavior. The behavior of the entire system is described by recording and summarizing all results of interest as the system is stepped through a series of simulated time periods. A schematic example of this approach applied to the behavior of consumers in response to a new product introduction is represented in example 3.3 of an interactive computer simulation model called Primer. (The SCANS system discussed in example 3.1 is another type of simulation application.) This method of process simulation has been a basic tool of operations research in studying

EXAMPLE 3.3

PRIMER: A MARKETING SIMULATION

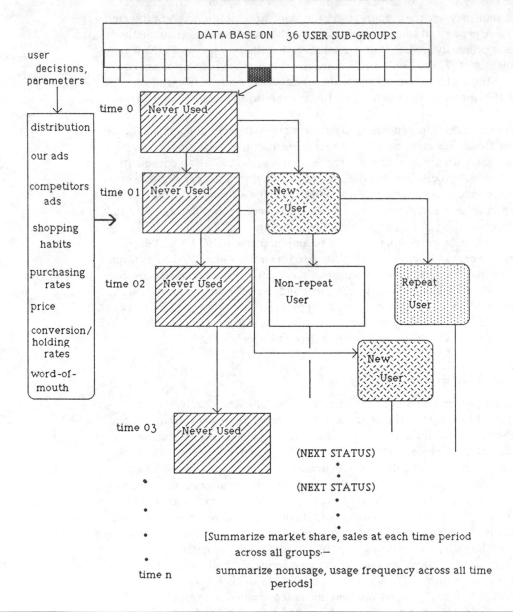

Models and End-User Modeling for DSS

many complex systems such as transportation networks, the growth and evolution of cities, marketing processes and consumer behavior, and nuclear war situations.

Process simulation is a decision strategy testing method. Given both controllable and uncontrollable impact variables as user-supplied trial initial conditions or policy constraints, the simulation process produces estimates of all outcomes of interest to the analyst or decision maker. Decision makers can assess the results, reset the variables representing their decisions and other general conditions, initiate the computer simulation process again, await the reported summary statistics of outcomes at the end of the simulation, and repeat the process as many times as is affordable and desired. While the system doesn't identify an optimal strategy, it provides the opportunity to test out a variety of strategies. The results may provide new insights to the decision maker in making a final choice of a strategy either from among those simulated or by constructing another strategy based on what has been learned about the behavior of the system.

While simulations of this kind have often been useful tools to aid decision makers when decision generating methods were infeasible, they too have a number of limitations, including the following:

1. Major system outcomes may often be unverifiable because of the infeasibility (technical or economic or social infeasibility) of obtaining sufficient actual empirical data (as in the case of nuclear warfare) to determine the validity of the simulation.
2. They often require large computer programs, large amounts of data storage capacity and computing time, and thus need considerable resources of large mainframe computers.
3. The approach requires considerable expertise and/or study time and effort in order to adequately represent the operation of each component of the system and to properly represent the linkages and flows between components. This often results in the development of a process simulation being too costly to justify.
4. Because of the monolithic nature of the computer processing needed and the complexity of the simulation model it may be difficult for a decision maker to have a sense of understanding and control of the simulation process. This may make it harder to gain credibility among policy makers for the results of the simulation.

Because of these factors, it is clear that process simulation is seldom the kind of method that general management users can develop and carry out for themselves unaided by specialists. It has been used with success in many instances, but it remains in the province of the OR specialists repertoire of methods rather than as an end-user built and controlled form of Decision Support System.

Another kind of decision strategy testing approach, however, is very much a basic DSS method that often can be developed and controlled more directly by manager users. When a decision situation can be modeled by a relatively few mathematical statements that describe key relationships and outcomes of interest, the user can test out many more situations and assumptions, continue to modify the model if desired, and rapidly obtain the new outcomes as changes are made. Smaller model size, lack of complexity, and rapid reaction to each user action increases the users understanding, sense of control, and confidence in the results. Less demand on computing resources, coupled with rapid interaction, also enables more thorough analysis to be carried out over a wider range of alternatives. The greater the number of alternatives that can be examined, the more likely it becomes that a significantly better alternative (closer to optimal, if not actually optimal) will be found.

This *aggregate model* approach, like the more elaborate *process simulation,* is a form of allowing the solving of the model's statements to imitate reality. The model processing of aggregate relationships does not separate out and simulate each subprocess, but it is still a simulation. This simpler, aggregate simulation may still step through time, but generally will consider fewer and generally longer time periods than will a more detailed process simulation. A process simulation, for example, may utilize the time increments of one day or one hour and simulate a full year while an aggregate simulation may directly compare outcomes for each of twelve months and add them up to show the year's totals.

Metaphorically, the more traditional OR process simulation approach pieces together many small snapshots each of which cover only a bit of ground, while the DSS simulation takes only one high altitude aerial photograph or only a few pictures with each one covering very large areas. The determination of which approach should be used should depend on the nature of the terrain, the atmospheric conditions, the relative costs and the user's need for precision. In some cases we can fly over and still see the ground well enough to take a fairly large and clear picture. In other cases we have to crawl around at ground level in order to see anything, taking small snapshots which then must be assembled like a huge jigsaw puzzle. We'd rather do the former if we can get good enough results that way.

It appears that many managerial situations do lend themselves to this aggregate form of simulation. Indeed, standard financial statements are calculated based on aggregate models that are a traditional way of gaining an overview of the state of an organization. When such models and the means to control their processing interactively are embedded in a computer system, a manager is given a dynamic tool to simulate a wide variety of assumptions and alternative financial states instead of a single static financial statement. The same dynamic means of gaining an overview can be obtained for marketing, production, human resource management, or any aspesct of an organization, so that the aggregate relationships can be varied and the manager can try out many alternatives.

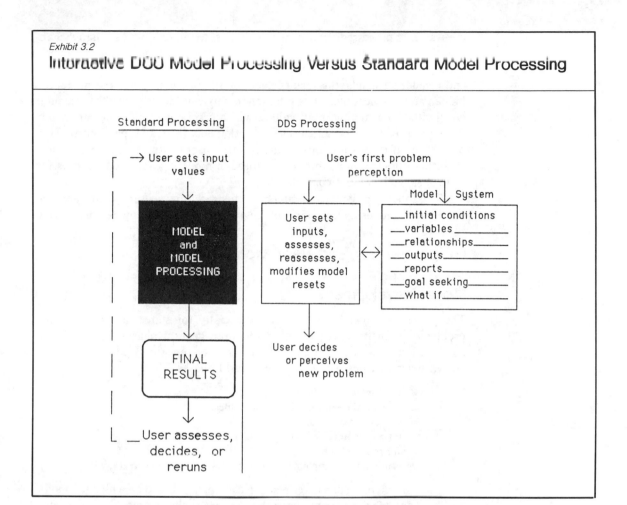

Exhibit 3.2
Interactive DSS Model Processing Versus Standard Model Processing

Standard Processing

→ User sets input values

↓

MODEL and MODEL PROCESSING

↓

FINAL RESULTS

↓

User assesses, decides, or reruns

DDS Processing

User's first problem perception

↓

Model System

User sets inputs, assesses, reassesses, modifies model resets

↔

—initial conditions
—variables_____
—relationships_____
—outputs_____
—reports_____
—goal seeking_____
—what if_____

↓

User decides or perceives new problem

The nature of the processing of such aggregate simulation (or "what if") models typically involves only straightforward calculation of each equation in the model, or, in some cases, the solution of sets of simultaneous equations to obtain values for some of the variables in the model.

A major difference between the DSS type of aggregate simulation approach versus the detailed process simulation form of strategy testing is the extent of interaction and control the user has over the processing. This is illustrated in exhibit 3.2. From the nonspecialist user's point of view, models and processing of both detailed process simulations and optimization-heuristic models are enclosed in impermeable "black boxes." The user can change inputs and some specified parameters but generally not the model itself or the processing method applied to it. These are imbedded in computer programs and are thus hidden within two technical layers of protective covering from the user: the layer of a complex mathematical and/or logical model; and the layer of the programming language and logic that represent the model and govern the way it is processed. In contrast, as illustrated in exhibit 3.2, the DSS approach tries to open up the model and the options available to control its processing. The user can change any part of the model, select a strategy of analysis and a mode of displaying results. Neither the processing nor the model are hidden and inaccessible. Thus interaction between the user and the system is not limited to changing input values, which can be done in either approach. Standard processing permits user interaction only through input control. DSS processing, if it lives up to its promise of true user control and ease of system evolution, should extend interaction through modeling and model processing control as well as input control.

The following sections discuss and illustrate how a user might approach developing and using this kind of aggregate DSS strategy testing model.

Guidelines for End-User Modeling

Model Development

The process of model development, especially for semistructured decision problems, is an iterative one in which three general phases can be distinguished, but in which the model developer/user repeatedly can loop back to any earlier phase desired. The three general phases are:

1. *Model content specification*
   Identifying the related relevant variables.
2. *Model relationships specification*
   Specifying required effects between model variables.
3. *Model processing*
   Determining and implementing an analysis or solution strategy.

Assessment of results takes place in each phase, based on which the model builder/user decides to continue with the current phase, go back to an earlier phase, or terminate the modeling process.

In the model content specification phase the user determines the identity of variables that are relevant to the decision problem as it is currently perceived. These variables can, of course, be subsequently deleted, added to, or modified in form. At this stage, specific relationships between variables need not be specified. Different approaches to initial variable identification may be followed. These include the following:

1. The traditional OR general qualitative general model approach;
2. The use of an available referent model;
3. The use of a standard "realm" area checklist;
4. Consultation with realm experts; and
5. Free-form personal viewpoints.

The traditional operations research approach to determining model content utilizes a qualitative model of the following form as a referent for hypothesizing the relevant variables.

Objective variables (payoffs or outcomes) are dependent on controllable decision variables and uncontrollable impact variables.

This verbal statement is more concisely expressed as:

Outcomes = f (controllable variables, uncontrollable variables)

The identification of each of the categories of outcome, controllable, and uncontrollable model variables is similar to the problem of identification of information requirements for an information system. The developer/user may find it helpful to use the critical success factor (Rockard 1979; Bullen and Rockard 1981) approach, similar to the earlier *key variable* (Drucker 1954) approach, often applied in information requirements analysis to identify the most relevant variables. This approach, as does the decision analysis approach to information systems requirements analysis first proposed by Ackoff (1967), concentrates on specifying what a manager's organizational unit is responsible to achieve, how performance will be assessed, and what must be carefully monitored in order to perform well in contributing to overall organizational objectives. That is, the manager/model builder answers the following kinds of questions:

1. Which outcomes will be the key ones that will (should) be used to measure the success of the functions and activities I am responsible for?
   (These are the objective variables.)
2. What resources do I control that are critical to carrying out my mission to reach my objectives?
   (These are the most relevant controllable variables.)
3. What external factors (outside my control) do I expect are, or will be, critical for me to take into account because they will affect key outcomes?
   (These are the most relevant uncontrollable variables.)

The key (or critical) variables identified by this approach will vary from one organization to another depending on the nature of the business, its organizational structure, and the scope of responsibility within the organization of the managers involved. An example is given in example 3.4 of factors worked out by a group of managers responsible for planning and control in a company producing automotive body paint. A more generic list of key variables is given in exhibit 3.3.

Other approaches to identifying model content may be desirable either as alternatives or as supplementary ways to assure more complete identification of relevant variables. The use of a referent model of the same or similar decision problem from a published source can help to identify relevant variables even if the model's relationships are not entirely applicable to one's own decision situation. Such models may be found in textbooks, journal articles, conference proceedings, and in manuals accompanying model generator packaged

EXAMPLE 3.4

A PLANNING MODEL CASE OF A QUALITATIVE MODEL FOR AN AUTOMOTIVE BODY PAINT PRODUCER

Model content:

Objective variables

CASH FLOW	GALLON SALES	MARKET SHARE
EARNINGS	MANAGEMENT DEVELOPMENT	SAFETY

Controllable impact variables

MARKETING SUPPORT	TECHNICAL SUPPORT	DIRECT SELLING
PRODUCTION PLANS	PLANT ASSETS	R & D ASSETS
SELLING TERMS	PRODUCTION PERFORMANCE	PRICE
STOCK LEVELS	INVENTORY TURNOVER	MARKET FORECASTS
PRODUCT IMPROVEMENT / INNOVATION		

Uncontrollable impact variables

COMPETITION	LITIGATION	RAW MATERIALS AVAILABLE
WEATHER	CAR REGISTRATION	STABILITY OF AUTO INDUSTRY
NEW CAR SALES	INTEREST RATES	GOVERNMENT REGULATIONS
GAS PRICES	DISTANCES DRIVEN	ACCIDENT RATES

software systems. Similarly, published texts and other literature in the specific functional area or realm of interest are sources of checklists of significant variables or factors defining a given area of responsibility. For example, the contents of a marketing text is likely to include chapters or sections corresponding to key variables in the realm of marketing such as sales, advertising, pricing, physical distribution, and promotion. These topics are themselves a good starting point for identifying the content of a marketing planning model. A short consultation with one or more experts in the functional realm, if the manager/model builder is a neophyte in the area, will have the same result of at least identifying key variables as a starting point.

Many manager/model builders will be able to tap their own knowledge of the realms they manage to identify the key variables or to add to and refine the variables identified by other sources. In some cases, however, it may not be entirely clear as to which variables are objectives, which are controllable

Exhibit 3.3

Key Variables to Consider for Model Content

Marketing key variables:

SALES VOLUME	ALLOCATION OF SALES	POTENTIAL BY MARKET
MARKET SHARE	EFFORTS	SEGMENT
SALES REVENUE	MARGIN ON SALES	NEW ORDERS
LOST ORDERS	NEW MARKETS	LOST CUSTOMERS
NUMBER OF NEW PRODUCTS	SELLING COSTS	ADVERTISING BUDGETS
PRICING DISTRIBUTION	SALES SUPPORT	SIZE OF SELLING FORCE

Production key variables:

EQUIPMENT UTILIZATION	WORKER UTILIZATION	MATERIALS UTILIZATION
MANUFACTURING COSTS	YIELDS	QUALITY REJECTS
BACKORDERS	IDLE EQUIPMENT	BACKLOGS
LEAD-TIME REQUIRED	ON-TIME/LATE COMPLETION	IN-PROCESS/FINISHED
SIZE OF WORKFORCE	RATES	INVENTORY
ABSENTEEISM	WORKFORCE SKILLS	WORKER TURNOVER
	INVENTORY	

Financial key variables:

RETURN ON INVESTMENT	PROFITS (NET/GROSS)	TOTAL COSTS
DIVIDENDS	CASH FLOW	WORKING CAPITAL RATIO
EARNINGS PER SHARE	ACCOUNTS RECEIVABLE	DEBT
INVENTORY TURNOVER	TURNOVER	CONTRIBUTIONS
TOTAL REVENUES	R&D INVESTMENT	

by the decision makers, and which are important but uncontrollable. The assignment of organizational authority or the exercise of contending power may be fluid and perceptions of needs and objectives may be dynamic. While such unstructured decision processes may make it difficult or impossible to utilize traditional operations research optimization methods, they should be the very areas in which a DSS approach is appropriate. Thus, the classification of variables is not essential at the outset of defining a DSS simulation model. It is only a useful framework for defining model content when these questions are not in doubt. If such a framework is not useful or feasible, a model builder can simply create a free-form listing of relevant variables according to expert sources and/or one's own personal view of the decision problem. When the model is subsequently completed and processed in a DSS simulation (or "what if") mode, there is no necessity for specifying an objective function as there would be in using an optimization model.

Model Relationships Specification

In the model relationships specification phase of model building, the variables must be linked together through explicit mathematical equations or logical statements. The main principle that should govern both the selection of variables to include in the model and the specification of relationships between them is to be as simple and parsimonious as possible consistent with maintaining a useful model. Both the specialist model builder as well as the nonspecialist manager should attempt to adhere to this principle. However, the specialist also may strive for elegance and conciseness of mathematical expression. This may necessitate the use of mathematical functions and notation that are unfamiliar to the nonspecialist. For much business decision modeling, elegant or advanced mathematics is unnecessary. The end-user manager/modeler should feel free to use familiar but less elegant, less concise, even less precise expressions, that adequately represent the relationship. But it is imperative that the model can stand up to a test of adequacy that explicitly compares the meaning of the model with what is known or believed to be true of the real situation. If relevance or logical consistency is unwittingly sacrificed for the sake of simplicity, the model will be worse than useless, it will be misleading.

In order to simply, but adequately, develop a useful set of model relationships, end-user modelers need to pay careful attention to the following basics:

1. Representing independent additive versus joint effects
2. Representing linear versus nonlinear effects
3. The setting of parameters, scaling and dimensional consistency
4. The treatment of time, leading and lagging effects

Independent versus Joint Effects

If a given variable has its own impact on an outcome *regardless of the magnitude of other variables,* it is said to have an independent, or additive effect on that outcome. For example, consider the following statements:

1. TOTAL COST = FIXED COST + VARIABLE COST
2. VARIABLE COST = VARIABLE MANUFACTURING COST + VARIABLE SELLING COST

In statement one, TOTAL COST will increase or decrease according to any change in *either* fixed or variable costs. If fixed or variable cost were to become nonexistent (zero in value), the total cost would not become zero unless both fixed and variable costs were zero. Each of the cost components contributes separately and independently to TOTAL COST. The same sort of independent effect is conveyed by statement two. The plus sign connecting variables is the mathematical way of saying that they contribute separately from one another to the outcome variable on the left side of the equation. Statement two, however, may not tell the whole story regarding independent effects. While each of the variable cost components contribute separately to total variable cost, they still may be linked and dependent on one another in some way. For example, VARIABLE MANUFACTURING COST may become larger when VARIABLE SELLING COSTS become lower under some circumstances. If, for example, selling costs are decreased when manufacturing reacts more rapidly to orders by using more overtime, such a dependent relationship would exist between these variable cost components. In this kind of situation, the model would not sufficiently represent reality without one, or perhaps more than one, other statement representing the dependency between the variable costs components. This might be done as follows:

3. VARIABLE MANUFACTURING
   COST = − PAR15 * VARIABLE SELLING COST

In this expression, PAR15 is the name of a parameter or multiplier that determines the extent to which each unit change in VARIABLE SELLING COST affects VARIABLE MANUFACTURING COST. The minus sign indicates that an increase in selling cost causes or enables a decrease in manufacturing cost. (Multiplication is indicated by the * sign.)

In other instances, an outcome may be affected by two or more variables directly acting in concert rather than separately. Such a joint effect, as illustrated in the following example, often requires a multiplicative linking of the variables:

CONSUMER SHOPPING = PERCEIVED NEED * RETAIL PROMOTION

Unlike the case of additive independent effects, the above statement says that *both* PERCEIVED NEED and RETAIL PROMOTION must be nonzero in order to affect CONSUMER SHOPPING. Specifying multiplication of these variables says that any increment or decrement in one of them causes more than a corresponding increment or decrement in the outcome; the effect is magnified because of the joint action (interaction) between them. Other statements in the model of consumer behavior might express the factors that determine the values of PERCEIVED NEED and RETAIL PROMOTION.

The examples above illustrate the basic modeling principles that:

1. Variables with independent effects on an outcome are usually linked by addition (or subtraction);
2. Variables that can be seen to affect a given outcome independently may still not be independent of one another; and
3. Variables that act in combination to jointly affect an outcome are (in the simplest form) linked together by multiplication (or division).

Linear versus Nonlinear Effects

The simplest mathematical relationship is a straight line or linear function. Example statements one, two, and three in the previous section all represent linear relationships in that each increment (or decrement) in any of the impact variables (the ones on the right hand side) has a given incremental effect on the outcome that remains constant over the full range of magnitudes of the impact variables. If VARIABLE MANUFACTURING COST in statement three were graphed against VARIABLE SELLING COST the result would be a straight line with a negative slope (a line running downwards toward the right). The steepness or shallowness of the line's slope would be equal to the value given to PAR15. The slope represents the ratio of the constant decrement in VARIABLE MANUFACTURING COST for each unit of increment in VARIABLE SELLING COST.

Suppose the relationship were not a straight line, but a curve as shown in example 3.5. Curvilinear relationships of many kinds could be represented by a variety of exponential, logarithmic, or multivariable multiplicative mathematical functions. The model builder specialist would utilize theory and statistical methods to determine the precise relationship and parameters that best fit observed or known data. Instead, a model builder who is personally knowledgeable in the behavior and history of the realm being modeled may not find it necessary to use such formal methods. Such a modeler may find it convenient to simply fit or assume a series of straight-line relationships, as shown in example 3.5, to approximate the curve relationship desired. Different straight-line segments which vary from one another in slope can together represent any curve with only some loss of precision. The amount of precision lost can be controlled by the modeler by using more straight line segments to gain more precision. The slope values applied to each successive line segment can vary in order to approximate the changing shape of a curve.

Both microcomputer spreadsheet software and mainframe modeling languages usually have language features to represent IF-THEN-ELSE conditions so that the use of different parameters, or the resetting of the value of one parameter, can be made conditional on a range of magnitude of a specified variable. Thus the conditions shown at the bottom of example 3.5 for the use of PAR16, PAR17, or PAR18, can be incorporated into the model itself. Examples of these language features are illustrated in chapter 5.

Setting Parameters, Scaling, and Dimensional Consistency

Examples of parameters (such as PAR15, PAR16, PAR17, etc.) and their use in a model have already been given in the previous section. While the *general form* of a relationship, such as a straight line or a particular kind of curve, may be apparent to the model builder, it is usually more difficult to specify a particular value for a parameter that determines exactly which of the infinite possible number of lines (or curves) applies to the particular situation being

EXAMPLE 3.5

A LINEAR APPROXIMATION

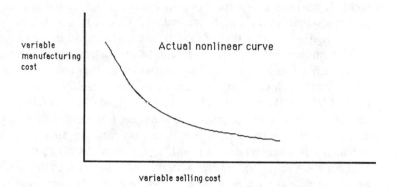

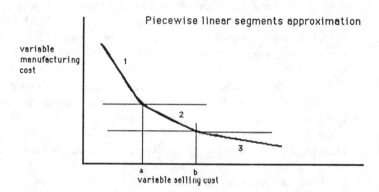

For Variable Selling Cost LessThan a :

VARIABLE MANUFACTURING COST = - PAR 16 * VARIABLE-SELLING
COST

For Variable Selling Cost Greater Than a But Less Than b :

VARIABLE MANUFACTURING COST = - PAR 17 * VARIABLE-SELLING
COST

For Variable Selling Cost Greater Than b:

VARIABLE MANUFACTURING COST = - PAR 18 * VARIABLE-SELLING
COST

modeled. As stated in the previous section, the parameters can be estimated by formal statistical regression methods using a set of actual observations, or can be specified by knowledgeable users according to their experience or judgment. It may be appropriate to combine a formal mathematical estimating procedure built into the software and an informal user judgment approach in an interactive process that is easy to use and control by the user. End-user DSS modeling software should facilitate such a combined approach by providing rapid feedback of outcomes based on mathematical parameter calculation from a few user supplied estimates. A sample dialogue illustrating this kind of interactive parameter calibration is given in example 3.6. In this example, the precise mathematical formula for the relationship between advertising and market share is built into the software in a manner similar to that of a standard financial or mathematical function. As with such a function, the user need not see or be familiar with the exact function in order to understand and control its implications. The necessary conditions for understanding and control are direct feedback to the user and the opportunity to change the estimates which determine the parameters to be used. With this approach, the model can be fine-tuned by the user until the parameter values are consistent with the user's best judgment about the way the realm being modeled actually works.

The order of magnitude of a parameter also needs to be consistent with differences in the units of measure used for the different variables being related. For example, a parameter may govern the degree of impact advertising expenditure has on market share, within various ranges of expenditure, as in example 3.6. Suppose it is appropriate to measure significant changes in market share in integer percentage points (to the nearest tenth of a point) and advertising expenditures are stated in units of one million dollars, as in the example. If within a given range, it takes about an increment of ten million dollars in advertising to gain two percentage points in market share, then the estimated slope parameter of a straight line relationship between market share and advertising expenditure in that range is 2/10 (two market share points per ten million dollars) or 0.2. If the parameter was instead stated as 2.0 and advertising expenditures stated in units of ten million dollars instead of one million dollars, nothing in the relationship would be really changed (two market share points per one ten-million dollar expenditure unit = 2/1 or 2.0). Thus a parameter reflects an arbitrary relative measurement scale relationship as well as a meaningful slope. The modeler-user needs to be aware of such scale effects on the magnitude of parameters and other variables in the model.

Similarly, a parameter is measured in *dimensional units* that depend on the dimensions of the variables being related to one another. The dimensional units in the example discussed above are *millions of dollars* (for ad expenditures) and *market share percentage points*. The dimensional units of the parameter is then millions of dollars per percentage point, or *$ millions/percentage point*. The modeler-user who controls the setting of a parameter needs

EXAMPLE 3.6

A MODEL CALIBRATION DIALOGUE

(System)   ENTER THE FOLLOWING

CURRENT MARKET SHARE in % = **20.0**   (User entries are **boldfaced**)

CURRENT AD BUDGET in ($ Millions) = **2.2**

ESTIMATED MARKET SHARE LIMITS in %

MAXIMUM **40**

MINIMUM **10**

ESTIMATE MARKET SHARE FOR 50 % INCREASE IN CURRENT AD BUDGET

FOR AD BUDGET OF $ 3.3 MILLION, MARKET SHARE = **25**

ESTIMATED RELATIONSHIP IS AS FOLLOWS:

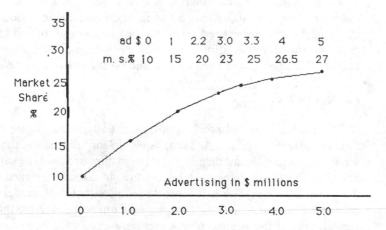

ad $	0	1	2.2	3.0	3.3	4	5
m. s.%	10	15	20	23	25	26.5	27

WOULD YOU LIKE TO CHANGE ESTIMATES? ENTER YES OR NO **YES**

ESTIMATE MARKET SHARE FOR 50 % INCREASE IN CURRENT AD BUDGET

FOR AD BUDGET OF $ 3.3 MILLION, MARKET SHARE = **23**

OTHER CHANGES? Y OR N **N**

to know its dimensional units of measurement (as well as its scale) in order to maintain consistency and understanding in using and modifying the model. But again, rapid feedback of results should enable the user to spot scale or dimensional errors by a test of reasonableness, without an extensive analysis. The user, however, should be alert (or made alert by the system) to look for such causes of unexpected or unreasonable results, before assuming more fundamental modeling changes are needed.

The Treatment of Time: Leading and Lagging Effects

An end-user aggregate DSS simulation model can, up to a point, represent a dynamic process while still retaining its relative simplicity. Different time periods, leading and lagging effects, can be represented by defining a fixed increment of time and identifying the variables in the model with regard to the time period in which they take on particular values. An example of a gross economic model that relates variables over three different time periods is given in example 3.7. The time periods in this instance might suitably be defined as three-month quarters of the year.

It can be seen in this model that a variable can be expressed as a function of other variables in the same time period, as a function of other variables in past time periods, or as a function of its own state in a past time period. For example, the model states that consumer expenditures in period t depends on the level of consumer expenditures one time period ago (period $t - 1$), as well as on government expenditures one time period ago, on the number of people employed in the current time period, and on the current prime interest rate.

Model Processing

A DSS model, as stated previously, is essentially an aggregate description of a real situation or system. As such, "solving," or "processing the model" generally means that the mathematical relationships are used to evaluate all symbolic variables used in the model that were not directly assigned values by the user/model builder. This often merely requires that each model statement be calculated to produce a value for the single unknown variable that appears on the left side of the equation, or somewhere else in the equation. (It is not a mathematical or general software system requirement that the unknown variables to be evaluated must appear on the left side of an equation. This is merely a conventional way of writing a model.) To be able to do this, the user either supplies values for all other variables in the equation, or these values are first calculated by the model processing computer program based on other model statements appearing in the model. This straight-forward evaluation of a model is applicable to the model given in example 1.1 in chapter 1. It can be noted in that example that REVENUE appears on the left side of the first model statement but that it cannot be given a value until the second model statement

EXAMPLE 3.7

TREATMENT OF TIME IN A SIMPLE ECONOMIC MODEL

Notation Used:

GNP_t Gross National Product in time period t
($ billions)

C_t Consumer expenditures in time period t
($ billions)

G_t Government expenditure in time period t
($ billions)

I_t Industrial expenditures in time period t
($ billions)

E_t Number of persons employed in time period
t (millions of persons)

R_t The prime interest rate in time period t
(in percentage points)

　　　Any of the above variables can be represented in up to two prior time periods by substi-
tuting $_{t-1}$ or $_{t-2}$ for t in the designation of the variable
name.

THE MODEL

$GNP_t = C_t + G_t + I_t$

$C_t = PARO1 * C_{t-1} + PAR02 * G_{t-1} + PAR03 * E_t - PAR04 * Rt$

$G_t = PAR05 * E_{t-1} + PAR06 * E_{t-2} - PAR07 * R_{t-1}$

$I_t = PAR08 * I_{t-1} + PAR09 * I_{t-2} + PAR10 * C_{t-2} + PAR11 * R_{t-1}$

$R_t = .12$

$R_{t-1} = .10$

$R_{t-2} = .13$

Note: This model could be extended to cover more time
periods, including time periods designated as being in the
future, using a notation such as t + 1, t + 2, etc., or simply
sequentially numbering time periods (t1, t2, t3, etc.) or
naming them (Q1-88, Q2-88, Q3-88, etc.)

for MY UNIT SALES is calculated. Similarly, the value of PROFIT depends on the value of COSTS and the statement that enables costs to be calculated appears in the model after the statement for PROFIT. Other variables such as COMPETITORS UNIT SALES, OTHER COSTS, MY MARKETING BUDGET, MY UNIT PRICE, and SALES UNITS GAINED PER MARKETING $ SPENT must also be assigned values before the model can be processed. In this example, all these variables are given values by the user after the model's relationships are all stated. In a procedural high-level programming language such as FORTRAN, this sequence of statements and variable value assignments would prevent processing from taking place and would represent several programming errors. But DSS modeling software, whether it is one of the more powerful spreadsheet packages for microcomputers (such as Multiplan or Lotus 1–2–3) or a mainframe modeling language (such as IFPS or EXPRESS), is mainly *nonprocedural* in nature. Nonprocedural means that the modeler need not tell the system a step-by-step processing logic, but that the user can place most model statements anywhere in the model relative to one another. The software itself, and not the user (or an application programmer), determines which statements have to be evaluated first before others can be evaluated. This generic software feature liberates the user-modeler to think only about the model's content and not about the required sequence of processing the model. (See Bodily [1985] on using DSS software for modeling.)

In some models, two or more groups of statements represent circular or simultaneous equations and thus cannot be solved in any single given one-at-a-time sequence. DSS model processing software has the ability to recognize such situations within a model without the user-modeler identifying or grouping such model statements in any special way. An illustration of this is given in a segment of a model shown in example 3.8.

Such circular references are usually solved by iterative methods built into the software package and automatically applied when needed. Of course, it is possible that circular references given in a particular model may not be solvable. This can occur when two or more statements are not mathematically independent (that is, when the statements do not really provide nonredundant information but are merely different ways of saying the same thing). The model processing software will usually notify the user of this situation after it has unsuccessfully tried to solve the model.

In addition to solving a model based on the initial values and relationships supplied by the user, the processing of a DSS model usually implies a considerable amount of user exploration is needed to seek preferred outcomes or to better understand the behavior of the system or situation simulated by the model. This type of "what if" analysis can take a variety of forms depending on the features of a particular software package. It is generally accomplished as indicated in example 1.1 by simply providing new values for one or more variables, and resolving the model. Instead of just changing the numerical value

EXAMPLE 3.8
CIRCULAR MODEL REFERENCES:
Simultaneous Equations A and B Are Found Within A Model

Statement A:

COMMISSIONS = 20% * NET SALES REVENUE

Statement B:

NET SALES REVENUE = 10000.0 − COMMISSIONS

Solution of simultaneous equations A and B:

COMMISSIONS = 1666.7
NET SALES REVENUE = 8333.3

(arrived at by successive iterations)

---

of one or more variables, the "what if" exploration could also take the form of changing one or more functional relationships. Such changes could apply to the mathematical nature of the function, the values assigned to parameters, or the addition or deletion of variables entirely. In many DSS modeling systems, the "what if" changes can be carried out while the system remembers the original, or "base" model, so that the changes do not become a permanent part of the model unless the user desires that. However, some modeling systems allow for a kind of temporary memory of "what if's" so that the user can add new trial changes on top of old ones, enabling the user to see the successive effects of cascaded "what if's." "What if" analysis applies to changing assumptions about relationships or the value of controllable or uncontrollable variables, and through resolving the model, seeing effects on the outcomes of interest to decision makers. Alternatively, the exploration of a DSS model can often be approached from the direction of setting a *goal* for a specified outcome variable and asking the system for the value that would have to be given to some other variable. This approach is called *goal seeking*. Some DSS modeling packages, mainly those running on mainframe computers, have special commands that enable the user to state the goal for a particular outcome and identify the variable to be changed in order to achieve the goal specified. This is illustrated near the end of the dialogue given in example 1.1 by the user entries of:

TARGET FOR PERCENT PROFIT RETURN ON REVENUE = 0%
SALES UNITS GAINED PER MARKETING $ SPENT = ?

The phrase TARGET FOR in the first statement may be established in a particular modeling system as a special command which sets up a goal seeking analysis, and is followed by the name of the outcome target variable and the value being sought. In this case a break-even value of zero percent is given by the user as the goal for the profit outcome. The second statement identifies the variable to be changed in order to achieve the specified target as SALES UNITS GAINED PER MARKETING $ SPENT. The user is asking what this marketing effectiveness variable would have to be, given the other values supplied to the model, in order to achieve break-even profit. The resulting value of 1.1 for SALES UNITS GAINED PER MARKETING $ SPENT could then be assessed by the user as to its attainability. If the user believes that such a level of marketing effectiveness is not likely to be attained, then the user may want to explore changing the values of different decision variables such as price or costs before further applying goal seeking analysis to marketing effectiveness.

It should be noted that goal seeking could be accomplished indirectly by performing a series of trial and error "what if's" for SALES UNITS GAINED PER MARKETING $ SPENT until the outcome of interest, PERCENT PROFIT RETURN ON REVENUE, reached the target of zero percent. A specific software feature to directly do goal seeking as a form of model processing represents a more convenient way of accomplishing the same end.

Conclusion

This chapter presented the fundamentals of modeling and model processing as a foundation for a two-pronged approach to advance end-user modeling in a DSS environment:

1. A user who is sufficiently knowledgeable to handle many basic DSS modeling needs, to avoid the most common pitfalls, and to recognize situations in which the aid of a specialist should be sought and in which more traditional Operations Research modeling approaches (such as optimization or heuristic models, or detailed process simulation models) might be more appropriate.
2. The enhancement of DSS software to include interactive modeling expertise modules based on the fundamentals presented in this chapter.

Review Questions, Exercises, and Discussion Topics

Review Questions

1. What are the general purposes of mathematical models?
2. Example 3.1 discusses a case in which both an optimization model and a simulation model were used in a complex system. Despite the fact that this was not a case of end-user modeling, what evidence is there in the case that

users' involvement resulted in learning something about the relationships included in the modeling system?

3. Distinguish between static and dynamic models. Which type of model is needed to evaluate the current or future state of a variable as a function of its own past state?

4. What is meant by the assertion that the model statement: PROFIT = REVENUE − COSTS, is *true by definition?* Is there any uncertainty involved in this statement of the relationships between the variables PROFIT, REVENUE, and COSTS? Is REVENUE a deterministic or stochastic (probabilistic) variable? Why?

5. Distinguish between the following categories of variables: (*a*) outcome variable, (*b*) controllable variables, and (*c*) uncontrollable variables? Why should a decision maker be concerned with all of these categories?

6. What are the essential nontechnical differences between the roles of decision strategy generation and decision strategy testing in aiding a manager?

7. In which category (decision strategy generation or decision strategy testing) are optimization and heuristic modeling? What is the main difference between optimization and heuristic modeling?

8. What are the main differences between a detailed process simulation model and a DSS aggregate simulation model?

9. What are the three general phases of DSS model development? In which phase is the testing of a model an integral part?

10. What approaches are available to a user-modeler to identify the relevant variables to include in a model?

11. What differences might there be between the way in which a specialist goes about specifying model relationships and an approach suitable for nonspecialists?

12. How would variables having independent linear, and separate effects on an outcome usually be linked in a model statement?

13. If two variables must act in concert and both must be present (have nonzero values) before an outcome is affected, in what way might these variables be linked in a model statement?

14. If a user has sufficient experience and judgment or historical data to determine a relationship that is not linear, how could that user represent the relationship in a model without knowing the mathematical form of a suitable curve (nonlinear function)?

15. What is the function of a parameter in a model? How might a user determine or control the value of a parameter without using formal statistical analysis tools?

16. What does *solving* a DSS aggregate simulation model imply? Does such a solution tell the decision maker the best strategy to follow?

17. Does a user have to know and specify which equations in a model comprise a set of simultaneous equations? What usually happens when such equations are included in a DSS modeling support environment?

18. How does *nonprocedurality* affect the way a user can state a model?

19. What is meant by a "what if" capability? By goal seeking?

20. If a goal seeking capability were not explicitly included as a feature of a DSS modeling system, what approach could the user take to achieve the same ends?

Exercises

1. Assume the role of a production manager in a computer manufacturing business and specify the variables you might consider important for possible inclusion in a production planning model. Specify which variables are directly controllable by you, which are uncontrollable, and which are important outcomes dependent on each of these other categories of variables.

2. How might you go about using the model that might be developed in the situation of this production manager? What variables might you use to do "what if" analysis and which outcomes would you want to see in this regard? What target variables might you select for "goal seeking" and which ones might be changed to achieve these goals?

3. Describe by means of a graph and a table of values a relationship in the above situation that is nonlinear. Show how this could be incorporated into a model using only linear segments to approximate the actual curve shown in your graph.

4. Describe the purposes and general features of a production planning model-based system that would be useful for this same manager but would be too complex for end-user DSS modeling and would most likely require specialists to develop.

5. Review each of the above questions and determine how your responses might have to be modified for a production planning model for the production manager in a different business which produces packaged bakery products for national distribution and retail sales mainly through supermarkets.

Discussion Topics

1. Discuss what is meant by the assertion that a mathematical model should *not* be as inclusive and detailed as the real phenomena it is intended to represent. Is the assertion correct? Why?

2. Discuss the proposition that the reductive approach of mathematical modeling is the only effective way to really understand a phenomenon. What are the essential characteristics of the reductive approach? What other approach exists?

3. Discuss the proposition: "An ideal DSS modeling system should enable intelligent users with realm knowledge but without advanced mathematical training to directly build, control, use, and modify their own models while at the same time guiding the user in avoiding misuse." Do you agree with the proposition? Why?

4. Discuss the correctness of an assertion that DSS modeling approaches have made Operations Research modeling methods obsolete? In what ways might a traditional Operations Research modeling approach be in conflict with a DSS end-user modeling approach? In what ways might they be complementary to one another?

5. Consider and discuss the potential benefits and the possible disadvantages of end-user modeling versus managers depending on specialist intermediaries.

The User-DSS Interface

4

There is your brother Aaron the Levite, is there not? I know that he is a good speaker. . . . You will speak to him and tell him what message to give. I shall help you to speak and him too, and instruct you what to do. He himself is to speak to the people in your place; he will be your mouthpiece, and you will be as the god inspiring him.
Exodus 4:5

The term *interface* was used in chapter 2 to refer to the point at which information flows between any two different system components. The user-DSS interface is composed of:

1. A *hardware set* consisting of the material tools which enable the user to activate the DSS (such as keyboard, mouse) and enable the DSS to communicate to the user (such as a display screen, audible signals); and
2. A *language set* consisting of signs, symbols, and rules for their arrangement used by the DSS to communicate information to the user and by the user to communicate commands and other information to the DSS.

The character of the interface is determined by the hardware set, the language set, and the underlying software that provides functionality to both of them. The user can directly perceive the hardware and language sets but can only get an indirect feel for the underlying software engine they drive and are driven by. The sense of the general character of the software, but not its detailed operational structure, is obtained through interaction with the surface hardware and language features of a system. To the user, the character of the interface can be said to result entirely from these surface features of a DSS. Indeed, the user's overall evaluation of the utility of the DSS is likely to be highly dependent on the character of these surface interface features. The actual power and scope of DSS functionality can only benefit a user if it is accessible and comprehensible. Ease of use and understanding are determined largely by the character of the interface. Furthermore, the difficulty of designing an effective interface depends on the extent of the capabilities of the

DSS. The more that the DSS can do, the more difficult it is to provide an interface that is easy to use and understandable. Because DSS usage is discretionary, the nature of the interface becomes a critical factor as either a barrier or a facilitative medium to any potential benefits of a DSS. For most nontechnical users a somewhat less powerful system with a more effective interface is likely to be preferable to a more powerful system with a cumbersome, difficult interface.

The term *interface* is used by the computer systems designer in an analogous way to the use of the term *medium* (or its plural, *media*) by mass communications specialists. In contrasting the effects of print versus television media, Marshall McCluhan argued that "the medium is the message," emphasizing the inseparability of what is conveyed from how it is conveyed and the often dominant communication role of the medium itself. A similar dictum may be applicable to the design or assessment of a DSS: *To the user, the interface is the DSS.*

In this chapter, the focus will be on characteristics of the user-DSS interface language (signs, symbols, and their arrangement). These will be identified and discussed with respect to how they relate to the functions to be performed and their effects on the user. Interface hardware features will generally be taken as a given, consisting of standard keyboards and display screens. Discussion of the human factors aspects of these are considered to be more appropriate for a computer engineering or human engineering text and will not be covered here.

The Dimensions of an Interface Language

The interface language is a medium for user-DSS communication. Communication flows in two directions. It includes:

1. Information that is originated by the user and transmitted to the DSS in order to control its operations, as well as
2. Information the DSS transmits to the user in order to convey the results of its operations as well as to solicit (or suggest, advise, or insist upon, . . . depending on the *strength* of the DSS design) further user command and control information.

As shown in exhibit 4.1, information flow within the interface is generated by separate but highly interdependent components of the interface. One component is part of the user and is comprised of a language repertoire the user must know. While the other component is part of the system's repertoire, it must speak in a manner that is more native to the user than to the DSS. The complete language interface is seen as overlapping the user and the DSS in order to provide the required communications link between them. An interface designer must thus keep the communications requirements of both the user and the system in mind.

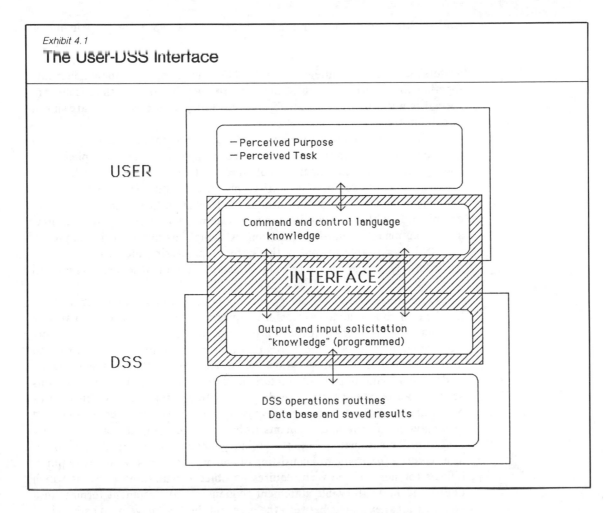

Exhibit 4.1
The User-DSS Interface

USER
- Perceived Purpose
- Perceived Task

Command and control language knowledge

INTERFACE

Output and input solicitation "knowledge" (programmed)

DSS

DSS operations routines
Data base and saved results

The dimensions of each interface language component are similar to those of any language and include:

1. A set of *elemental symbols,* or the "alphabet" of the language,
2. A set of *words,* or allowable symbol configurations that correspond to some conceptual or material entities in the user's world (which includes entities in the DSS's world that must be known to the user), and
3. The allowable patterns or rules by which "words" can be combined in order to comprise *statements* and by which statements can be related to one another.

The symbols or "alphabet" of the language are most often actual alphabetic or numeric characters, or pictoral elements comprised of particular line or point segments. These elements are combined to comprise "words," which can be actual words found in the dictionary, special words, or graphic line or dot configurations used as quantitative analogs. Other pictoral elements can be used in their entirety, similar to Chinese ideograms or ancient cave-wall writers pictograms, as integral "words" (without stringing alphabet elements together to comprise a word). Such picture "words," often called icons, are special symbols standing for an object or an action. Some examples are shown in exhibit 4.2.

Other special picture elements that have been called *metri-glyphs* can also be used (although they have rarely been applied in a DSS) to pictorially convey quantitative characteristics of an entity (usually an object rather than an action). Some examples of metri-glyphs are given in exhibit 4.3.

Words (in the sense of this term as used here), in turn, either singly or in combination with other words comprise statements that convey an interpretable or actionable unit of information. Although, as discussed in chapter 2, the DSS user is able to control the system's processing indirectly in a nonprocedural language, logical rules for allowable statement sequences may still be required within the interface language.

For example, within a user-system dialogue, it would usually be illogical for the user to give an answer before a question has been asked or to answer questions in a different sequence to that in which they were asked. In a user-DSS language interface, the words that a user may utilize in a statement to initiate particular system operations are called *commands*. The data elements or data sets containing the characteristics or status of objects that operations are to be performed upon are also identified within a statement by either words or picture symbols. A statement always specifies one or more commands and also may specify the data elements to be operated upon, if that is logically necessary. This is analogous to the ordinary language meaning of a statement as a sentence (or predicate) consisting of one or more verbs, with any required objects (or none, if the verb requires no object). Rules and patterns which define and limit allowable statement sequences and statement formats in a conversational exchange between the user and the DSS have been categorized into a relatively few types. These include the following main types:

1. Menu formats.
2. Question-answer formats
3. Command language formats
4. Input/output structured formats
5. Free-format natural lnguage

These conversational format types can be modified and combined with each other in a large variety of ways as well as used in conjunction with different modes of representing DSS output information (in ordered lists, tabular numeric reports, as graphics, etc.).

The following sections will give examples and discuss the relative merits of using these conversational formats, both individually and in combinations found to be useful in practice.

Exhibit 4.2

Picture "Words" (Icons)

ICON	MEANING

Letter01-4/15/85

Word processing document
named "Letter01-4/15/85"

Create a bar chart

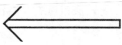

Transmit current screen
display

Move input(output) to the
right

Move input(output) to the
left

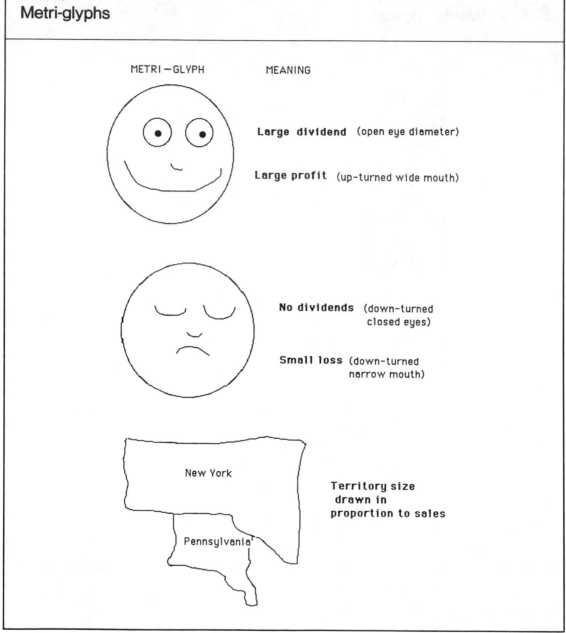

Exhibit 4.3
Metri-glyphs

METRI—GLYPH   MEANING

Large dividend (open eye diameter)

Large profit (up-turned wide mouth)

No dividends (down-turned closed eyes)

Small loss (down-turned narrow mouth)

New York

Pennsylvania

Territory size drawn in proportion to sales

Menu Formats

Menu formats (one type of which is illustrated in exhibit 4.4), as the name implies, simply display one or more finite lists of alternatives from which the user can choose in communicating to the system. The menu items can include commands which determine the nature of the analysis or output format desired as well as the data set (or variables) that are to be the objects of the commands. Command menus can be separated from data set object menus or they can be combined within a single menu list. When required, a series of menus can be nested in a logical sequence and presented to the user in a predetermined logical order or in an order that is determined by the user's selection from a prior menu. For fairly extensive menus, it is also useful to structure menus by grouping choices under category headings that are familiar to users and to sequence the menu items in some logical order (alphabetical, quantitatively ascending or descending, by frequency of usual or expected choice, etc.).

A menu format places little demand on the user in terms of interface language rules since only a simple selection is required. It is only necessary that the menu items be clearly stated, understandable, easily found in the list, and that the user be familiar with the mechanical means of selection. Commonly used mechanical means of selection include the movement of a keyboard controlled cursor, the manual movement and "clicking" of a mouse, or the typing of a particular number or letter that identifies the menu item. Because of their simplicity, menu formats are widely used and often preferred for inexperienced users. However, the simplicity of fixed menus, when this interface type is not combined with other types, has a negative side. As in other contexts, simplicity is the enemy of power and flexibility.

If the number of options to be chosen via menus becomes extensive, the menu format can become too tedious and time consuming for the user. While careful design of nested menus can often mitigate the burden of too lengthy individual menu lists, a different interface format type (such as a command language) often can enable the user to completely specify what is desired to the system in a much faster and concise manner. Also, if the user learns from the experience of using the system that new kinds of analyses and data are needed, the menus (as well as the DSS main functional routines) may have to be extended and restructured. This typically cannot be accomplished by a nonprogramming user and therefore may lead to greater dependency and the need for more intensive continuing support for still evolving menu-driven systems. Thus an entirely menu-driven interface is most appropriate for systems that can be well-specified with greater certainty in advance and for systems that only require a limited number of identifiable choices.

Exhibit 4.4

Menu Formats

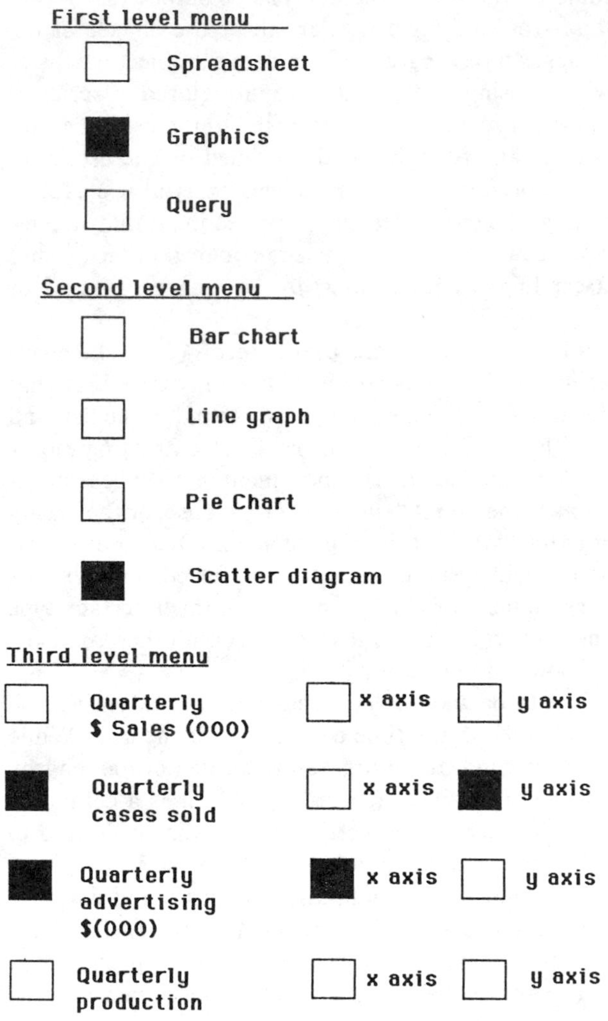

First level menu

☐ Spreadsheet

■ Graphics

☐ Query

Second level menu

☐ Bar chart

☐ Line graph

☐ Pie Chart

■ Scatter diagram

Third level menu

☐ Quarterly $ Sales (000)	☐ x axis	☐ y axis
■ Quarterly cases sold	☐ x axis	■ y axis
■ Quarterly advertising $(000)	■ x axis	☐ y axis
☐ Quarterly production	☐ x axis	☐ y axis

Question-Answer Formats

In the question-answer (Q-A) type of interface language, the computer system asks the questions and the user provides the answers. Because of this, the dialogue is quite one-sided in that the system actively controls the course of the interactive session much more than the user does. In terms of the nature of the *system-user dialectic* described by Young (1978) to distinguish the extent to which each party in a dialogue *initiates* (requests, questions, or commands) versus *responds* (provides information to the other party), a purely question-answer interface is characterized by the system doing all the initating and the user doing all the responding except for the culminating system response of displaying final results.

The user's control over the system in Q-A mode is implicit in the answers provided to the system, which consist of choosing action options (often by a yes-no selection) and keying in variable input data. The sequence and format of questioning is usually relatively fixed, sometimes providing limited user-selected options such as an abbreviated versus a full text mode, and a degree of branching to alternative question sequences based on prior user answers. This is illustrated in exhibit 4.5.

Exhibit 4.5
Question-answer Format (Q-A)

Long Version

Q. *Do you want to display a report?*

A. Yes (Note: if response is "No," branches to 2nd sequence shown below)

Q. *Which report?*

A. April 1986 Sales by Territory

Q. *Do you want standard or special format?*

A. Special format

Q. *What line spacing do you want?*

A. Double space

Q. *What column width do you want? Enter number of spaces.*

A. 15

Q. *Special heading?*

A. No

Exhibit 4.5   (continued)

*Q. If ready to display report, enter DISPLAY. If
you want to change any prior responses,
type CHANGE.*

A. DISPLAY

(2nd sequence branched to from line two above if entry was No)

Q. Do you want to create a report?

A. Yes

Q. *Enter the Report Name*

A. Inventory Movement Analysis

(etc. until report content and format is defined)

Abbreviated Version

Q. *Enter Display or Create, Report Name,
(optional) Line Spacing, (optional) Column
Width*

A. Display, April 1986 Sales by Territory,
double, 15

(Note: If user entered Create instead of Display, system would
procede to request report content as follows, and go on for
any other required report specifications)

*Q. Enter data elements to display in order of
columns as follows:*

ITEM1NAME, ITEM2NAME, ITEM3NAME, etc.

Because of this relative rigidity and strong design (the system leading the user), Q-A formats are most often appropriate for inexperienced users performing tasks that are relatively structured with respect to the sequential logic of processing. If the application problem is not merely the automation of a structured task (and therefore not truly a DSS application), the semistructured aspect of a purely Q-A dialogue comes about only by the user repeating part or all of the interactive session and modifying the answers given to the system. Because the user generally cannot directly control the session by initiating action at any point in a dialogue, the user's desire to change an answer

to a previous question must usually wait for the completion of the system controlled Q-A sequence or requires the user to end the dialogue prematurely and
begin it anew. Either of these alternatives can be quite frustrating for the user.

More frequent users will be able to anticipate the question sequence and
therefore become impatient with the delays inherent with one at a time questions and answers. A Q-A format can mitigate this problem to a degree by
allowing the user to choose between two style options:

1. One at a time questions in full text (for infrequent users); or
2. Grouped and abbreviated questions (for frequent user).

These options are illustrated in exhibit 4.5.

As implied by the processing sequence rigidity already mentioned, Q-A
formats, like the menu approach, are not appropriate when a large variety of
new and unanticipated modes of analysis may be desired as the user learns
from experience. All changes in both the repertoire of operations and choice
in the sequence of their performance will require changing the underlying
software. In this respect, both Q-A and menu formats imply a continuing reliance on programming support to a greater degree than less rigid, more powerful interface formats such as command languages and natural language. The
nature of both menu and Q-A formats also implies that they cannot be efficiently used for most modeling (creating and modifying models), although
they can be used to *process* models (that is, to provide input data and cause
the processing of previously defined models that are already stored in the
system).

Command Language Formats

A command language consists of user constructed statements containing verb-
noun pairings or verbs alone selected from a predefined set. Command languages vary with respect to the repertoire of verbs that cause the system to
perform operations and the categories of nouns that identify information to
be displayed or used as input for the operations specified. Exhibit 4.6 provides
a sample of command language style statements. Because commands to be
issued at any point in an interactive session are chosen by the user, a command
language type of interface enables the user to more directly control the kind
of system operations that are performed, the information sets that they are
performed on, and the selection of output content and mode of presentation.
Unlike a Q-A interface, the user usually has wide latitude in determining the
sequence of operations either as the system responds to a single prior command
or to a user-specified string of commands. The command language interface
can be used for mathematical modeling and model processing, as well as for
data base querying, interactive graphics, and statistical analysis.

Command Language Format Type

(Note: Command "verbs" are shown in capital letters, data names and modifiers are shown in mixed or lower case letters, notes to the reader are in smaller type.)

DISPLAY REPORT April 1986 Sales By Territory

(Previously prepared and saved report is shown on the screen)

PRINT

(Report is printed.)

NEW REPORT Inventory Movement
COLUMNS Jan thru Dec
ROWS In, Out, On hand, Net Change = On hand − Previous On hand
DISPLAY
NEW ROW Percent change = (Net Change/Previous On hand) * 100
HEADER 1987 Monthly Inventory Analysis
DISPLAY DOUBLE-SPACE, 15 COLWIDTH
SAVE, PRINT
GRAPH x = COLUMNS, y = On hand, Line graph, DISPLAY
GRAPH Bar Chart, DISPLAY
PRINT
SAVE GRAPH Bar Chart
END

Unless a command language interface is combined with a menu format mode of presentation, the user must remember the verbs, nouns, and legitimate verb-noun pairing rules, if any, as well as any other syntactical rules for structuring a command statement. In this regard, the system can (and should) provide a HELP option as an auxiliary memory aid for optional use. But even with such aids, a greater burden of system knowledge is placed upon the user with a command language in comparison with the previously described types of interface styles. The extent of this knowledge burden is proportional to the *power* of the system, where power is a measure of the functional scope and usage flexibility of the system. In general, the more powerful the system, the greater is the extent of the verb command repertoire, the larger the noun inventory that reflects the extent of the accessible information base, and the more flexible and extensive are the syntactical rules.

In order to mitigate the knowledge burden on the user, an extensive command language can be designed in levels (or layers) so that a limited basic level of commands cover the functions most often required. Many users may be able to utilize only the basic level of commands until and unless they progress to more extensive requirements. To accomplish this, the command language repertoire can often be structured in a hierarchical manner, with certain major commands identifying a family of one or more ancillary command types that can be used when needed to elaborate on or modify the major command. For example, the verb REPORT can cause the display of information in a standard default format unless it is modified or followed by related forms such as REPORT OPEN FORMAT, REPORT NO HEADINGS, REPORT WITH GRAPHS, OR DUMMY REPORT, each of which causes a different kind of report output to be displayed. In addition, command language interfaces often enable users to define new commands sometimes referred to as *macros* (or macrocommands), one of which causes a sequence of predefined ordinary commands to be called into operation. This feature enables users, as experience is gained and an analysis approach evolves, to avoid the repetition of frequently used sequences of individual commands by defining them as a single macro. Macros, in turn, can include other macros. Thus the levels of a command language can dynamically evolve along with user learning.

Because of the step by step user control provided by a command language, it is a more appropriate format to use when the mode of analysis desired during an interactive session is less predictable and needs to be more flexible. But providing greater control to the user demands more of users in terms of both language knowledge as well as ability to determine the most appropriate mode of analysis for themselves. It is a less *strong* design approach in that it does not inherently lead the user as much as a Q-A or menu format. In terms of Young's system-user dialectic (1978) previously referred to, it falls into the opposite classification from that of a purely question-answer interface, in that in a pure command language it is the user that does all the initiating and the system that does all the responding.

Input-Output Structured Formats

In the input-output structured format type of interface the user is presented with displays resembling a series of forms in which certain areas are filled in by the system and related areas are left open for the user to fill in. The spreadsheet format shown and discussed in example 2.3 in chapter 2 is an example of one variation of this type of interface used for model definition and processing. In the spreadsheet format, the user makes input entries in cells within the column and row grid displayed by the system. Output results are also presented within the same format.

The approach has also been used for query software such as IBM's QBE (query-by-example) package. In this package, the user supplies column headings and makes entries under these headings in order to indicate operations which define the output report to be displayed. Thus, although the system may not actually fill in a part of the user's input form, the format is implied by the system's envisioned response of a columnar report which also provides the general format for the user's query input. (See exhibit 4.7 for an example of this type of query interface.)

The principle assumption behind both spreadsheet and QBE-type interface designs is that they facilitate the user's communication of what is wanted and eliminate as much abstract thinking as possible by making the system's response resemble the way in which the user initiates the operations which produce it. The initiating input is given in context with the already visible format of the desired output.

However, this is not the only way in which input forms can be designed. An alternate way to utilize a form-style interface is to enable the user to initiate action and provide input data within a form displayed by the system, but one which does not resemble the form of the system's response. This alternative may be suitable when the varying proportions of input to output do not make it convenient to utilize similar formats. But even in this case, the need to think abstractly about the input needed in relation to the output desired is reduced by the system's provision of a guiding form for the user. The feasibility of using such a form is limited by the degree to which the type of input categories can be predefined and structured conveniently for display within a form framework.

In its pure form (using no commands or menu items), this type of interface is similar to the Q-A interface in that the system provides prompts (either through the questions presented or the displayed framework of the form) for the user's responses. It differs from the Q-A interface, however, in that all, or many, of the user's entries can be considered at once rather than sequentially, and users thereby can exercise greater control over the sequence of their inputs. While this may be less frustrating, it also provides less guidance for more complex cases.

Free-format Natural Language

The term *natural language* in the context of computer systems means that the human-computer dialogue appears, more or less, to be the same in its style as a human-human dialogue in ordinary English.* Of course, no commercial computer software package has reached the point of passing the well-known Turing test (1956) for artificial intelligence; that is, being able to respond and

---

*The assumption that it is natural to speak English is either a mark of the ethnocentricity of Americans and other, more or less, English speakers, and / or tacit recognition of the dominance of English as the modern international *lingua franca* of business and technology (especially computer technology).

Exhibit 4.7

Query Example Use of Input/Output—Structured Interface

(Note: User enters a report heading and the names of data elements as column headings. The entry of *D.* entered and copied across the line under the column names is a command which causes the items named to be displayed under their headings.)

1987 Monthly inventory analysis

Warehouse	Jan			Feb			March			April		
	In	*Out*	*Onhand*	*In*	*Out*	*Onhand*	*In*	*Out*	*Onhand*	*In*	*Out*	*Onhand*

D. --

(continue for May thru December)

System Response

1987 Monthly inventory analysis

Warehouse	Jan			Feb			March			April		
	In	*Out*	*Onhand*	*In*	*Out*	*Onhand*	*In*	*Out*	*Onhand*	*In*	*Out*	*Onhand*
Northeast	5	10	80	10	20	70	5	30	45	0	25	20
South	0	5	35	21	10	46	0	10	36	5	10	31

(Note: In this query the entry of *Sum* entered and copied across the line, along with *D.* for display under the column names causes the items named to be totaled under their headings, the results displayed and the *Print* entry causes the entire report to be printed.)

1987 Monthly inventory analysis

Warehouse	Jan			Feb			March			April		
	In	*Out*	*Onhand*	*In*	*Out*	*Onhand*	*In*	*Out*	*Onhand*	*In*	*Out*	*Onhand*

D., Sum, Print --

System Response

1987 Monthly inventory analysis

Warehouse	Jan			Feb			March			April		
	In	*Out*	*Onhand*	*In*	*Out*	*Onhand*	*In*	*Out*	*Onhand*	*In*	*Out*	*Onhand*
Northeast	5	10	80	10	20	70	5	30	45	0	25	20
South	0	5	35	21	10	46	0	10	36	5	10	31
Totals	5	15	115	31	30	116	5	40	81	5	35	51

carry out a dialogue with a human being in a manner indistinguishable from that of a human-human dialogue. Bennett (1983) concluded that "the size of 'knowledge base' resources needed and the difficulty of constructing the dialogue manager have precluded widespread use of Natural Language techniques." But limited context, more or less natural, human information queries can be processed by some software packages. A most notably used main frame query package in this category is called INTELLECT (Artificial Intelligence Corp.).*

The requirements for naturalness in a user's statements to a query package are limited by the scope of the functions of the query ad hoc "what is" reporting function. In using this kind of capability the user mainly must make statements consisting of only predicates, that is:

1. Action words (verb commands) that specify what operations are desired, with or without the following components;
2. Names of information items (object nouns) to which the commands refer; and
3. Words or phrases that modify the verb commands or object nouns.

In this regard, the meaningful content of a natural language query would be the same as that contained in a command language but for differences in syntax, usage, and style. In a natural language query interface, in contrast to a command language query system, users can:

1. Punctuate statements according to standard English usage, rather than in software-prescribed spacing and punctuation formats;
2. Use a variety of synonyms to refer to the same commands, information items, and modifiers; and
3. Arrange their statements in any number of ways according to their choice, all of which have the same logical interpretation.

For example, the following natural language (NL) query can be compared to its command language (CL) counterpart:

NL: PRINT THE SALARY IN DESCENDING ORDER OF ALL EMPLOYEES WHO ARE CHEMISTS WITH SALARIES GREATER THAN $50,000.
CL: PRI NAME, SALARY (DO); IF (JOB = CHEMIST AND SALARY GT 50000);

---

*INTELLECT has also been incorporated into a Cullinet data base system under the name of On-Line English.

(Note: PRI is an abbreviated command form for PRINT, (DO) stands for descending order, GT for "greater than," and rules for use of commas, semicolons, spacing, etc. must be followed.)

Naturalness of this kind, it can be argued, minimizes the special knowledge a user must have to only being aware of the extent of the data base. The need for special training in the use of the system is therefore, in theory, eliminated or at least minimized to a few short demonstrations. Because of this, the time required to prepare for usage appears to be minimum and therefore the desire to be up and running quickly with little or no training expense often attracts an organization to this kind of system. In practice, however, the elimination or minimization of training is counterbalanced by the need to perform an analysis of terminology usage and the preparation of a special system file (often called a *lexicon*) to define all synonyms that may be used, especially with respect to information items. For example, a number of command-type statements such as the following one are made by a specialist (the specialist must learn this command language) to define synonyms in a preparatory computer run:

SYN PEOPLE/ANYONE/EVERYONE/EVERYBODY/PERSONNEL/EMPLOYEES

Also, it is often necessary, if the system is to operate efficiently, to preextract information items from numerous computer files and create a special single data base file for use with this software. If users' needs subsequently change, this data extraction must be repeated. These and other efforts and their associated costs are often hidden to potential users, who are typically more impressed with the apparent ease of use and novelty of the natural language interface.

However, even this apparent advantage to users is not without any trade-offs. The following users' problems have been observed in the early usage stages of this kind of natural query interface:

1. Users have difficulty in phrasing unambiguous queries that produce the reports they desire (the trade-off for open format freedom of expression is the need to know how to say what you really mean);
2. Users are sometimes dissatisfied with system response time (often due to the need to have the computer interpret the natural language query coupled with the extra processing needed to retrieve data for unnecessarily complex queries that might be inadmissible in a more structured command language); and
3. Users begin to tire of keying in complete English sentences and full verbs rather than abbreviated forms.

The latter problem of long-winded typing fatigue is often partially rectified by building into the system an ability to include abbreviated terms as synonyms for full words or phrases. This, of course, enables system usage to naturally evolve into something that more closely resembles a command language than natural language. One may wonder why it isn't nearly as well to begin with a command language. This is less a criticism of the ability to design clever enough natural language dialogue processors than it is an observation that human repetitive exposure to and interaction in any given work environment tends to evolve more efficient specialized languages rather than continue usage of general purpose English. (Anyone who ever started work in a new field and a new company can testify to this assertion.) Thus it might be said that natural language is often unnatural.

A user-DSS interface with a greater amount of structure may actually be easier for the user after an initial (often small) investment in learning, than an open format that places a greater burden on other user communications skills. In human-human dialogue, the human receiver of an unclear communication can often fill in gaps and eliminate ambiguity through reference to past experience. If still uncertain, the human receiver can ask a relevant question. The computer software, as yet, is largely incapable of using experience for intelligent interpretation and is very limited even in its ability to ask to-the-point questions. In other words, current natural language systems have only a rudimentary form of intelligence, namely the ability to parse (divide up) a statement and match its parts against a limited stored vocabulary.

Mixed Interface Formats

Many highly structured limited scope user-interactive computing applications are not in the category of decision support. For example, these include applications such as:

1. The selection of the report for display from a limited number of preprogrammed, preprocessed standard reports (using a menu format);
2. The entry of a limited amount of input data into a transaction system (using an input-output structured format); and
3. The on-demand computation and printing out of a standard process, such as preparation of a fixed content, fixed format cost estimate or the grading of an examination (using an input-output structured format or a command format).

As indicated, these interactive automation applications can often effectively utilize a single type of interface format. However, the greater scope and flexibility demanded by most true DSS applications is likely to require a mixed interface which combines the features of two or more of the basic types of interface formats (Carlson 1983).

A dialogue within a continous interactive session can be thought of as a flexible linked series of paired steps or phases, each of which should use the most appropriate type of interface for its intended purpose. For example, consider the following paired phase sequences and their respective interface formats:

Sequence A

First Phase: Enables the user to select the mode of analysis to be carried out from among a limited number of choices such as modeling, query, statistics, and graphics operations.
Interface Format: Menu
Second Phase: Enables the user to choose which operations within the previously selected analysis mode are to be performed on which items of data.
Interface Format: Command

Sequence B

First Step: Query requests are made by the user which often require a list of input data before they are responded to, unless they can be interpreted in several ways and thereby require clarification or cancellation.
Interface Format: Natural language user requests
Second Step: As prompted by the system, data and/or clarifying information is supplied by the user when required.
Interface Format: Question and answer

Sequence C

First Phase: Data and formulas are entered into a spreadsheet model.
Interface Format: Input-Output structured format
Second Phase: Final numerical results are to be printed out in a selected format.
Interface Format: Menu

In addition to such paired sequences of mixed interface types, it is often convenient to use a combination of interface types within the same step of a dialogue. For example, a question and answer sequence could, in addition to single entry responses such as yes-no or single numeric quantities, require the user to make a multiple choice response in which the choices are displayed in a typical menu format. A menu or question and answer segment could also be made a part of an input-in-context-of-output form, such as a choice of graphing options shown on a two-axis plotting display. A natural free format interface may also utilize certain reserved key command terms that are always used in their special functional meanings within the otherwise natural style of the interface.

The interface designer is faced with a large variety of choices to mix and combine interface types as well as to select among choices within each type, such as the choice of commands, sequence of menu items, grouping or layering of commands or menus, the structure of input-output formats, and the use of special symbols or icons in combination with or instead of ordinary words. While some research has been done on ease of use for varying interface features,* few guidelines for DSS interface designers have been derived from

*P. Reisner on the human factors of grammar complexity (1981), H. Lehmann (1978) on the complexities sometimes caused by simple natural language statements, Benbasat and Wand (1984) on the preference of users for truncated abbreviation forms of commands, and other findings summarized by Branscomb and Thomas (1984).

such research. As Branscomb and Thomas (1984) point out, prediction of ease of use depends on controlled experiments involving actual use by representative end users. This is obviously difficult to arrange and in the absence of such research, designers must rely on available user reactions to existing systems, limited testing among small numbers of possibly nonrepresentative users, and their own best judgments. The point has also been made (Huber 1983) that research directed toward finding an "optimal" DSS design is probably inappropriate and irrelevant because DSS packages need to be flexible, friendly, and provide a variety of options for multiple users with different styles, performing different tasks at different times. Since the effectiveness of the interface depends on both the user and the tasks to be performed, system flexibility should include user-controlled choices in the nature of the interface language format. This makes the interface design task for wider scope, integrated DSS even more difficult if the inclusion of a variety of interface options and multiple paths is not to confuse users rather than enhance ease of use.

Advanced and Emerging Interface Language Features

Currently available advanced interface features include the use of keyboard macros and voice input. Emerging new developments may include new interface features that are appropriate for software with more intelligence to infer more from *softer, fuzzier* user statements, as well as do more to lead the user into more effective analysis without taking a tedious series of baby steps through lengthy sequences of Q-A, menus, and HELP screens.

The currently available features of keyboard macros and voice input are, because of their inherent limitations, used mainly by either neophyte computer users who require relatively few functions to be performed, or by leading-edge sophisticates who want to become virtuosos and wring every last drop of functionality out of the computer. The vast majority of middle-range users as yet do not have a voice input capability and make only limited use of advanced keyboard macros. Keyboard macros are the use of special function keys or key combinations in order to initiate computer operations that would otherwise require a series of individual steps (whether these steps utilized an ordinary command language or menus, Q-A, or any standard interface language mix). For neophyte users performing more structured tasks, keyboard macros may be designed for them by an expert in order to speed up operations and thereby increase usage efficiency. Advanced users may be able to define their own keyboard macros for use in much the same way as previously described for the use of macros within a command language.

Voice input system enhancements are available but fall into two general categories:

1. Speaker-independent systems intended for the use of many clerks at work stations; and
2. One speaker dedicated systems that are automatically calibrated to that speaker before general usage.

The first type of systems are generally limited in their ability to being able to recognize only a few words (such as "yes," "no," and the numeric digits from zero through nine), which may be sufficient for such applications as simple data entry in certain transaction processing or transaction control operations. The second type of user-dedicated system can be much more flexible and able to recognize a much larger vocabulary such as that used in a query language set of commands. These systems usually need to be "trained" by each speaker to recognize that speaker's pronunciation of some vocabulary of, typically, up to a few hundred words. The speaker can "retrain" the system if the vocabulary is to be changed. Ordinary and advanced English speakers have vocabularies of many thousands of words, and voice recognition appears to be advancing toward closing the gap in human versus computer vocabularies. However, one cannot have a meaningful open-ended conversation with, say, a DSS query system anyway, without a much greater artificial intelligence capability to interpret ordinary language. The repertoire of commands of a query language may well be accommodated within the limits of voice recognition systems but the limits may not be able to include recognition of all the names of elements in an extensive data base. It seems likely that better voice recognition systems will become increasingly available and their costs will decrease as their range of voice type and vocabulary recognition capabilities increase. Thus such systems can be expected to become more cost-effective. If cost-effectiveness continues to increase, at some point voice input will become commonplace as an optional input if not a replacement for keyboard input. When that occurs, thereby eliminating the tedium of typing lengthy and highly redundant English sentences, an added impetus is likely to be given to a spoken form of natural language interface. It is even possible that some limitation in a voice recognition capability could be used advantageously for a natural language query system if the system is only capable of understanding the key command phrases, data names, and logical modifiers, while ignoring as "noise" the redundant parts of a complete natural statement.

As advances in artificial intelligence for coping with fuzzy attributes and incorporating more expertise into software also come to fruition, the style and content of interface languages may change to reflect these new capabilities. This kind of more interpretively intelligent software should enable users to know less about how to formulate and communicate a precise and sensible analysis and concentrate more on communicating what they know to be relevant about the circumstances of their problem situation. A *fuzzy* command capability, for example, could enable a user to make the following kind of request:

COMPARE LARGE CUSTOMERS' ORDERS TO SMALL CUSTOMERS' ORDERS

In a standard language the terms LARGE and SMALL would have to either be replaced by precise numerical qualifiers (eg. "Greater than $10,000,000," "Less than or equal to $10,000,000") or else be preassigned as synonyms for those qualifying expressions in a lexicon. An intelligent fuzzy command processor, given a sufficient data base and knowledge base, could determine a sensible context-dependent operational definition for LARGE and SMALL in much the same way as a human analyst would approach this task. COMPARE could be a built-in command with a standard meaning known to the user, or it could have been predefined by the user as a macro-command, or, with some additional built-in expertise, the system could interpret COMPARE to simply mean that the user is making a vague request to an expert self-organizing mechanism to determine and execute some sensible mode of comparative analysis. If the simulated expert requires more situation context information before determining a suitable analysis mode, it will ask for it. These forms of artificial intelligence capabilities could continue to utilize the basic forms of interface formats presently in use, but different kinds of information will be required from users and communicated to them from an expert system which is leading the user in new ways to prepare for its higher level self-definition of an appropriate analytical response. While the precise implications for new interface styles and contents are difficult to predict, it seems likely that modifications will be made in each type of interface format as well as in the nature of effectively mixed interface formats.

Review Questions, Exercises, and Discussion Topics

Review Questions

1. To what aspect of a system (any system) does the term "interface" refer?
2. In a DSS-user interface, what kinds of information does the system communicate to the user? What does the user communicate to the system?
3. What relationships exist, if any, between the scope of functionality (power) of a DSS and its ease of use?
4. Name five different types of interface formats that have been used in interactive systems.
5. List the main advantages and limitations of each of the types of interface formats you identified in the previous question.
6. What interface features might be included in order to mitigate the knowledge burden on a user of an extensive command language?

7. In which types of interface does the system take the strongest role of leading the user and constraining the users flexibility in initiating operations?
8. Which types of interface provide the user more flexibility and control over initiating operations in any desired order?
9. What kinds of functional requirements should be included in a natural language query system? What are the main differences between such a language and a command language interface for the same query functions?
10. Why is it unlikely that a powerful DSS could effectively utilize only a single type of interface format?
11. What are keyboard macros and what kinds of users may they be most appropriate for?
12. What are the potential advantages and current limitations of voice input?
13. What is an example of a "fuzzy" command and how might the ability of a system to accept such commands be helpful to users?

Exercises

1. A special DSS query system is being designed to aid ardent sports fans, sports writers, and other interested parties in retrieving and analyzing a wide range of recent historical data on sports events, players performance records, etc.
   a) Name and define the functions of a set of commands for a suitable Command Language for this system.
   b) Sketch and describe the appearance and functions of a set of visual symbols or icons that might be useful in this system.
2. A system is intended to aid students in selecting elective courses to take. Describe a series of questions and examples of student responses such a system might effectively utilize in a Q-A interface format.
3. A lexicon is to be developed for a natural language interface for a query system to be used by a group of marketing managers and analysts. Give a list of synonyms (single words or short phrases) you believe will be most required for the following basic kinds of commands, data items, and modifiers:

COMMANDS	DATA ITEMS	MODIFIERS
a. LIST	1. SALES	i. LARGEST
b. SUMMARIZE	2. PRODUCTS	ii. SMALLEST
c. SORT	3. CUSTOMERS	iii. ALL

4. Briefly describe a planning task you have some familiarity with and write a sample DSS-user dialogue which utilizes a mixed format interface suitable in supporting this task.

Discussion Topics

1. In a survey of microcomputer users, attitudes toward two different DSS software packages were compared. The users that were sampled to evaluate each package were matched in terms of their backgrounds, present job tasks, and their general approaches to problem solving. The packages

performed the same functions, yet user attitudes and assessments of the packages varied markedly. What might explain this result? Give examples and present your reasoning in justifying your answer.

2. In human-machine communication, what is most "natural" for the machine (a present day computer) is least "natural" for the human, and vice versa. What approaches seem best to overcoming this "natural language gap?" Discuss pros and cons of different approaches.

3. Some would argue that according to a strict definition of DSS, a system which provides a menu of predefined reports is not really a DSS, but might still be very useful and justified whatever name we might call it. Discuss when such a system might be a useful approach to take? Take into account in your discussion characteristics of the organization, the user(s), their jobs, the type of business, and any other factors you consider to be relevant. What might be expected regarding maintenance needs of such a system, the expected life of the system, and what might follow in a next system version?

4. *a*) Discuss the prospects for designing the ideal (or optimal) DSS-user interface.

   b) What questions would need to be answered in order to accomplish this and how could these questions be answered?

   c) If you were a DSS software developer what would you do with respect to developing the best interface possible in a real and competitive business situation?

References

Benbasat, I., Wand, Y. 1984. "Command Abbreviation Behavior in Human-Computer Interaction." *Human Aspects of Computing, Communications of the ACM 27*(April)4:376–83.

Bennett, J. L. 1983. *Building Decision Support Systems*. Chapter 1, Reading, Mass.: Addison-Wesley. 12.

Branscom, L. M., Thomas, J. C. 1984. "Ease of Use: A System Design Challenge." *IBM Systems Journal* 23(3):224–35.

Carlson, E. D. 1983. *Building Decision Support Systems*. Chapter 4, Reading, Mass.: Addison-Wesley. 70.

Huber, G. P. 1983. "Cognitive Style As a Basis for MIS and DSS Designs." *Management Science* 29(May)5:567–79.

Lehmann, H. 1978. "Interpretation of Natural Language in an Information System." *IBM Journal of Research and Development* 22(5):560–72.

Reisner, P. 1981. "Formal Grammar and Human Factors Design of an Interactive Graphics System." *IEEE Transactions on Software Engineering* SE–7(2):229–40.

Turning, A. M. 1956. "Can A Machine Think." in *The World of Mathematics* New York: Simon and Schuster.

Young, L. F. 1978. "Another Look at Man-Computer Interaction." *INTERFACES* 8(February)2:67–69.

Microcomputer and Mainframe* DSS

I had three hundred cooks to dress my victuals, in little convenient huts built round my house, whereby they and their families lived, and prepared me two dishes apiece. A dish of their meat was a good mouthful, and a barrel of their liquor a reasonable draught. . . . Their geese and turkeys I usually ate at a mouthful . . . of their smaller foul I could take up twenty or thirty at the end of my knife.
Jonathan Swift, "A Voyage To Lilliput" in *Gulliver's Travels,* International Collectors Library, Doubleday & Company, 1945.

In the earliest days of commercial computers, when the term "business application" was almost synonymous with the tireless, accurate, automated processing of large volumes of transaction data, *big was beautiful.* For the few operations research number crunching applications such as large scale linear programming models for transportation networks and refinery mix problems, a big computer was not only beautiful, but it meant that solving these large models became feasible for the first time. In the 1970s, the microcomputer came on the scene, but not to compete with the large mainframe, which is still king for its ability to ingest and digest large volumes of data at unsurpassed speeds. The micros found their own niche, in which smaller is, if not beautiful, more convenient and cost-effective for a different set of needs.

*The term "mainframe" is used here to cover a wide range of computer sizes in categories that, for other purposes, are variously classified as minicomputers up through supercomputers. For purposes of this discussion all of these are grouped together under the heading of mainframes. This is not intended to minimize the important differences between the various sizes and models included in this category of computers. Various sizes and models of microcomputers also exist. But the microcomputer-mainframe dichotomy is useful as a means of generally comparing differences and trends in the DSS software package capabilities that have been developed for each of these groups of computers.

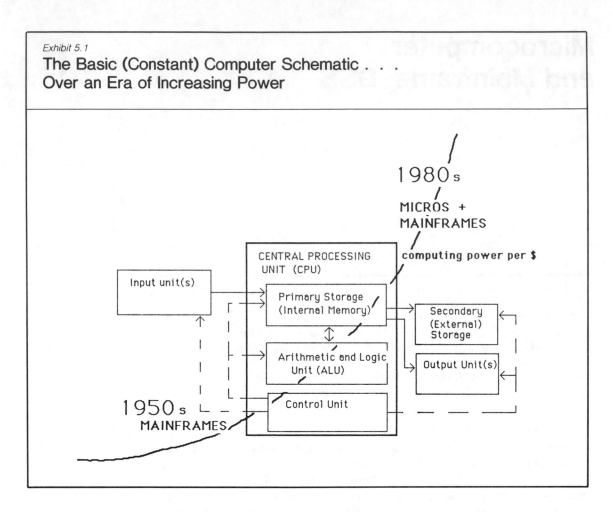

Exhibit 5.1

The Basic (Constant) Computer Schematic . . .
Over an Era of Increasing Power

But despite the changes wrought by new computer technology, the well-known maxim of history—*the more things change, the more they remain the same*—seems to hold for at least some aspects of computers. One such constant over the short but dynamic history of computers, is that the general schematic representation of the functional components of 1950s mainframe computers would look exactly like that of today's microcomputers. They would all include the basic components in the central processing unit (CPU), as well as secondary storage, input, and output units shown in exhibit 5.1. Although the details of computer engineering vary, these same generic components make a modern computer (at least as we currently understand the concept of *computer*) able to perform the wide variety of applications the human mind can identify and specify.

Within this constant framework, however, advances in microprocessor technology radically changed the size and the cost of hardware circuitry required to operationalize the functions represented in this standard schematic. These advances made the microcomputer feasible and the mainframe able to handle more computing at lower unit costs. Today's microcomputers have the computing power of many of yesterday's mainframes. In addition, it is important to note that microcomputers have had, and it appears will continue to have, an advantage over mainframes in their ratio of cost to processing speed. The internal processing speed of computers is commonly measured in "MIPS," millions of instructions executed per second. Dividing the dollar cost of the computer by MIPS ($/MIPS) provides a measure of the unit cost of computing. On this measure the microcomputer is a relative bargain.

Accompanying the cost-effectiveness impact of changes in operationalizing hardware functions, new software approaches became feasible. Software that would take too long to run and require too much of the available internal memory space within the old technology, now had bigger and faster computer resources available at affordable costs. The resulting new hardware-software-micro-mainframe environment has changed all the cost-benefit and feasibility equations, as well as the psychological factors, that determine scope of usage and accessibility of computing power. This new environment has had a significant impact on the management of information resources in both large and small organizations.

Although the type of computer application that has come to be called DSS predates the introduction of microcomputers, the use of DSS has been particularly affected by the increasing penetration of microcomputers and their evolving relationships with larger computer systems. This chapter examines the ways in which DSS applications have been affected by the new hardware-software-micro-mainframe environment. It will look at this environment's affect on DSS application identification and growth within the framework of the three varying dependency relationships illustrated in exhibit 5.2. As this exhibit indicates, issues related to the identification and assessment of potential DSS applications are seen as falling into the following categories:

1. Those issues that are *independent* of the choice of mainframe versus microcomputer as the tool for implementation;
2. Those issues that are *dependent* on the availability or choice of microcomputer and mainframe resources; and
3. Those issues that require a role for both these types of computer resources, and are thus seen as related to *interdependent* micro-mainframe functions.

Exhibit 5.2

DSS Requirements Versus Micro-Mainframe Dependency

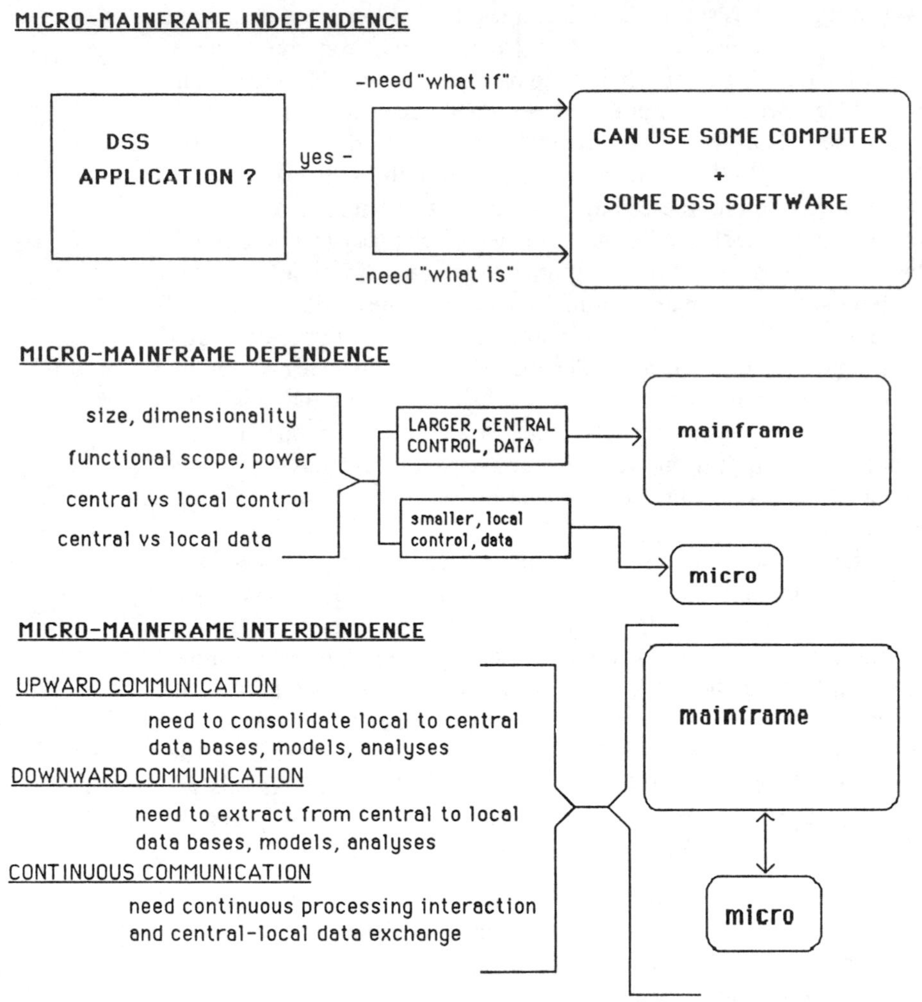

MICRO-MAINFRAME INDEPENDENCE

DSS APPLICATION ?

yes –

–need "what if"

–need "what is"

CAN USE SOME COMPUTER + SOME DSS SOFTWARE

MICRO-MAINFRAME DEPENDENCE

size, dimensionality
functional scope, power
central vs local control
central vs local data

LARGER, CENTRAL CONTROL, DATA → mainframe

smaller, local control, data → micro

MICRO-MAINFRAME INTERDENDENCE

UPWARD COMMUNICATION
    need to consolidate local to central
    data bases, models, analyses
DOWNWARD COMMUNICATION
    need to extract from central to local
    data bases, models, analyses
CONTINUOUS COMMUNICATION
    need continuous processing interaction
    and central-local data exchange

mainframe

micro

DSS Micro-Mainframe Independencies

In the 1960s, given the impetus of mainframe time-sharing services, applications that provided staff analysts with the kind of control and flexibility needed for exploring semistructured business problems became more frequent and visible. Perhaps some applications we would now consider to have the attributes of DSS began even earlier, in the 1950s before the general availability of mainframe time-sharing. Although we tend to equate *interaction* with either mainframe time-sharing or the use of microcomputers, in a general sense, all computers are devices that can be programmed to perform certain processes that interact with human thought processes. In management information systems, the difference between remote computer processing, unconnected via direct communication to users sitting at input or output devices, and time-sharing systems using communication terminals, is essentially the *media* and *speed* of interaction, not interaction itself. As long as humans are involved as providers of computer inputs and interpreters of computer outputs, human-machine interaction is taking place. Computer specialists have merely adapted the term *interaction* as a shorthand way to differentiate between the much more rapid and direct exchanges that time-sharing or microcomputers provide, and the longer interval interruptions of indirect input-output exchanges that are provided by computers operating in so-called *batch mode*. Interactive problem analysis, however, does not always require rapid, immediate interaction. Sometimes, the delay in receiving computer printouts in batch mode, which may be only a day, or a few hours or even minutes, may be beneficial. A short delay could provide the analyst-user with an opportunity to digest interim results, think through the next step in an analysis, or to break out of the mind-set resulting from concentrating on one problem continuously, thereby allowing time for subconscious idea germination to take place. On the other hand, there is no doubt that, whether rapid interaction is needed or not for any analytical advantage, it is nearly always more *convenient* to be able to communicate directly with a computer. The direct input-output facility of communication terminals and CRTs eliminates the physical steps and extra handling involved with preparing and transmitting remote input forms and receiving, handling, storing, and retrieving hardcopy computer printouts of a series of interim results. The processing efficiencies afforded by modern, cost-effective direct communications has led to the increased use of input and output terminals and data communications for in-house time-sharing on mainframe computer systems for a wide variety of applications, including those of a transaction processing or standard reporting nature, as well as DSS applications.

Thus, in the typical large organization, any need for rapid interaction as well as the convenience and efficiency of direct communication can be provided by either microcomputers used in stand-alone mode, or by in-house time-sharing or outside time-sharing service bureaus using mainframes serving multiple users and multiple types of applications. Given the convenience-efficiency justification of direct communications and its widespread availability on mainframes, users working in direct communications mode can utilize rapid interaction or not, as long as they can work at their own discretion and pace. DSS applications are discretionary applications, which should enable users to determine their own pace of interaction as well as to flexibly control the analysis process itself. Choosing between a microcomputer and mainframe time-sharing for DSS applications is therefore not dependent on the need for interaction itself or (within general limits) the speed of interaction desired, since both options provide user-controlled interaction.

Also, one cannot determine an absolute application requirement for either a mainframe or microcomputer based solely on which general DSS basic functions are to be used. Although many of their usage characteristics and specific features differ, a variety of modeling software packages for "what if" types of analysis are available for both microcomputers and mainframes. The same is true for the "what is" type of data base software capability and the "why" facilities of statistical analysis or knowledge-based rule processing. Therefore, no general restrictions determine that a particular type of DSS function dictates the use of one or another type of computer. Specific packages, however, run only on specific models of micro or mainframe computers, depending usually on their size requirements and always on their specified software *operating system* (such as PC DOS for IBM personal computers or Apple's DOS for microcomputers; DOS/VSE for an IBM mainframe or PRIMOS for a Prime 50 series computer). For the latter reason, given that a micro package or a mainframe package can each do the job, the type of computer and operating system that has already been acquired may be the sole reason that dictates which package will be compatible and therefore which will be selected.

However, there often are other significant differences between microcomputer and mainframe DSS software and processing modes. So even though the general characteristics that identify an application as suitable for a DSS (that is, a semistructured problem that can utilize a semistructured analysis process) do not automatically indicate which kind of computer is needed, more specific factors should be taken into account to decide whether a micro alone, a mainframe alone, or a combination of both, will be most cost-effective. These factors are discussed in the following sections.

DSS Micro-Mainframe Dependencies

Micro and mainframe resources for DSS may differ on the following dimensions:

1. Cost of software/hardware resources
2. Size limitations
   —of models
   —of data bases
3. Functional scope and power
   —nature and extent of built-in functions
   —model and data base management capabilities
   —processing time differences
4. Extent of integration of functions
   —scope and power of individual functions in one package
   —use of multiple functions
5. Ease of use (usability)
6. Local personal control or central control
   —psychological environment differences
   —privacy, data integrity, and security
7. Directness of linkages with other systems and data access
   —dependencies on and accessibility of data produced elsewhere

If it were true that mainframe resources always delivered more benefits to DSS users, then their relatively higher costs would still have to be taken into account to complete a cost-benefit comparison. (These varying cost ranges are illustrated in exhibit 5.3.)

But as the following discussion will indicate, it is not always the case that mainframe DSS resources always deliver more usable benefits. In addition to examining cost differentials, real requirements and usable benefits will have to be taken into account in order to justify a choice between using mainframe or micro software.

Model and Data Base Size Dependencies

In general, mainframe systems have accommodated larger models and data bases, and/or a larger number of individual models and data bases that can be consolidated or combined in a single analysis. However, this is changing rapidly and it appears that in the near future microcomputer software and hardware will be able to handle problems large enough so that the size factor will rarely determine by itself that a mainframe is needed for a particular DSS application. For example, the original VisiCalc spreadsheet package could accommodate 16,002 cells (63 columns × 254 rows). Lotus 1–2–3 subsequently

---

Exhibit 5.3

Sample Costs for Mainframe and Microcomputer DSS Resources*

Microcomputer DSS Packages

    General per copy price range for spreadsheet/query systems:

        $195–$2,500

Mainframe DSS Packages

    General per copy price range for modeling/query systems:

        $25,000–$320,000

Microcomputer Hardware

    Microcomputer + printer + hard-disk + modem:

        $3,500–$15,000

Basic Mainframe Hardware Costs

    Telecommunications terminal:

        $1,500–$3,500

Allocated charges for CPU time + storage:

        $1 to $20 per average interactive session

*Discounts for volume purchases of microcomputer hardware and software can generally be obtained in the range of 10–20 percent. Software prices are generally trending downward, all prices change rapidly and current sources should be checked at the time of purchase. All price ranges given are for relative illustration only.

---

provided a capability to handle 524,000 cells (254 columns × 2048 rows). A more recent version of Lotus 1–2–3 raised its row capacity to 8000 and thereby is capable of including just over two million cells. In the past, it would have been necessary to consider a mainframe package such as IFPS (which had maximum dimensional limits of 250 columns by 8192 rows) if one wanted to be able to develop a model of up to two million cells. Mainframe packages (such as IFPS) can be expected to keep pace in raising their own size limits. But it would seem that only rare situations would give rise to DSS applications (as opposed to large structured OR models) that would require such large models. At present, the size of internal memory (RAM, random-addressable memory) of microcomputers in use and their operating systems provide an upper limit to the size of models or data bases that can be programmed at one time. Thus a software package may allow for two million cells but a microcomputer with only a 512,000 byte RAM cannot process such a spreadsheet model. (The package would run but provide a message when the computer's capacity was reached.) But there is an equally rapid trend toward larger microcomputer memories and software developers are apparently trying to stay ahead of the curve. For example, the Macintosh was initially a 128K machine, then an upgraded 512K version was released, and subsequently the MacPlus machine provided over a million bytes of RAM. It is expected that a new version of the IBM DOS operating system for their PCs will raise the limit it places on memory from 640K to 16 megabytes (16 million bytes).

Similarly, data base software for microcomputers had considerably smaller limits than mainframe packages in the past. The same limits for a Lotus 1–2–3 spreadsheet apply to a Lotus data base, for example. By comparison, the natural language query system called INTELLECT can extract data from virtually unlimited size files and, as a practical matter, can directly access an extracted data base of several million data elements.

The size requirement for DSS is seldom known in advance with great accuracy and thus it may be important to provide for considerable excess capacity. As with the other dimensions of differences, a user's initially expected requirements may be satisfied within the limits of smaller-dimensioned (and less expensive) microcomputer hardware/software. But, given the increasing availability of much larger software and hardware capacities at small cost increments, it may be economically worthwhile to obtain more than one expects to need and avoid potential future costs of transferring smaller systems applications into larger systems. (Two cases of small and large DSS planning applications are shown in example 5.1.)

A newer category of personal computers, the so-called supermicro *work stations* such as the Sun and Apollo Microsystems, have larger memories and faster processing speeds (and bigger price tags) than the more usual microcomputers such as the IBM PC or the Macintosh. These and even newer versions of such workstations using reduced instruction set (RISC) technology to obtain faster processing speeds will continue to encourage development of DSS software at the personal desktop level with the size capacities and functional scope and power currently associated only with mainframes. RISC personal work stations are being developed by IBM, Hewlett Packard, by AT&T (via their "C" machine), and by Digital Equipment Corporation.

Thus size limitations are a factor for many microcomputers and software packages in use but is tending to diminish as a categorical distinction between personally controlled microcomputers and centrally operated mainframes.

EXAMPLE 5.1
LARGE AND SMALL DSS PLANNING APPLICATIONS

LARGE PLANNING SYSTEM CHARACTERISTICS

Purpose: Corporate financial planning support for a large international multidivisional company.

Scope of system: System consists of several submodels:

1. An econometric domestic demand forecasting model (approximately 350 equations and 600 variables*) of the industry segments that purchase the company's major industrial products.
2. A foreign demand statistical time series forecasting model of the foreign purchases of the company's major industrial products.
3. A set of divisional product models (12 models of about 500 variables each) that translate forecasted demand, pricing policy and internal cost factors into divisional financial plans.
4. A corporate financial model (about 350 equations and 800 variables) that integrates divisional financial models into a comprehensive consolidated statement.

General Requirements:

1. Divisional model inputs include cost and historical data extracted from transaction data files and past financial records.
2. A great many judgmental assumptions need to be explored and revisions made within both the divisional and consolidated corporate models before final plans are accepted.

*Note: More variables than equations characterizes an under-determined model requiring many variables to be given values as input data or assumptions rather than solved for mathematically.

3. Convenient and powerful data management facilities are required because of the need to consolidate and pass data between system components.

CONCLUSION:

A microcomputer spreadsheet package could handle separate components, but overall system size, needs for data management, statistical and analytical power call for mainframe software or a mainframe-micro combination.

SMALL PLANNING SYSTEM CHARACTERISTICS

Purpose: Financial modeling support for a single product regional consumer food product distributor.

Scope of system: The system consists of two models:

1. An internal operations model (50 equations and 80 variables) that includes relationships between operating costs and aggregate financial results.
2. A model that produces a final financial statement (40 equations and 65 variables) based on a few key outputs of the prior model and alternative assumptions about external factors such as taxes and borrowing interest rates.

General Requirements:

The system is used mainly at annual planning time and adjusted once each quarter. Data entry and reentry volume is considered small enough for manual key-entry by an assistant.

CONCLUSION:

A microcomputer spreadsheet package can meet needs.

Differences in Functional Scope and Power

As in the case of the size capacities previously discussed, most analysts and users would probably agree that the scope and power of mainframe software for both data base and modeling support functions has been significantly greater than these microcomputer software capabilities, but also that this gap is narrowing. In order to examine more closely what this means and how one can make such assessments, it should be pointed out that:

1. Functional *scope* can be defined as the extent of the list of commands and functions that a system can perform, and functional *power* can be defined as a concept related to how much useful work a user can obtain by concise communication of what is desired, but as a practical matter these concepts are hard to separate and it is probably not useful to do so in an assessment of software functionality;
2. There is no standard recognized way of measuring and comparing the relative functional scope and power of two different software packages or of different categories of packages; and
3. Most single quantitative dimensions of comparison (such as the number of built in financial or mathematical functions of a modeling package) can be misleading.

To illustrate the need to jointly consider scope and power, and not to be misled by single quantitative dimensions, we can examine the comparison of modeling packages in example 5.2 on the basis of the number and type of built-in functions they respectively include.

EXAMPLE 5.2

A COMPARISON OF NUMBER OF BUILT-IN FUNCTIONS

Number of built-in functions of the following types:

	Financial	Mathematical	Statistical
Mainframe packages			
A	15	19	—
B	8	11	9
Micro Packages			
C	6	12	2
D	—	15	—

What the numbers alone, in this example, do not reveal is that:

1. In mainframe package A no distinction is made between statistical and general mathematical functions, and some basic kinds of statistical results can be easily obtained with the use of some of the functions classified as "mathematical";

2. While it appears that mainframe package A contains a more extensive repertoire of financial functions than does any one of the other packages, a closer examination of the details of what these functions actually do would reveal that mainframe package B's financial functions have a wider scope of applicability and greater power because they utilize certain parameter arguments to the functions in order to cover a wider scope of situations whereas the other packages utilize a different function for each of these situations or do not include them at all. For example, packages A, B, and C all include a net present value financial function. Only package B, however, can handle variable future payments as well as fixed payments, and variable as well as constant future interest rates;

3. Micro package D appears not to include any financial functions at all, but an examination of its repertoire of mathematical functions would reveal that one of these can indeed compute the net present value of a series of fixed future payments, given an interest rate; and

4. The fairly wide scope of micro package D's "mathematical" functions can often be easily utilized in various combinations to obtain the same results as using a given single "statistical" or "financial" function of one of the other packages, or to perform a "statistical" or "financial" function that is *not* included in one of these other packages. (How then can one, merely by counting categorized functions, assess the loss of some "power" for the gain of some "scope?")

The above discussion considered the number and nature of built-in functions. Functional scope and power, however, is not only affected by these characteristics, but also by size and dimensionality limitations, and by the range of functionality provided by the repertoire of processing command modes included in the software. The range of processing command modes is determined by what users can make the system do in operating upon either data bases or models or both. If the user-system interface utilizes a command type of language in order to initiate operations, the extent of processing command mode capabilities could be determined by inventorying the number and type of built-in commands. These could be assessed in a manner similar to the consideration of built-in functions provided in a modeling language. Often, however, system operations utilize other interface styles such as operation menus, or question and answer formats, as well as commands and mixed interface types. Such variety makes it difficult to identify and inventory all of the modes of processing available at the user's fingertips from one package to another in order to make a simple direct quantitative comparison. Example 5.3 illustrates some of the dimensions and limitations of a comparison based on the number and type of processing command modes included in a modeling package.

EXAMPLE 5.3

COMPARISON ON SELECTED PROCESSING MODES

Availability/number of processing modes of the following types:

	Model consolidation commands	"What if"	Goal seeking	Sensitivity analysis	Output options
Mainframe packages					
A	8	2	yes	2	4
B	4	1	yes	2	6
Micro packages					
C	1	1	no	no	2
D	—	1	yes	no	3

As with the prior example comparing built-in functions, no simple numeric summary inventory such as given above is sufficient. Examination of the specifics of these processing mode capabilities would reveal the following:

1. The more directly interactive micro spreadsheet type of interface makes it relatively fast and easy to carry out a variety of sensitivity analyses even though no specialized commands are provided for this purpose as in the command language type of interface used by the mainframe packages (the summary display of such results, however, is not as compact or fast to print out in the spreadsheet package);

2. The two types of "what if" commands of package A are used to differentiate between *cumulative* "what if's" (in which one or more prior "what if" variable value changes are retained along with a subsequent change of another variable's value) and "this one time only" stand-alone type of "what if," but the same two modes of "what if" analysis can be obtained in the micro spreadsheet packages by the user specifying when temporary results are to be saved (either under different names or replacing previous results under the same name) or merely displayed temporarily.

These specific differences illustrate that often the nature of a non-command interface language provides more or less power in carrying out different modes of processing, but that these differences are not always easy to identify and compare to specific command repertoire items.

End-user data base ("what is") packages also vary considerably in their scope and power, with mainframe software generally providing the more extensive and powerful repertoire for this kind of analysis than earlier versions of micro query systems. This is currently no longer the case for all microcomputer data base query software. For example, the Oracle and FOCUS packages previously ran only on mainframes but have added fully-functioned microcomputer versions that run on IBM compatible personal computers.

Purists have argued that some past microcomputer packages using the designation of data base management systems (DBMS) were really not data base systems at all, but should instead have been called file managers. A survey reported in 1981 found that only two out of twenty self-proclaimed data base management systems for microcomputers upon examination proved to really provide this kind of capability (Barley and Driscoll 1981). Essentially, a file management system enables a user to update and maintain a single file of like-constructed records, and to sort and list the file, but to do little or nothing more in terms of data manipulation or to selectively project a part of the file or to join selected data items from two or more different files that can be logically linked. The design, structure, and use of data base management systems is a specialized subject that is beyond the scope of this text, but the particular capabilities of such a system that are most relevant to end-user DSS are those associated with their query language capabilities. In many cases, DSS software packages are called "query packages" rather than a DBMS. The use of this kind of capability was illustrated in chapter 2 and the nature of user-system interfaces in which queries can be conveyed to the system were discussed in chapter 4. The following query capabilities are most significant for DSS and vary in terms of functional power and scope from one package to another:

1. The ability of users to retrieve and display selected data elements (representing attributes or characteristics) of one or more entities from a data base depending on their characteristics meeting a user-supplied set of logical qualifications;
2. The ability to control the sequence (ascending or descending sorted order) of a selected and displayed list of entity attributes;
3. The ability to produce summary statistics (such as the mean average, maximum and minimum values, a count of entities meeting a qualification, totals and subtotals) and to calculate percentages;
4. The ability to refer in a query to different types of entities (such as "employees," "projects," and "customers") from two or more data base files that can be logically associated with one another; and
5. The ability to mathematically combine numerical data elements (entity attributes) contained in the data base in order to generate new data for display to the user.

To the extent that one can generalize regarding these features, it is likely that a mainframe package will have all or most of these capabilities (some mainframe packages can only extract information from a single "flat file" or a relational data base referring to a common entity such as "customer accounts," rather than being capable of linking different logically associated entities as in item 4). In contrast, many micro packages are limited to the capabilities included in 1 and 2 above, and some of the capabilities in category 3, while others such as the micro version of FOCUS include the same capabilities as mainframe packages.

Extent of Function Integration

Packages differ significantly from one another with respect to the extent to which basic capabilities such as modeling, data base querying, graphics, and word processing are integrated within a single package. In this regard, however, one cannot so easily generalize as to whether mainframe software or microcomputer software is categorically more integrated. More or less integrated DSS software exists for both types of computers and more or less single function software also exists for both types of computers.

As stated with regard to assessing functional power and scope, the degree of integration of multipurpose software cannot be measured by a standard single scale on order to facilitate comparison. Integration, at one extreme, may mean little more than that the final output of one mode of analysis can be patched or "pasted" into the output of another application as a monolithic chunk rather than as a set of data that can continue to be operated upon in the receiving application as individually accessible data elements. For example, in this kind of integration a graphic display could not be edited or recomputed within a text document it has been "pasted" into. In order to change the graph itself or its textual labels and headings it would be necessary to return to the graphics mode and operate on or reproduce the graph before patching the new graph back into the receiving text document. At an opposite extreme of integrated functions, the transition from function to function would seem to be all part of a continuous flexibly flowing conversation, and the user would not need to be aware at all of leaving one mode of processing, such as modeling, to enter another mode, such as graphing, or vice versa. This kind of perfect integration would, in effect, make the interface between basic functions so natural that it would be "transparent" (translate: "invisible" and of no concern) to the user. Although no categorical claim can be made in this regard for the superiority of all micro software to that of mainframe packages or vice versa, the ease of crossing such functional interfaces seems to have been pioneered by some particular micro packages. Given the general competitiveness and continuing search for advances in software design and ease of use, it is likely that many of these and other features found to be desirable by users will be adapted into both micro and mainframe software.

In addition to the extent of integration as distinguished above, packages vary in terms of the problem-size trade-offs integration usually implies. The presence of several general capabilities within a single package usually means more internal storage is required for the software itself, thereby representing a trade-off with regard to the size limitations of applications data and models. However, the design of a particular package determines the extent of the size sacrifice implied by broader functionality, and, as noted earlier, size dimensions for software and hardware are generally increasing.

Another aspect of integration is more related to the ease of acquisition, volume discounts, and convenience of supporting users and providing maintenance than to the actual need for integrated applications. Rather than selecting and acquiring different numbers of packages for individual needs, a number of copies of a single all-purpose package can be acquired by a central purchasing agent in the information systems department. Even if individual users only utilize a part of the integrated packages capabilities, advantages of central volume acquisition and maintenance may offset the lower individual utilization. Also, as mentioned earlier with respect to the evolutionary growth in size and scope of power needs of a given kind of general function, users will often grow into entirely new categories of applications. If an integrated package was initially obtained, these new needs can often be met with the software already in place. The perception of beneficial new applications even may be stimulated by the presence of the software and its availability for user experimentation.

Ease of Use

"User friendly" has become the unofficial "seal of approval" claim nearly all end-user software vendors feel they must bestow upon their own package. Since a standard measure of ease of use is lacking, anyone can interpret its meaning and claim its abundant presence. The over-claims and misuse of the term "user friendly" has given it buzzword status. Serious attempts to preserve its utility generally define the degree of user friendliness (or ease of use) as being measurable according to the training and practice time necessary to attain an acceptable or average level of competence. A package requiring two hours of learning to reach that prescribed level would presumably be ten times "friendlier" than one requiring twenty hours of training before a user could properly perform the same operations. However, this definition is still lacking a precise criterion for acceptable or proper performance, and it is seldom, if ever, operationalized. Any available ratings of learning times tend to be subjective assessments, and thus not reproducible, not audited, and not printed on package labels.

But if functional power is a dimension in which mainframe systems have the edge, most observers would probably agree that in any contest for ease of use a jury of users would give the blue ribbons to microcomputer packages. This is probably the result of the influence of several factors, including the following:

1. A primary marketing target for microcomputers was (and is) end-users without prior programming or computing experience, who require a lower learning barrier to usage than programmers or other experienced technical users such as engineers;

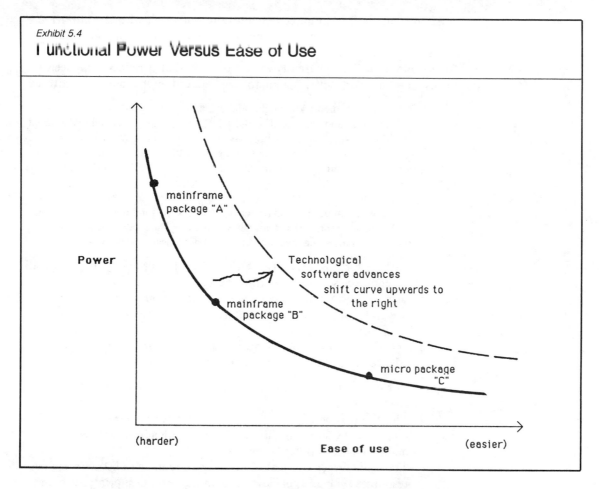

Exhibit 5.4

Functional Power Versus Ease of Use

Power

mainframe
package "A"

Technological
software advances
shift curve upwards to
the right

mainframe
package "B"

micro package
"C"

(harder)

Ease of use

(easier)

2. New best-seller applications such as spreadsheet packages were conceived and born within the microcomputer environment, and were designed on a "clean piece of paper" unencumbered with traditional interface design thinking; and

3. The generally more limited functional requirements (lower functional scope and power) of micro software had the built-in advantage of making these packages easier to learn and use, especially for less dedicated or infrequent users (see exhibit 5.4 for general relationship between functional power and ease of use).

Early and subsequent spreadsheet packages, if they didn't entirely innovate a new interface style, certainly popularized it and clearly demonstrated its appeal to users. The input-output structured format interface of a spreadsheet package (discussed in chapter 4, examples also given in chapter 2) was not commonly used in interactive mainframe software, with the latter more commonly utilizing command language and question and answer interface styles. A major reason the spreadsheet interface structure of "input in the context of output" is apparently easier to use is that it reduces the need for the user to think abstractly. Abstractness is reduced by the following features:

1. A common framework for input and output
   —Input data and functional model relationships can be defined and entered by the user one at a time, within a visual framework of the larger spreadsheet, rather than defining a model within a separate and different format from that of the results of "solving" (numerically evaluating) the model; and
2. Immediate response
   —The user can get immediate feedback of results for each entry or change in the spreadsheet, rather than delaying solving the model and seeing results until after the model definition mode is terminated.

The earliest spreadsheet software (VisiCalc) has probably influenced all subsequent end-user software interface design. A more reactive and natural interface is now considered a major requirement, not only for the spreadsheet type of capability, but for microcomputer DSS software applications in general.

Factors other than the main features of the interface language that may influence the relative ease of use of micro systems usage are:

1. The omission of sign on, sign off protocols in the stand-alone micro environment;
2. The elimination of remote, application unrelated system interruptions due to mainframe usage overloads, scheduled maintenance, or other factors; and
3. The more direct physical control (again reducing abstractness) over resources such as application programs, data files, printer, etc. in the microcomputing environment, as opposed to the remote command language manipulated mainframe environment.

Given the general "friendliness" advantage of the microcomputer user's world, if a natural language interface is desired on the grounds that it provides ease of use and requires little prior training, then this would generally be a plus for mainframe systems. Mainframe software originally provided this kind of query capability and mainframes are still better able to implement the natural language approach without sacrificing too much in data base size restrictions or in processing time needed to react to a query. However, well-designed query systems using other interface styles may offer nearly as much ease of use and require only marginally longer introductory training session or a brief self-training exploratory exercise session.

Personal Control

A greater sense of privacy, lower psychological threat, and greater personal control seems to be key appeals of working in the self-contained micro world. In contrast, in the world of mainframe time-sharing one may have a sense (real or imagined) that "Big Brother" may be watching, or "we might cause some damage or be culpable for some unknown offense." Some specific real contributing factors to this generalized higher psychological "comfort quotient" of the microcomputing environment can be identified as including:

1. The direct control over physical resources not only contributes to ease of use (as pointed out above) by reducing abstract command language dependency, but enhances a sense of independent control through one's own physical and private action, rather than through communicating action requests to another entity (albeit an impersonal entity);
2. The knowledge that in a time-sharing environment one's usage is usually being monitored to some extent in order to charge time and/or cost against an individual or organizational account; and
3. The knowledge that other users are "out there" and simultaneously communicating over something like a shared "party line" with the same computer (even if their applications are entirely independent of one another's).

In some cases, the lack of privacy and independence in time-sharing is made much more evident through a system which monitors the usage of specific applications and data bases (and not just total connect time and CPU usage time), through password and security procedures, through system messages conveyed, and through interuser communications.

In addition to the psychological user appeal provided by the microcomputer environment, real threats to the security and privacy of user-owned data and personal analyses can be reduced in this more private world. The stand-alone noncommunications environment eliminates remote electronic access over a wide network of potential infiltrators that exists in time-sharing despite security procedures. While stand-alone microcomputer work is still vulnerable to theft and unauthorized exposure, only direct contact in the immediate physical locus of the user must be guarded against. These threats may cumulatively across an entire organization loom as large as the dangers inherent in protecting centralized mainframe facilities. But this is mainly the headache of central management and information system executives, while individual users are concerned mostly with their own data and comforted by their sense of more direct control over it. From an organizational point of view, information system managers are often discomfited by the inability to enforce security measures over microcomputer users compared to time-sharing users. But they may take some comfort from the lesser impact of the loss of local microcomputer data here and there than the impact of losing all the eggs in the central computer basket. This spread-and-diffuse-the-impact advantage, however, disappears in a computing environment in which micros communicate with mainframes and with one another. From the point of view of a central information resource executive's security concerns, this is the worst of worlds. As the next section discusses, this world of micro-mainframe interdependency is fast becoming the norm for large organizations.

DSS Micro-Mainframe Interdependencies Evolving Needs for Communications Links

A few experienced "old-hand" DSS users have been using mainframe timesharing tools for many years. It is more common for newer DSS users in a large organization to start out as users through the relatively recent acquisition of a personal microcomputer. (Indicative of the rapid growth of microcomputer acquisition and usage, it is estimated that by 1989 expenditures on personal computers will exceed expenditures on mainframes and that end-user computing will account for 50 percent of a large corporations computing resources [Klein 1985].) This comes about usually because new users themselves have perceived a particular limited need for a single type of application such as a spreadsheet capability, or because they have a general notion that the set of personal analysis tools in a particular multifunction microcomputer package would be useful to them, or because they have been allocated a microcomputer with some software to use in any way they may see fit.

Justification procedures for microcomputer resources have typically not been as rigorous, specific, or extensively analyzed and reviewed as are large scale new mainframe systems and hardware acquisitions. Often, the pattern of getting started using microcomputer DSS tools is the reverse of the traditional one for large projects, in that the acquisition of the resource *precedes* any specifically documentable and well-understood application. Availability leads to new demands, rather than the reverse more-traditional view of demand justifying availability (Young 1981). While some justification procedure is needed, its nature is, and should be, different for DSS tools than for automation because of the DSS focus on evolving, semistructured analysis leading to greater effectiveness and *added* value, rather than only (or mainly) seeking direct *cost reduction* for repetitive structured processes (Carlson 1983; Keen and Scott Morton 1978; Klein 1985; Young 1984). (This issue of economic justification is discussed further in chapter 7.) But the evolving new demands that the availability of relatively low unit cost micro resources initiates often eventually outgrow the capabilities of personal computing working in isolation. When that occurs, the cycle of experience leading to new demands changes its *nature* and not merely the size dimension of data and application requirements. The new demands are for *interdependent* micro and mainframe facilities in a communications environment.

The data bases that need to be entered and used for most initial user-perceived applications are typically small and consist of items selected from regular mainframe produced report printouts, manually kept personal files, or externally published sources such as trade journals. As these initially perceived needs are met and experienced is gained, however, the self-sufficient microcomputer user evolves into a different kind of information consumer. These more advanced information consumers widen the scope of their demands, requiring the ability to select data items from a larger universe than that which is already at hand in locally available files and reports. Because of the variety of information needed, the information demands of this more advanced consumer now exceed levels that can be efficiently and conveniently accommodated by local data entry from hard copy sources. Direct access to existing corporate and externally maintained computer data bases is now needed and the individual, initially a self-sufficient user, comes back to ask for support from the MIS department. At an earlier stage, computer specialists and information systems managers may have thought that the availability of microcomputer resources would ward off users and get the MIS department "off the hook" of backlogged demands for new application programs. They then discovered that one set of user demands have only been traded for a new set of demands. End-users demands may initially have been satisfied only by microcomputer hardware and software acquisition and the offering of some introductory training. But now they also require the option of a communications link to the mainframe and a "data counseling" form of support. Data counseling is a form of user support that:

1. Informs users of data sources by communicating the existence and contents of both internal and external data bases;
2. Facilitates access to the contents of these data bases by instructing users on how to obtain them; and
3. Counsels users on effective strategies of data search, information acquisition, and analysis for varying application needs.

As described above, the need to access remote data bases and "download" selected data elements from mainframe files into micro files is a common path for evolving individual user needs. It is often motivated by the escalation of user demands through the evolutionary learning process of usage experience. A variation on this general theme of microcomputer usage evolving into mainframe-micro linkage is the evolution of independent *parallel usage* of both microcomputer resources and mainframe time-sharing for DSS needs such as query systems and modeling. The impetus to link these two separate parallel capabilities in some cases comes from the MIS manager. The motive is to encourage users to do more of their analyses on the micro and less on the mainframe whenever that is feasible. In this case, initially separate micro and mainframe capabilities were put in place in order to serve different end-user computing needs that were independently justified. For example, a natural language query capability may have been installed on the mainframe in order to enable users to easily access a large corporate data base. Separately, typical microcomputer capabilities sprung up using an integrated spreadsheet-data base package. After an initial usage phase, it has become clearer that time-sharing processing due to the natural language query processing has grown beyond expectations and is causing contention for mainframe resources. A study of usage by the MIS department reveals that many of the query demands in any given usage session consist of a variety of ways of reprocessing (summarizing, sorting, grouping, etc.) the same subset of elements selected from the larger data base. This need, it is then clear, could be met by downloading that selected data subset to the microcomputer where it can be processed further while the mainframe is free to handle other needs. Of course, there is also the possibility that users may not know in advance which subset of data is going to be needed. In this situation they may resort to repeated download requests that could defeat the intention of freeing up more mainframe time. This risk aside, in the parallel mainframe-micro facility situation, the combination of user demand evolution and the MIS department's concern with efficient utilization of mainframe facilities often leads to the establishment of a micro-mainframe communications link. A further saving is made available by the replacement of specialized time-sharing terminals with microcomputer-modem combinations. (A modem is required at each end of the communication line in order to convert the digital computer-generated signals into analog telephone line signals and back again. For a discussion of other technical linkage factors see Klenk [1985].) With the use of a modem and required communications software to enable the microcomputer to emulate a terminal, the microcomputer can be used as both a terminal and as stand-alone computer.

However the linkage has come about, the initially desired downloading capability opens a path for two-way data communication to take place. Data and the results of analyses processed on micros can also be "uploaded" into mainframe maintained data bases and models. The ability to upload can be a two-edged sword. On the positive side, some organizational needs for consolidating models and data can be well-served by this capability. But this avenue also carries the potential for a new threat to data integrity unless it is controlled. If any local user can—whether accidentally or intentionally—modify, replace, or blank out data in a corporate data base through bypassing the usual editing and verification controls that operate within the mainframe data base management system (Perry 1984), then the integrity of the data is compromised. Because of the difficulty of enforcing local microcomputer user practices (Ward and Perkins 1985), adequate controls mainly depend on MIS planners and technical specialists providing them through automatic mainframe procedures included in the data base management system, the operating system, and communications control hardware and software. Often, the main provision of such control will be that multipurpose corporate internal data bases will be accessible in read only (downloading) mode, and cannot be written into except by the few systems and files that serve as primary data sources (typically these will be transaction processing applications and summary data distilled from transaction data). Important exceptions to the *read only* access rule would apply to special data bases and models that are intended to serve as consolidated outputs of separate but related planning and analysis applications, as illustrated in exhibit 5.5. Such consolidated outputs could, for example, represent:

1. A corporate consolidation of divisional proposed financial plans and budgets in a multidivisional corporation;
2. An aggregation of marketing plans created by individual product managers in a multiproduct company; and
3. A consolidation of departmental personnel turnover and requirements forecasts.

In these cases, local semistructured DSS analysis is carried out in a first phase but the results must be put into a structured format so that they can be combined into a consolidated plan. The consolidated plan may itself then undergo further analysis at the higher organizational level through "what if" types of trial assumptions. This, in turn, may trigger a request to the lower organizational level to perform further analysis within new constraints and to submit a revised plan for final consolidation. For this kind of iterative planning cycle, DSS tools are used for both individual or local applications as well as for organizational or group decision making. While it would be possible to complete such a process by the dispatch of hard copy intermediate outputs between the parties involved, this would require reentry of data and would obviously be an inefficient and time-consuming process. The need for such a consolidated DSS planning process is thus a further key justification for the mainframe-micro link.

In addition to these requirements for linking microcomputers to mainframes, there are also evolving needs and capabilities to:

1. Link micro users to one another in a local area network (LAN) environment; and
2. To provide more continuous communications between a group of micro users and a mainframe than are needed for merely downloading data or uploading and consolidating final results.

Communication between micro users can be used for support of a group decision process in which all members of the group are able to send messages to each other about their common problem and to simultaneously view the same data base query or model-based analysis. This linkage can also support the trading of local data bases, models, and analysis procedures between individual users.

Exhibit 5.5

Download Only Versus Integrated Organizational DSS

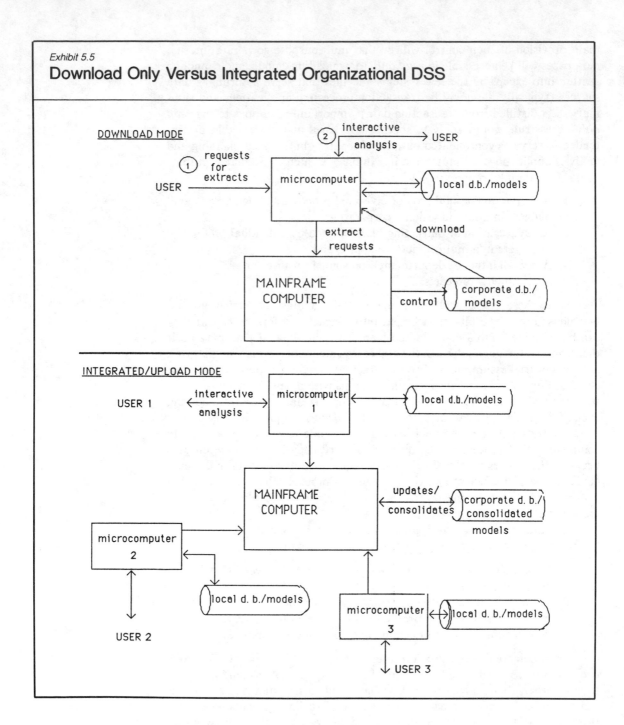

Continuous communication linkages between a central mainframe and local microcomputer users could be used to facilitate an environment in which the system itself (through appropriate software) determines where computing is to be done and which software is required in a computer-managed distributed processing environment. Such an environment could also ultimately be used to provide an automatic *decision alerting* capability. Such a capability may be based on a standard control reporting and status monitoring system that includes a diagnostic feature that sends signals or messages to managers with particular responsibilities. These managers may thus be prompted to seek further information and understanding through their query and analysis DSS functions.

In summary the main reasons for mainframe-micro (and micro-micro) linkage in relation to DSS are:

1. Evolving demands of microcomputer users for access to corporate and external data bases;
2. The need and potential for more efficient computing resource utilization by reallocating a higher proportion of exploratory processing of limited subsets of corporate data from the mainframe to the microcomputer and by generally controlling the distribution of processing;
3. The need for upward consolidation of local analyses and plans;
4. Support of group decision processes involving multiple micro users; and
5. Providing the basis for emerging methods for alerting managers by more directly tieing standard control reporting systems into DSS capabilities.

Management Implications of a DSS Communications Environment

Once mainframe-micro links are established, a new set of management issues and cost considerations become manifest. While the more effective utilization of computing resources is often one of the motivating factors in establishing the link, maintaining an efficient mix of micro-mainframe computing is problematic in a user-controlled discretionary usage environment. Automatic central computer control over the distribution of processing would not be likely to provide a complete solution for optimal usage. It would itself place a new demand on the central computer and is also limited by individual users' willingness to operate on line. An appropriate form of user education is needed to ensure proper usage whenever users have the choice of getting their analyses done on either the micro or mainframe facility. Such education can only succeed if it goes beyond "how to" and can demonstrate that it is to the advantage of users to opt for microcomputer processing when it can more efficiently get the job done. Often, the psychological comfort as well as more tangible ease of use advantages of microcomputer usage will be sufficient to sell users. While positive incentives are generally more effective, a suitable policy of charging mainframe usage against local users budgets is also helpful in making this case. Least desirable as control measures are relying solely on arbitrary time cutoffs for mainframe applications. Although such constraints may be necessary as fail-safe devices, they should rarely have to be activated because intelligent, educated, self-motivated users generally avoid these situations.

It should also be noted that for some applications MIS management should seek to educate and encourage users in the direction of using mainframe systems rather than stand-alone microcomputer systems. Such applications may include those that need the greater control and security usually provided on mainframe systems as well as those that require a more organizationally disciplined and coordinated decision process than an individual approach can provide.

The pricing structure of micro software also seems likely to be affected when the communications environment becomes the general rule in multiple user organizations. Currently, micro software is mostly priced by the copy (a heritage of its beginnings as a home computer or stand-alone personal computer tool). Corporations can gain volume discounts by centralizing their purchases. Mainframe software, in contrast, is generally sold as a right to use a single copy that can serve a multitude of individual users. In a communications environment in which local users can gain access to the use of centrally stored software as well as data, and exchange data, models, and software with one another via communications networks, one can question the logic of a per copy micro software pricing policy. Regardless of where software is stored and which computer it runs on, the value to an organization in a multiuser communications network environment is the *capability,* not the number of copies. Moreover, it is common for vendors of mainframe packages to also provide a linked microcomputer version of their package or a linking option to commonly available micro software. Since they are selling the combination of micro-mainframe software, it seems more reasonable to formulate or negotiate a package price for the full capability rather than a per copy price. In the modern "wired" organizational environment, it seems inappropriate to acquire software mainly as if it were the same as books and records for individual collections as opposed to an integrated central library resource that can be almost instantly copied or used via electronic means.

Other issues related to mainframe and microcomputer software selection and management policies for its effective use are discussed in the next two chapters.

Review Questions, Exercises, and Discussion Topics

Review Questions

1. *a*) How did advances in microprocessor technology influence the development of new kinds of applications software?
   b) How does the history of DSS applications relate to the evolution from batch processing mainframes, through time-sharing, to microcomputers?

2. *a*) Is the schematic architecture of microcomputers essentially different from that of mainframes?
   b) Which types of computer applications are most suited to mainframe computers rather than to microcomputers in a large organization?

3. Is it true or false that true DSS applications require the unique features of a microcomputer? Explain.

4. In computer jargon, interactive systems generally refer to microcomputer and time-sharing applications support. Are there other forms of useful user-computer interaction? Explain.

5. What benefits might be obtained by pauses or delays in human-computer interaction?

6. *a*) In what ways do microcomputer and mainframe DSS resources differ?
   b) If it is technically feasible to carry out a DSS application using either a micro or a mainframe, what criteria should determine which option is preferable?

7. *a*) Which features and requirements of DSS applications determine whether a microcomputer system will suffice or a mainframe system is needed?
   b) Which DSS application characteristics do not strictly dictate whether a microcomputer or a mainframe should be utilized?

8. Which of the following ratios generally reflects the ratio of popular microcomputer to mainframe DSS unit package costs:
   a) 1/1000 *b*) 1/10 to 1/100 *c*) 1/ 10,000

9. What reasons might be given for using a microcomputer even though many spreadsheet applications evolve into larger models and one cannot be sure that eventually a mainframe might be more suitable?

10. *a*) On what dimensions have mainframe DSS software packages often been superior to micro DSS software?
    b) On what dimensions are micro DSS software packages generally superior to mainframe DSS software?

11. What factors might cause a comparison between software packages based on the number of built-in functions to be misleading?

12. How might the nature of the user-system interface make up for the lack of direct commands for carrying out certain modes of analysis in a software package?

13. What basic capabilities should a DSS end-user query package have?

14. What factors might be hidden in the claim that a package "integrates" the three different capabilities of modeling, data base query, and graphics?

15. Which features would be present and which absent if a multifunction package could be perfectly integrated from the user's point of view?

16. How are the factors of problem size limitations and function integration related?

17. *a)* How is ease of use generally related to the functional scope and power of software?

    b) What trend exists in this regard ? Explain the significance of this trend.

18. What apparent advantages in terms of ease of use does a spreadsheet package have in relation to most mainframe modeling languages for the nonmathematician user?

19. What factors other than the specific nature of the software interface might contribute to the user friendliness of microcomputers?

20. Compare microcomputer and mainframe usage from the point of view of security and privacy. How might the user and the information systems executive differ in this regard?

21. What factors contributed to the need to link microcomputers to a mainframe capability in order to support DSS applications?

22. What is meant by data counseling and what brings about the need for this function?

23. What equipment utilization efficiency concerns might motivate MIS executives to foster the mainframe-micro link?

24. Describe what is meant by downloading a set of data. Why is it relevant to DSS users.

25. How does the need for integrated organizational plans relate to micro-mainframe linkage?

26. What new issues are likely to arise after experience with a micro-mainframe-communications environment is gained?

Exercises

1. Describe a DSS query type of application need that could be run on *either* a mainframe or a microcomputer with appropriate generally available software that we can assume is already accessible in the company. Include in your description a profile of the tasks and responsibilities of the user, the nature of the business and relevant organizational characteristics, and identify others in the organization that are relevant to the user. If you personally were the user in this situation, what factors might cause you to have a personal preference as to which option (mainframe or micro) to follow? What factors might cause the vice president in charge of information system resources to have a preference?

2. Describe a spreadsheet modeling application that is unlikely to grow and evolve to proportions and functional requirements that would justify moving the application into a mainframe environment.

3. Prepare an outline for an educational user workshop/seminar intended to facilitate and encourage the appropriate use of micro versus mainframe data base query facilities.

4. Compare the relative costs of providing 150 users with a typical integrated microcomputer package and a stand alone microcomputer with versus providing them with dumb terminals and time-sharing access to a mainframe and software to perform similar functions. Make any necessary assumptions needed to complete your analysis. What other factors and alternatives would you examine in order to decide which alternative should be followed?
5. Describe a situation in which communications, data and model sharing, and output transmission between individual microcomputer users would be useful. Describe the functions and job tasks of the users and the nature of the organization. Might it also be useful in this situation to provide access for one or more users to a mainframe data base and/or to mainframe software?

Discussion Topics

1. Considering the various modes and speeds of human-human interaction (person to person, or person to many people via different media), in what ways are these forms of interaction like human-computer types of interaction and in what ways do they differ? Discuss which kinds of human-computer interaction are best suited for different kinds of situations (eg., conveying messages or transmitting data versus thinking through a creative process versus exploratory "what if" or "what is" analysis).
2. Discuss reasons for retaining versus reasons for changing the basis on which microcomputer software is sold by vendors of mainframe software and/or by others. What pricing policy do you believe would be best for those involved?
3. Assuming it will be necessary for nonprogrammers to use mainframe resources for some DSS applications, what might be done to make them more user friendly and less threatening while also following good information resource management practices.
4. To what degree does the need to provide a common structure for a consolidated corporate model inhibit semistructured user-controlled analysis at local levels which provide component inputs to the corporate model? Does the framework of a consolidated corporate model imply that a semistructured planning process will evolve into a highly structured process? Does this also imply that micro-mainframe linkage is (can be) instrumental in the evolution of semistructured individual DSS into structured organizational computer processing? Are both desirable and undesirable outcomes of such linkage and consolidated planning models possible?

References

Barley, K., Driscoll, J. 1981. "A Survey of Database Management Systems for Microcomputers." *Byte* 6 (November) 11.

Carlson, E. D. 1983. "An Approach for Designing Decision Support Systems." in *Building Decision Support Systems,* edited by J. L. Bennett, Reading, Mass.: Addison-Wesley. 15.

Keen, P. G. W., Scott Morton, M. S. 1978. *Decision Support Systems: An Organizational Perspective.* Reading, Mass.: Addison-Wesley. 221–23.

Klein, M. 1985. "Information Politics." *Datamation* 31(August 1)15:87–92.

Klenk, R. 1985. "The Benefits and Pitfalls of the Microcomputer-Mainframe Link." *Journal of Information Systems Management* 2(Spring)2:3–9.

Perry, W. E. 1984. "How To Maintain Control in the Data Base Environment." *Journal of Information Systems Management* 1(Spring)2:46–54.

Ward, G. M., Perkins, W. M. 1985. "A Three-Step Approach to Microcomputer Security Controls." *Journal of Information Systems Management* 2(Spring)2:17–23.

Young, L. F. 1981. "The Golden Scope Syndrome, the Availability Effect and MIS," *MIS Quarterly* 5(September)3:29–33.

Young, L. F. 1984. "Justifying Information Systems." (Online: The Editor's Forum), *Journal of Information Systems Management* 1(Summer)1:93–95.

DSS Development and Software Selection

6

Show me he ordered, I'm willing to help you. I've done what I could so far. If necessary I'll go ahead blindfolded, but I can't do it without more confidence in you than I've got now. You've got to convince me that you know what it's all about, that you're not simply fiddling around by guess and by God, hoping it'll come out all right somehow in the end.
Sam Spade, p. 60 in Dashiell Hammett's *The Maltese Falcon*. New York: Vantage Books, 1972

In the early days of business computer systems, practitioners had little by way of standard methodology to approach the development of new computer applications. At best, developers borrowed the general descriptions of what had been called "the engineering method", which consisted mainly of guidelines for a logical sequence of steps comprised of: (*a*) define the problem; (*b*) gather data; (*c*) design a solution; (*d*) implement and test the solution. At worst, many early practitioners seemed to be "fiddling around by guess and by God, hoping it'll come out all right somehow in the end." As experience accumulated however, practitioners of large-scale engineering development projects defined the "systems approach" for studying a complex system as a whole, including both its internal relations as well as its interaction with its environment. Systems approach thinking began to affect commercial computer systems development as data processing projects shifted their focus from individual applications toward integration of applications into more comprehensive organizational information systems.

Computer project development methodologies also were further refined into more detailed phases and procedures. The "systems development life cycle" of (*1*) requirements analysis; (*2*) general and detailed design; (*3*) system construction; (*4*) systems testing and installation; and (*5*) operations and maintenance, was defined in both broad terms as well as in terms of its specific subprocesses and procedures. Charting, analysis, and documentation techniques were developed or adapted for computer systems work. Better project management practices were defined and applied and the concepts of "structured design" and "structured programming" were enunciated. While many practitioners continued (and still go on even now) to ignore such developments and persist in following less disciplined practices, structured approaches and professional project management have often demonstrated that applications software could be developed in a significantly more efficient way. In addition to these improved project development methods, many organizations have also adapted overall systems planning processes, so that master plans for MIS spanning several years into the future could be integrated with the strategic needs and longer range plans of the organization as a whole.

Then along came the rapid expansion of DSS, followed and augmented by the dissemination of microcomputers, giving rise to a new category of applications in which the painfully evolved formal systems development methods initially seemed not to apply. In a dynamic technical and business environment, new computer systems methodology apparently begins to become obsolete even before it has been completely disseminated and adopted as standard practice. The velocity of technological "push" toward usage seems to exceed the velocity of adaptation of management methods, thus producing considerable turbulence for managers to cope with as best they can.

A still evolving methodology for DSS development and management planning is a moving target. Despite the difficulties such change creates for managers, college instructors, textbook authors, and students, it is a positive sign of a continuing effort to find better DSS development methods. This chapter will attempt to present a DSS development methodology and directions in which practice seems to be headed (the following chapter will deal with planning and organizing for DSS).

Recognizing that organizations today will rarely develop their own DSS software systems from the ground up using third generation programming languages, this chapter will also discuss the selection of DSS generators (fourth generation language packages). In DSS, as in other categories of computer applications, package selection should be recognized as the key activity preliminary to the development of specific systems. Since DSS applications were first defined and built, the availability of a variety of DSS generator packages has radically increased. This increased package availability is the key factor in enabling the DSS concept of rapid evolutionary DSS application development to be feasibly realized in a wider number of cases. DSS generator packages have simplified the development of DSS applications by creating a ready-made repertoire of generic capabilities within a general interface environment that could be tailored into specific applications. However, the elimination of a part of the design problem for each individual application is replaced by the problem of selecting the most appropriate DSS generator package (or packages) for the family of applications that are likely to arise. This problem is somewhat analogous to the selection of the third generation programming languages (eg., COBOL, PL–1, or FORTRAN) to be used for developing standard data processing applications in a large organization.

An Overview of Requirements
for DSS Development Approaches

As discussed in chapter 1, automation in general differs fundamentally from the concept of support. More specifically, the DSS approach to supporting semistructured decision problems and decision processes differs significantly from the automation of structured decision model algorithms. This special character of DSS applications gives rise to a need for different development practices. Because DSS modes of computer support do not consist of prescribed repetitive fixed sequence processing, DSS design cannot utilize the static detailed processing logic "blueprints" (as expressed in flow diagrams or structured pseudo-code) required by traditional forms of automation. A DSS application is typically not merely another computer application with a limited number of output options provided. A true DSS application (as opposed to merely on line forms of traditional automation) requires a variable length user-system conversation in which the possible sequences of computer processing steps depend on dynamic user decisions and are therefore so varied and large that all allowable branching alternatives cannot be prespecified.

The user is expected to learn and evolve new forms of analysis through system usage, and not through prior nonsystem experience with a repetitive standard process. The DSS should be a means of *gaining experience and learning* whereas a traditional automated application is a means of *freezing and standardizing* processing logic that has already been learned or accepted. This special purpose of DSS effectively contradicts the premises of traditional systems development practice in which a careful, thoroughly detailed set of information requirements must be prepared through extensive analysis prior to systems design and implementation. Traditional systems, although modifiable within limits, are meant to remain relatively fixed "data processing factories," with standard products and processing sequences for the life of the repetitive application being served. DSS are meant to be modifiable upon and within each usage occasion, as often as desired by the user, without delays to respecify and rebuild the system.

Because of these basic differences, a DSS development methodology must meet special general requirements consisting of the following:

1. Verification of the DSS approach
   Prior to, or early in the development process, it is necessary to reliably discriminate between those situations in which a DSS approach is called for and those requiring an entirely different approach (such as an operations research model-based systems development effort or an information system development cycle approach), or situations that may require a combined approach.

2. Identification of functional DSS components needed
   Given that any DSS approach may be appropriate, initial problem analysis must aim at identifying generic functional DSS "toolkit" requirements (such as a query capability, a modeling language capability, an integrated modeling-graphics-data base capability, etc.)
3. Approximation of the "rich-poor" information design boundary
   The extent of information requirements (*what* and *how much* information the system must contain and enable the user to see) is basic and as important to identify as early as possible during DSS development as it is for standard reporting systems. Although information needs can be expected to evolve with usage and are difficult to specify in advance, DSS development methods must enable systems builders to determine at least the relative scope of information needed as a minimal usable starting point (ranging from a "rich" world described by many variables measured in a variety of ways to a "poor" problem environment that is sparsely described by few variables or data base items).
4. Base system development versus next version multistage development
   While it is necessary to complete a standard development cycle of requirements specification, design, and system implementation, in order to produce an initial working model or "base system", this initial version can be expected to evolve through further development iterations that are interspersed with and often indistinguishable from actual system usage. This bears a certain similarity to providing for system modification after development of a traditional information system, but differs significantly with respect to the extent, ease, and rapidity of modifiability of the initial base system. DSS development methodology must typically go further toward accommodating and facilitating an evolutionary, variable length, multicycle, fast redevelopment process built onto the development of a base system.
5. User capability-style assessment and usage projection
   Although DSS redevelopment is expected to evolve with usage, in order to provide a more effective base system the DSS development process must go further than traditional systems analysis in initially assessing users' capabilities, problem-solving styles, state of knowledge and analytical skills repertoire. It should also include projecting and reassessing how these are likely to change as experience in using the system accumulates.
6. Approximation of the "hard-soft" design boundary
   DSS package selection and development methodology should include ways to utilize the user capability-style assessment in setting an appropriate level between relatively "soft" design that must be tailored extensively by the user in order to implement a specific support application and more specific "hard" design functionality that allows for or requires relatively little user modification.

7. Approximation of the "strong-weak" design boundary
   DSS package selection and development methodology should also include
   ways to utilize the user capability-style assessment in setting an
   appropriately designed level between a very high degree of user freedom
   and control over the sequence of system operations ("weak" design) and a
   design in which the system leads the user to a higher degree ("strong"
   design). (It should be noted that in the extreme, "strong design" that would
   not allow for *any* user control would take an application out of the category
   of computer *support* and instead classify it as *automation*.)
8. Integration of user training and education into development
   DSS development methodology should include ways to utilize the user
   capability-style assessment and reassessment in establishing and
   maintaining a suitable user education and training support program to
   enable and facilitate the learning-through-usage process.

The remainder of this chapter will discuss DSS development methods and
how they address these needs.

An Outline of the DSS Development Process

Before discussing the specifics of DSS development for particular applications, we note that an overview of organizational needs for DSS should be part
of the MIS planning process. General DSS resources and application areas
should be identified within the MIS master plan after a general organization-
wide needs survey has been conducted. The organizational needs survey will
be discussed further in the next chapter. It can be assumed that in most large
organizations, whether through such a planning process or because of evolutionary past applications, some inventory of DSS resources such as DSS generator packages, microcomputer software and equipment, etc. is already
available in the organization. While these facilities may be found to be applicable or not applicable to a particular new application, they must be taken
into account in the application development process. It is also taken as a basic
premise, that regardless of how particular potential DSS applications are
identified, (whether through a planned process or on an ad hoc basis), it is
useful to adapt, follow, and attempt to continually improve an application development methodology in order to avoid a profusion of inefficiently developed
and ineffective DSS applications. The inapplicability of the particular methods
developed for more traditional systems development should not take us back
to the uncontrolled wasteful development practices that prevailed among inexperienced computer users in the 1950s.

The main phases of a DSS application development process are shown in
exhibit 6.1. These are, in turn, partitioned into three major phases, each of
which is shown respectively in exhibits 6.2, 6.3, and 6.4.

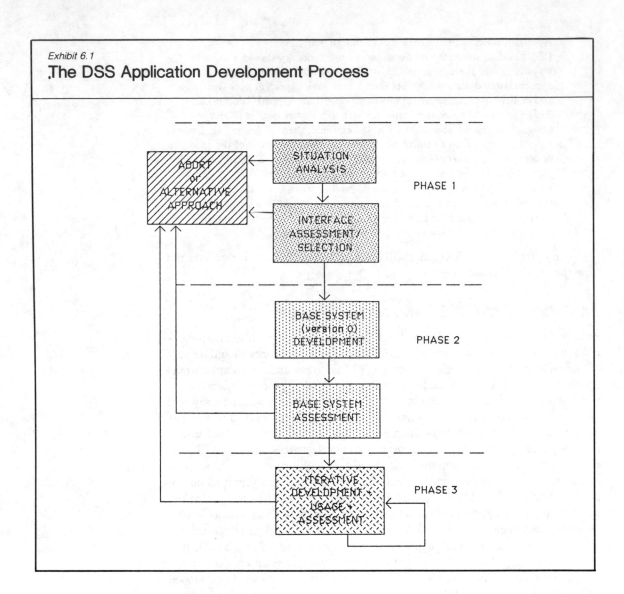

Exhibit 6.1
The DSS Application Development Process

SITUATION ANALYSIS

ABORT or ALTERNATIVE APPROACH

INTERFACE ASSESSMENT/ SELECTION

PHASE 1

BASE SYSTEM (version 0) DEVELOPMENT

PHASE 2

BASE SYSTEM ASSESSMENT

ITERATIVE DEVELOPMENT + USAGE + ASSESSMENT

PHASE 3

The first major phase of DSS development, phase 1: preliminary assessment, consists of:

1. Situation analysis, and
2. Interface assessment and selection.

Situation analysis corresponds roughly to general requirements "fact-finding" and feasibility assessment in traditional systems development. More specifically, situation analysis for a DSS application has the following two main objectives:

1. To gather sufficient information about the relevant characteristics of the organizational setting, the user(s), and their decision-related tasks, to provide a basis for assessing the applicability of any DSS approach and for subsequently selecting specific DSS tools; and
2. To identify which generic DSS functional components (if any) can feasibly and appropriately be applied to the situation.

Interface assessment and selection, the second part of phase 1, corresponds roughly to the functional specification and cost-benefit analysis steps in traditional systems development. Its main purposes are:

1. To assess available or acquirable hardware tools and language interfaces (packages) and select those most appropriate for the situational characteristics and applicable generic DSS functions; and
2. To estimate the potential value* of using a DSS of the type indicated and assess whether or not acquiring that value appears to merit the expenditures and efforts associated with system acquisition and use.

The second major phase of DSS development consists of developing and assessing the base system or first version ("version 0") of the DSS. Base system development differs somewhat from the iterative development/usage of subsequent versions of a DSS. Base system development consists of the steps shown in exhibit 6.3. The purposes of this phase are:

1. To relatively quickly create a working system that can serve as a basis for further problem analysis and modification; and
2. To enable immediate assessment through actual use to determine whether or not it appears worthwhile to continue to use and/or develop the DSS.

---

*The term *value* (as discussed later in this chapter and more fully in Chapter 12) has a different usage here than that of the term *benefit,* as in *cost-benefit* analysis.

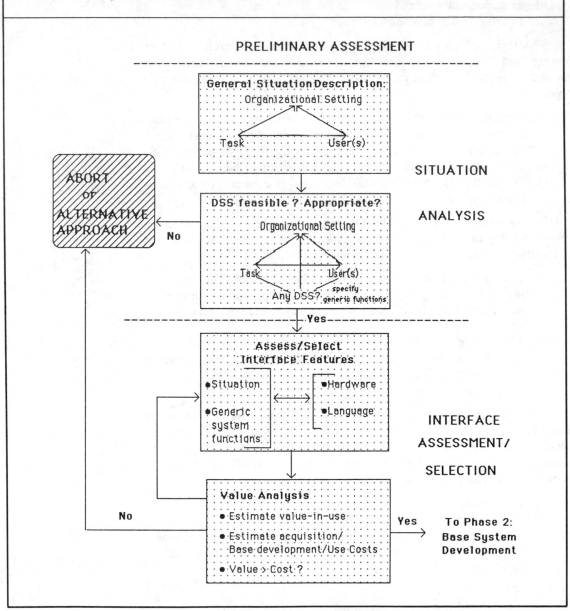

Exhibit 6.2

DSS Development Phase 1: Preliminary Assessment

PRELIMINARY ASSESSMENT

General Situation Description:
Organizational Setting

Task   User(s)

SITUATION

ANALYSIS

DSS feasible? Appropriate?

Organizational Setting

Task   User(s)

specify
generic functions

Any DSS?

ABORT
or
ALTERNATIVE
APPROACH

No

Yes

Assess/Select
Interface Features

• Situation   • Hardware

• Generic   • Language
  system
  functions

INTERFACE

ASSESSMENT/

SELECTION

Value Analysis

• Estimate value-in-use

• Estimate acquisition/
  Base development/Use Costs

• Value > Cost?

No

Yes

To Phase 2:
Base System
Development

Exhibit 6.3

DSS Development Phase 2: Base System (Version 0) Development / Assessment

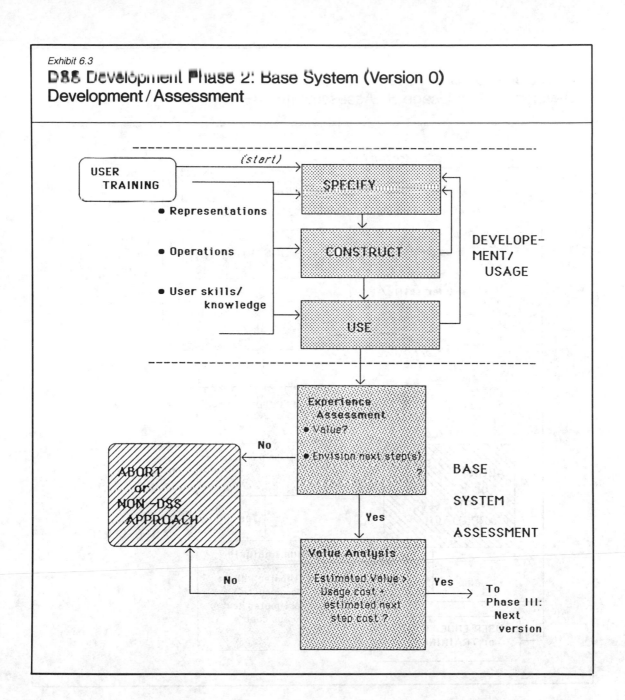

Exhibit 6.4

DSS Development Phase 3: Iterative Development + Usage + Assessment

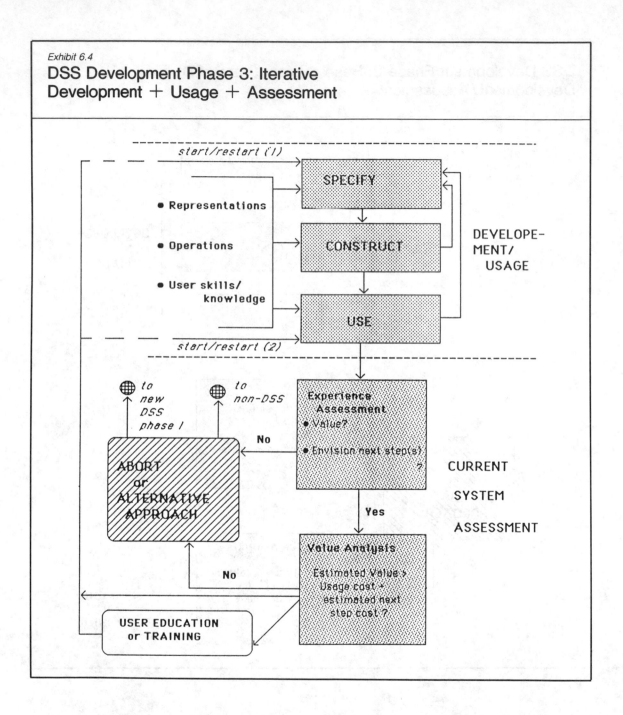

Phase 3, iterative development + usage + assessment, is shown in exhibit 6.4, as consisting of steps similar to those carried out in basic system development, but carried out at a more advanced detailed level and entered into at more than one starting point. Iterative development may continue as a consequence of repeated usage and assessment.

It is noted that in all three major phases, assessment can result in not continuing in the development or use of the DSS, but instead either abandoning the application of any computer-based approach to the problem entirely or pursuing an alternative approach such as using a traditional information system or a formal operations research model-based system. This result of not pursuing a DSS approach should not be considered a negative outcome. If a DSS approach is examined and rejected as inappropiate or infeasible early in the process, unproductive effort and development costs are avoided. Discontinuing DSS usage and development later in the process may result from having attained sufficient learning through the DSS experience so that the problem can now be restructured sufficiently to make other approaches more appropriate. In this case the DSS has served its purpose and the new state of knowledge of the user has reduced the marginal value of continued usage below an acceptable threshhold. Of course, DSS applications, like all other computer applications, may also become obsolete because the problems they address are simply no longer relevant to a changed organizational situation. DSS usage should not be allowed to become bureaucratic by setting arbitrary objectives of high usage levels or the self-perpetuation of a staff group, or to provide computer "toys" for devotees. The only legitimate objective for DSS is the likelihood of enhancing organizational effectiveness.

The succeeding sections will discuss the methodology used in each of these phases in greater detail and indicate possible directions for its improvement.

Methods for Phase I: Preliminary Assessment— Situation Analysis: Describing the Situation

The methods for carrying out a situation analysis for a DSS application utilize the same tools that are commonly used for fact-finding for other types of applications, but their manner of usage and content vary considerably. A DSS analyst-builder must typically interview perspective users and/or design and apply questionnaires, document collection methods, and use direct observation in order to gather enough information about the organizational situation, the nature of the decision-related tasks that must be performed, and the personal characteristics of the users. In some cases, the perspective users may be sufficiently knowledgeable about DSS methods and tools to effectively serve as their own analysts, and in effect "interview" themselves and otherwise analyze their own situations. When this is not the case (and it is probably still most often not the case), it is important that organizational procedures and resources exist that facilitate access to a DSS analyst so that perspective users who may be eager to apply the easily obtainable user friendly software package they have heard about do not go ahead on their own without counsel and guidance. This is a special problem aspect of DSS management in a microcomputer, end-user language environment, that will be discussed further in chapter 7. But it has direct implications for DSS development methods in that lengthy and complex formal approaches to new applications development will effectively assure that users will simply bypass the formal approach to development and go their own way. The initial situation analysis methods must be especially fast and easy to apply, without sacrificing effectiveness. If they are sufficiently fast and easy to apply, they can also probably be taught to new users so that when subsequent needs arise, dependence on an analyst is lessened and may be reduced to a minimum contact for purposes of checking results and coordinating the use of hardware and software resources.

Interviews and other investigative methods for a DSS application situation description are not intended to produce information sufficient to produce highly detailed flow charts of highly structured operational procedures. If such detailed, structured, repeated processes are utilized and the goal is to automate them, then such an application can quickly be reclassified as a traditional computer project and not a DSS application. Because such detailed documentation is not required for DSS, the relevant content matter for a situation description can usually be obtained quickly by a competent analyst, often through a single interview of less than two hours duration. The most relevant aspects of the situation description needed are as follows:

1. Organizational setting
   a) A description of the organizational level, structure, size, objectives and functional scope of the organizational unit involved. (Note that the "organizational unit" can be a department, a work group within a department, a single individual role, or any other functional entity with definable boundaries.)
   b) Informal practices and "cultural" atmospherics relevant to the way in which the organizational unit operates.
   c) Relevant relationships of the organizational unit with the rest of the organization or with other organizational units with which it significantly interacts.
2. Task
   a) The focus of the decision related tasks being addressed. As one guideline for identifying focus, reference should be made to Simon's classification of decision-making phases into intelligence (scanning, monitoring, and seeking to identify problems, opportunities, trends, patterns or other relationships that may require decisions to be made), design (identifying or constructing alternative strategies), and choice (assessing alternative strategies and selecting one).

b) The nature of the tasks with respect to the degree of structure, variability, length and frequency of the processes currently applied.

c) The feasibility of accomplishing the objectives of the tasks in whole or in part through alternative structured means such as optimization models, regular computer reporting systems, formal computer forecasting methods, etc. (This is an area in which specialized knowledge is particularly needed and often inadequately applied.)

d) The main dependent, independent and interdependent aspects of the decision-related tasks being addressed with respect to other tasks carried out within and outside of the organizational unit. These dependency relationships should refer to information sources, information access and information sharing, authority constraints, and functional coordination requirements (including both individual and team functions).

3. User characteristics
   a) The level and extent of skills, experience and knowledge of the user(s) that are directly relevant to the tasks currently being performed.
   b) The experience and background of users with respect to DSS tools and other analytical methods (such as operations research model building, statistical methods, etc.).
   c) Readily identifiable attitudes, preferences, and styles related to problem solving, decision making, information seeking, analytical versus intuitive approaches, or willingness to directly learn and use computers and other new methods.

An example of a situation description making reference to these categories is given in example 6.1.

Situation Analysis: Is DSS Feasible and Appropriate?

Given this kind of situation description, an initial assessment can then be made of the feasibility and appropriateness of following a DSS approach. As part of this assessment, particular generic DSS functions such as modeling support, data base query support, graphics support, or combinations of these should be identified as applicable or not. Chapter 2 presented descriptions and examples of these support functions. (See, for instance, exhibit 2.4: Examples of Status Access and Analysis Questions.) This general inventory of the kinds of things a user can do with DSS should be used as a checklist against the salient questions and needs arising out of the problem situation. With respect to the situation described in example 6.1, such an assessment is given in example 6.2. This assessment concludes the situation analysis, and if it indicates that a DSS approach is functionally feasible and appropriate, leads into the second stage of the preliminary assessment, the interface assessment/selection stage.

EXAMPLE 6.1

A SITUATION DESCRIPTION:

Planning Support for the President of UAU University

THE ORGANIZATIONAL SETTING

Utopian Atlantis University (UAU) has approximately 7000 students in four Colleges: the College of Humanities and Science, the College of Engineering, the College of Business, and the School of Law. UAU has recently acquired a new president after a twenty-five year term in office of the now-retired last president.

The president of the university is responsible for long range planning, has final responsibility for all top-level decisions requiring capital expenditures, and is the highest level of appeal for all other academic and administrative matters. UAU has a total budget approaching $100 million per year, approximately 60 percent of which is covered by full and part-time students' paid tuition. The stated objectives of the university are to strive for excellence in both teaching and research, and to attain national recognition. The university is currently well-known regionally, mainly for its Engineering programs, although other programs are generally thought of as good to excellent. All programs have produced many professionals working predominantly within the region. In the past, the university was run by a strong authoritative president, with little substantive sharing of power with other administrative officers or with the faculty. Administrative officers tended to be cautious, noninnovative and to await the president's decisions. The faculty was a mixture of some old-timers who were competent instructors but did little or no research, others who were more recently recruited ambitious and promising researchers and educators, and a few already recognized outstanding scholars.

THE TASK

The new president desired to make the quest for excellence more substantive than it had actually been in the past. To do so, he intended to prepare well thought-out, feasible short range (two-year) and long range (ten-year) strategic plans and to do so

with the widest possible participation of the faculty as well as administrative officers. While concerned with increasing meaningful participation and wide commitment to new directions, the president was also worried about avoiding an unwieldy process unable to reach consensus and unable to react to changing conditions without overly lengthy debate. The president wanted to establish a process in which new proposals could rapidly be made sufficiently explicit so that their implications could be determined according to quantifiable assumptions and other measurable criteria rather than by argumentation alone.

The strategic plan, among other aims found to be relevant, was to focus upon three general goals:

1. Improving the academic level of incoming students;
2. Significantly increasing funded research; and
3. Increased financial stability through increasing the university's endowment fund.

There was uniform support among the faculty and administration for all of these general goals, but a wide range of opinions existed on specific objectives, policies, priorities, and strategies.

Recognizing that effective planning is not a one-time exercise, the president wanted to establish a foundation for an on-going process of planning, modifying the plan as required, and monitoring progress against the plan. A new position of assistant to the president for planning was established and a person with past experience in a consulting firm and an MBA degree from AUA was hired. It was decided that an initial planning process would consist of having the planning assistant set up an outline structure for each academic department to follow in summarizing their professional goals, current status, and proposed methods of reaching their goals over the next two years (in some detail) and over a ten-year planning horizon (in less detail). Administrative officers (mainly the chief financial officer and his top assistants, and the academic vice president) were asked to follow a similar format in summarizing their outlooks on their respective areas of responsibility. Everyone was asked to particularly state the things they saw as primary objectives, to quantify them or state them in measurable terms as much as possible, and to identify the most critical limiting constraints on reaching these objectives. Each group was asked to address these items by specifying three distinct levels of objectives and the resources needed to achieve them: (1) A maximum effort level; (2) A significant (but lower) effort level; and (3) A maintenance (little or no change) level.

It was the planning assistant's responsibility to integrate these into a coherent analysis that would clarify several key issues, including:

1. Financial implications for the entire university of various priorities and levels of effort;
2. Feasibility and consistency of alternative actions and assumptions with external factors such as student population trends and demographics, competitive, economic, social and legal factors; and
3. Overall synergy, thematic clarity, general policy consistency, opportunities for greater collaboration or pooling of resources, and avoidance of ineffective duplication.

In terms of Simon's model of the decision-making process, these tasks and the overall process has its main focus within the design phase (developing and analyzing alternatives) and the choice phase (selecting a final plan from among the alternatives identified). To a lesser extent, the intelligence phase is also served by virtue of giving initial and periodic consideration to the external trends (such as the demographic population trends affecting the size of the student market pool) in order to assess their impact upon current policies and future plans. The variables involved, however, are limited and do not normally require searching through extensive amounts of data or large varieties of data sources.

THE USER(S)

If any form of computer support for this planning process were to be utilized, the primary user would be the new planning assistant, who was knowledgeable and experienced in a variety of analytical techniques including mathematical modeling and statistics. He had used computer support tools before, including a major mainframe modeling support system, a mainframe data base query system, and microcomputer spreadsheet software.

It was the planning assistant's desire, however, that if it were found to be feasible, computer support tools also be made available at some point to all of the other participating faculty and administrative groups so that:

1. Each participating party could perform their own prior analysis in developing their own plans and proposals;
2. Each participating party could analyze and understand the university plan, so as to foster support and facilitate making and testing new proposals or modifications of their own plans as the need might arise; and
3. Efforts to integrate plans could be facilitated through at least partial computer-assisted plan consolidation.

The faculty and administration varied widely in their familiarity with and attitudes toward using computer support tools. Recognizing this and also aware of the need to complete a first planning cycle without a lengthy development and training program, the planning assistant felt that for the development of initial plans he might be the sole user. However, he also felt that any system adopted should be capable of, in the future, supporting all the participants in prior and post-planning analyses, consolidation and modification functions described above.

EXAMPLE 6.2

DSS APPLICABILITY FOR AUA PLANNING SITUATION

DECISION(S)/TASK STRUCTURE

Objectives: Multiple, trade-offs not clearly specifiable in advance.

Internal and external impact variables: Generally known or identifiable.

Functional relationships:

1. Many definitional (or accounting identity) known relationships, for example
    Tuition revenue = (Number of students — number receiving tuition remission) * Annual tuition $
2. Many other cause-effect estimated relationships, for example
    Number of applicants = f (Target population size, Annual tuition $, state of economy, reputation of UAU, competitive institutions offerings)

Analysis/Problem Processing: Need to explore many cut and try assumptions and trial strategies, no apparent formal optimization process.

Conclusion:

This appears to be a typical semistructured decision situation and therefore from a technical point of view, an appropriate DSS application.

APPLICABLE/FEASIBLE DSS GENERIC FUNCTIONS

Task/Organizational Setting Viewpoint

A modeling and "what if?" analysis approach appears to be most appropriate to testing out the implications of alternative plans and assumptions as called for by the problem situation. The future need to integrate and consolidate plans seems to call for a modeling language and model processing component with these capabilities.

A data base "what is?" status access or query capability would appear to be only marginally useful for initial planning given that the volume of hard numerical data needed is probably not very large and that most of the relevant data is not now available on existing computer readable files. Most of the required input data is in the form of already summarized published statistics or requires user estimates to be made. However, future monitoring of progress against plans for purposes of control would probably benefit from an ad hoc query capability against a redesigned and implemented administrative data base which would also be used for regular control reporting.

Interface Assessment/Selection—An Overview

In the interface assessment selection stage, the DSS development analyst makes use of knowledge of another inventory of choices, those alternative features of hardware and language interfaces described in chapter 4. This inventory of alternative interfaces is matched against the needs arising out the situation analysis. The first step is to identify software that will meet the general DSS functional requirements. The selection of an interface that seems most appropriate to the user, task, organizational setting, and required DSS functions, should first be undertaken by reviewing the DSS generators already acquired

A statistical analysis capability would appear to be useful for estimating a limited number of key relationships needed for modeling such as correlations between applications and relative tuition costs as well as economic conditions.

Given the need to facilitate communications between different stakeholder groups, some graphic display capability would appear to be useful to support communications in presentations, meetings, and report illustrations. However, this form of support is not seen to be sufficiently urgent to justify any delay in the first round of initial plans development.

CONCLUSIONS:

In order of apparent importance and priority:

1. The priority need appears to be for *modeling* support.
2. A statistics capability would augment modeling (or could be of marginal use without any formal modeling as a source of information for general guidance).
3. A graphics capability would be useful, but at a lower priority.

4. A data base query capability would be of future use but requires developing a new administrative processing and reporting system as a prerequisite.

Users' Characteristics Viewpoint

The main initial user, the planning assistant, is familiar with and receptive to the use of a modeling support system as well as the use of other analytical tools. As the key initial user, he could develop a base system and later modify it in order to facilitate usage by a wider group of potential users.

CONCLUSION:

The applicable forms of support would not only be accepted by the key initial user, but would be seen by him as an extremely useful means for accomplishing his immediate task and enabling the future enhanced participation and continuing planning and monitoring needs to be met.

OVERALL CONCLUSION:

A DSS approach appears to be appropriate and feasible. Within the general guidelines for its generic capabilities given above, the more precise features of such a system remain to be assessed and selected in the next stage (see example 6.5).

by the organization through an overall continuous DSS planning and needs assessment process. General criteria for assessment and selection of the "best-fit" match between the interface and the situational requirements are:

1. Functional scope and power
2. Ease of use;
3. Extent of data base requirements;
4. "Soft" versus "hard" design;
5. "Strong" versus "weak" design.

These criteria are discussed further in the sections following. They will be seen to be related to one another and not independent considerations.

If none of the already acquired software packages prove to be suitable, then other commercially available DSS software packages can be identified and reviewed. If one of these are found to be acceptable, then in-house designing and programming of a support system may be considered. This sequential consideration of commercial packages before considering building your own is generally more efficient than considering all make-or-buy alternatives simultaneously. It is becoming less and less frequent that some existing package alternative is not more cost effective than building your own. It also is generally more desirable for an organization to acquire a robust set of DSS resources to serve many applications without duplicating essentially similar functions. A different second package than one already acquired for the same kind of DSS function (e.g., two different mainframe modeling languages) may be marginally better suited for a particular application, but a small added advantage will not justify the additional costs of acquisition, maintenance, user support and support staff training. Thus the selection of a set of packages as a general DSS corproate resource should be part of the general planning process (discussed more fully in the next chapter). However, a fresh review of these resources to assess the use of a particular package for a particular application should occur (whether *again,* in greater detail, or for the first time) when the application is actually being implemented.

The appropriate software choices will generally also identify the hardware alternatives. Hardware selection is therefore carried out after the language interface features provided by the software choices have been initially assessed.

Value Analysis

An interface should not be finally chosen without carrying out a value analysis in order to economically weigh and justify one interface alternative against another and to determine whether *any* available choice appears to be worthwhile. A fuller discussion of value analysis and other aspects of the economics of computer support will be given later in chapter 12, but a summary of key points is presented here, in the context of DSS development methods, because the establishment of the value of an application should be an integral part of the development process.

Value analysis, as shown earlier in exhibit 6.2, often requires recycling through the assessment/selection of interface features in order to explicitly compare trade-offs between two or more different packages. The first review of packages is typically a screening step in which a group of eligible packages is identified for subsequent value analysis. Under some circumstances, a particular interface alternative will be seen to clearly represent high potential value relative to its cost and it may not appear to be worthwhile to search any further for other alternatives.

Value analysis differs from the usual cost-benefit analysis associated with more traditional applications. The *main focus of value analysis is typically on* those factors that were only considered to be *secondary* and relatively "intangible" in traditional cost-benefit analysis. While traditional systems are assessed mainly on processing efficiencies, DSS are intended to add value to a decision-making process by improving organizational effectiveness. The contribution a particular DSS may make to improved decision outcomes is usally very difficult (or even impossible) to measure directly and in advance of usage. Estimates of value must therefore usually be made by judgmental assumptions, often making use of similar or analogous past experience and extrapolating these into future situations. DSS value analysis can itself be seen as addressing a semistructured problem that can be modeled and assessed in a variety of ways.

Value is what a rational and knowledgeable user should be willing to expend both directly and indirectly to acquire and use the system. While some may use the term *benefit* in a similar manner, as has been pointed out above, it is not typically the practice to do so. The broader concept of value includes *all* outcomes of usage relevant to users, including some outcomes often not considered to be economic. Recognizing that users often will be willing to expend a considerable amount for indirect outcomes, a value analysis depends on the particular users involved and the full situational context. Attitudes toward risk and information value, for example, vary with individuals and probably are inseparable from their skills and performance as decision makers. Factors such as usage convenience or increased confidence may be of value not only because they demonstrably can result in saving time and cost, but because they are important to and inseparable from the user's approach to the task at hand, including the user's willingness to use a support system at all.

The concept of *expenditure* or *cost* in value analysis should also be broad and user-dependent. It should not only take direct monetary expenses such as package costs and formal training costs into account, but also include an assessment of how much time and personal effort users will be willing to expend (of their own volition and because of personal preferences) in order to learn and improve their usage skills through their own efforts.

Interface Selection/Design Criteria: Consideration of Scope and Power versus Ease of Use

In the previous chapter (chapter 5) the concepts of *scope* and *power* were generally defined and seen to be usually related to one another. *Scope* was defined as the extent of the functions a system can perform and *power* is a measure of how much useful work can be initiated by concise user communication. In chapter 4 a basic set of types of conversational interface formats were described, which consisted of:

1. Menus;
2. Question-answer;
3. Command language;
4. Input/output structures;
5. Natural language;
6. Combinations of these.

These interface formats were seen to vary in their suitability for varying levels of functional power and scope as well as in their ease of use. In general, the interface types that are easiest to use but most limited in power and scope are menus and question-answer formats.

Functional scope and power (treated as a composite) was seen to be related generally to *ease of use* (see exhibit 5.4 in the previous chapter) in the form of a trade-off providing more functional scope and power at the expense of ease of use (although in a nonlinear manner). Of course, this trade-off curve expresses only a general tendency and not a precisely measurable set of dimensions on which specific package designs can be pinpointed. But figuratively speaking, an approximate region on this trade-off curve must be selected in the light of the results of the situation analysis. Such an approximation can serve to classify those interface alternatives that can be considered to be at least acceptable with respect to both functional scope/power and ease of use. Within this acceptable category, preferences between two or more alternatives can then be based on a more detailed analysis of trade-offs. This procedure can be extended to include consideration not only of functional scope/power and ease of use, but also of the related dimensions of the extent of the data base required, hard-soft design, and strong-weak design that are discussed in the sections below.

Thus the assessment and selection of a "best-fit" software interface can be seen as a two-step process consisting of:

1. Screening by classification into the acceptable region of a multidimensional criteria space; and
2. Preferential trade-off analysis within the acceptable region.

It would be convenient if all of the design selection criteria dimensions could be mathematically measured and the selection process reduced to the processing of a mathematical model, but this isn't feasible. Instead, it is more practical to use the criteria as general guidelines. How this might be done in practice is illustrated by example 6.5 following the general discussion of the other interface hardware and software selection criteria.

Consideration of Data Base Requirements

As previously stated, information needs for DSS can be expected to evolve with actual usage, but it is possible and necessary to at least roughly categorize the extent and sources of data required. Based on a general knowledge of the situation and task, an estimate can determine whether initial data needs will be extensive and require representing a "rich" and complex environment in which many variables must be considered, a very "poor" world of very few variables, or somewhere in between. Such a categorization and rough estimate is necessary and must suffice to determine the following:

1. Is the required scope of data minimal and can it be efficiently obtained with only a few user-entered inputs at the time of usage? If not, what other data sources must be accessed and for about how much data?

2. Will access to administrative systems' files be necessary and, if so, for about how many data items of what approximate length? Must more than one source or file be accessed or consolidated?
3. What is required as to the age of required data and how can it be kept up to date? Can the user easily do any required updating or must this be accomplished with the support of other departments, assistants, etc.?
4. To what extent can additional functional scope and power of a support system be substituted for some stored or user-entered data? (That is, which information can be calculated or created by the processing of source or other stored data when it is needed rather than itself be included in a previously stored data base?)

If the situation description and the direct additional knowledge of the analyst is insufficient to make these approximate determinations, then it will be necessary for the analyst and main user to return to the situation analysis phase in order to answer these questions. A useful method is to "mock up" some examples, either on paper or using any available software aid to create some sample prototype information representations. If the user can at least identify some relevant representations (what the system can show the user), these can serve as a basis for determining what changes, variations, calculated results, additions, or reformatting can be used in order to produce new representations. The utility of these trial representations can be rapidly assessed by the user and the source data required can then be identified. In this manner a glimpse ahead at actual usage can take place without actually building a full prototype base system. This partial prototype need not contain computer support for the analytical functions and the envisioned support operations, but merely must aid in mocking up displays of relevant representations of the sole purpose of approximating the extent of the initial data base required to produce these representations. This can be accomplished with many microcomputer word processing or drawing packages, or can be done with manual media (eg., paper or chalkboards).

Consideration of "Hard-Soft" Design

In the context of DSS, the terms "hard" versus "soft" system capabilities have been used to distinguish between the relative degree of *general* functions versus *application specific* operations directly built into the software. Softer capabilities are more generic functions which require a user to follow a process of tailoring or "hardening" them into a particular application. This hardening process is analogous, although by no means technically identical, to programming in a relatively soft third generation language such as COBOL in order to produce a specific application program. Although DSS generator packages are (unlike COBOL) relatively nonprocedural fourth generation languages, they may provide very generic soft capabilities such as general commands and symbolic language elements and a grammer for combining them into any logical or mathematical statement. In contrast, a relatively hard capability might consist of a predefined set of functions for a particular business application (such as financial planning, investment analysis, or advertising planning) with no user option to add to or modify these built-in specialized functions. The same contrast between hard and soft capabilities can apply not only to modeling and model-based analysis but also to other DSS functions such as a data base query capability.

When considering the hard-soft design criterion, the following general trade-off relationships can be taken into account in selecting a suitable interface:

1. Harder DSS capabilities versus learning requirements.

    Harder DSS capabilities, for systems that are not extremely extensive in functional scope, are usually easier to learn and use for those who are already experienced in the subject area of the application.

    Because harder system design includes functions specifically related to the user's application realm and less of a general nature, there is less for a user to learn about how to tailor the system in order to get a particular mode of analysis accomplished. On the other hand, if the system is functionally very extensive, the user must learn how to find and select the precisely desired functions rather than learning how to modify or tailor fewer more generic functions.

    Not only the extent, but also the nature of learning required is affected by hard-soft design. In general, harder design requires less abstract thinking about how to formulate an analysis or processing strategy and how to tailor the system in order to implement it and more concrete thinking about selecting specific well-defined functions. The style and capability of the user in this regard, as well as the nature and extent of the task, should therefore be taken into account.

2. Harder capabilities versus scope and power.

    Harder capabilities are less flexible (less modifiable and less extendable). A hard set of fundamental capabilities for the average user, in order to provide a new mode of analysis or a higher degree of functional scope, must have its basic repertoire of operations extended through rebuilding the basic software into a new version instead of enabling the user to directly derive new forms of functionality by retailoring the system. If a hard design is intended from the outset to satisfy more advanced users demanding a wide range of analysis, it must usually include a lengthier repertoire of functions. If a system is to be used by novices requiring only basic functions, average users, and advanced users, a hard design should also include some segmentation or classification of functionality into the subsets most likely to be required by each of these categories of users in order to facilitate user identification of and access to the particular functions needed. The manner in which a system merely facilitates or strongly directs users toward proper or efficient usage is another design dimension, the strong versus weak dimension, discussed below.

Consideration of "Strong-Weak" Design

The strong versus weak design dimension, as previously mentioned in chapter 4, is a relative measure of the extent to which the system leads or forces the user into a particular procedure (strong) or leaves it to the user to select or define what procedure to follow during any usage session (weak). It should again be noted that, if carried to the extreme of forcing the user into a standard processing procedure allowing for no deviations, strong design moves over the boundary between support and automation according to a strict definition of computer support systems. But within the bounds of providing some user control over processing, support systems can vary considerably with regard to how much control is provided to the user and how easy it is for the user to exercise control.

Examples of alternative design approaches in this regard are illustrated in example 6.3 and in the cases presented in example 6.4.

When considering the strong-weak design criterion, the following general trade-off relationships can be taken into account in selecting a suitable interface.

1. Stronger DSS capabilities versus ease of use and learning requirements. Stronger DSS capabilities are easier to learn and use. There is less to be learned because the system will take a stronger role in leading the user through prescribed or suggested steps. If the system usually takes users along a path that serves their needs, it is easier for them to use because the system requires little effort from them to steer it.

On the other hand, if the system does not make it easy for the user to deviate from its usual prescribed path, a strong design can be very frustrating for users who know what they want to do differently. Even when a relatively strong design allows users to override the recommended mode of processing, the need to wait for the system to provide an opportunity for breaking out of a usual processing sequence introduces an unwanted delay for such self-directed users.

2. Weaker capabilities versus scope and power. A relatively weak system that allows users great flexibility in actively steering is only useful if that degree of user control has a payoff in terms of increased or more effectively utilized scope and power. If providing flexible steering does not result in delivering or using more scope and power the user is, in effect, driving the system in a narrow lane along the same roadway and arriving at the same destination that could have been identified in advance and built into a stronger automatic pilot. The user will quickly tire of any thrill initially involved in steering the system once it is seen to be steering to no avail.

EXAMPLE 6.3

HARD VERSUS SOFT CAPABILITIES

SOFT DESIGN FOR A PLANNING MODEL SUPPORT SYSTEM

Built-in commands cover basic control functions only:

START NEW MODEL, SOLVE, WHAT IF, etc.

User may enter mathematical and logical relationships in a flexible modeling language:

eg. Statement 125 REPORT A IF SALES LESS
THAN 250, ELSE REPORT B;

eg. Statement 130 RETURN = 100 *
PRESVALUE (SALES/COSTS), etc.

User may create new functions for future reference:

SAVE 130 AS RETURN FUNCTION OF (SALES,COSTS)

User may specify report contents and formats:

SPECIFY REPORT (Report Name/ Report
Heading Line1, Report Heading Line2,Report
Heading Line3/ Number of Columns/
ColumnHeadings/ ColumnWidths/
MaxLinesperPage(optional)/
PageNumbering(parameter1,parameter2)

HARD DESIGN FOR A FINANCIAL PLANNING SUPPORT SYSTEM

Control command repertoire:

SHOW, PRINT, COMPUTE, ENTER DATA, PREPARE REPORT

Built-in function repertoire (No user defined modeling language):
includes 56 standard financial functions such as

PRESENT VALUE (Time seriesName)

Report type options (includes four standard system defined reports):

P&L; BALANCE SHEET; CASHFLOW; ROI

Includes a standard format to display or print up to
six at a time of results of computation of any of the
built-in functions.

EXAMPLE 6.4

STRONG-WEAK CASE EXAMPLES

CASE A. (A STRONG DESIGN APPROACH)

System A always forces usage to move through four sequential phases of (1) analysis mode specification; (2) data entry or selection; (3) analysis; and (4) reporting. The analysis mode specification phase allows the user to select from an extensive menu of *predefined* modes of data analysis (note that this is a hard design approach) or to *add any number of user defined* new analysis modes through a special language for this purpose (note that this is a soft capability). If the user does not define a new mode of analysis or select any mode from the menu, but instead merely allows the system to procede by pressing a "return" key, the system follows its own built-in default option for analysis and goes on. According to the analysis mode specified, the system requires data entry to follow a particular format within prescribed parameters. Also according to the selected analysis mode, the user is provided with a limited number of report content options. If the user breaks off a usage session, data and analysis results can be saved for a subsequent session. However, any subsequent session will always begin with the same sequence of (1) analysis mode specification; (2) data entry or selection; (3) analysis; and (4) reporting. During the data entry phase the user must either select a previously saved set of data or enter a new set in the required format. Saved sets of data are associated with the specified analysis mode for which they were initially created and cannot be directly used by a different analysis mode.

This system is very strong in leading the user through a prescribed processing sequence, but it has extensive power and scope resulting from its extensive hard menu of analytical modes and its soft user defined analysis capability. Thus users have a great deal of control over the mode of analysis but no control over the sequential phases of an interactive session.

CASE B. (A STRONG DESIGN APPROACH)

System B is similar to *system A* described above in that it has a strong design leading users through the same four phases of (1) analysis mode specification; (2) data entry or selection; (3) analysis; and (4) reporting. However, *system B* differs in that it has no capability for supporting user-defined analysis modes and its built-in menu of analysis modes is limited to only three alternatives.

Like *system A* this system is very strong in leading the user through a prescribed processing sequence, but it has limited power and scope resulting from its hard menu of only three analytical modes. Thus users have some control over the mode of analysis but no control over the sequential phases of an interactive session. This system has only a limited degree of flexibility and support capability that differs from batch mode analysis through combining rapid on-line response and display along with some optional modes of analysis.

CASE C. (A WEAK DESIGN APPROACH)

Case C is similar to *case B* in that it has a limited number of modes of analysis built into a hard menu. But these are different modes of analysis than those of *cases A* or *B* and they accept their respective sets of input data in less structured formats that are independent from the analysis mode. In *case C*, processing phases also consist of (1) analysis mode specification; (2) data entry or selection; (3) analysis; and (4) reporting, but unlike the prior cases these can be usefully carried out in varying user-controlled sequences. For example, because of the looser constraints on data formats, selected report contents resulting from carrying out an analysis can be accepted as input data to a subsequent analysis. Thus a session may start by selecting the saved report of a prior session and then going directly into a new analysis, or alternatively, modifying the report data by going into a data entry phase in which new data is added or changed prior to analysis. In addition, the analysis mode need not be specified prior to data entry. Multiple analysis modes can also be specified at the same time and applied to either the same single set of data or applied to any group of data sets. Thus any combination of analyses can, at the user's option, be applied to any combination of data sets through a command language of the form: ANALYSIS (analysis mode list), DATA (data set list), where a "list" is of the form (first list item, next list item, . . . last list item), ANALYSIS (analysis mode list), DATA (data set list), . . . etc. to last ANALYSIS (analysis mode list), DATA (data set list).

But, as previously discussed, a high degree of scope and power can be derived from flexible user tailoring of soft capabilities or from an extensive repertoire of hard capabilities. Thus a relatively weak design can be combined effectively with either hard or soft capabilities. It is also possible that a system with a limited hard designed repertoire of basic functions can deliver some increase in scope and power by means of a weaker and therefore more flexible control interface. This is illustrated by case C in example 6.4.

But what can be said about a strong design capability allowing little user control over the sequence of processing in a system with extensive scope and power (whether derived from a soft tailoring of generic functions or an extensive hard repertoire)? Can a general sequence of processing be prescribed regardless of the extent of the systems functional scope and power ? In many modes of support this is possible and a situation of this kind is illustrated by case A in example 6.4.

In summary, what can be said about the relationship between the soft-hard dimension and the strong-weak dimension is that all combinations of these relative categories are possible and may be useful in particular situations, but a weak design is not suited for a system requiring little scope and power.

It should also be noted that although a weak interface allows the user greater flexibility in steering the system, that does not mean that this approach must leave the user without guidance aids. The extent to which a system presents options or suggests paths for users to follow without forcing them to do so is another important design dimension. The need for guidance is, of course, related directly to the strong-weak dimension in that the stronger the design the less is the need for guidance and the weaker the design the greater the need for guidance. Moreover, user guidance should generally be provided in a weak or highly user-controlled manner so that users can obtain it when desired and easily ignore it when automatically offered by the system. In other words, guidance, to the extent it may be needed, should be accessible but unobtrusive.

Selection of Hardware Interface Features

As previously stated, the appropriate software choices will generally identify which hardware alternatives are feasible and acceptable. The relative scope and power and ease of use differences associated with mainframe and microcomputer DSS software were discussed in chapter 5. Taken together with these dimensions, other differences between mainframe and microcomputer software capabilities with respect to data base limitations, hard-soft and strong-weak capabilities, will serve to identify which computer models within the general categories of computer sizes will be able to run the software deemed appropriate and acceptable for the application. As with the assessment of software, the feasible hardware choices must also be assessed with regard to costs, availability, and usability for other existing or planned applications (including office automation as well as DSS) in the organization.

Linkage of DSS, under some circumstances, with data arising out of transaction processing and regular reporting systems was discussed in chapter 2. The need for such an interface in order to access data should have been identified earlier in estimating data base requirements, as discussed previously. This need, taken together with any need to exchange information and analyses or to consolidate models between a group of users, will determine the need for communications facilities.

A general assessment of both hardware and the software interface features for the situation analysis case presented in examples 6.1 and 6.2 is illustrated in example 6.5.

Methods for Phase II:
Base System Development and Assessment

Given the selection of DSS software and hardware based on the situation analysis and value analysis, a base system (or "version 0") must next be implemented. The extent and nature of the work involved in base system development depends on the specific interface features of the software being used. As previously discussed, a soft and weak interface design will require extensive tailoring and user selection of an approach to initial development and application of the system and a harder and stronger interface will allow and require less effort. In any case, specific DSS application development means that some effort must be expended to harden system capabilities and exercise user strength over control options. This is necessary in order to use a generic package or DSS generator as a tool to create and use a working specific DSS application. This can be assessed further in terms of the benefits derived and the need for any further iterative use and development.

This first system version starts without a system that will run. While phase 2 starts with a "clean piece of paper," phase 3 starts with a specified working base system as a foundation. Development/usage methodology differs somewhat between these two phases because of these different initial conditions. Phase 2 development/usage is seen as a sequence of steps with some looping back, as shown previously in exhibit 6.3. The basic sequence of specify-construct-use is concerned with selecting, setting up, and applying an initial set of operations that manipulate some data base or set of information representations, whether user supplied or previously stored. The identification and implementation of any initial and subsequent set of operations and the representations they refer to depend on the current state of knowledge and skills of the user. For this reason, development and usage of a specific DSS cannot be separated from the state of user knowledge and process of learning taking place within the user. For any step of specification, construction, or use, the user's state of knowledge may be the critical barrier to carrying out the step, and therefore this barrier must first be removed before development can proceed. For this reason, basic user training should precede the DSS development

EXAMPLE 6.5

INTERFACE FEATURES FOR UAU PLANNING SUPPORT

LANGUAGE FEATURES AND SOFTWARE SELECTION

Functional Scope and Power Consideration

General Requirements

1. Flexibility and scope
   a) A modeling language is required that will allow the user to express and easily change a variety of mathematical and logical relationships.
   b) Only basic built-in mathematical and logical functions such as square root, logarithms, logical value and magnitude comparisons are needed (trigonometric functions are unlikely to be useful)
   c) Approximately seven built-in financial functions would be useful for basic calculations on the two most common methods of depreciation of capital expenditures, present value of future positive and negative cash flows, rate of return or interest rate of positive and negative cash flows, and the amount of annuities or future payment of present loans.
2. Communications and readability
   a) In order to facilitate understandability, the language should be easily readable by those familiar with basic mathematical notation without having to use a manual or receive training in a special computer notation.
   b) While analyses and final results will need to be communicated between participants, speed of communications is not essential for these planning and analysis needs that will typically occur over a period of some months, with the major usage being the first year, some additional annual re-analysis and revision, and further major re-analysis and revision at five year intervals.

c) Some graphics capability will be useful but need not be highly integrated with model analysis. Graphics will mainly be useful to facilitate understanding of the final results of individual analyses.

Ease of Use Consideration

Most potential participating users already have some experience in at least using microcomputer spreadsheet packages and the major user, the planning assistant, has experience with mainframe modeling software usage as well. A system meeting the scope and power characteristics required as well as the need for understandable communications, should present no inherent ease of use problems. Any systems that are approximately equal on functional grounds can then be compared for the ease of use of their control command features, interactive procedures, editing features, reporting features, and other ancillary capabilities such as on line help. Since the users will not be computer novices, however, the system selected need not sacrifice much in the way of compact expression and efficient operations for the sake of simplicity.

Scope and Size of Data Base Consideration

1. Models
   a) Number of models
      There will be one major consolidated model for the entire university, and four submodels, one for each of the four colleges respectively. Each of these models may be further segmented into component submodels.
   b) Size of models
      The integrated planning model for the university as a whole will probably consist of about 50 statements in its initial version and may grow in the future to about 100 statements. Each statement is expected to represent a function of up to

10 terms. Therefore each model could be represented as a matrix of up to about 10 × 100 = 1000 elements. Actual storage however can be considerably larger than this if expressed as a spreadsheet (variable by time matrix) with storage elements required (even if their values are zero) for each time period even though these can be expressed in a more compact mathematical notation (see 2. regarding file sizes below).

Each of the four college submodels are expected to be of about the same magnitude. These college submodels will be used separately and independently from the university model but will be related in terms of some of the college model variables being common to corresponding variables in the university model. Thus certain variable values must be transferred at some time but each model can be used independently and need not be directly linked at the time of usage.

2. Number, size of active files

No administrative files need to be directly linked. Data can be conveniently segmented into two or three files at most for each model. Each file can be expected to contain values for up to 200 model input variables or parameters in a time series form. The volume of data can be approximated as follows:

Maximum number of time periods: 12 months for each of 10 years = 120 time periods
Maximum number of variables: 200
Maximum total data required per model (total of all files) = 120 time periods × 200 variables = 24,000 data elements (fields)

Files capacity required per model (assuming each data element requires 10 characters) = 24,000 × 10 = 240,000 bytes

Hard-Soft Capabilities Consideration

The nature of the flexible modeling functions requires a relatively soft capability to formulate and modify most of the relationships that will be found relevant. No standard (harder capability) university planning package exists that specifically covers the scope needed.

Strong-Weak Capabilities Consideration

A relatively weak capability is needed in which the users can perform a variety of what if and sensitivity analyses during initial and subsequent model development and usage. The main object is not to produce an automated planning report generator or a mechanical method of planning, but to explore and adapt assumptions to various perceived trends and possible scenarios in order to more thoroughly analyze and select policies and strategies.

In addition, users are familiar with analytical methods and have abstract thinking skills needed to evolve their own approaches to modeling and analysis. A strong system pushing users into particular modes of analysis would probably not be used or useful.

Over-all Software Assessment and Acceptability

1. Available modeling software
   a) Mainframe Package "Z"
      The university already had an interactive mainframe planning model package used via terminals by students in a number of business courses. This package had much more capacity (in terms of model sizes and data handling capability) than required. It contained all the built-in functions needed as well and considerable more mathematical functions than required. It also included a fairly rudimentary but adequate graphic capability. It met other requirements of general ease of use, although it had some

EXAMPLE 6.5 continued

weakness in its text editing capabilities. Its design was relatively weak and soft as required.

It was clearly usable for the identified needs, but its usage had the following drawbacks:

—Although the usage licensing agreement did not restrict the system's use to teaching only (as did some other commercial packages available under special favorable terms to educational institutions), the policy of the university restricted the computer hardware system it ran on to teaching use only.

—The university did not have a compatible modeling language that could run on the microcomputers available to all faculty for purposes of off line development and analysis. (System "Z" had a micro version available but the university had not acquired it and it did not run on the micros generally available on campus.) Although terminals were available at several campus locations, it was desirable not to use mainframe time-sharing resources for nonteaching purposes on this hardware system. The use of microcomputers for some off line development and analysis could minimize the demand for the mainframe resource. Several microcomputer spreadsheet packages were available (see below) to all faculty members but these languages were not directly compatible with the language of package "Z." Two other mainframe facilities were available at the university; one for faculty research and some limited student use, and a second system dedicated to administrative data processing. However, the version of package "Z" in use did not run on these systems.

b) Micro spreadsheet packages
As mentioned, several spreadsheet packages were available at the university and most faculty members and many administrative officers had their own copies of a particular package. These packages were all user friendly and could meet the initial expected "first version" size requirements for this planning application. However the most generally available package could not handle the 200 variable (one for each spreadsheet row) maximum that might be required for future versions. All of the micro packages were relatively easy to use, and allowed for a great deal of user control and flexible modeling. However, several drawbacks (in addition to the size restriction mentioned) existed for their use, as follows:

—The most commonly available package had no graphics capability. (Several of the other micro packages did include graphics. Although integrated graphics would have been convenient it was not considered essential.)

—None of these packages had all of the built-in financial functions needed, although they did contain four or five of them.

—Their modeling languages included a "relative referencing" notation that was not standard and easily understandable only for the user familiar with basic common mathematical notation.

—None of these micro package modeling languages were directly compatible with the mainframe package "Z" language, although it was possible to save numerical data resulting from their calculation that could be transmitted to the mainframe system and saved as a package "Z" file.

2. Other (acquirable) modeling packages
    a) Other mainframe packages.
       Several other mainframe packages were
       available and could easily fulfill the
       requirements. Two of these could be seen
       to have some ease of use advantages,
       but these were considered to be of
       marginal value. These packages also had
       some greater functional flexibility in
       representing modeling dimensions
       beyond two dimensions, but this also was
       considered to be of marginal value. All of
       these had micro versions compatible with
       their mainframe package.
       It was also possible to acquire a
       mainframe version of package "Z" that
       would run on the research computer
       system hardware.
    b) Other micro packages
       The only micro package that had any
       advantage over those already acquired
       was the micro version of package "Z." Its
       advantage was its greater readability and
       its direct compatability with the
       mainframe version, but (as stated above)
       it did not run on the microcomputer model
       generally in use on campus.

HARDWARE FEATURES CONSIDERATION

Considering hardware features independently from
that of software package capabilities, the general
preferences were as follows:

1. The most desirable alternative would be a
   system utilizing the commonly available
   micros already familiar to most users. Most of
   these micros already had comunications
   capability with a mainframe time-sharing
   system and in the future would also be able
   to be linked directly with one another.

2. The next best alternative would utilize a
   mainframe system that would not interfere
   with student use and that could be used in
   conjunction with the transmission of data
   downward for off line micro analysis and
   upward for consolidation into a mainframe
   model.

FINAL ASSESSMENT AND SELECTION

Considering all of the factors discussed above as
well as the costs of acquiring either new software
or hardware, the following assessment and decisions resulted:

1. For purposes of completing the initial
   planning on time and without delays for
   acquiring and setting up new resources it
   was best to utilize package "Z." This would
   meet all of the absolute requirements and it
   would represent only a minor limited period
   drain on computer teaching resources to use
   package "Z" on the time-shared computer
   system on which it currently was running.
   This system could be used both by the main
   planning assistant user and was already
   available to all and familiar to several faculty
   members who could participate in this first
   (and considered critical) planning effort.

2. Although it would be a benefit to be able, in
   the future, to use micros for at least off line
   analysis, all of these alternatives had
   significant drawbacks. All except micro
   package "Z" would require constructing
   some of the basic financial functions needed,
   but micro package "Z" would not run on the
   available microcomputers. If they were used
   as the primary planning tool and not merely
   for off line analysis, the less readable
   modeling conventions they used would be a
   drawback. For at least the first round of
   planning it was decided not to rely on any of
   the micro alternatives.

EXAMPLE 6.5 continued

3. For future rounds of annual planning, the following steps were decided on:

   a) A version of package "Z" that would run on the research mainframe computer would be acquired. This entailed a moderate one time charge and only a 15 percent increase in the annual maintenance charge already applied to the use of the one mainframe teaching system. This had the added advantage of making package "Z" available for any faculty research need (as well as for the planning application) without having any impact on computer resources for teaching. Although the planning application alone would only represent a periodic and probably moderate drain on these resources, it was felt that it was not desirable to set up a continuing precedent for this violation of policy.

   b) The planning models developed would be published and made available to all parties involved along with some samples and guidelines for the translation of the package "Z" models into spreadsheet form, as well as suggested feasible procedures for segmenting a model into smaller components in case the complete model exceeded size limits for the generally used spreadsheet package.

   c) Spreadsheet versions of the missing financial functions would be created as student projects and distributed for general use. This could have additional utility beyond this one application.

   d) A general procedure and supporting software would also be developed and distributed to facilitate the transfer of data (not model statements, but numerical data) between package "Z" on the mainframe and the commonly used micro package. This also could have additional utility beyond this one application.

   This short term and longer term follow-up approach appeared to deliver the most value for the lowest additional cost considering the needs of this application. In addition, it was clear that a larger consideration of values and costs beyond this single application were relevant and these also influenced the alternative chosen.

process, and should continue as needed during any stage of development. This continual training can be accomplished through a variety of means including using self-training published reference materials, through the personal guidance of staff support specialists, through user exchange groups, and through the help and guidance features built into the software itself.

The earlier situation analysis and interface assessment generally identified the nature of the DSS, but a specific DSS application must now be constructed using the general interface tools that have been put into place. Because the development of a specific DSS includes its actual usage and an assessment of that usage, the end-user (or one or more particular users in the case of many users) must either also fill the role of the DSS builder or else work closely with an experienced specialist DSS builder. When a specialist DSS builder is involved, that person should play the dual role of:

1. Specifying and constructing the specific DSS in close consultation with the user; and
2. Providing training and tutoring (or building upon prior training) in order to enable the user to use the system effectively.

A convenient starting point for creating the specific DSS is to refer to any information representations previously identified during the data base requirements assessment carried out in the interface selection stage. Starting with such a basis, or else creating such a basis at this stage, the development proceeds by further specifying the specific information representations that will be relevant to the user to see. Depending on the nature of the support to be provided, this can include tabular displays of data, graphics, or logical or mathematical relationships in the context of a set of such relationships. These representations can be constructed or entered into the specific DSS in whichever manner the software requires. They can be specified and entered one at a time, or alternatively a group of representations can first be identified and entered into the system as a group, according to whichever style suits the builder/user. Interspersed with the construction and further specification of representations, the builder/user can attempt to specify useful operations that can be carried out upon these representations (such as solving a set of equations, sorting a set of data, graphing data, correlating data, assessing sensitivity of some relationships, etc.). After specifying such operations the builder can construct them (enter them into the DSS in the language provided by the software for doing so). The process of building the base system can continue by a further sequence of specifying additional representations and operations. This can go on until the specific DSS contains sufficient representations and operations to enable some processing to be initiated and completed by displaying meaningful results to the user. The point at which system use should be initiated can either be thought out in advance or simply tried out according to two tests:

1. Computability
   A minimal set of representations and operations must be specified and constructed before the system can process anything.
2. Situational utility
   Assessing whether the user can learn anything of any value in the problem situation based on the results of usage.

If system usage doesn't pass the test of computability, the system is underspecified and the builder must return to specify and construct either or both additional representations or operations. If the system usage passes the first test of computability but not the second test of situational utility, then the base system has again not been sufficiently developed, but this time on pragmatic grounds determined not by the system but by the user.

When both tests have been passed sufficiently (according to the user's judgment) to enable completion of an assessment of usage value, the base system development can be considered to be completed.

An assessment of the usage experience should then be carried out to determine whether or not any value has been attained and whether any next steps of further usage/development can be identified and assessed as likely to yield any further value.

Methods for Phase III:
Iterative Development + Usage + Assessment

As noted, system versions evolved in phase 3 begin with the working base system as a foundation. The user can therefore continue development by further usage and by specifying and constructing new or modified specific representations and operations. The basic sequence of specify-construct-use shown previously in exhibit 6.3 for development of the base system is modified in exhibit 6.4 in order to show these optional starting and restarting entry points for iterative development. Because usage is integrated with further development, it is highly desirable that users can now carry out changes and additions to the system largely on their own with minimal assistance from specialist DSS builders.

Once again, after some period of usage that may involve several changes in the system, the user may reassess the problem situation and the value of continuing to use and evolve the DSS. Such an assessment may be formal and carried out with the assistance of a DSS specialist (or even at the request of a DSS staff group) or it may be informal and implicit in a user's discontinuance of usage of the specific DSS. The assessment may result in:

1. A new round of development/usage (restart at (1) or (2) in exhibit 6.4);
2. Discontinuance of the application entirely (the "abort" option); or
3. Recasting and transporting the system into the category of a regular (non-DSS) information system or into a different DSS because the situation has grown beyond the originally assessed needs and capabilities (the "alternative approach" option).

The choice and efficacy of any of these options depends on both changes in the problem situation and on the user's state of knowledge about the problem and the DSS. User learning is the critical issue and it should be clear what learning can and cannot be attributed to the use of the DSS. The user's experience in developing and using the DSS can result in three different kinds of learning:

1. Learning more about the problem situation.
   This kind of learning represents the most direct potential payoff resulting from the DSS experience. It should also be recognized that the DSS is seldom the sole source of learning more about the problem situation.
2. Learning more about how to analyze the problem situation.
   This kind of learning increases the user's analytical skills and thereby can provide a less direct, future payoff in formulating more effective analytical strategies. The use of a DSS by itself usually isn't capable of adding complex technical new analytical

approaches to the user's repertoire but can sharpen judgments in selecting already familiar or nontechnical analytical methods through experience.

3. Learning more about how to use the DSS to efficiently operationalize any further analysis.

    This kind of learning enables the user to more easily "drive" the DSS and obtain greater utilization of its inherent power. It is enhanced by frequency of use and by intensity of use of the DSS as well as by formal training.

The last kind of learning (item 3 above) is typically the first area of formal DSS training offered to users prior to their involvement with a specific application. It is concerned with training in the tools themselves and how to use them in a mechanical or technical sense. It includes such things as how to enter data, select menu options, the content and rules of a command language, or which keys to press to initiate or terminate particular operations.

However, the second type of learning (item 2 above), that of learning more about useful analytical approaches, is not usually provided as part of DSS user training. It is actually more appropriate to consider this to be *education* in more general abilities and not as *training* in specific skills. It is too often assumed that the user already has sufficient prior education and knows enough about analytical methods to make good use of a DSS if trained in how to use it. A specific assessment of the user's level of analytical knowledge should be part of a thorough situation analysis. However, education of this kind may arise again as a critical factor as the user gains experience and learning about the problem itself through iterative DSS use. As shown previously in exhibit 6.4, a form of *advanced analytical education* should therefore be explicitly considered as an option, along with advanced training in the more specific system usage skills. This consideration usually requires the assistance of a specialist as part of the experience assessment stage.

The iterative development/usage process continues for the life of the specific DSS. As noted above, its life may end because the DSS has yielded whatever learning it can and similar new situations can be handled without carrying out the exploratory type of analysis which is the hallmark of DSS. In this regard, the success of a DSS application may lead to its own demise. The application may also become obsolete because, like other computer applications, it simply no longer applies to a new dissimilar business situation.

Much in this iterative development/usage process depends for its effectiveness upon a set of organizational background factors that have only been touched upon in this chapter. These factors include organizational resources, policies and practices involving training and education, the DSS supporting staff, and overall integration of DSS planning and acquisition of hardware and software into the master planning process for MIS and for the organization as a whole. These organizational issues are discussed in chapter 7.

Review Questions, Exercises, and Discussion Topics

Review Questions

1. Why should the development of a base system for a DSS application not attempt to use a detailed process flow chart of the current method as a first step in determining system requirements?

2. Shouldn't all systems be easily modifiable when modifications are called for? In what way does a DSS application differ from other applications in this regard?

3. *a*) What is meant by the hard-soft capabilities of a DSS generator package?
   b) What effect does this dimension have on ease of use?
   c) What effect does this dimension have on functional scope and power?

4. *a*) What is meant by the strong-weak capabilities of a DSS generator package?
   b) What effect does this dimension have on ease of use?
   c) What effect does this dimension have on functional scope and power?

5. What is the relevance of a user's skills, style, and knowledge have on the selection of DSS software ? What trade-offs does this dimension imply with regard to functional scope and power and ease of use?

6. *a*) Identify and describe the three major phases of DSS application development.
   b) What are the main objectives of each of these main phases?
   c) What major subphases or stages do each of these consist of?

7. In what way(s) does the development of a base system differ from the iterative further development of a DSS application?

8. Why should hardware selection come after software selection?

9. What arguments can you make for *not* searching for the optimal DSS generator for each application independently from any other applications?

10. Does the rejection or abandonment of a DSS approach represent a failure of analysis? Give reasons for your answer.

11. What role should the user play during the development of a base system? Give reasons.

12. What role should the user play during the any iterative development beyond that of a base system? Give reasons.

13. *a*) What kinds of user learning may take place prior to and during development and use of a DSS application?
    b) How may each of these kinds of learning be facilitated and accomplished?

14. What is the purpose of a value analysis, when should it be carried out during development/usage of a DSS, and how does its emphasis differ from that of traditional cost-benefit analysis for automation systems?

15. What effect might the need to interact with and share decision making among different people have on the selection of hardware and software for DSS?

Exercises

1. Develop a situation description for a real situation familiar to you that you think might be an opportunity for a DSS application.
2. For the same situation, write an assessment of the applicability and feasibility of a DSS approach, identifying the general kinds of DSS capabilities (if any) that would be appropriate.
3. Complete a software and hardware interface assessment and selection for the same situation or for an alternative situation in which a DSS approach is deemed to be appropriate.
4. Select two different DSS packages (either for a mainframe or a microcomputer) that purport to do similar functions and compare them with respect to ease of use, functional scope and power, problem size and data base limitations, the hard-soft dimension, and the strong-weak dimension.
5. Analyze the DSS training provided by a real company in your area for its content, cost, scope of user coverage, and effectiveness. Distinguish between general educational objectives and specific skills training in your analysis.
6. Design an interface for a new specialized software package for a specific application following a relatively hard design approach in order to minimize the work a group of users (inexperienced with computers) would have to do. Select and outline an application situation in which this kind of approach is likely to be appropriate as opposed to adapting a more general DSS generator package. In documenting your interface design, include the following:
   a) An inventory of the types of *representations* (displayed information) the users would consider to be basic needs.
   b) An inventory of the types of *operations* (command language vocabulary, menu options, etc.) the users would consider to be basic needs.
   c) A sample of a typical interactive conversational usage session showing user inputs and computer responses (in the form of a script clearly differentiating between the user's statements and computer responses and other displays, annotated with explanatory stage directions).
   d) A discussion of the main features of the interface and reasons why they appear to most appropriate for these users and this application.
   e) An estimate of how such an application and user needs and desires might evolve in the future after experience in using the DSS.

Discussion Topics

1. Discuss the possibility for using more structured development methods (such as hierarchy diagramming and other forms of modular structured analysis) for at least some aspects of DSS application development that utilizes general DSS generator packages. Is this an inherently contradictory notion or do you think such methods might be developed and prove useful?

2. Discuss the proposition that the availability of general DSS software tools has caused a considerable amount of inappropriate, inefficient and ineffective use because of the failure of adequate educational and training resources to keep up. Is the remedy for any "knowledge" gap most likely to be solved by different software design approaches (what kinds) or by more education (what kinds) or by other factors (which)?
3. What kinds of skills seem to be most needed by DSS builder specialists and how can such individuals best be found and developed? Is it reasonable to expect the relevant attributes and knowledge needed in one person or is some form of team approach to user support more practical ? How might either an individual consultant or a team approach be organized and how might it be carried out effectively in a typical large organization? Are organizations likely to extend their expenditures for DSS support groups?
4. What improved methods and practices might be developed to identify and transport DSS applications into standard computer systems if they evolve to a point where they become essentially structured computer applications? Discuss whether or not this is an important issue.

References

Ahituv, N., Neumann, S. 1982. "Software and Hardware Tools of a DSS." *Principles of Information Systems for Management,* Dubuque, Ia.: Wm. C. Brown. 339–420.

Bahl, H. C., Hunt, R. G. 1985. "Problem-Solving Strategies for DSS Design." *Information and Management* 8(February)2:81–88.

Benbasat, I., Wand, Y. 1982. "A Dialogue Generator and Its Use in DSS Design." *Information and Management,* New York: North-Holland. 5(September/November):231–41.

Bodily, S. E. 1985. "Creating and Using a Model in a High Level Language." Chapters 4 and 5 in *Modern Decision Making: A Guide to Modeling with Decision Support Systems,* New York: McGraw-Hill Book Company.

Carlson, E. D. 1983. *Building Decision Support Systems* edited by J. L. Bennett, Reading, Mass.: Addison-Wesley.

Carlson, E. D. 1979. "An Approach for Designing Decision Support Systems." *DATA BASE* 10(Winter)?:? 15.

Huber, G. P. 1983. "Cognitive Style as a Basis for MIS and DSS Designs: Much Ado About Nothing?" *Management Science* 29(May):567–82.

Keen, P. G. W. 1981. "Value Analysis: Justifying Decision Support Systems." *Management Information Systems Quarterly* 5(March)1:1–15.

Keen, P. G. W. 1980. "Adaptive Design for Decision Support Systems." *DATA BASE* 12(Fall)1, 2:15–25.

Keen, P. G. W., Scott Morton, M. S. 1978. "The Design Process: Decision Analysis and Evolution." Chapter 6 in *Decision Support Systems: An Organizational Perspective,* Reading, Mass.: Addison-Wesley.

Leary, E. J. 1985. "Decision Support Systems: A Look at Hardware, Software and Planning Procedures." *Industrial Engineering,* 17(October)10:82–94.

McCosh, A. M., Scott Morton, M. S. 1978. "The Design Process." Chapter 4 in *Management Decision Support Systems,* New York: John Wiley & Sons.

McNurlin, B. C. 1981. "Developing Systems By Prototyping." *EDP Analyzer,* 19(September)9.

Martin, M. P. 1982. "Determining Information Requirements for DSS." *Journal of Systems Management* 33(December):14–21.

Menkus, B. 1983. "Practical Considerations in Decision Support System Design." *Journal of Systems Management* 34(June):32–33.

Naylor, T. H., Gattis, D. R. 1976. "The Future of Corporate Modeling." (on the need for user-oriented nonprogramming languages) in "Corporate Planning Models." *California Management Review* 27:4:69–78.

Norgaard, B. 1984. "Pitfalls To Avoid With Modelling Languages," *Management Decision* 22:2:25–30.

Reimann, B. C. 1985. "Decision Support for Planners: How To Pick the Right DSS Generator Software." *Managerial Planning* 33(May–June):22–26.

Sprague, R. H. 1980. "A Framework for the Development of Decision Support Systems." *Management Information Systems Quarterly* 4(December)4:1–26.

Sprague, R. H., Carlson, E. D. 1982. *Building Effective Decision Support Systems.* Englewood Cliffs, N.J.: Prentice-Hall, Inc.

Sussman, P. N. 1984. "Evaluating Decision Support Software." *Datamation* 30(October 15):171–72.

Planning and Organizing for DSS: Rebalancing Control in the New Environment

7

And thus your freedom when it loses its fetters becomes itself the fetter of a greater freedom.
Kahlil Gibran, *The Prophet,* p. 56, Alfred A. Knopf, 1923

As noted in chapter 5, the sudden appearance and growth of microcomputers in large organizations in the late 1970s and early 1980s hastened the growth of DSS applications. Initially, this phenomenon usually occurred in an uncoordinated, unplanned way. Some MIS directors saw the new opportunities for end-user computing as a means of "getting off the hook" of user pressure to develop new applications to support management. These MIS executives were content to let users go their own way in using their microcomputers to fill the gaps for managerial planning and analysis support while allowing the central computer staff to concentrate on maintaining and developing new administrative data processing applications for the corporate mainframe computers. The application backlog was long enough, they felt, without attempting to centralize all microcomputer acquisition and programming or setting up new kinds of support applications.

Other information systems managers saw the independent growth of end-user computing as, at best, a mixed blessing that could return to haunt them. Their concerns often centered around two issues:

1. The total cost of acquiring microcomputers and software was initially hidden because it showed up only on many individual budgets instead of as part of the corporate investment in information processing resources. Eventually the aggregate cost may become visible to higher management and lead to questions as to the reasons for the circumvention of central control over computer resources. These questions might eventually be delivered to the door of the MIS director.

2. The uncontrolled processing of data by many individuals may also lead to one or more highly visible catastrophes of the breakdown of information integrity and security. Such an eventuality would also require answers from the MIS director as to "How did you let this happen?" These managers fretted over how to regain complete control over computing resources and all applications.

Eventually it became clearer to both the *laissez-faire* MIS directors and the "tight control" advocates, that the new computing environment and the new DSS applications required a different third approach, an approach which found a new middle ground of central coordination, support, and planning as well as a large degree of local freedom. It also became clearer to users who started by going their own way independently of the central computer department, that they had to come back to the corporate computer specialists as their data, communications, and software needs outgrew the scope of their private individual resources. Complete independence from the experts, these users discovered, could have its negative side of limited access to required corporate data and other forms of useful support. As all of the key parties learned from experience, new approaches evolved for the integration of DSS into MIS planning, and, in turn, the integration of MIS plans with DSS as a key component into the strategic plans of the organization. Exhibit 7.1 illustrates these basic relationships.

This chapter will discuss and present:

1. The need for establishing such a DSS organizational strategy;
2. The components of a DSS organizational strategy;
3. Examples of how some organizations have handled DSS planning and the organization of DSS staff support; and
4. Contrasting methods and characteristics of early DSS organized support versus those suitable for later stages.

The Need for a DSS Organizational Strategy

A strategy to plan and organize resources for the effective use of DSS is needed because of four interrelated major factors:

1. Systems integration and compatibility;
2. Economic acquisition and use of information resources;
3. Effective individual use and avoidance of misuse of DSS; and
4. Support of group and organizational decision processes.

Without an overall plan and structure for DSS, these factors will limit the effectiveness and increase the cost of DSS to the organization in ways described below.

Exhibit 7.1

Integrated DSS-MIS-Corporate Plans

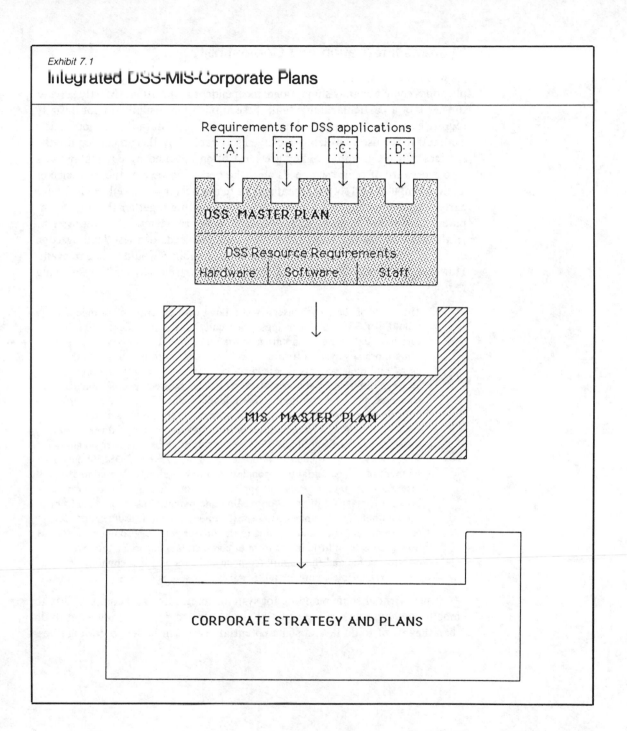

Requirements for DSS applications

A   B   C   D

DSS MASTER PLAN

DSS Resource Requirements

Hardware | Software | Staff

MIS MASTER PLAN

CORPORATE STRATEGY AND PLANS

Systems Integration and Compatibility

As was the case with early data processing applications, many early DSS applications come about as stand-alone, independent applications. Mostly serving the needs of a particular individual, these applications usually do not initially require extensive amounts of data nor do they require data that is not readily available to the user. Utilizing packaged software, they also do not require the services of a programmer. They are most often initiated by particular users who are aware of their own needs and who become aware of the existence of a microcomputer and software that appear to meet their perceived needs. These early users are willing to take the initiative in putting together the microcomputer and software, entering their own data, and learning how to use the system. If all that was desired was to meet these initial needs of these leading edge users, the issue of systems integration and compatibility would not be relevant. However, systems integration and compatibility *is* relevant for the following reasons:

1. The *needs* of these early users evolve along with experience (as indeed they should, if DSS fosters learning). Eventually they require access to corporate data bases, adaptation or the replacement of software, help in using more advanced software capabilities, and coordination with other users' and their systems. These needs call for communications (both between different computer systems as well as between people) and can no longer be met by stand-alone independent systems. They become more difficult or impossible to meet within acceptable time delays as they arise, even with the aid of technical specialists, if a large range of diverse software and hardware tools must be supported across the user population.

2. The "everyone for themself" approach limits the *reach* of DSS to only a segment of the potential user population. Lack of standard or compatible resources for similar needs and applications inhibits the diffusion process because it makes it difficult for existing and potential users to learn from one another. The less pioneering spirits among potential users cannot rely on formal education and training in the *laissez-faire* environment. Informal user groups have little in the form of common languages for the exchange of information and the uninitiated nonuser hears only a cacophony of incomprehensible computer talk.

Thus, without some planning for systems integration and compatibility to smooth the way, users will eventually not be able to do what they want to do when they want to do it, and some potential users will be left out altogether.

Economic Acquisition and Use of Information Resources

The lack of planning and coordination for DSS also will increase the direct costs of acquiring hardware, software, and data and using these resources efficiently. Significant volume discounts are obtainable for pooled purchases of microcomputers and microcomputer software. Users who are aware of data existing among other users and available for sharing can save valuable time and effort by avoiding the reentry of data already captured in machine-readable files. Common data standards and sources would also enhance data integrity, thereby avoiding costs related to incorrect data. The avoidance of needlessly proliferating local data bases and planning models would enhance security and thereby avoid costs associated with data losses and violations of confidentiality. Centrally coordinated and pooled training and other forms of staff specialist support can also be significantly more cost effective than the separate acquisition of these expensive professional resources.

A coordinated approach can also more effectively perform value analysis on applications and apply what has been learned about payoffs and costs from shared organizational experiences. In addition, the assessment and selection of software and hardware should often be based on a set of similar or related needs rather than on individual applications taken one at a time. Organizational practices and policies of cost justification (discussed further in chapter 12) are difficult to apply effectively without a corporate system-wide DSS planning strategy.

Effective Individual Use and Avoidance of Misuse of DSS

Without organized support personnel and policies and guidelines for their use, it is much more difficult to avoid the pitfalls of potential misuse of DSS resources. While it is desirable for users to learn about their business problem realm by experience and, to a degree, by experimentation, "trial and error" in choosing methods or software often stems from lack of expertise and knowledge of more appropriate and directly effective alternatives. The potential misuse of support systems (discussed further in chapter 12) cannot be completely eliminated without a form of tight control that would also inhibit and provide bottlenecks to the general use of DSS. But complete freedom to apply easy-to-use systems without any coordinated advise and counsel would not liberate users so much as it would leave them in uncertainty as to whether or not there was a more effective way to approach their problems. A DSS strategy should aim at significantly reducing, if not eliminating, this kind of uncertainty.

Support of Group and Organizational Decision Processes

Many, if not most, DSS applications support the individual decision maker or individual participant in a decision process. Even when it is necessary to obtain the approval or concurrence of others before decisions can be implemented, it is often useful for individuals to use a DSS to independently analyze a problem situation and develop their own proposed plans and strategies. However, it can be helpful if each participant adheres to certain common guidelines and uses a common language that will facilitate communication as well as the eventual development of an integrated final group or organizational plan. Other decision processes require interaction between members of a group who are jointly responsible for decisions. These situations often require special methods and new support functions to be put in place in a "Group Decision Support System" (De Sanctis and Gallupe 1985). (These are discussed further in chapter 13.)

In order to be in a position to effectively support group decision processes and the development of coordinated organizational plans, an organizational perspective must be taken in planning and organizing for DSS.

The Components of a DSS Organizational Strategy

A DSS corporate strategy will include many of the same components included in a general MIS master plan for other types of computer applications. However, because of the special characteristics of DSS, planners must deal with these common components in a different manner. The components are as follows:

1. Users and their needs
2. Specialist staff support
3. Computer hardware
4. Software
5. Data
6. Communications facilities

The strategic plan for DSS should be incorporated into the MIS master plan, and like it, should take an organization-wide perspective. This requires looking across the entire organization to identify, at least in broad brush categorical terms, the needs for support applications and how they are likely to grow and change over the planning horizon. Two different views of the planning horizon are useful, one shorter range view of one to two years, and a somewhat longer range view of up to about five years. The various segments and types of potential users across the organization should first be identified, and estimates made of the kinds and numbers of applications needs that may be expected to arise within each user segment over the planning horizons. User segments can be defined according to varying organizational functions and tasks within those functions, as well as according to a knowledge of the attitudes and propensities of groups and individuals toward using computer support. Estimates of supporting staff, hardware, software, data, and communications resource requirements can be based on a knowledge of the number, type, and application needs of the user population. The DSS strategic plan should provide:

1. A comprehensive and cohesive view of the *characteristics* of each of the DSS resource components (supporting staff, hardware, software, data, and communications facilities) needed;
2. The *quantities* of resources required (how many support specialists of each kind identified are needed, how many microcomputers, terminals, etc.);
3. The estimated *costs* associated with the acquisition and maintenance of the resources;
4. The *timing* of significant phases of DSS applications and the consequent scheduling of the types, quantities, and cost budgeting of the required resources; and
5. The *organizational structure, policies, and procedures* needed to coordinate the availability and usage of common DSS resources.

In theory, it would be ideal to work out all of these aspects of a DSS–MIS strategy before ad hoc individual actions toward implementing local applications took place. However, the real world seldom presents planners with a neat situation which makes the ideal feasible. For a variety of reasons, large companies often do not find it practical to develop the complete MIS–DSS master plan before other organizational factors are first clarified and resolved. During such a period of working out general policies and setting the stage for completing plans, interim incomplete strategies must often be improvised while a management dialogue is fostered to help clarify the issues and provide a common understanding leading to complete plans. Such a case is illustrated in example 7.1, which involves a company in the process of reorganizing and modernizing its computer systems while trying to work out an integrated approach to information resource management covering both traditional and decision support applications.

The various aspects of strategic planning for DSS are discussed further and illustrated in the sections that follow.

EXAMPLE 7.1

AN IRM FRAMEWORK FOR DECISION SUPPORT

THE ZYX INFORMATION RESOURCE MANAGEMENT CONCEPT

Definition and Scope of Information Resource Management (IRM)

The basic concept of IRM is that a definable set of information within an organization is (or should be) viewed and managed as a major organizational resource (rather than as the personal or local property of individual managers or local organizational units). The essential elements of information resource management should include

1. The existence of a corporate or organizational data base;
2. A data base administration function;
3. Computing resources and support functions that make the central data base accessible to managers throughout the organization in an appropriate manner and within suitable controls.

The above practices are necessary in order to operationalize the concept so that it is not merely a concept. It is one thing to state that information is a corporate resource in the same sense that money is a corporate resource. It is another to formulate policies and practices that make that statement meaningful. The basic elements needed, as enumerated above, are analogous to the elements of financial resource management, in that corporate monetary resources must also be centrally managed and controlled, but accessible to (not owned by) local managers in a controlled environment that enables the business as a whole to function both effectively and efficiently. The manner in which each organization implements the basic themes of IRM will vary with the character and needs of that organization. The purpose of this position paper is to define the main threads of IRM at the ZYX Corporation.

Corporate Background and General Requirements

ZYX is a corporation currently in the midst of a major transition to a new mode of management. Moving from a centralized management style into a form of divisionalization, ZYX is working out the meaning and practice of "divisionalization", as it best suits the corporate objectives, realities of the business environment, and an evolving corporate style and culture. Such major corporate management transitions have been seen to generally require about a five year period before a large complex organization can evolve, absorb and internalize (make its own in a real and psychological sense, as well as in a formal sense) a radically new identity and way of operating. The need to institute new IRM practices is complicated by the uncertainties and inherent conflicts that generally accompany such major management transition periods. IRM development generally requires existing or definable corporate policies and operating procedures in order to provide criteria for designing effective IRM. But in the transitional corporate state, IRM must contribute to, and often serve as the cutting edge of evolving corporate operating policies. This dual role of leading and following places severe strains and challenges on the MIS staff and the rest of the management team. Because these additional situationally inherent strains can block successful evolution, a positive mode of clear and continuous communications between general managers throughout the organization and those charged directly with IRM becomes doubly important. Rather than serving as any final set of answers, it is hoped that this position paper will further a dialogue contributing to IRM development.

The Strategic Role of IRM

The first prerequisite for a team effort is the need to recognize that IRM must play a central, key, *strategic* role in running the business effectively from both corporate and divisional viewpoints. The generally accepted notion of what is meant by "strategic" in a business context is that which defines and follows a central theme as to how the business addresses its competitive marketplace. It should be apparent that certain kinds of information from both internal and external sources is essential in order to monitor the competitive marketplace and continually assess the position of the business within it.

Several factors dictate that modern business strategy must rely more heavily than ever before on computer-processed and computer-communications delivery systems for strategic information rather than exclusively on informal and personal sources.

These factors include:

1. Market-driven flexibility while retaining consistency.
   The need for consistent views of business operations within the context of a variety of definitions of segmentation. Because of competitive trends and new technology-driven and economy-driven usage patterns, market segment definitions may have to change flexibly for different analytical purposes and not remain fixed within current internal organization structure boundaries and definitions. Internal control reporting and administrative processes must remain relatively constant while also feeding input to a flexible strategic analysis capability.

2. Recognition of new trends and rapid response to both trends and discontinuities.
   The need for continuous monitoring, interpretation and early warning signals of developments that could directly and indirectly affect the business from a growing number and increasingly complex interlocking network of external factors. Complexity requires that a new marriage must take place between computer support and personal analysis rather than relying on the latter alone.

Both of the above dimensioins require a new perception of computer support that goes beyond the out-dated notion that computers are simply inhumanly fast and tireless clerks. Computers now are both back-room automation devices as well as executive staff professional analysis support resources. In order to justify the use of the former we have to assess cost replacement by means of automation. In order to justify the use of the latter we have to assess its contribution to *value-added strategic management.*

More specifically, these factors imply that divisions in a multidivisional corporation such as ZYX must manage their own business strategically, but also that the corporation must do so with respect to an overall portfolio management view of the entire business as a complete system. Strategic information and analysis for both divisional and corporate management is likely to cut across divisional lines and address common external variables. For both divisional and corporate management, it will require cross-comparison of different business segments and the means to aggregate the parts into a whole. This kind of capability requires advance planning and a common system of data base resources. It should be emphasized in this regard that a common system does not imply an inflexible system. A common system must not be implemented in a way that inhibits or prevents flexible modes of analysis by multiple users for multiple purposes. Indeed, a cost-effective means of providing such a flexible capability is one of the key reasons for establishing corporate IRM. Disjoint and uncoordinated local data management blocks flexibility to merge and extend information as well as to uneconomically duplicate efforts. Commonality is thus not merely an efficiency or economy of scale issue. IRM is essential to enhance *strategic effectiveness.*

ZYX's Key Corporate-Divisional Data Bases

Commonality and the ability to access for multiple purposes at both corporate and divisional management levels is essential for two major data base components:

1. Sales and marketing information
2. Manufacturing information

The complete master set of data would be maintained as a corporate resource and be accessible to both corporate and divisional managers for the extraction of subsets of context-relevant information. That is, on any occasion in which a subset of the data base is needed, a facility will be in place to extract that data and transmit it to either an individual local microcomputer for local analysis or to a local network of microcomputers for joint use. Thus

EXAMPLE 7.1 continued

the central data base will not place limits upon the ability to perform any desired local analysis but will instead extend the reach of access beyond that of strictly local data bases. There is, in any case, a need for a central data base extracted from both manufacturing and sales operations related to transaction processing. These systems must adhere to some common requirements both for legal reasons as well as because of the need for maintaining an integrated financial reporting system. Both these requirements and the economies of acquiring and maintaining a common software system represent sufficiently compelling reasons for a common system. The related factor of providing common fundamental data bases for management analysis is an additional reason for commonality. Neither the efficiency factor nor the IRM factor stand in the way of local flexibility in reporting or in ad hoc information access. The ways in which flexibility is retained are discussed further in the next section on software acquisition and maintenance.

Software Acquisition and Maintenance

A procedure for the acquisition of common key software packages has been evolved in which divisional participation plays a key role. The acquisition of such software represents a significant investment with and impact on profit and loss performance and P/L reporting. Both software and hardware are capitalized and written-off over a five year period. The corporation, acting in effect as the agent of the divisions, buys an unlimited license to mainframe software packages that allows each of the divisions to use the software. The actual selection of key basic packages is done by representatives of the divisional users sitting in a common committee which is advised by members of the MIS staff. The acquisition process follows the following stages:

1. Committee representatives are chosen by each division.
2. The committee meets and discusses their common key requirements, facilitated by MIS staff who also act as recorders of the requirements specified by the divisional user representatives.

3. A subtask group of user representatives is chosen from the larger committee and meets, along with an MIS staff member, in order to develop a request for proposal document.
4. The RFP is distributed to all mainframe software vendors with an offering in the application area and proposals are received.
5. Proposals are screened for whether or not they meet basic criteria established by the user committee, and the best proposals, not to exceed five vendors, are selected to be invited in to make presentations to the committee.
6. After these presentations, the committee discusses the presentations and votes on their choice of the best three.
7. Those who pass this level of screening are invited to prepare actual computer demonstration tests for the committee.
8. The Committee then votes on their final selection. At the same time each divisional representative prepares specifications on any special modifications that may be required to meet divisional needs.
9. MIS integrates the modification requirements and negotiates both the acquisition and modification agreement with the vendor.
10. MIS supervises the actual delivery and acceptance testing process and distributes the software to the divisional users.

Operations and maintenance then are conducted as follows:

1. Each division maintains its own data processing facilities and runs its own computer operations for basic transaction-oriented processing utilizing the common mainframe packages acquired for those purposes.
2. Divisions receive "object code" versions of the software, which is suitable for production processing rather than convenient program modification. "Source code" package versions, convenient for making modifications, is retained by corporate MIS.
3. A single version of the software is maintained; no uncoordinated local changes are made that would destroy the integrity of the package.

4. Divisions can, however, utilize the common outputs of the package as inputs to any other local program developed to carry out additional special processing. Divisions, however, are encouraged to confer with other divisional users through MIS on all subsequently identified special needs in order to coordinate further programming and eliminate duplicated efforts.

5. As the need for modifications to the package itself are identified, MIS will coordinate divisional agreement on the desired modifications, and will determine through consultation and agreement with the users, which divisional computer group will actually make the modifications. That division will complete the changes and act as the pilot site before all other divisions accept the changes as being completed.

6. The finally accepted modified package will be retained, as was the original package, by corporate MIS in source code form and updated object code versions will be distributed to the divisions.

Management Information and Decision Support Capabilities

The "bread and butter" data processing applications needed for order processing, manufacturing control, other transaction oriented data processing applications, and financial reporting are all served through the acquisition and use of packages, as described above. But we distinguish between these *data processing* needs and *management information support* functions. As discussed at the outset of this paper, it is the strategic support functions that require an IRM policy and a special set of resources. These IRM support resources include the following:

1. Data base management software maintained at the corporate computing facilities to serve both corporate users and to provide access for divisional users to corporate data bases derived from divisional transaction processing systems and external sources.

2. As part of the above capability, user-oriented query software will be centrally maintained and accessible for local use via microcomputers used as terminals.

3. Central corporate acquisition of microcomputers and general purpose microcomputer software as the agent of local users in order to obtain volume discounts and ensure compatibility and maintainability.

4. The distribution of microcomputers for use as work stations for individual productivity as well as analysis and decision support tools. In addition to operating as stand-alone individual computing devices for both office automation (word processing and local report generation) and for management analysis and decision support, these microcomputers will be chosen so that the option to use them as communications terminals is also maintained.

5. Corporate MIS will facilitate the *Information Center* concept of supported end-user computing. End-user computing is supported through educational and consulting services which provide "help" but not "do" staff assistance.

6. Corporate planning and maintenance of communications facilities. Computer communications resources will include:
   a) Mainframe-microcomputer linkage for the downloading of mainframe maintained data base subsets;
   b) The linkage of users to one another through local area networks; and
   c) Wider area networks where they are needed for such applications as the transmission of divisional transaction data outputs into corporate data bases.

Unresolved Specifics

The above discussion outlines the current general concept of IRM and data processing management objectives and practices at ZYX. It is recognized however, that many specifics of operating procedure, division of responsibilities, and coordination of activities remain to be worked out. With an understanding of mutual needs and interests and an open line of communications, we feel confident that ZYX can continue to refine an IRM concept that fits the new ZYX management style and serves a strategic role in attaining success.

Categories of Users, User Needs, Training and Education

Users can be usefully categorized in several ways. The amount and type of support they will require from staff specialists for training and consultation, as well as the type and design of software that will be suitable for them will depend on their experience and attitudes toward computers in general as well as their familiarity with analytical methods. Combining some of these factors, the following user categorization can be made:

Type 1: The Leading Edge Superusers

Experienced computer users for DSS type applications, they know what they want. They may have extensive knowledge of analytical methods. They need little assistance in determining the suitability of DSS or in using DSS software. They do not want to be held back in getting the resources they need to get on with their applications.

Type 2: The Moderates

These users have some experience in one or a few limited applications. They do not have extensive knowledge of analytical methods or of a wide range of software capabilities. They are not sure if they can get more out of using a computer in their work but are generally receptive and quite positive about learning more.

Type 3: The Encourageables

This group of potential users are trepidatious and cautious but willing to try if given sufficient help and encouragement. They have little or no experience and no clear idea of what they can do with a computer.

Type 4: The Die-hard Resistors

These are the "over-my-dead-body" hard core anticomputer people. They never want to touch one and prefer not even to be in the same room as one. They have a negative image of the computer based on little or no specific knowledge, but they insist that a real professional has no need for an electronic crutch and would only be inhibited from true creativity by using what they think of as a semiconductor straightjacket.

It is useful for planning user training and DSS resource acquisition to identify and quantify these user types by department and by job function. As a first screening device to gather some of this information, a general user survey by questionnaire may be helpful. An illustration of this kind of questionnaire, accompanied by an explanatory cover memo, is given in example 7.2. While such a questionnaire is limited in its ability to identify all DSS application

EXAMPLE 7.2

END-USER COMPUTING PLANNING SURVEY

Name _____ Title _____

1. Do you currently, either personally or via an assistant, use a microcomputer for any aspect of your work?
   Yes _____ No _____

2. Please indicate (by an "X") which of the following best applies:

   With regard to anything related to my job, (beyond regular processing or reporting that would normally be carried out by a technical data processing staff). . . .

   a) I *do not* feel the need for any new or additional personal computer support. . . .
   (*a-1*) either currently or in the foreseeable future _____
   (*a-2*) at present, but may have a future need _____

   b) I *do* currently feel I need my own additional computer support, but . . .
   (*b-1*) I would want my assistant to actually operate the computer _____
   (*b-2*) I would want to receive sufficient training and help so that I could use the computer myself _____
   (*b-3*) I'm not sure if I'd want to operate it myself or not, I'd like to know more about it before deciding _____
   (*b-4*) I have other considerations not covered above. (Please elaborate in the following space)

   _____
   _____

3. If you do feel you need additional computer support, please describe (in general terms) the nature of your need(s) as you see them:

   _____
   _____
   _____

4. I (would) _____ (would not) _____ be interested in attending a brief (half day) seminar with other ZYX managers at my level for an introductory overview of the scope of personal computer support capabilities.

   (If you are interested in attending such an introductory seminar, please indicate a range of preferred dates during the next few months)
   July (best days) _____
   August (best days) _____

5. Subjects I would like to know more about, either through a seminar or by other means, Include: _____
   _____
   _____

6. I (would) _____ (would not) _____ be interested in obtaining individual private counsel or aid to determine my own needs for computer support and how to fulfill these needs.

MEMO ACCOMPANYING QUESTIONNAIRE

From: MIS Dept.
To: All Corporate and Divisional Managers and Professional Staffs:
Subject: Survey for Planning End-User Computing Support

A few minutes of your time is requested in responding to the attached brief questionnaire.

Its purpose is to provide some initial data to help in our efforts to support effective end-user computing. (*As a reminder, the term "end-user computing" means managers or their staffs using a computer directly for their own needs without the need to work through technical intermediaries.*)

Planning for effective end-user computing must be based on a total picture of currently perceived needs and on expected future needs. Our aim is to provide those ZYX managers who may need and want support with the most appropriate computer tools, and with the know-how required to use them, at the appropriate time.

Effective managerial end-user computing is largely *discretionary* and individual in nature. It would serve no useful purpose and there is no intention to force, pressure, or even to sell all managers to use computers. The objective is to plan a coordinated approach to *support* managers when and as they may be prepared to become users.

Please take a few minutes now to respond to the questionnaire. If you have any questions in this regard please call Art Johnson (MIS–x 1794).
Kindly return the questionnaire to: Art Johnson, MIS
PLEASE RETURN BY JULY _____

opportunities, it can serve as a means to uncover first priority support needs and opportunities and to concentrate follow-up user interviews in departments and job function categories for which some positive results have been obtained.

Initial training should be aimed primarily at type 2 and type 3 users. Given appropriate recognition and release from other duties, type 1 superusers can often be enlisted as effective supporting agents in either participating in training sessions for others or in providing on-site assistance to less advanced users after initial training. Type 4 users should not be met head-on and coerced, but provided with an open door should they change their minds. If they do not join up in the early stages, many of them will eventually be influenced by the example of their coworkers as usage increases and becomes the norm rather than the exception. In any case, 100 percent usage should not become an end in itself and coercive practices are inconsistent with supporting users in their discretionary use of DSS.

Training users is often considered a primary task of a DSS support group, but it may be cost-effective to use outside training services and consultants either to supplement an internal staff or to provide complete training management and training delivery services. Training not only needs planning and proper selection of the recipients of training, but also involves a great deal of effort and experience to create effective written materials, demonstrations, visual aids, and trainee exercises. A good program should also be followed up by tracking new user needs as they arise after training. Examples 7.3 and 7.4 illustrate one company's initial efforts in setting up its own training program.

Initial training generally concentrates on learning the mechanics of using the DSS tools, first in elemental exercises illustrating the functionality of hardware and software features and then in complete sample problems. After demonstrating and walking through generic sample problems, a workshop session should be included for at least one fundamental application that has previously been identified as directly related to the work of the trainees. As was the case of ZYX, Inc. referred to in the examples in this chapter, a brief initial training session of a few hours is limited to the physical use of the microcomputer or terminal (or combined terminal-micro) as a workstation that can be used for a variety of tasks. These workstation accessed tasks may include office automation applications such as word processing and electronic mail as well as decision support, with each type of application typically being selected from a menu of applications built into the workstation's basic software interface.

EXAMPLE 7.3

ZTX COMPANY INC. END-USER
COMPUTING EDUCATION

PROPOSED MANAGEMENT TOOLS

1. Scheduling spreadsheet. (Status: Initial version prepared by John L. Sullivan, needs next step development via Lotus)

   Purpose: To project workshops into future, see total required elapsed time, effects of changing priorities between user groups, changing facilities (number of instructors, PCs). To rapidly revise plans, see implications of alternatives, print out schedules. Tool to balance between ad hoc reaction and operating with feasible, flexible general plan.

2. Evolving User Needs Feedback System
   a. Post-training follow-up questionnaire (Status: First draft prepared and attached. See *example 7.4*)

   Purpose: To gain perspective of user on needs for additional training about one month after completion of initial workshops.

   b. Hot-Line (and other) Request Monitoring and Reporting System

   (Status: Needs development, should run via Lotus.)

   A system to capture, categorize, summarize, and report on user requests via Hot-Line and other means.

   Purpose: Spot general needs, recurring problems by user groups, to serve as a basis of planning additional training, modifying current workshops, providing other forms of both preventative and remedial assistance.

3. Pre-training User Questionnaire (*Feed-forward*)

   Capturing user background, computer experience, etc. via personnel records and brief questionnaire derived user perceptions of needs and attitudes toward micro support.

   Purpose: Serve as base line for assessing user evaluations of training, for tailoring workshops to extent possible and segregating users by needs, and as an initial milestone for comparison and measurement purposes in assessing post-training evolving needs.

This is followed up by a second training session on the use of specific DSS software packages such as an integrated spreadsheet–data-base–graphics package. These two phases of initial training (introduction to the work station and introduction to one or more basic packages) can be scheduled as a continuous introductory program on consecutive days or on separate days (without more than a week's delay between them), as dictated by the demands of the working situation.

EXAMPLE 7.4

POST-WORKSHOP FOLLOW-UP QUESTIONNAIRE

This section to be prepared by MIS prior to distribution to the respondent:

NAME: MARIO CUOMO
DEPT. FINANCIAL ADMIN.
Workshop: LOTUS (or Multimate or other—not workstation intro alone)

Completed on: 4/15/88
    Please take a few moments to respond to the following questions with regard to the microcomputer application for which you recently completed the workshop identified above.

---

1. Please consider your most recently completed full work-week and indicate the number of days on which you used this application (LOTUS) to any extent. (check the appropriate space)
   0 days _____ 1 day _____ 2 days _____ 3 days _____ 4 days _____ 5 days _____
2. Please consider your usage of *this application* during the most recent four (4) week period and indicate how many days per week you used this application on average. (check the appropriate space)
   0 days _____ 1 day _____ 2 days _____ 3 days _____ 4 days _____ 5 days _____
3. *a)* Considering your recent four weeks' experience, about how many hours per day of usage of *this application* would you estimate to be most typical or average. (check the appropriate space)
       Less than 1 hour _____   1–2 hours _____   2–3 hours _____   3–4 hours _____
                    4–5 hours _____   5–6 hours _____   6–7 hours _____   7–8 hours _____
       More than 8 hours _____

   b) Please indicate about how many hours you used this application on your *heaviest* (maximum) usage day during this same four week period.
       Less than 1 hour _____   1–2 hours _____   2–3 hours _____   3–4 hours _____
                    4–5 hours _____   5–6 hours _____   6–7 hours _____   7–8 hours _____
       More than 8 hours _____

   c) Please indicate about how many hours you used *this application* on your *lightest* (minimum) usage day during this same 4 week period.
       Less than 1 hour _____   1–2 hours _____   2–3 hours _____   3–4 hours _____
                    4–5 hours _____   5–6 hours _____   6–7 hours _____   7–8 hours _____
       More than 8 hours _____
4. Please describe (in the space below) the nature of the business task(s) for which you used this application during this four week period: (use the back of the page also if needed). Please include in your description the features of the application you used to carry out the task(s).

5. Please use the space below (and the other side of the page if needed) to describe any positive benefits or any negative effects on you and/or your job performance you think have resulted from your use of this application to date:
   Benefits/positive effects:

   Negative effects:

6. Please use the space below (and reverse side of page) to identify and describe any aspects of this application on which you feel you would like to have additional training. Include any problems you may have in using the application as well as any new things you'd be interested in doing.
   If there are any tasks, applications, or problems that you are interested in but you are not certain whether or not they can be done with this kind of software package, please describe them.

7. Please indicate how many hours per typical day you yourself used a personal computer in total *for any and all applications and purposes* (not just the application referred to above), during the most recent full work-week.
   (check the appropriate space)
   0 hours _____
   1–3 hours _____   3–5 hours _____   5–8 hours _____
   8 + hours _____
8. Please use the following space to make any additional comments you feel might be helpful for improving support or training for your use of personal computers for any purpose.

As mentioned previously, this kind of initial training is intended to introduce users to the tools of DSS and get them started in using them on applications that have already been identified. But the fully effective utilization of DSS resources should not rest entirely on the already obvious applications. Managers and staff users who are not specialists in analytical methods need additional educational support so that they can recognize opportunities for effective support, avoid the misuse of a DSS approach, and evolve less obvious applications. An illustration of a management seminar intended to serve this broader educational purpose is illustrated in example 7.5.

Functions and Organization of DSS Supporting Personnel

A supporting staff for DSS, consisting of internal or external consultants, or a mixture of both, is needed for the following functions:

1. Surveying and counseling users to assess the suitability and opportunity for new DSS applications;
2. Planning a DSS strategy, developing implementation procedures and monitoring implementation;
3. Assessing and acquiring DSS hardware and software tools;
4. Planning, administering, and conducting a training and educational program for users;
5. Assisting users in the process of developing specific DSS applications;
6. Providing quick response to "hot line" user requests for help in overcoming typical minor problems of hardware and software usage;
7. Providing liaison with the technical support that may be needed from computer operations specialists (for installation of communications facilities, access to corporate main frame data bases, etc.);
8. Keeping users informed on news and developments from external sources that may foster more effective and efficient usage of DSS tools;
9. Facilitating the exchange of information and sharing of resources between users;
10. Conducting special organizational studies on user satisfaction, evolving needs, the effectiveness and value of the training-educational program and from DSS usage, and recommending revised plans and policies accordingly;
11. Tracking technical and commercial developments and assessing their implications for the organization.

EXAMPLE 7.5

MIS-SPONSORED EDUCATIONAL PROGRAMS
IN COMPUTER-BASED SYSTEMS ANNOUNCES—
AN EXECUTIVE BRIEFING-WORKSHOP

FOR SENIOR ZYX MANAGERS

*Decision Support Systems
for Strategic Planning*

The new "user friendly" computer-based capabilities called Decision Support Systems (DSS) are growing in usage by top level corporate leaders including CEOs, CFOs, and other senior members of strategic management. DSS helps these managers cope with "semistructured" (somewhat fuzzy) planning and analysis problems without requiring them to become either mathematicians or computer scientists. They use their own intuition and experience while using the computer as a "mind lever" to more thoroughly explore alternatives.

This introductory two day series will introduce DSS concepts and applications within the context of the key strategic planning function . . . *and it will provide an opportunity to get started in using DSS for your immediate needs.*

Sessions are scheduled on two successive Saturdays in order to avoid work interruptions and provide a relaxed "out-of-the-office" atmosphere, further enhanced by informal interaction within your executive peer group and with the seminar leader, an experienced executive consultant, researcher, author and lecturer in DSS.

The Schedule

Day 1, Saturday, November 10,
9:00 A.M.–4:30 P.M.

The morning session will introduce the basic concepts and definitions of Decision Support Systems, review case examples, and survey DSS software components and packages that are available for both large (mainframe) computers and personal microcomputers.

The afternoon will be used for a workshop session to mutually explore the needs and potential DSS aids for the attending managers both individually as well as with respect to common corporate planning concerns. Key issues and critical informational and analytical planning requirements will be specified through group discussion. Next steps needed to provide DSS for the attending managers will be identified.

Day 2, Saturday, November 17,
9:00 A.M.–4:00 P.M.

The morning session will include walk-throughs of DSS planning models. Emphasis will be on how to create and develop your own models using only basic math and logical methods. Methods of using models for "what if" and "goal seeking" analysis will be demonstrated. The role of such analysis in the planning process will be discussed.

The afternoon session will consist of a workshop in actually using a Lotus 1–2–3 planning model on IBM personal computers.

The mix of basic abilities and knowledge needed in a DSS support staff includes the following:

1. The ability to communicate well with users, technical specialists and outside vendors;
2. A good basic knowledge of management functions and the nature of business needs;
3. A knowledge of the underlying principles and basic capabilities of DSS and the distinguishing characteristics of DSS development and application methods from those of other approaches (mainly those of traditional computer information systems and of operations research);
4. A knowledge of the basic types of DSS software packages and their use on microcomputers and mainframes.

The first two of these are fundamental to the user-management-business orientation that is needed as opposed to the computer-tools focus of the technical specialist. While the latter two areas of knowledge can be learned from specific formal training courses and experience in the specifics of DSS, the first two stem from basic abilities, attitudes and broad prior educational background. New DSS staff members should be selected from among those who are already strong on the first two points and if not already strong on the latter two, have the interest and ability to learn them quickly through training.

As mentioned in the prior section with regard to training, the best new DSS support people may come from the ranks of the more experienced (usually self-taught) DSS users (the type 1 superusers). They can best understand users needs and communicate in the user's language because they *are* users. They have often informally been playing the role of consultant to less experienced users because their proximity while working in the same department makes them visible and accessible. In effect, this informally evolved situation causes the superuser-consultant to do two jobs at once, the work of his formally assigned responsibilities as well as the work of the on-site consultant. Eventually this becomes formally recognized and the superuser may be reassigned to the DSS support staff, often as the original nucleus of such a staff.

Other candidates for new DSS staff positions can be sought from among those systems analysts (or even programmers) in the MIS department who may have above average people-communications skills and some knowledge or interest in end-user computing and DSS as a next career step out of traditional data processing. If suitable candidates of this kind can be found, their reassignment to a DSS staff group can have the dual benefit of retaining them in the company by proving a desired new opportunity; and including added liaison or informal links with the MIS department and bringing some additional systems knowledge into the DSS planning and support function.

It is also useful to recruit or have access to at least some DSS support consultants with considerable knowledge of operations research methods, particularly optimization methods, model building, and statistical analysis.

Knowledge of these background disciplines is important in spotting situations in which their use is appropriate to supplement or to replace less direct DSS trial and error "what if" type analysis. If extensive expertise of this kind is not available on a regular basis within a DSS group, the DSS group should, at a minimum, be trained in understanding the nature of operations research capabilities and in recognizing problem characteristics that call for OR methods to be applied. Given this kind of training and understanding, they may not be able to apply OR techniques themselves but should be able to determine when to call in OR specialists to aid users.

Beyond recruiting a DSS support group, two related organizational issues are:

1. Where should DSS support groups be placed in the organization? (This includes associated questions regarding the size of such groups, and their responsibility and authority relationships with other groups and departments.)
2. What are suitable career paths and means of motivating DSS staff personnel?

The question of where to place DSS staff within the organization can be discussed in abstract terms which logically relate the DSS functional role to other functions. But theoretical considerations of structure are often of less importance than the question of the specific individual executive that has overall responsibility for DSS in the organization. That individual should ideally have a high position in the MIS department or at least good knowledge of MIS functions and a close working relationship with the director of MIS. Ideally, responsibility and authority for planning and supporting DSS should ultimately reside in the top MIS executive. Obviously, the top DSS authority needs to have at least a broad knowledge of DSS but need not be an expert in the technical details of DSS software. The DSS executive particularly needs to recognize distinctions between the DSS mission and staff functions from those of office automation, as well as understanding that DSS and office automation use common resources such as microcomputers, terminals, data bases, printers, or communications networks.

Given the linkage of DSS to MIS and to organizational strategic planning at the top of the organizational hierarchy, there are several alternatives for the location of DSS staff personnel. As shown in exhibit 7.2, the most common ones are:

1. A central DSS support group within a corporate or divisional MIS department.
2. A distributed DSS staff of one or more people placed within each major user department or user group.
3. A combination of the above, often with a "matrix" form of dual reporting relationships.

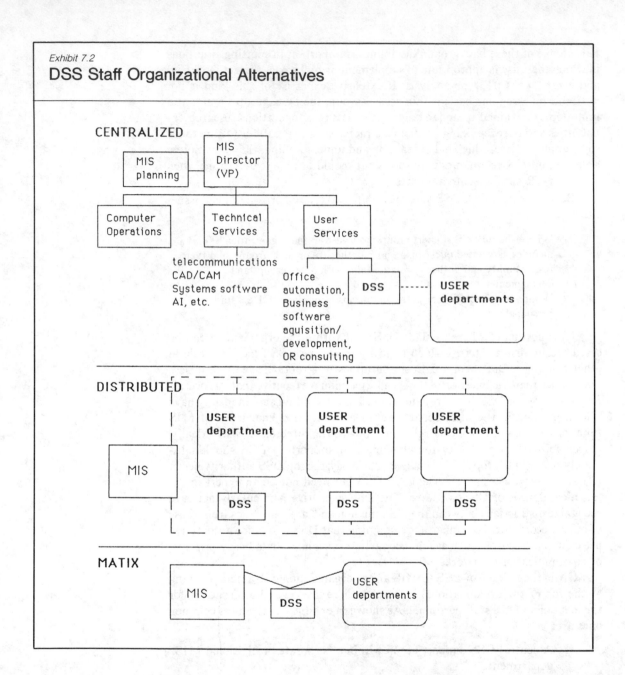

Exhibit 7.2
DSS Staff Organizational Alternatives

CENTRALIZED

MIS planning

MIS Director (VP)

Computer Operations

Technical Services

telecommunications
CAD/CAM
Systems software
AI, etc.

User Services

Office automation,
Business software
aquisition/
development,
OR consulting

DSS

USER departments

DISTRIBUTED

MIS

USER department

USER department

USER department

DSS

DSS

DSS

MATIX

MIS

DSS

USER departments

The advantages and disadvantages of each, and the factors determining their respective suitability for different situations, are similar to those for the organizational placement of MIS systems development staffs. These are as follows:

Advantages for a Centralized DSS Support Group

1. Easier to maintain a high level of relatively uniform professional standards;
2. The total size and cost of DSS staff resources are more visible and easier to control;
3. Uniform distribution of work load and staff utilization levels are easier to control because of pooling of demands;
4. Greater affordability for including a wider scope of staff expertise among staff members with complementary capabilities (expertise on OR model building, statistical techniques, mainframe packages, microcomputer packages, data base software, specialized management applications experience, systems analysis and software evaluation background, special knowledge of training and education, etc.);
5. Facilitates the exchange of professional information and the creation of a "professional culture";
6. Greater size of the central DSS group and proximity to other central information system groups increases opportunities for advancement into related technical and management areas.

Disadvantages for a Centralized DSS Support Group

1. Less continuous and informal contact and communications with users;
2. Less specialization by user function and more limited cumulative learning of user functional areas;
3. May be prone to a more technical orientation as opposed to a user service orientation;
4. Limits opportunities for transfer and pursuing career paths in the users' functional areas of management;
5. May be vulnerable to political pressures in the allocation of their services and criticism about disproportionate attention to some user groups at the expense of others.

The advantages and disadvantages of a distributed staff approach, in which each sufficiently large group of users or each user department maintains their own DSS support group, are the mirror image of the advantages and disadvantages for a centralized organization. Where a centralized group may have the disadvantage of less informal user contact, for example, the local user DSS group has the advantage of more contact, and so on with regard to each of the factors enumerated above.

The matrix form of organization may moderate the disadvantages, and hence also may moderate the corresponding advantages of each of the other alternatives. This may be seen as a reasonable middle-ground approach, but it also has the special disadvantage of balancing between two lines of authority and responsibility that may be in conflict with one another.

Situational factors that are most relevant in choosing between the organizational alternatives are as follows:

1. The current and expected number of users.

   The number of DSS support staff people needed obviously should depend on the number of users that need support. Some observers estimate that there should be one staff person for about forty or fifty users. The right ratio will vary with factors such as the experience of users and the importance of their tasks. Economic considerations will limit the feasibility of assigning even one DSS staff person, let alone a DSS group, to every user department. User departments that have closely related functions may be combined in assigning a distributed DSS staff. In general, smaller organizations and organizations with relatively small (fewer than forty) numbers of users in closely related functional areas, will find a centralized alternative to be more suitable. On the other hand, only one high level executive may justify the attention of one regularly assigned staff assistant to provide DSS support, possibly combined with other duties for that executive.

2. Organizational structure and culture.

   Organizations that are highly centralized with respect to managerial control and the provision and control of most other supporting staff functions (such as financial services, information systems, or personnel services) are most likely to find it appropriate to centralize DSS support as well. Decentralized or divisionalized organizations that allocate a great deal of autonomy to local managers in planning, controlling and implementing business operations will find a distributed DSS approach more suitable.

3. Task and technological dependencies.

   In looking at an entire organization as a system of interrelated tasks and functions, some subsystems consisting of highly interdependent functions can often be discerned. The support of these functions should be organized accordingly, with separate resources being controlled within each highly interdependent subsystem. This systems view of factoring a large complex organization into its parts may generally follow the lines of formal organizational units such as departments, but it may also cut across these lines in grouping highly related tasks. For example, in some organizations manufacturing management may be highly interdependent with sales in a dynamic environment requiring very close planning and control between these two functions. In this case, a single DSS support group for both manufacturing and sales would be appropriate.

   Technical considerations such as the need for access to data and the available computer communications and networking facilities should also be taken into account and may dominate other considerations. A DSS support group that is isolated from the resources and knowledge needed to access required data is limited in its ability to counsel users. The DSS group may need to coordinate closely with telecommunications specialists and therefore may benefit from being located within the same chain of command.

It should be clear that even when locally distributed DSS groups are found to be suitable it is still important, as indicated by the dotted line connections shown in exhibit 7.2, to maintain close coordination with MIS because of the need to plan for and utilize a common set of computing resources.

The motivation and career paths open to DSS staff people is still an open question. As mentioned above, each form of organization tends to make it easier for DSS staff members to advance in either a general management direction within user organizational areas or in more closely computer-related positions. It is desirable for both the organization and the individuals involved to maintain open paths in either of these directions.

Policies and Practices for the Acquisition of DSS Hardware and Software

As stated in chapter 6, software and microcomputer acquisition should not be approached independently as each particular user application arises. Instead, a systems view should be taken as part of overall DSS planning and strategy. In the planned systems approach, an overview of the needs across the broad spectrum of users and applications is first obtained. Then a set of complementary packages is selected in such a manner as to minimize duplication of functionality while cost-effectively meeting the needs of users and their tasks. Hardware selection then follows from software and other systems requirements as discussed in chapters 5 and 6. Often, a single microcomputer brand and model is selected as the corporate standard or particular compatible makes arc specified.

User needs surveys supplemented with a minimal number of "key user" interviews can serve to obtain the broad view of needs required in a short period of time. Key users are either high ranking managers with already identified application needs of their own or persons (often the managers in charge) who are knowledgeable about the needs of an identifiable major group or department of potential users. If the planned systems approach is to succeed and not be circumvented by individual users obtaining their own resources without waiting for the conclusions of DSS planners, it is essential that:

1. The prior understanding and cooperation of users is obtained; and
2. The planning and acquisition process be carried out quickly and in a phased manner so that the most urgent needs are met without delay.

Example 7.6 describes a user meeting announcement at an early stage of DSS planning to explain the benefits of the systems approach to acquisition and to gain the voluntary cooperation of users.

EXAMPLE 7.6

ANNOUNCEMENT MEETING TO DISCUSS EFFECTIVE SUPPORT OF END USER COMPUTING WITH PERSONAL COMPUTERS AND THE INFORMATION CENTER

Purpose:

Certain corporate practices need to be established with regard to the acquisition and use of personal computers. Plans and activities are already underway which will extend the use of personal computers and will establish an Information Center approach to supporting users.

The purpose of this and subsequent presentations is to clarify critical issues that are at stake in adhering to uniform practices. The intent in establishing uniform practices and central coordination is to most effectively support both individual users and the company as a whole. This cannot be achieved without cooperative compliance in the acquisition of personal computers.

It is assumed that compliance to established procedures will be assured by a more complete common understanding of the underlying reasons why central coordination is *essential* for effective support. This is perhaps an unusual situation in that compliance will not limit the individual. On the contrary, only compliance will guarantee each individual user of maximum support in effectively meeting his/her needs.

MAIN ASPECTS OF POLICY:

Previously announced and currently practiced policy provides an avenue for the acquisition of personal computers. This requires that a Capital Expense Appropriation Request (CEAR) be made and forwarded to MIS. Upon request, MIS will also provide assistance in completing a CEAR.

The need for a ZYX policy of central coordination of personal computer acquisition is based on the following factors:

1. Providing for the telecommunications compatibility that will be needed by users;
2. Providing corporate economies of scale in acquisition and maintenance of personal computers;

3. Enabling users to "buy in" with respect to staff consulting support and the facilitation of the learning process;
4. Relieving users of the time consuming and confusing burden of hardware and software searching, assessment, and acquisition;
5. Establishing a common foundation for integrating organizational data, analysis methods, planning and decision processes, where such integrated approaches are needed.

In order to elaborate on the above points, the following issues are relevant and will be introduced in today's meeting:

1. The kinds of applications that can be effectively supported with the use of personal computers and direct user computing;

2. The capabilities of personal computers and the software (packaged programs) that run on them.

3. The Information Center concept.

4. Relationships and the need for communications between personal computers and a larger (mainframe) computer.

5. What is at stake for users and the corporation in coordinating user computing. That is, establishing the right balance between:
   a) managerial control, compatibility, and the economic use of information resources; and
   b) supporting individual users in being creative and flexible, and in taking individual initiative and responsibility without sacrificing organizational coordination.

It will usually be most cost-effective if a single package is selected as the standard for each generic category of DSS functions, rather than obtaining multiple packages from different vendors whose functional differences are of marginal importance to most users. The needs of each organization will, of course, vary, but an example of a basic software resource set for a large corporation might consist of one each of the following:

1. A mainframe modeling language package;
2. A mainframe user language for database queries;
3. A mainframe statistics, forecasting, and graphics display system;
4. A microcomputer integrated spreadsheet-database-graphics package (with at least download linkage to the above three mainframe systems);
5. A management graphics and information display system suitable for conference room presentations.

Considering the common use of microcomputers and some software resources for both decision support and office automation applications, considerable savings can be obtained through centralized negotiation and purchasing of both microcomputers and software packages. An illustration of savings is given in example 7.7. As enumerated in the example, in addition to the reduced acquisition costs, important but less tangible benefits are also derived by centrally obtained standardized systems. These include:

1. Saving individuals' time and effort in acquiring hardware and software.
2. Maintaining compatibility of equipment and software between different locations, thereby facilitating not only mainframe-micro data communications, but also facilitating user to user informal communications and interdepartmental user transfers without crossing over software language barriers.
3. Lowering the cost of future training, educational, and maintenance support by using standardized equipment and software.

The Information Center as Part of a DSS Strategy

The information center, a concept initially defined and implemented by IBM Canada in 1976, is essentially an organizational unit with the physical and staff facilities to help users to help themselves in DSS or other aspects of end-user computing. Originally associated with the establishment of a single central place to which users could go in order to utilize microcomputers or interactive terminals, software, data, and staff help, the term has been extended to apply to any other physical distribution of these same resources and services. It can be said that a central means to carry out the mission of the DSS support group, as described previously in this chapter, is to provide information center facilities to users. Nearly all companies still use the term "information center" to mean one or more walk-in facilities for users who may not

EXAMPLE 7.7

THE ZYX ACCOUNTABILITY COST/BENEFIT LETTER

Application Report Number 85-1   July, 1985

MICROCOMPUTER INITIAL ACQUISITION PHASE

Application Description:

The consolidated initial corporate purchase of 50 units of IBM PC/AT Workstations and associated set of basic software. Set up work to make the ZYX Workstation operational and distribution to users. USER(S): Corporate management and staff

Benefits:

I. Cost Reductions and Avoidance $ value/year
   1. 50 unit IBM PC/AT purchase negotiated discount, saving $1593 per unit over individual purchase 79,650
   2. 50 unit software purchase of DunsPlus menu utility product, including LOTUS, Multimate, menu utilities, saving $294 per unit over individual purchase 14,700
   3. Replacement of need for Hewlett-Packard terminals by adding emulator to PC, substituting for 50 terminals and saving $2640 per terminal 132,000
   4. Replacement of need for 15 IBM-3278 terminals by adding emulator to PC, saving $1290 per terminal 19,350

5. Replacement of need for 10 units of IBM Displaywriters and Multimate software by means of PC with software, avoiding cost per unit of $9,740 97,400

TOTAL TANGIBLE BENEFITS (Cost reductions /Avoidance) $343,100

II. Intangible or Less Tangible Benefits
   1. Avoidance of individuals' time and effort for searching for, acquiring, and setting up hardware and software.
   2. Avoidance of incompatibility of equipment and software between different locations, and for mainframe and micro communications.
   3. Facilitation of educational support and maintenance support for standardized equipment and software.

Cumulative Benefits (Applications 85-1 through Current Report)
CUMULATIVE TOTAL TANGIBLE
BENEFITS   **$ 343,100**
CUM TOTAL TANGIBLE BENEFITS PER SHARE $/share __.045__

Reported by DSS Staff   Estimate source(s): ZYX DSS Group

---

have (or may need help before they can use) their own hardware-software-data facilities. Whether there is one central information center or several locations, the essential feature of the information center is its *service-oriented* approach to *facilitate* rather than take over responsibility for running users' applications.

A particularly important role that information centers have played within a DSS strategy is as the first avenue of experimentation and gaining experience in the initial applications of key users who then return to their departments to demonstrate, educate, and counsel other users with the same or similar applications. Thus the information center is not merely the means of letting users get a particular analysis done, but is a major means of influencing and disseminating effective end-user computing know how. Although some organizations have attempted to force usage of an information center instead of providing users with their own facilities, they are in the minority. The information center usually tries to promote effective end-user computing through attracting users with easily accessible and high levels of good service rather than attempting to coerce users into standard practices and procedures. Most new information centers have found that demand for their services grows rapidly and there is often difficulty keeping up with the demand. This is especially the case when information centers, as some do, go beyond their theoretical charter to help but not do, and provide development and operations services. A segment of users would much rather have these things done for them even at the price of retaining their dependency on others for all future applications. There is thus the danger that uncontrolled information centers and less than adequate user education and training may result in the information center merely becoming another kind of data processing operations center instead of supporting end-user computing.

Stages of DSS Advancement

Getting Started

The early introductory stage is critical for the successful establishment of the "third approach," that is, an organizational DSS strategy embodying the right balance between local freedom and central planning and coordinated support. The first step in getting started should be gaining wide consensus on a general mission statement for the DSS support function that clearly states the objectives. The MIS management steering committee is usually the most useful forum for working out a consensus on DSS support objectives. These should not only spell out the nature of support systems and a rationale for their use in the company but should include a general timetable for attaining specific levels of results. For example, a first priority objective might be to provide personal microcomputers and financial and marketing data base query capabilities to enhance a basic menu of standard corporate status reports for each of the twenty top level corporate and divisional executives within two months. A second priority objective might be to extend these services with additional modeling analysis and planning capabilities to the next level of fifty marketing and manufacturing managers within five months. In order to provide a factual basis for setting such objectives, it is often useful to assign appropriate MIS management analysts (or an outside consultant working through MIS) to conduct a short pilot study of support needs and opportunities.

Once such a mission statement is accepted, the steering committee is then in position to review and approve the specific steps necessary to formulate and implement a strategy to achieve the stated objectives. The most common first steps that should be considered and tailored to each particular organizational situation include the following:

1. Formulate policy for the organizational location and reporting relationships of DSS support personnel and procedures for the acquisition of microcomputers and DSS software.
2. Select or recruit suitable support personnel and establish one or more DSS support groups (located at corporate and/or divisional headquarters).
3. Identify the first category of applications (if this has not already been done through a pilot study) as quickly as possible obtain the resources necessary for their implementation, and get them up and running.
4. Prepare the ground for the earliest wave of users through a communications program to inform them of plans and enlist their cooperation.
5. Provide initial training to the first group of priority users and complete plans for a full training and educational program.
6. Establish a pilot information center with facilities for an identified set or category of applications.
7. Formulate methods and procedures for user feedback and monitoring support effectiveness and evolving DSS application needs.
8. Formulate methods for estimating CPU load implications, corporate data base access requirements, and other computing resource requirements for the next wave of expected DSS usage and establish the organizational practices necessary to integrate these DSS resource requirements into MIS plans.

This first stage of getting started can usually be accomplished within a four to six month period, with completion being marked mainly by the acquisition of basic resources and their use for the first wave of high visibility DSS applications. The stage is then set for a new wave of needs and action steps to be taken.

The Mid-Life and Mature Stages of DSS Advancement

The start-up stage is followed by a "mid-life" period of several months in which the early applications are consolidated or extended, new users are identified and trained, the scope of DSS applications is extended, and the policies and practices previously worked out are put into practice and refined as needed. Common steps initiated in this stage include:

1. Adding additional DSS support staff personnel, establishing additional DSS groups, or assigning local DSS group-user group liaison persons.
2. Obtaining additional microcomputers and software packages to round out the DSS capabilities repertoire.

3. Establishing an information center–DSS newsletter to inform users of new facilities, successful applications and helpful practices.
4. Implementing advanced training and educational programs.
5. Fostering the establishment of user exchange support groups to meet periodically and share experience and know-how.
6. Setting up micro-mainframe communications links, especially for the downloading of portions of a corporate data base into microcomputer storage accessible to microcomputer spreadsheet and data base software packages.
7. Conducting formal studies to assess experience in utilizing the information center and reviewing the current status of user needs and future requirements.
8. Review and refine DSS resource acquisition practices and plans as required and integrate these into MIS plans.

A "mature" organizational stage for DSS may be reached after several years of evolutionary practice. Such a stage can be marked by certain advanced practices that go beyond the mere extension and growth of DSS applications. These may include some of the following:

1. Establishing formal methods of diagnosis, modification and transfer of DSS applications that have evolved and "hardened" into standard computer systems.
2. Greater integration of DSS support group operations with MIS systems development staff operations and the further establishment of "in-between" special applications fast development groups. Such groups may do development and operations for ad hoc applications that are too complex for end-user development but not calling for the use of standard programming languages and full scale software development projects.
3. Establishing practices and facilities to further the sharing of user model libraries (or *model bases*) for prototype categories of planning and analysis.
4. Development of formal methods for consolidating individual planning models into corporate models as well as decomposing corporate models to enable portions of them to be used for local planning and analysis.
5. Providing for automatic "transparent" to the user allocation of computer processing between mainframes and microcomputers in a communications, software, and data base sharing environment.
6. Integrating new forms of computer support into the current DSS functional repertoire, including:
   a) Query access to text bases derived from electronic mail and word processing systems;
   b) Idea processing forms of qualitative support described in the subsequent chapters of this book;
   c) The integration of expert systems and knowledge base modules into other types of support software packages.

Review Questions, Exercises, and Discussion Topics

Review Questions

1. Some MIS directors initially welcomed end-user computing and others had anxieties about it. Describe the thinking behind each of these attitudes and comment on the degree to which it may have been a correct position.
2. List four major factors which dictate the need for a planned organizational strategy for DSS.
3. What are the characteristics of those DSS applications which can effectively stand alone as independent applications not requiring integration with or the use of centrally operated corporate facilities?
4. *a)* What are the characteristics of DSS applications which *cannot* effectively stand alone as independent applications and which do benefit from integration with corporately operated facilities?
   b) What kinds of negative results stem from the lack of a coordinated approach in implementing these applications?
5. Identify economic reasons for a coordinated approach to acquiring DSS hardware and software resources.
6. What technical and human components are common to both general MIS planning as well as to DSS planning?
7. *a)* Identify and describe the four main categories of users described in this chapter with regard to their experience and attitudes.
   b) What are the main differences in the approach that should be taken toward each of these user types with regard to training and support?
8. What should be the main focus and objectives of initial training in DSS?
9. List the main functions of a DSS support group.
10. What advantages may be derived by transferring superusers into a DSS support group?
11. What advantages may be derived by transferring some MIS systems analysts into a DSS support group? Which aspects of their MIS and personal skills and experience are most useful for this new assignment and which are not likely to be very important?
12. What is the relevance of operations research knowledge to the mission of a DSS support group?
13. What are the main alternatives for the organizational positioning of DSS support staff personnel?
14. Where should the ultimate responsibility for DSS resources and support ideally reside and what characteristics and capabilities should the top DSS support manager possess?
15. Describe the main advantages and disadvantages of a distributed DSS staff form of organization.
16. What special disadvantage may be associated with a matrix form of DSS staff organization?

17. About how many DSS staff members should there be, on average, for a user community of 100 managers?

18. What situational factors are relevant in choosing among the alternative ways of organizing a DSS staff?

19. What are the characteristics of "key users" and why is it important to gain their understanding and support of DSS policies?

20. What economic benefits may be obtained by coordinating planning for DSS and office automation resource acquisition?

21. What role does the information center play in formulating and implementing a DSS strategy?

22. What are common first steps taken in getting DSS started in a large organization?

23. What steps are commonly taken in the "mid-life" stage immediately following the introductory stage of DSS?

Exercises

1. Describe an organization and identify its characteristics which would dictate that a centralized DSS group would be the best approach (assuming that is the case).

2. Find and describe a case example of a successful initial DSS application for (*a*) a very high level executive and (*b*) a middle-level manager. What organizational factors can be identified as contributing to these successes and which factors may have represented difficulties to be overcome?

3. Write a critique of the position paper given in example 7.1 which was prepared by the ZYX MIS department and circulated among corporate and divisional executives. Identify and explain factors which may underlie the kinds of reactions various managers may have to it, given the situation of a transition from a centrally run to a more divisionalized company.

4. *a*) Design a brief questionnaire that might be used to uncover potential new DSS applications for the use of college students in matters relating to their studies, their career plans, or to other personal needs.

   b) Assuming the college would consider providing DSS resources for the personal use of students because of the educational value of offering this kind of experience, what organizational, technical, and economic factors would have to be considered in planning to establish such a DSS facility for students? Prepare an outline for such a plan.

5. Do a literature search on the experience of companies in using information centers and describing variations and commonalities across different approaches to establishing and operating an information center.

6. Write a job description for a new position as director of DSS in a large multidivisional corporation. State any assumptions you find it necessary to make about the structure and policies of the organization.

7. Write a brief memo inviting key middle-level financial managers to a first one day seminar on DSS. Include enough information to answer the question they may have about why it would be worth their while to attend.

Discussion Topics

1. Assume you are a new plant manager of a chemical factory with considerable prior experience in using a microcomputer to do your own management analyses and planning. Your new company is large and has a centralized MIS department that tries to tightly control all computer hardware and software acquisition. They have stated that eventually all plants will be supplied with DSS resources but as of the present none have yet been made available to you. You decide to act immediately and buy three microcomputers and some software for your plant. You and your chief engineer are the main users and within a few months attribute several thousands of dollars of savings and improvements in plant operations to your analyses carried out with the aid of these resources. With a partner, each of you role-play and simulate a discussion that might take place between the plant manager and the corporate MIS director over the "rights" and "wrongs" of the plant manager's actions.

2. Discuss the relative advantages and disadvantages of hiring computer science majors versus hiring business majors for some beginner positions in a corporate DSS group.

3. Assume you are offered two different jobs, one as a DSS staff consultant in a marketing department's information center and the other as a systems analyst in a corporate MIS department. Discuss the pros and cons of accepting each of these jobs (assuming equal starting salaries).

4. Argue for or against the proposition that the respective missions of a DSS support staff and of an office automation group are so different from each other that these two functioins should not be combined in a single department for the support of end-user computing.

References

Camillus, J. E., Lederer, A. L. 1985. "Corporate Strategy and the Design of Computerized Information Systems." *Sloan Management Review* 26(Spring)3:35–42.

DeSanctis, G., Gallupe, B. 1985. "Group Decision Support Systems—A New Frontier." *DATA BASE* 16(Winter)2:3–10.

Diprimio, A. 1984. "Develop A Five-Step Plan To Launch Decision Support Systems." *Bank Systems and Equipment* 21(September)9:56–58.

Guimaraes, T. 1984. "The Benefits and Problems of User Computing." *Journal of Information Systems Management* 1(Fall)4:3–9.

Kendall, G. 1984. "Decision Support for the Information Center." *Canadian Datasystems* 16(May)5:65–67.

King, W. R. 1983. "Planning for Strategic Decision Support Systems." *Long Range Planning* 16(October)5:73–78.

Mazursky, A. D. 1984. "Acquiring and Using Microcomputers." *Journal of Information Systems Management* 1(Winter)1:47–57.

Meador, C. L., Keen, P. G. W., Guyote, M. J. 1984. "Personal Computers and Distributed Decision Support." *Computerworld* 18(May 7)19:7–16.

Multinovich, J. S., Vlahovich, V. 1984. "A Strategy for a Successful MIS/DSS Implementation." *Journal of Systems Management* 35(August):8–15.

Myers, K. A., Schonberger, R. J., Ansari, A. 1983. "Requirements Planning for Control of Information Resources." *Decision Sciences* 14(January)1:19–33.

Vacca, J. R. 1985. "The Information Center's Critical Post-Start-Up Phase." *Journal of Information Systems Management* 2(Spring)2:50–56.

Wetherbe, J. C., Leitheiser, R. L. 1985. "Information Centers: A Survey of Services, Decisions, Problems, and Successes." *Journal of Information Systems Management* 2(Summer)3:3–10.

Young, L. F. 1984. "A Corporate Strategy for Decision Support Systems." *Journal of Information Systems Management* 1(Winter)1:58–62.

Young, L. F. 1985. "Has DSS Moved Into Its Adolescence?" *Journal of Information Systems Management* 2(Fall)4:78–80.

Support For Qualitative Thinking and Creative Processes:

Part **2**

Idea Processing Concepts and Definitions, Functional Specifications, Software.

Idea Processing Support: Definitions and Concepts

8

> *I paused, examining and analysing all the minutiae of causation, as exemplified in the change from life to death, and death to life, until from the midst of this darkness a sudden light broke in upon me—a light so brilliant and wondrous, yet so simple, that while I became dizzy with the immensity of the prospect which it illustrated, I was surprised that among so many men of genius who had directed their inquiries toward the same science, that I alone should be reserved to discover so astonishing a secret.*
> Chapter 4, *Frankenstein*, Mary W. Shelley, Bantam Books, 1981

This chapter will explore what is meant by idea processing support and its relevance to practical decision making and to the DSS approach discussed in the first part of this book. To do this, it will be necessary to clarify what is meant by an *idea* and the relationship of *creativity* to the generation and refinement of ideas. The nature of analytical methods of problem formulation and problem solving (DSS concerns) will be contrasted with methods of synthesis of ideas into problem contexts and exploratory problem definition (idea processing concerns). In support of the latter, the role of the computer as a *thought organizing aid* and *meaning manipulator* will be discussed. The concepts explored in this chapter will set the stage for presenting various means of operationalizing idea processing support functions in the following chapter.

Ideas, Knowledge, and Creativity

The term *idea* is used in a variety of senses. What is implied in everyday statements such as "I just had an idea about how we should spend our vacation," or "She has a great idea for a new business," is quite different from the psychologist's or philosopher's notion of ideas as elemental mental images presented to human consciousness as the raw material of the thought process. In the latter sense, the roots of the scientist-philosopher's notion of an idea stems from empiricism. John Locke (1690) expressed the viewpoint of empiricism in statements such as the following:

"Every man being conscious to himself that he thinks; and that which his mind is applied about whilst thinking being the ideas that are there, it is past doubt that men have in their minds several ideas, such as those expressed by the words *whiteness, hardness, sweetness, thinking, motion, man, elephant, army, drunkenness*, and others. . . ."

Locke goes on to assert that the source of all ideas is human experience and observation:

"Our observation employed either about external sensible objects or about the internal operations of our minds perceived and reflected on by ourselves, is that which supplies our understanding with all the materials of thinking. These two are the fountains of *knowledge*, from whence all the ideas we have, or can naturally have, do spring."

Our present concern is consistent with this latter notion of ideas as elemental mental representations of meaningful objects or concepts rather than as complete plans for action. Ideas, as Locke saw them, spring from *knowledge*, which in turn is derived from observation of the external world as well as awareness of our own internal ruminations on these observations. Knowledge itself remains a somewhat vague notion, but implies more than just the raw data storage of remembered observations and includes some form of *interpretation* of these observations. Ideas are then the *conscious* expression of these interpretations. In this sense, ideas are individual notions that we become conscious of but which may not be relevant to any specific predefined purpose. However, individual ideas can become further refined. Ideas may not merely come into and go out of our awareness like randomly retrieved and displayed data elements, but instead can be consciously related to each other in ways that we begin to find useful, interesting, satisfying or entertaining. Idea processing takes individual ideas and manipulates, synthesizes, and associates them with one another until they form a larger contextual pattern that we can consciously relate to some human concern or problem. Thus, as illustrated in exhibit 8.1, idea processing can be defined as that process which takes ideas as inputs and produces as outputs the contextual frameworks we identify as decision problems or as plans. Science does not know precisely how this mental process occurs, nor do we know precisely how the underlying knowledge base is organized in the human mind. The organization of knowledge into knowledge bases, the ways in which knowledge bases can be accessed, and the development of inferences derived from extracted knowledge (ideas), are subjects of continuing research for both cognitive psychologists and for computer scientists who attempt to imitate such functions within a computer.

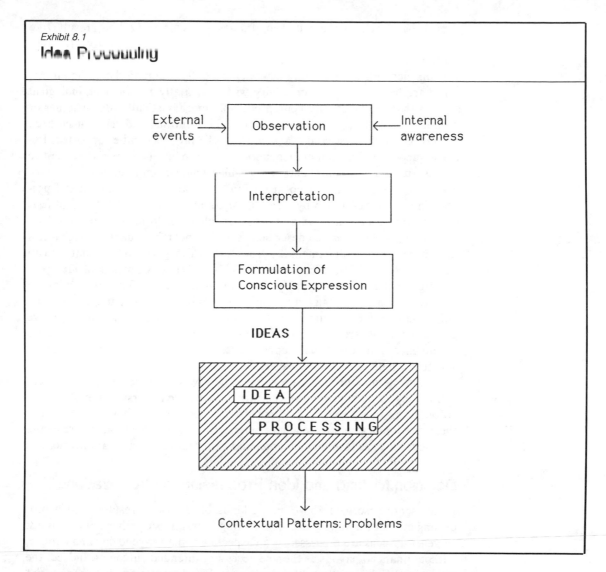

Exhibit 8.1
Idea Processing

External events → Observation ← Internal awareness

Observation → Interpretation

Interpretation → Formulation of Conscious Expression

IDEAS

IDEA PROCESSING

Contextual Patterns: Problems

The concerns of artificial intelligence (AI) with *knowledge representation,* with how to derive and design *inference processes* that can represent human expertise (*knowledge engineering*) and package these capabilities within interactive computer systems (*expert systems*) are fundamentally different from the problem of how to support idea processing. (The contrasting concerns of expert systems development and idea processing support will be discussed further later in this chapter.) Without knowing exactly how it occurs, we can observe that ideas sometimes come together to provide us with insights leading to the solution of practical problems or to the creation of new forms of cultural expression. When novel and meaningful new ways of seeing things result from this process, we refer to the process and its results as being *creative*. Because we are not able to articulate exactly how the general process of synthesizing existing elements in interesting new ways actually occurs in the human mind, some are led to associate creativity with essentially mystical or biological sources that are inherently nonreproducible mechanistically. But whether or not all aspects of idea processing can ever be identified and reproduced need not prevent us from seeking ways in which the process can be supported. Because support, unlike automation, does not seek to imitate or replace an entire process, it does not require detailed specification and reproduction of the process. Moreover, whether or not it faithfully imitates any human mental process, in some cases a step by step logical computer process for the synthesis of ideas into useful new ways to define problems or to identify potential solutions to problems *can* be described. Such a linearly sequential mechanical process may differ fundamentally from that which gives rise to what we call human creativity, but it can nevertheless be an effective means of idea processing whether or not we apply the term creative to it. Thus, particular instances of idea processing may or may not require creativity, and may or may not be susceptible to automation. But if aspects of idea processing (creative and noncreative) are supportable by interactive computer-based systems, the development and use of such support systems are relevant concerns for management scientists and to managers.

Some methods of such support have already been implemented and others seem likely to be developed in the future. A better understanding of the relationship of idea processing support to decision support should help further these development efforts, encourage receptivity to the exploratory use of the new support tools that may emerge, and foster more effective application.

Decision Making and Idea Processing in Organizations

In the sense described above, many kinds of ideas and results of idea processing are not relevant to decision making in business or other organizations. In general, ideas are processed as an aspect of human psychology and culture, without financial payoffs as the sole necessary intended outcomes. Indeed, the ultimate underlying impetus for the human thought processes that shape social systems may have no conscious connection to identifiable payoffs of any kind, but may simply be the inherent consequence of the structure of biological and social systems. According to systems theory, living systems are *open systems* that may seem to be purposive and goal seeking but actually are equilibrium seeking and equilibrium maintaining mechanisms (Bertalanffy 1951). Equilibrium is sought because that is the nature of systems that survive. Even survival itself need not be a conscious goal of the system or of an invisible intelligence-driven hand guiding the system. It is merely a logical outcome that those systems we have ever been able to observe are able to survive and those that have not survived are unobservable. Thus the expressed profit seeking objective of a business organization as well as any other explicit goal may be the conscious medium of expression for the more essential and unconscious metagoal of maintaining the equilibrium of the organization as a system. Other means, besides that of profit seeking as a unique or dominant purpose, are available as media for maintaining organizational equilibrium, given a particular environment. In this theoretical view of systems behavior, idea processing may merely be an aspect of natural "wired-in" human systems activity, necessary to some inner sense of well-being and equilibrium, whether or not it is goal directed.

However, at least at the conscious level at which we explain our own behavior to ourselves and others, organizational decision making is defined as a goal seeking, purposive activity. The expression and communication of goals, whatever form they take, seem to be a necessary means of coordinating systems decision making in ways that facilitate equilibrium. Thus, nontrivial forms of individual and group idea processing in organizational settings are purposely directed at, or involved in decision making in a variety of ways:

1. Extensive idea processing is directed at the recognition of significant decision problems or opportunities requiring decision making and action.
2. Extensive idea processing is necessary in defining and continuously redefining the scope and components of complex decision problems; that is, identifying the objectives and the factors that may affect achieving objectives.
3. Extensive idea processing is necessary to identify alternative strategies or action plans in complex decision problem situations.
4. Idea processing, rather than following predefined rules or logical mathematical algorithms, is often the means by which a decision is made among alternative strategies.

As previously noted, idea processing includes nonspecific (and perhaps nonspecifiable mental processes), and its applicability to the formulation and solution of decision problems does not rely on either mathematical algorithms or on other kinds of structured logical step by step solution methods. Many researchers have observed that the nonspecifiable type of idea processing appears to be the more dominant approach of expert high-level decision makers. The following are typical of this viewpoint:

1. Mintzberg, H. (1976) contrasts the analytical reasoning process of management science with the intuitive thought process of the manager and concludes that analytic planning had little impact on how top management functions.
2. Dreyfus, S. E. (1981) argues that "formal models do not represent abstractions and simplifications of expert understanding, but rather that a model represents a type of understanding that is typical of inexperienced beginners and that this type of understanding is, after sufficient real-world experience, supplanted by a much superior mode of human situational understanding totally different from that represented by a model."

3. Isenberg, D. (1984) reports that "thought sampling" statements describing how senior managers think indicate that they do not engage in solving isolated problems but deal with interconnected networks of problems and use what he calls "high intuition" (as opposed to "low intuition" which is mere guesswork) in which rapid pattern recognition takes place and solutions are generated and regenerated as new information is obtained.
4. Cowan, T. A. (1963) states that scientists could learn that "intuition has a more important role to play in even simple and apparently trivial decisions than the rational constraints of present day decision procedures allow . . . the constraints imposed by general logic and generalizing mathematics upon decision procedures virtually rule out the study of truly creative decisions and tend to restrict decision science to mechanical and therefore dull and repetitive instances of decision-making. . . ."

If idea processing related to decision making is to be supported, what can we base such support upon if all we can say is that this kind of decision making involves a highly developed level of "intuition" and "creativity?" We need to examine more closely what has been observed about creative problem solving in determining whether or not there may be a technically feasible role for computer-based support.

What Is Known about Creative Problem Solving?

While a gap remains in the literature with respect to a complete taxonomy of problems and their relationship to the dynamics of problem solving (Sackman and Citrenbaum 1972), it is generally recognized that *creativity* often is key to the formulation and development of ideas. A descriptive model of the creative process was formulated by Wallas (1926). In Wallas' model, four phases of the creative process are postulated as: (1) preparation, (2) incubation, (3) illumination, and (4) verification. These stages are described in the following paragraphs and related to Simon's (1960) descriptive model of the decision making process, which consists of the three stages of intelligence, design, and choice. These models are shown side by side in exhibit 8.2.

Wallas' preparation phase bears some similarity to the first part of the intelligence stage of Simon's model. It consists of gathering facts, knowledge, and ideas that may be relevant to some question of interest.

The incubation and illumination phases of creativity involve respectively, first a pause (incubation), in which some unconscious sifting and relating of the information gathered during preparation takes place, followed by (often sudden) recognition or awareness of a new relationship that has importance to the thinker (illumination). Illumination appears relevant in its result, but not necessarily in its means (which usually are at a subconscious level), to the latter portion of Simon's intelligence phase, in which the information gathered is interpreted and understood to comprise a situation which is relevant and

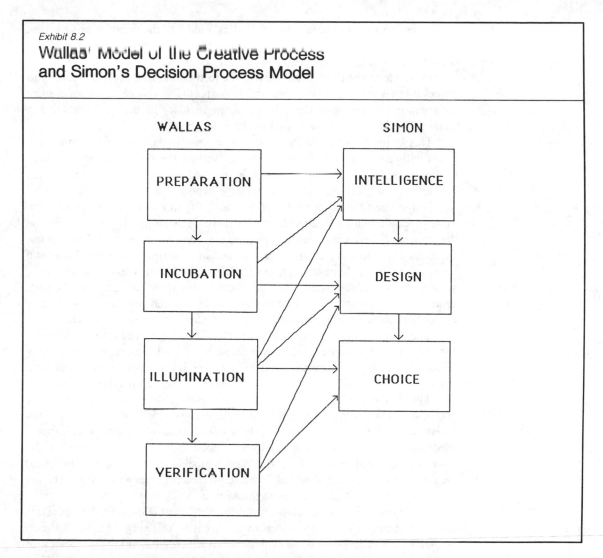

Exhibit 8.2

Wallas' Model of the Creative Process and Simon's Decision Process Model

WALLAS   SIMON

PREPARATION → INTELLIGENCE

INCUBATION → DESIGN

ILLUMINATION → CHOICE

VERIFICATION

requires a strategy to be formulated and decided upon. Sudden illumination may also be the the means of revealing new alternative strategies as well as the most preferred strategy, which are, respectively, the aims of Simon's design and choice stages.

Incubation is related to the search for and identification of alternatives at a subconscious level (discussed later with respect to divergent search processes). In this respect, incubation can be seen to be the creative process stage that may be relevant to Simon's design phase, which is directed at the formulation of one or more strategies to cope with a decision situation.

In verification, the final stage of Wallas' model of the creative process, the insight gained (in illumination) is tested and seen to be pragmatic and acceptable, or is rejected, or reworked until it becomes acceptable. In this phase of idea development the thinker relates the initial notion to other concepts and places it into some logical and pragmatic context. The thinker imposes closure by accepting or rejecting the validity of the idea for its utility for achieving some goal or for clarifying a broader knowledge model.

This latter phase of verification can be seen to have some common purposes with both Simon's design stage as well as the choice stage, in which strategies are assessed and accepted or rejected with respect to the decision maker's preferences between their relative expected outcomes.

Despite certain similarities and applicability of one to the other, the creative process to which Wallas referred and the decision-making process Simon described are clearly not identical in purpose, content, or method. But it is not farfetched to find connections between the two descriptive models. Ideas and decisions problem elements such as variables, relationships, and strategies, are sometimes merely different semantic labels for the identical conceptual entity. One can, for example, have and develop an idea about how to bring about a desired outcome by a new arrangement of decision problem variables.

The decision-making process, in each of its stages, requires ideas to be formulated and processed, often in creative ways, and the creative processing of ideas requires decisions to be made. Thus each process is intertwined with the other at lower levels of detail within each of their respective phases.

The Wallas model provides a commonly used set of terms and a reference framework for describing what happens in creative idea processing in broad brush terms. This framework may be useful in considering how to support creative idea processing, just as Simon's model has been with respect to decision support. However, neither the Wallas model nor the work of subsequent researchers in the psychology of creative processes go very far in prescribing precisely *how* the steps of creative thinking actually work.

Other observers can be consulted, however, for at least identifying certain common themes that recur in describing creative thinking. One such theme is that which claims and cites evidence that *divergent* thinking processes, as opposed to *convergent* thinking, are relevant to creativity (Guilford 1967). Divergent thinking involves a broad search for alternatives, usually in an "open problem," a problem for which there is no unique answer. Tasks involving divergent thinking were examined by Fulgosi and Guilford (1968) with respect to short-term incubation (assuming a subconscious form of divergent thinking occurs as in Wallas' description of incubation). In divergent processes, the generation of alternatives involves finding many combinations of elements that may provide possible answers. Fluency of thinking and originality characterize a divergent search for alternatives, rather than rigorous adherence to prescribed steps and criteria for finding some uniquely "correct" result. In a convergent search, the opposite is true; that is, there is a unique solution to meet prescribed criteria that is sought. As Guilford points out (1975) however, these two methods are not necessarily used in isolation and can be intermixed in that a "guessing" or divergent approach can be used on the way to a convergent solution. The degree to which the entire process can be characterized as divergent or convergent is relative rather than absolute and depends on the degree of limitations imposed on the answer. We would go further in claiming that convergent subprocesses can be imbedded within a larger divergent process. That is, unique answers to well-defined subproblems can be sought through structured methods, and then used in combination with other answers to other subproblems in a wide-ranging synthesis of answers to subproblems that may comprise more open and complete answers to larger problems. Some examples of divergent, convergent, and mixed problems are given in exhibit 8.3.

Although the research base is sparse, another recurring theme is the relevance of creativity to *problem discovery* and *formulation* as opposed to finding problem solutions. Taylor (1972) observed that those high in creativity tended to gravitate toward more generic problems in an attempt to understand underlying general relationships as opposed to the more direct approach of solving more well-defined and specific problem manifestations. Other investigators (Csikszentmihalyi and Getzels 1971) also found that originality in artists was highly related to the problem discovery orientation. Problem discovery is another way of expressing the purpose of Simon's intelligence phase of decision processes, thus pointing to a further link of creativity (as applied to problem discovery) to the decision process.

Another pervasive theme in relation to creativity is the role of metaphorical thinking. Metaphors are figures of speech in which one kind of object or idea is used in place of another to suggest some kind of likeness between them. They serve us to make connections between things which are not usually seen as connected in any literal way. Through such nonliteral connections we are able to see things in a new way. Poetic uses of metaphor, such as "my love is a red rose," or "my soul is an enchanted boat," evoke feelings and associations that help to convey the nonliteral or extraliteral emotions and thoughts of the author's mind to the mind of the reader. In the world of politics and business, metaphors are also commonly used to emphasize, famialiarize, and to explain. For example, computer science teachers often explain the function of the control unit in a computer's central processing unit by saying it is "the traffic policeman of the computer." The general use of the term "memory" to denote computer storage is metaphoric. Metaphors are instruments of divergent processes because they synthesize disparate ideas. They include and integrate possibilities that would be excluded by referring only to literal standard categories. For this reason metaphors are useful in extending the search for discovering and understanding new problems and in identifying potential new solutions.

Exhibit 8.3
Divergent-Convergent-Mixed Problems

Divergent Examples:

- Find potential uses for space satellites.
- Name a new polyester fabric.
- Formulate a means of helping the poor without fostering dependency.
- Create plans for fostering involvement in systems development.
- Identify ways to use computers to support creativity.

Convergent Examples:

- Find a solution for x and y for two given linear independent equations.
- Minimize the cost objective function in a linear programming model.
- Find all checks in a batch for more than $500.
- Find the shortest round trip route possible.

Mixed Examples:

- Identify the six lowest cost cross country trips and assess their market potential and ways of selling them.
- Take the prescribed subject matter for a DSS course and find a new way to teach them within time and cost limits.

Metaphors have been observed to be used spontaneously by creative thinkers. Based on the assumption that metaphors can also be used intentionally to foster creativity, the generation of metaphors are a key device in Gordon's (1961) "synectics" process for developing creativity (see example 8.1). Gordon uses metaphorical aids to first "make the familiar strange" so that the usual constraints of literal logic and fixed perceptions of the familiar can be broken through. In another phase of the synectics process, metaphors are further used to "make the strange familiar" as a means of seeing new relevance in the unfamiliar to the problem at hand.

Other methods developed and used to foster creativity include the following heuristics (methodological devices to aid in generating new ideas):

1. Deferment of judgment and aiming at larger quantity of ideas.
   Osborn (1963) developed and described the process he called *brainstorming*, in which personal interaction in groups constrained from the exercise of premature judgment was used to generate larger lists of possibilities which were only subsequently assessed. Underlying hypotheses are that premature judgment inhibits creativity and that higher quantity of ideas ultimately leads to higher quality.
2. Use of *verb checklists* to build on prior ideas.
   Parnes (1967) developed a creative problem solving (noncomputer) program utilizing both group and individual processes.
   In generating ideas checklists of verbs are used to build on previous suggestions. These include the following transformation devices:

   —*put to other use,*   —*substitute,*
   —*adapt,*   —*rearrange,*
   —*modify,*   —*reverse, and*
   —*magnify,*   —*combine.*
   —*minify,*

3. Redefinition and generalization.
   The conscious identification of problem boundaries and subsequent stretching or removal of these boundaries is another technique of creative problem solving.

A related mode of getting to the heart of things and removing unnecessary constraints associated with specific known solutions is a technique of successively generalizing until the most generic problem statement is reached. (For example: pencil—writing implement—input device.)

In summary, the following general statements can be made in regard to what is known about creative problem solving:

1. The Wallas model, although not accepted by some scientists and modified and elaborated upon by others, is still the most generally accepted descriptive model of the creative process.

SYNECTICS AND THE USE OF METAPHOR

The Synectics Process follows the following general phases:

Phase 1:

Problem As Given (Developing or identifying the original understanding of the problem or general concern.)

Phase 2:

Making the Strange Familiar (Uncovering and revealing hidden or contrary elements not previously identified.)

Phase 3:

Problem as Understood (Analysis and digestion of the initial problem in order to redefine the problem in a more appropriate new way.)

Phase 4:

Operational Mechanisms (Metaphors are developed which are relevant to the problem as understood. The purpose is to open up the problem and escape from rigid, overly constrained thinking.)

Phase 5:

The Familiar Made Strange (Uses the metaphors to see the problem in a strange new way.)

Phase 6:

Psychological States (Creates the psychological atmosphere, including involvement and detachment, most conducive to creativity according to synectics theory.)

Phase 7:

States Integrated With Problem (The most pertinent analogy is conceptually compared with the problem and used to liberate the problem from its old form.)

Phase 8:

Viewpoint (Stating a technical insight obtained through the prior steps.)

Phase 9:

Solution or Research Target (The viewpoint is made operational by testing the underlying principle or defining the necessary further research.)

---

2. The specific mechanisms of mental activity underlying creative mental processes have not been verified and perhaps are unverifiable, but certain manifestations of creative thinking have been observed and incorporated into consciously directed individual and group efforts to enhance creativity.
3. These mechanisms involve divergent search processes, the use of metaphor, and the use of certain logical transformational methods used to modify, build upon, and redefine existing problem elements.

Creativity and Right Brain Processes

Research on the functioning of the human brain associates processes related to creativity to hemispheric specialization of the right side of the brain. While some new evidence casts doubt on strict specialization, the differences hypothesized by left/right hemispheric brain researchers are still useful as descriptors of dichotomous human mental capabilities and idea processing

The following brief excerpt (Gordon 1961, 54–56) illustrates the use of metaphor or analogy in Phase 4 in a session aimed at inventing a new kind of roof. Prior steps had led to the notion that there might be an economic advantage in having a roof white in summer and black in winter.

A: What in nature changes color?
B: A weasel—white in winter, brown in summer; camouflage.
C: Not only that. It's not voluntary and the weasel only changes color twice a year. I think our roof should change color with the heat of the sun. There are hot days in the Spring and Fall and cold ones too.
B: OK, how about a chameleon?
D. That is a better example because he can change back and forth without losing any skin or hair.
E: How does the chameleon do it?
A: A flounder must do it the same way.
E: Do what?
A: Hell! A flounder turns white if he lies on white sand and then he turns dark if he lands on black sand . . . mud.

D: Yeah, that's right! But how does he do it?
B: Chromatophores. I'm not sure if it's voluntary or involuntary. Wait a minute; it's a little of each.
D. How does he do it? I still don't plug in.
(B goes on to explain how a reflex action adapts to surrounding conditions through bringing black pigment chromatophores from the deeepest layer of the cutis to the surface as black spots which appear solid from a distance.)
C: I've got an idea. Let's flip the flounder over to the roof problem. Let's say we make up a black roofing material, except buried in the black stuff are little white plastic balls. When the sun comes out and the roof gets hot the little white balls expand according to Boyle's law. They pop through the black roofing vehicle. Now the roof is white.

The flounder analogy and other metaphors were explored in order to see new relationships and possible approaches to the problem.

---

modes.* This section summarizes these right-brained process descriptions in order to extend our understanding of creative idea processing as a foundation for defining the potential for computer support.

While the left brain is credited with the ability to use language through direct literal association of words and objects, the right hemisphere apparently perceives patterns, images, and makes the type of imaginative connections associated with divergent thinking and the use of metaphor.

*In personal correspondence with me (Nov. 9, 1981), Professor William Taggart (who has written about right/left brain differences and their relationship to information systems [1981, 1982]) stated that he treats these differences as . . . "*metaphors* for dimensions of creative decision making. Whether the model is a physiological reality is not as significant as whether it is a useful problem solving paradigm."

The right hemisphere, according to Zaidel (1980), has the special function of initially developing concepts and context as a particular aspect of intelligence called "crystallized intelligence". Zaidel states:

> "When you present a new symbol to someone, and he has to learn new associations between visual symbols and linguistic material, the right brain is dominant in the beginning. But as he becomes more familiar with the system, the action moves over to the left brain. Now why that is, is not clear. *Perhaps because the right hemisphere provides the context for the new information, through its rich associative network.*"

Zaidel's speculations are based on a survey of the literature, which in turn rests upon clinical evidence derived from studies of patients who suffered accidental severance of the connection between their brain hemispheres or on patients undergoing brain surgery. Bogen (1977) compiled a list of terms used by psychologists to characterize right versus left brain functions. These lists are given in exhibit 8.4. A generalization that can be made regarding these lists is that the left-brained items suggest a more structured, prescribed, and constrained way of thinking. The right-brained list suggests the opposite; not the absence of structure, but its relaxation into a more loosely constrained semistructured style of thinking.

The contrast of more structured processing in the left hemisphere mode and less structured in the right hemisphere mode brings us back to the essence of the concept of computer support systems as facilitating semistructured processes rather than automating structured processes. This suggests that the right hemisphere list can serve designers and developers of support systems as a check list to help identify or suggest new, untapped modes of computer support.

The most common vehicles for the communication of information between computers and human users are words, numbers, and pictures. What can be said about the way in which the right and left brain hemispheres deal with each of these? The left hemisphere is the literal language and number processor, taking the individual words or numbers and linearly processing each one within some framework of analytical rules. The right side deals more with holistic patterns such as spaces, shapes, pictures, and larger chunks of language such as phrases, sentences, and paragraphs. Thus each side deals with words and language, but the left side does so in a more unitary, sequential, "bottom-up," building-the-whole-from-the-pieces, manner. The right side operates in a more "top-down" way, accepting the larger pattern in order to extract general meaning. Numbers, or more generally, the concept of quantity, may be similarly handled as individual items on the left side and as related patterns on the right, with the right side also able to interpret pictorial patterns as quantitative analogs. Recognition of entire pictures may be exclusive to the right side. But language (qualitative statements) and numbers (quantitative statements) apparently are processed by both halves, but in different chunk sizes and in different manners.

Exhibit 8.4

Right and Left Brain Styles of Knowing

Left brain	Right brain
Intellect	Intuition
Convergent	Divergent
Intellectual	Sensuous
Deductive	Imaginative
Active (preceptive)	Receptive
Discrete	Continuous
Abstract	Concrete
Realistic (planned)	Impulsive
Propositional	Imaginative
Transformational	Associative
Lineal (Sequential)	Nonlineal (Simultaneous)
Historical	Timeless
Explicit	Tacit
Objective	Subjective
Structured	Semistructured

(Based on Bogen 1977)

The different descriptors of right and left hemisphere ways of processing are aspects of human cognitive style. Cognitive styles are made up of a multiple number of dimensions, which are only dimly understood and generally described by the lists of descriptors and general observations previously given in the above discussion. Thus cognitive style is still an open subject in need of more definitive research before it can be more precisely defined. On the other hand, computer systems designers must procede on the best available knowledge and assumptions about cognitive style and how it might best be supported. The danger is that cognitive style, including the left-right brain paradigm, may be prematurely dismissed as a significant consideration in developing support systems. As Taggart and Robey (1982) have pointed out, much of the MIS/DSS literature on cognitive style and its implications for systems design draws upon Huysmann's (1970) distinction between "analytic" and "heuristic" approaches to decision making. Huber (1983), for example, points out the difficulties in using this analytic-heuristic dichotomy as a design factor and suggests that it may not be a useful concept for system design. In contrast, it appears to us that part of the difficulty in finding relevance of cognitive style to DSS design is that the notion of support systems has been too limited. Another part of the difficulty is that the notion of cognitive style has also been too narrowly defined. It may be that many types of DSS and MIS applications can do little or nothing to effectively accommodate either heuristic or more creative aspects of right brain cognitive styles, but it also may be that we simply have overlooked or failed to invent new forms of right-brained support because we didn't know about them.

Several social observers have pointed out a general cultural bias in our educational system and professions toward left-brained approaches. This may be another factor inhibiting the recognition of the opportunity and development of right-brained oriented support systems.

Artificial Intelligence and Creative Processes

Artificial intelligence (AI) is concerned with designing and implementing computer systems (essentially software) that will appear to operate in ways that are associated with intelligent human thinking processes. The kinds of intelligent processes addressed in the many computer programs developed include understanding and responding to ordinary (natural) language, language translation, learning, reasoning, problem solving and some types of decision making (as in playing chess and other games). Although many AI applications are impressive and involve innovative techniques of data organization and programming, no claim is made that computers have, as yet, been enabled to "think," in the general sense. After much debate, analysis, and theorizing, whether or not computers are inherently unable to "think" in human terms is still an unanswered question. Among other aspects of this question, one difficulty is to determine whether or not being conscious or self-aware is a necessary aspect of thinking, and further, what is really meant by consciousness and how its presence or absence can be objectly tested. Another related part of the debate on this question has centered on the question: *Can a computer be creative or is creativity inseparable from the human mind?*

To answer this question unequivocally in a theoretical sense, a better understanding of creativity and creative processes is needed than is available, as well as a better knowledge of the limits of computability. However, the general AI approach does not require that intelligent processing behavior in a computer must mirror the logic (or illogic) of the associated human thinking process. The observable computer outputs must merely be indistinguishable from human outputs in comparable circumstances (the so-called Turing test for computer intelligence proposed by mathematician Alan Turing [1950]). In this type of pragmatic test for creativity, the product of a computer can be assessed to be a creative work such as a good novel or play if knowledgeable literary critics considered it to be comparable in quality to accepted literary works such as those of Shakespeare or Proust, for example. If the test for creativity is whether or not a computer can produce such literary works, then we must conclude that, thus far, computers have not been programmed to successfully perform such literary feats, nor do techniques yet exist to do so. Like other AI research, efforts to manifest creativity in computers may, even if not entirely successful, shed some light on what we mean by creativity. While a computer can be (and has been) programmed to produce a credible, grammatically correct English sentence given a data base of categorized words and rules for putting them together, the ability to judge and assess the creative value of such a sentence, and if necesssary, to modify it to improve its creative value, seems to involve an extremely extensive base of experience and complex logic that is, thus far, unique to human cognition. (Not only can a computer not be relied upon to show good creative judgement, but it also can not be relied upon to avoid nonsense when given a very wide-ranging domain.)

As pointed out in chapter 1 and in the introduction to this chapter, some AI researchers may continue to be concerned with these issues of whether or not human cognition and creativity (involving a higher or deeper level of awareness and judgement) can be automated, but our concern is with the *supportability* of idea processing, not its total automation. An area of more recent AI concern, that of expert systems, may be more relevant to discuss in the context of idea processing and creativity support systems. Unlike the issue of whether or not AI techniques can automate the production of a complete creative work, expert systems are intended to manifest intelligence in providing expert consultation to a user, and not to replace the user.

The earlier question of whether or not computers can be creative can be reformulated in the spirit of expert systems as follows: *Can expertise on creativity be captured and effectively utilized within an interactive, user-controlled computer support system?*

In the light of the summary given earlier in this chapter on what is known and not known about processes to develop and enhance creativity, it would seem reasonable to conclude that there is no deep expertise on this subject, but there are a number of useful methods and guidelines. A system that could interactively guide the user in the use of such methods may be a useful teaching device for the novice, but such a system would hardly seem to be worthy of being called an expert system. Experts and expert systems (which manifest human expertise) must possess a large repertoire of complex knowledge and be able to *utilize* and *operationalize* it within a problem situation, not merely guide or teach the user in the principles that may be applied. While it is, or should be, true that expert systems support rather than replace the user's final judgments, they do so by offering directly *executable* advise, and not merely prescriptions for how users can arrive at their own conclusions. An expert system must also be able to explain, at the user's request, its own reasoning as to how it reached its conclusions and advice so that the user can assess the value of the advice and maintain control. However, expert systems should be convertible into automated decision-making systems, if users chose to transfer power and abdicate their interactive control. In most domains in which expert systems have been developed or proposed, such a conversion of the system from the role of consultant into the role of executive would not be acceptable. The automation of very important decisions is not likely to be acceptable on social, political, and psychological, as well as technical grounds. That is, even if machines could be demonstrated to possess as much versatility, knowledge, and judgment ability as top human experts, which they cannot yet do in any area involving deep expertise, valid reasons may remain for not turning final decision implementation over to them.

An expert system that could act as a creative consultant would have to have the capability to generate novel problem definitions, for example, and offer them to human users for their judgment or reaction, and then to react to these human reactions with further explanations or improving modifications. This would imply that an experience base as extensive as that of a highly experienced human adult could be represented in the knowledge base of the computer system. Unlike expert systems dealing in an extensive but limited domain such as that related to medical diagnosis, the knowledge base that would be potentially useful for the creative generation of useful ideas would not be limited to any particular domain. Many of the techniques mentioned earlier (such as the use of metaphors, the removal of boundaries, and the formation of unusual new combinations) are premised on the notion that creativity requires the breaking down of overly constraining categories of knowledge and finding previously undefined associations. The creation of such an unstructured and far-reaching knowledge base and the formulation of inference processes necessary to utilize it would require that knowledge engineering (a methodologically undefined field) be capable of mirroring the complexities of creative human processes.

Thus, starting from the point of view of expert systems as interactive support systems rather than the more traditional AI approach to completely automating creativity, we appear to arrive at the same dead end. Idea processing and creativity support, if it is feasible at all, given current technology and knowledge, must take a different tack than that of either traditional AI or the newer AI expert system approach.

Creativity in Imagined Context Development

Another means of idea processing is the imaginative creation and exploration of a complete situational context. These full situational contexts and the event sequences flowing from them are known as scenarios or historical sequences. Scenarios are constructed in order to more fully understand the dynamics of events and to use this enhanced understanding in the formulation of policy and strategies for future contingencies.

Scenarios are based on stated initial conditions and specified assumptions about the way in which the major "players" in the situation are likely to behave. If the future outcomes projected by this method include critically undesirable results, the events and sequential actions are retraced to determine what could have been done differently to avoid the undesired results (Kahn and Wiener 1967). A brief example of a scenario is given in example 8.2.

EXAMPLE 8.2
A SUMMARIZED WORLD CRISIS SCENARIO
(An Imagined, But Plausible Sequence of Events.)

INITIAL CONDITIONS:

Time: 1990

Assumptions: The world's energy usage cycle has returned to a point where oil, once again, is in short supply. The ruling Ayatollah in Iran has just died, and several forces are vying for control in a chaotic civil war. The Soviet Union has massed troops along the Iranian border.

SEQUENTIAL EVENTS:

Day 1

The top U.S. security advisors have been called into session by the President. It is agreed that no immediate military action be taken but that the Soviets be told of American "concern" regarding any potential interference. Much debate has taken place over whether such a message should be sent and over its precise wording.

Day 3

It appears that pro-Soviet Iranian factions are gaining the upper hand. Soviet troops remain poised at the border. The Soviets have not responded to the American message. The security advisors meet and agree that an American naval force be ordered immediately into the area and placed on alert, but that other U. S. forces should not yet be conspicuously alerted or moved. A debate is opened on what alternatives might be considered should a) pro-Soviet internal groups take over and b) the Soviets themselves should openly intervene with their own troops. No agreement is reached.

Day 4

Earlier reports that pro-Soviet forces seem to be winning are refuted by US Intelligence. It now appears that a pro-Western faction is in the ascendancy. There are also reports of the use of Soviet artillery and planes against these forces.

Day 5

The American UN delegate is instructed to propose a resolution that all foreign forces be kept out of Iran and the Iranians allowed to settle their own affairs. The resolution is vetoed in the Security Council by the Soviet Union. It is introduced into the Assembly, where a debate ensues.

(This scenario continues with significant local events, plausible Soviet and American reactions being chronicaled. If the scenario ends in a disaster, such as a superpower exchange of nuclear missles, it is reviewed and analyzed from the point of view of how the disaster might have been averted by altering the U.S. actions taken at seemingly critical junctures. If the scenario ends well from the American point of view, it is analyzed in order to identify which moves were critical to the outcome, and what contingencies could have arisen and how they might have been handled in order to preserve the desired outcome. Alternative scenarios can be formulated and analyzed varying some of the initial conditions.

It should be noted that the nature of this particular type of scenario calls for a day by day, or perhaps even an hour by hour, treatment of time. Other kinds of scenarios relevant to a business situation may find a longer time period or a more collapsed treatment of time into only a few major phases to be appropriate.)

EXAMPLES FOR SCENARIO TOPICS
OTHER THAN CRISIS MANAGEMENT:

I. *A Microcomputer Manufacturer's Strategy and The Future Market For Microcomputers Under Alternative Assumptions of Technological and Economic Conditions.*

II. *Alternative Assumptions Of Future Social Conditions and Plausible Outcomes for Alternative Models and Policies for Higher Education*

III. *Implications for Communications Systems of Social, Technological, and World Political and Economic Alternative Futures*

A variation of scenario development as applied to organizational or national policy analysis is the formulation of likely future sequential social, economic, and cultural processes in different societies based on previously observed phases of development in other societies that have already passed through these phases. These historically projected sequences are examined for their implications about outcomes of concern to policy makers and used in policy formulation in a manner similar to that of general scenario analysis.

While creativity may play a role in specifying the initial conditions of scenarios, the development and analyis of these imagined contexts must be governed by knowledge and reason in order to maintain plausibility rather than by creatively searching for novel but highly unlikely or fanciful occurrences. Scenarios are thus seen as a significant aid to idea processing, but as a very different approach than the methods of creativity enhancement previously discussed.

Premises for Idea Processing Support Development

The search for and development of useful computer-based methods to support idea processing can best be founded through an *engineering* approach, that is: derive new designs from theory to the degree that this is possible, but do not wait for a complete, proven theory to build and try out a variety of new software functions. Points of departure for the functional design of idea processing software can be sought by means of:

1. Analysis of descriptive models and theories of creativity and thinking processes;
2. Analysis of the body of experience that has accumulated from individual and group processes and heuristics (behavioral, group dynamic, nonanalytic, as well as analytic approaches not previously involving computer support);
3. New insights and ideas of systems designers on approaches not previously tried;
4. Assessment and experimental modification of existing and new (as more becomes available) commercial and experimental computer software for idea processing support.

The guiding principle for development should be to find and build upon what seems to work well, and to clearly separate this pragmatic objective from the worthwhile, related, but different objectives of research and theory building on human thinking processes. In analyzing noncomputerized processes for assessing the potential for computer support, it should be borne in mind that the objective is not to enable the computer to manifest either intelligence or creativity for their own sake, but to support the *user's* intelligence and creativity. The analysis of noncomputer processes thus aims at breaking these processes into their components so that we may be able to identify those functions that can advantageously be performed by the computer, while the user continues to remain in control of what is done and to concentrate more attention on those unstructured or unspecified mental activities that lie at the heart of creative thinking.

A basic step that aids thinking through the use of external tools has long been practiced; that is, physically recording one's thoughts in writing (in words, pictures, or special symbols) and using implements such as paper and pencil or chalkboards, as external memory devices and work buffers for trying out and recording modifications. Writing (and rewriting) original works is a means of developing ideas. Therefore, it can be argued, computerized word processing is also idea processing support when it is used not merely to record, reproduce, retrieve, and edit already developed material, but to aid in developing new ideas as part of a problem context.

One can, however, seek to extend support methods by looking more closely at the special characteristics of the idea processing methods previously discussed in this chapter, methods which do not rely merely on the open-ended creation of textual material. Words are the well-established symbolic vehicles for conveying ideas to ourselves and to others. But in the context of idea processing, the computer need not be limited to the production of bulk text, but can be used as a more basic word-symbol manipulator. In seeking specific modes of idea processing support, the following three generic levels of idea processing support can be distinguished and examined:

Level 1 Support: The "Secretarial" Level

At this level, the computer can be used essentially as a convenient vehicle for capturing, recording, and mirroring back an individual's thoughts in order to facilitate their further development. The extent of storage of words (or phrases) in formats that represent and interlink ideas is limited to the working inputs originated by the user within a given work session (or a continued work session) on the same problem. Thus the storage requirements are limited and represent a working buffer rather than a comprehensive knowledge base. No provision need be made in the system at this level for building more complex logical linkages between different work buffers in order to construct a network of associations. Each work buffer can merely be "tagged" or coded with "key word" subject category designations in order to facilitate retrieval under a user-directed strategy of search and association.

Level 2 Support: The "Framework-Paradigm" Level

At this level, the computer provides the user with selected frameworks that may be appropriate to the organization of the user's thoughts. Such frameworks may consist of logical structures and identified categories or dimensions of the problem or problem description method, within which the user can supply specific inputs under each supplied or implied heading. These frameworks serve the user as thought-organizing aids, in a manner similar to checklists and forms, in that they call attention to relevant problem aspects and provide a formatted vehicle for entry of detail. In addition to the frameworks themselves, this level of support may include a limited number of examples or sample entries within a given framework. These entries need not comprise an extensive base of ideas, but can be limited to providing the user with some thought-starting concrete examples or to providing limited paradigms (exemplifying models) for certain common problems.

Level 3 Support: The "Generative" Level

At this level, the computer is used to actually generate and display word-ideas for the user's consideration, either by means of synthesizing or associating word elements previously stored or currently entered by the user. The processing algorithms and storage structures required for this level of support may or may not include methods of artificial intelligence, but the active generative functions of the computer are intended to comprise only certain steps within a user-controlled dialogue. The user remains as the initiator and judge of what is to be retained and further developed as potentially creative and of value.

These three levels of support can be considered to represent a hierarchy in terms of the degree and sophistication of support. But it should be noted that a higher level of support does not necessarily comprise a more *effective* level of support (and certainly does not automatically imply a more *cost-effective* level). The appropriate level of support must be determined by problem requirements, user preferences and style, and the economic assessment of values delivered relative to costs incurred.

A word-idea base, whether previously stored, currently entered by a user, or currently generated by the computer under user control, can be thought of as a special kind of data base (in which no numeric quantitative data appears). The elements of a word-idea base are to be placed within certain logical frameworks, associated with one another in certain ways, and selected for display under certain rules according to user initiated requests. Idea processing support may thus be likened more fruitfully to data base concepts than it can to word processing. Word processing (which is really text-document processing) deals in much larger chunks of data than idea processing need consider. In idea processing, the elemental word-symbol chunks need to be related by the user to one another in a variety of ways, but the user need not be concerned with extensive grammatical structures for sentences and stylistic concerns for sentences, paragraphs, and larger text segments. The associative linkages between word-symbols in idea processing are supported more by means of simple format than by complete context. Relevant context is elaborated upon in the mind of the human thinker rather than made explicit. Formats are simple, sparse, and more structured, relying on variety of content and on relative position and juxtaposition to aid idea search and development rather than the style and context of larger chunks of text. The system must support the synthesis of relatively short word-symbol strings, but be able to place or list them in potentially large categories.

Based on the above general considerations, the concepts, terminology, and functions of computer data base organization and data base processing can be examined for their applicability to the special cases of idea processing support. The following chapter will refer to the noncomputer methods and theoretical models mentioned in this chapter in order to derive and present more specific functional specifications for a variety of idea processing support modules.

Review Questions, Exercises, and Discussion Topics

Review Questions

1. What is the source of ideas, according to Locke?
2. As defined in this chapter, idea processing is a process with inputs and outputs. What are its inputs and what are its outputs?
3. In order to support creative idea processing, is it essential that AI methods be used to simulate the human thinking process? State the reasoning behind your answer.
4. Must all human idea processing activity be goal directed? Is all human idea processing directed at decision making?
5. Identify several ways in which idea processing is necessary or can be relevant to the decision process.
6. What, if any, evidence is there that high level executive decision making depend on forms of idea processing other than structured analytical methods?
7. What are the four stages of a creative process described by Wallas?
8. What relationships, if any, do each of the stages of Wallas' model of a creative process have to the stages of Simon's model of a decision process?
9. Describe what is meant by "divergent thinking." How is divergent thinking related, if at all, to creativity?
10. Is there any connection between problem discovery and creativity? Describe any connection there might be.
11. What is a metaphor? How is metaphorical thinking related to creativity? How is it related to problem discover or problem solving?
12. What two hypotheses underlie Osborn's brainstorming process?
13. Name nine verb checklist items used in Parnes' creative problem solving method.
14. How might the technique of successive generalization aid in problem solving?
15. Which type of brain hemispheric thinking, right or left, are the processes of metaphorical and divergent thinking associated with?

16. Which brain hemispheric thinking style, left or right, can be characterized as being less linearly structured? Explain your answer.
17. What can be concluded, if anything, about the relevance of cognitive style to the design of support systems?
18. In what ways might creativity be relevant, and in what ways might it be irrelevant, to the development and analysis of scenarios?
19. What is meant by an "engineering approach" to finding and developing computer methods for idea processing support?
20. What can be utilized as points of departure for developing idea processing support software?
21. What are the three generic levels of support for idea processing proposed in this chapter?
22. In what way might standard word processing software serve to support idea processing?
23. What aspects of idea processing seem to lend themselves to support by means of a data base type of system?

Exercises

1. Describe a problem derived from your own experience that could most appropriately utilize divergent thinking. Create as long a list as you can of potential alternative solutions to the problem.
2. Develop a summarized set of three scenarios for a particular business situation: each one starting from different initial conditions that can be respectively characterized as optimistic, pessimistic, and most likely.
3. List several metaphors for (a) the entity "computer," (b) the entity "executive." Next to each metaphor, briefly note the essence of the connection between the metaphor and the original entity.
4. Describe an instance from your own experience, or interview someone else to obtain a description of an instance from their experience, in which a complex, poorly defined problem situation was ultimately resolved through finding a creative solution. Describe the stages of the process that took place. In what ways do they relate to the Wallas model?

Discussion Topics

1. Argue either for or against this proposition: A computer can ultimately be made to demonstrate human intelligence.
2. Argue either for or against this proposition: A computer can ultimately be made to demonstrate human creativity.
3. Argue either for or against this proposition: A computer-based expert system to be used as an expert creative consultant can now be designed and implemented.
4. Argue either for or against this proposition: A computer-based idea processing support system can now be designed and implemented based on what is known about noncomputer individual and group methods of supporting creative thinking.

References

Bertalanffy, L. von. 1951. "General Systems Theory: A New Approach Unity of Science." *Human Biology* December:303–61.

Bogen, J. E. 1977. "Some Educational Implications of Hemispheric Specialization." *The Human Brain* edited by M. C. Wittrock, Englewood Cliffs, N.J.: Prentice-Hall.

Cowan, T. A. 1963. "Decision Theory in Law, Science and Technology." *Rutgers Law Review* 17(Spring)3.

Csikszentmihalyi, M., Getzels, J. W. 1971. "Discovery Oriented Behavior and the Originality of Creative Products: A Study with Artists." *Journal of Personality and Social Psychology* 19:47–51.

Dreyfus, S. A. 1981. *Formal Models vs. Human Situational Understanding; Inherent Limitations on the Modeling of Business Expertise. ORC 81–3,* Berkeley: University of California, February.

Fulgosi, A., Guilford, J. P. 1968. "Short Term Incubation In Divergent Production." *American Journal of Psychology* 81:241–46.

Gordon, W. 1961. *Synectics: The Development of Creative Capacity.* New York: Harper & Row.

Guilford, J. P. 1967. *The Nature of Human Intelligence.* New York: McGraw-Hill.

Guilford, J. P. 1975. "Creativity: A Quarter Century of Progress." In *"Perspectives in Creativity",* edited by I. A. Taylor, and J. W. Getzels, Chicago: Aldine Publishing Company.

Huber, G. P. 1983. "Cognitive Style As a Basis for MIS and DSS Designs: Much Ado About Nothing?" *Management Science* 29(May)5:567–97.

Huysmans, J. H. B. M. 1970. *The Implementation of Operations Research.* New York: John Wiley & Sons.

Isenberg, D. J. 1984. *Field Research On Managerial Thinking: Seven Findings, Seven Puzzles.* Working Paper 9–785–040, Division of Research, Harvard Business School, August.

Kahn, H., Wiener, A. J. 1967. *The Year 2000.* New York: The Macmillan Company.

Locke, John. 1690. "An Essay Concerning Human Understanding." in *Readings In the Theory of Knowledge,* edited by J. V. Canfield and F. H. Donnell, Jr. 155–69 Appleton-Century-Crofts, division of Meredith Corporation.

Mintzberg, H. 1976. "Planning On the Left Side and Managing On the Right." *Harvard Business Review,* July–August.

Osborn, A. 1963. *Applied Imagination: Principles and Procedures of Creative Thinking.* New York: Scribner's.

Parnes, S. 1967. *Creative Behavior Guidebook.* New York: Scribner's.

Rickards, T. 1974. *Problem Solving Through Creative Analysis.* Reading, Mass.: John Wiley and Sons.

Sackman, Harold, Citrenbaum, Ronald L. 1972. *Online Planning—Towards Creative Problem-Solving.* Englewood Cliffs, N.J.: Prentice-Hall, Inc.

Simon, Herbert A. 1960. *The New Science of Management*. New York: Harper and Row.

Taggart, W., Robey, D. 1981. "Minds and Managers: On the Duel Nature of Human Information Processing and Management. *Academy of Management Review,* 6:2:187–95.

Taggart, W., Robey, D. 1982. "Human Information Processing in Information and Decision Support Systems." *MIS Quarterly* 6(June)2:61–73.

Taylor, I. A. 1972. "A Theory of Creative Transactualization: A Systematic Approach to Creativity with Implications for Creative Leadership." *Occasional Paper* 8, Buffalo, N.Y.: Creative Education Foundation.

Turing, A. "Computing Machinery and Intelligence." *Mind* 59:236.

Wallas, Graham. 1926. *Art of Thought*. New York: Harcourt Brace.

Zaidel, E. 1980. quoted by Scmeck, H. M. Jr. "Two Brains of Man: Complex Teamwork." *New York Times* January 8:C1–C3.

Toward Functional Specifications for Idea Processing Support Systems

9

This chapter describes the functions of a potential set of computer support modules for idea processing (IP)* based on the concepts and methods presented in chapter 8. The framework for formulating and discussing these functional modules will be to:

1. Identify potentially computer-supportable IP functions;
2. For these functions, identify support tasks at each of the three levels of IP support defined in chapter 8, (level 1, secretarial support—level 2, framework-paradigm support—level 3, generative support);
3. Illustrate the allocation of tasks between the computer and the user at each of the supportable levels.

The purpose of the material presented in this chapter will be to serve as a basis for the development of IP software and to provide a framework for positioning, understanding and assessing current and future IP software as it becomes available.

---

*An earlier discussion of support for creative processes can be found in Young (1983).

General Supportability of Human Idea Processing

Idea processing has been described in the previous chapter as the capturing, relating, and synthesizing of individual ideas into larger contexts of meaningful problems. As stated previously, the origination of ideas and the creation and recall of mental associations that link them are human processes that may not be rendered as explicit logical operations in all cases. But once ideas, individually and in larger associated sets, become available as conscious entities, many standard data processing operations can be seen to become applicable. Basic data operations commonly recognized as logical steps (Burch et al. 1983) used in converting data to information include:

1. *Capturing* Recording data reflecting an event or occurrence in some form that enables it to be subsequently retrieved and processed further.
2. *Verifying* Checking to assure that data was captured and recorded correctly.
3. *Classifying* Classifying data into categories that are meaningful to a user.
4. *Arranging* Placing data into some specified sequence or relative juxtaposition.
5. *Summarizing* Combining data in a mathematical sense by means of arithmetic aggregation or logically reducing data by extracting only certain elements from a larger set to represent some desired aspect of interest to the user.
6. *Calculating* Mathematical and/or logical computation.
7. *Storing* Places data onto some storage medium for its retention and availability for retrieval.
8. *Retrieving* Searching out data, gaining access to it, and making it available for subsequent processing and/or display to a user.
9. *Reproducing* Duplicates data within the same medium or between different media for purposes of convenience, back-up, record keeping, or serving different processes in different ways according to their respective needs.
10. *Disseminating/communicating* Transferring data from one place to another and ultimately to one or more users.

Representations of ideas, seen as nonnumeric data with special meanings, can be the object of each of the above data operations except for the mathematical forms of *summarizing* and *calculating*. The processing of ideas into larger contextual patterns that are meaningful to a problem area of concern to a user, can be seen as being analogous, at least in part, to the processing of raw data into meaningful information in more traditional computer applications. Because of the semistructured and variable nature of human idea processing, interactive user control is essential, as it is in the more quantitative forms of decision support. The broad outline of idea processing support should then consist of a dynamic process in which the user can selectively and repeatedly refer to certain functional commands or desired results and thereby initiate a series of data processing operations, each of which acts upon idea representations as the raw data of the process. While the commonality of idea processing support with other computer applications is their mutual use of generic data processing operations at a basic processing level, its uniqueness is the nature of the particular functions and desired results that these operations comprise and operationalize. The functions of idea processing support systems can be derived from noncomputerized methods of idea processing already known to be useful, just as the functions of DSS software are derived from previously known methods of quantitative and logical analysis.

Supportable Idea Processing Functions

Based on a review of methods of idea processing discussed in chapter 8, particular functions requiring readily identifiable data processing operations as central to their utility include the following:

1. *Divergent searches for alternative ideas.*
   This function centers on the *classification* of ideas and *arranging* combinations of juxtaposed ideas.
2. *Problem redefinition and generalization.*
   This function focuses on *classifying* and *arranging* ideas into logical hierarchies reflecting relative degrees of generality and specificity with respect to associated dimensions.
3. *Idea manipulation (transformation) aids (Parnes' list).*
   This series of functions require certain logical operations (*calculating* in the logical sense) to be performed based on particular kinds of *classifying* schemes.
4. *Metaphorical association.*
   This function depends on the association of ideas by *classifying* and *arranging* ideas in a variety of unusual ways.
5. *Scenario building and analysis.*
   This method requires *summarizing, storing, retrieving,* and *communicating* certain key events or situational elements in a historical sequence.

In addition to the central data processing operations noted above, all of the above methods normally require the data operations of *capturing, verifying, storing, retrieving,* and *communicating* to be performed, whether this is done manually using chalkboards, paper and pencil, or by other means to extend human memory. The following sections will describe how these functions can be supported by particular computer support modules. To facilitate reference, each module discussed will be uniquely identified by a classification code comprised of three numerical components:

1. A method type number,
2. A support level number (1, 2, or 3)
3. A unique module number, sequentially numbering each functional module within method-support level classification prefixes.

While functional modules for each method will be described and their use illustrated at each particular level of support, it should be noted that, in practice, mixed levels of support are desirable and often necessary, and should be accommodated within a single support system. In the discussion which follows, it is assumed that higher levels of support are provided by utilizing all lower level modules as well as current level modules, in a cumulative manner. Thus, level 3 support, for example, is made available through the use of at least some level 3 modules, but also can utilize level 2 and level 1 modules.

Moreover, just as functionally integrated DSS software has become attractive, IP support systems comprising integrated combinations of functions supporting more than one IP method are also likely to be found to be highly desirable after users become familiar with such systems.

Divergent Search Support Modules (Method Type 1)

Divergent search in open problems that have no unique solution requires finding combinations of ideas or elements of ideas that can subsequently be assessed for their utility. A noncomputer approach to supporting divergent search in engineering design problems has been called "morphological analysis" (Allen 1952). This approach can be generalized for use in a wide variety of divergent problems and can serve as the basis for the computer support functions discussed below. Morphological analysis involves: (*a*) defining the main dimensions of a problem, (*b*) listing as many alternative levels or states within each dimension as can be identified, (*c*) forming combinations across all dimensions of these individual dimensional alternatives in order to generate all or a large variety of problem approaches, and (*d*) reviewing and assessing these combinations in order to select a feasible and preferred solution. This general approach is illustrated in exhibit 9.1.

Using this framework as a general reference, computer support functions for divergent search at each of the three levels previously defined are described in the following discussion and illustrative examples.

Divergent Search Support Level 1—The Secretarial Level

At this lowest support level, the support system should be able to perform, in an analogous way, all those tasks that could be usefully done by a skilled stenographer taking dictation, transcribing the material captured for subsequent review, modification, and integration with additional newly-dictated material, according to the user's directions.

At this level of divergent search support, the user provides the dimensions (or category headings) and the idea elements within them. These elements are entered and are to be combined within an input format provided by the computer. The input format should facilitate the user's task of classifying the idea

Exhibit 9.1

Morphological Analysis Method Illustration

STATE PROBLEM: (Example) *Seek a new transportation system.*
IDENTIFY RELEVANT DIMENSIONS:

A. POWER SOURCE   B. CONTAINER-VEHICLE
C. CONTROL MECHANISM   D. PATHWAY

LIST ALTERNATIVES WITHIN EACH DIMENSION

A. Power source	B. Container-veh.	C. Control mechanism	D. Pathway/ medium
1. electric	1. conveyor belt	1. user-driven	1. paved road
2. gasoline	2. wheeled vehicle	2. chaffeured	2. airways
3. nuclear	3. suspended "basket"	3. automated	3. waterways
4. steam	4. wheel-less container	4. semiautomated	4. space trajectory
5. solar			5. fixed track

FORM COMBINATIONS (400 possible combinations in this case)* 80 "A1" Combinations

A1-B1-C1-D1	A1-B1-C2-D1	A1-B1-C3-D1	A1-B1-C4-D1
A1-B1-C1-D2	A1-B1-C2-D2	A1-B1-C3-D2	A1-B1-C4-D2
A1-B1-C1-D3	A1-B1-C2-D3	A1-B1-C3-D3	A1-B1-C4-D3
A1-B1-C1-D4	A1-B1-C2-D4	A1-B1-C3-D4	A1-B1-C4-D4
A1-B1-C1-D5	A1-B1-C2-D5	A1-B1-C3-D5	A1-B1-C4-D5
A1-B2-C1-D1	A1-B2-C2-D1	A1-B2-C3-D1	A1-B2-C4-D1
A1-B2-C1-D2	A1-B2-C2-D2	A1-B2-C3-D2	A1-B2-C4-D2
A1-B2-C1-D3	A1-B2-C2-D3	A1-B2-C3-D3	A1-B2-C4-D2
A1-B2-C1-D4	A1-B2-C2-D4	A1-B2-C3-D4	A1-B2-C4-D4
A1-B2-C1-D5	A1-B2-C2-D5	A1-B2-C3-D5	A1-B2-C4-D5

(Group of 20 more "A1" combinations including "B3")
(Group of 20 more "A1" combinations including "B4")
80 "A2" Combinations (similar to above)
80 "A3" Combinations (similar to above)
80 "A4" Combinations (similar to above)
80 "A5" Combinations (similar to above)
ASSESS ABOVE COMBINATIONS FOR FEASIBILITY/DESIRABILITY

*Note: Finding "good" solutions depends on dimensions and alternatives included.

elements and arranging them within categorical dimensions. The computer should also provide a working format for the subsequent display of these classified idea elements in a manner that will aid the user in visually associating idea elements and in physically selecting the components to be synthesized into a combination that can be saved at the user's direction. Level 1 support should also provide the user with a convenient means of subsequently retrieving previously saved combinations, editing these by altering one or more components of the combination, rejecting or saving any combinations in the work area display, and selecting, formatting, and editing any desired combinations for hard copy printing at the user's option.

An example application of level 1 divergent search support is given in example 9.1.

Level 1 Modules

Module 1–1–1 Input Interface Manager

This software module manages the dialogue in which the user supplies idea elements and categorical dimension headings as inputs.

Module 1–1–2 Format/Display Manager

This module formats and displays the input elements and dimension headings supplied by the user in a form that facilitates association and provides options for displaying modified or retrieved idea combinations at various stages of an interactive work session.

Module 1–1–3 Synthesis Manager

This module facilitates the user's selection of idea elements that are to be combined into more complete multidimensional ideas.

Module 1–1–4 Edit/Modify Manager

This module enables the user to change, delete, or add idea elements that are part of previously formed combinations.

Module 1–1–5 Save/Retrieve Manager

This module supports the user in causing work in progress to be saved and in retrieving previously saved work.

Module 1–1–6 Print Manager

This module implements the user's option to print out hard copy representations of selected results.

EXAMPLE 9.1

DIVERGENT SEARCH- LEVEL 1 SUPPORT

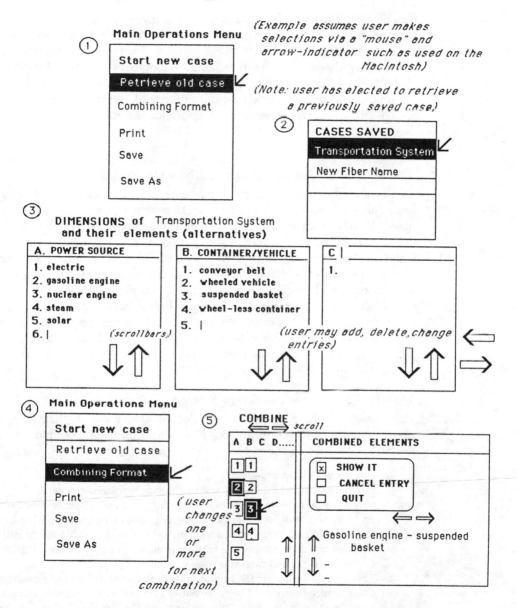

(Example assumes user makes selections via a "mouse" and arrow-indicator such as used on the MacIntosh)

(Note: user has elected to retrieve a previously saved case.)

① Main Operations Menu

- Start new case
- Retrieve old case
- Combining Format
- Print
- Save
- Save As

② CASES SAVED

- Transportation System
- New Fiber Name

③ DIMENSIONS of Transportation System and their elements (alternatives)

A. POWER SOURCE
1. electric
2. gasoline engine
3. nuclear engine
4. steam
5. solar
6. |
(scrollbars)

B. CONTAINER/VEHICLE
1. conveyor belt
2. wheeled vehicle
3. suspended basket
4. wheel-less container
5. |

C |
1. |

(user may add, delete, change entries)

④ Main Operations Menu

- Start new case
- Retrieve old case
- Combining Format
- Print
- Save
- Save As

(user changes one or more for next combination)

⑤ COMBINE scroll

| A B C D..... | COMBINED ELEMENTS |

1 1
2 2
3 3
4 4
5

- [x] SHOW IT
- [ ] CANCEL ENTRY
- [ ] QUIT

Gasoline engine - suspended basket

Divergent Search Support Level 2—The Framework-Paradigm Level

At this level the system provides the user with examples of dimensions for certain frequently encountered or generally useful problem paradigms. Sample idea element entries and sample idea combinations may also be provided by the system in order to illustrate alternative strategies for the user to follow in the search-synthesis process. Level 2 support also facilitates different user search or synthesis strategies in forming combinations. The use of level 2 divergent search support is illustrated in example 9.2. It should be noted that the uniquely level 2 functional modules described below are used in combination with some level 1 modules previously identified.

Level 2 Modules

Module 1–2–1 Reference Dimensions/Examples Provider

This module displays user selected reference dimensions and sample entries for commonly encountered problem areas within basic management functional domains such as strategic corporate planning, new product development, marketing planning and analysis, production, personnel, and financial planning. The limits of the problem area and extent of the reference frameworks provided can be determined by the data base associated with this software module while the module itself can be generically designed to retrieve and display reference material according to user selection. While the integrity of the basic reference frameworks and entries is maintained, the examples provided should be transferrable to working storage and accessible for modification and further processing by the user using any of the level 1 modules 1–1–2 through 1–1–6.

Module 1–2–2 Synthesis—Search Strategy Guide

This module can support the user in selecting among and implementing optional approaches to the formation of combinations. For example, the following options may be supported:

1. *Free form random browsing*
   In this approach the user may want to randomly scan entries across dimensions without following any particular preference order or orderly procedure for systematically examining sequenced combinations according to any predefined iterative method. This may be most suitable for an initial trial and error exploration of a very large number of possible combinations.
2. *Constrained Nucleus Scanning*
   This approach supports the user in first scanning the entries individually in order to specify any fixed requirement or primary preference with respect to any particular element or subcombination. This "nucleus" of one or more elements can be specified by the user before other dimensional elements are scanned for possible combination with this fixed starting basis.

EXAMPLE 9.2

DIVERGENT SEARCH—LEVEL 2 SUPPORT

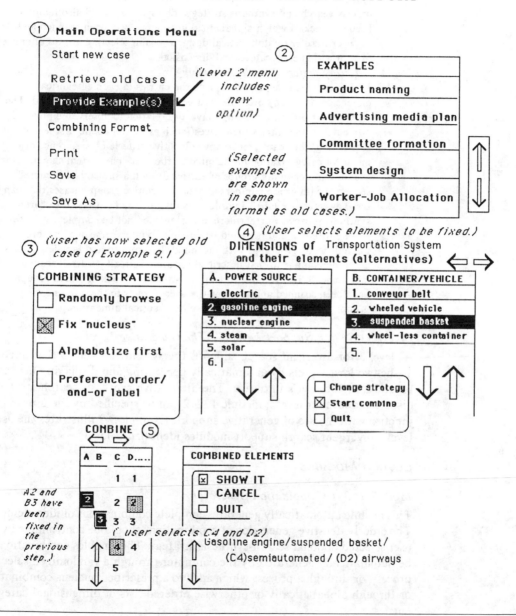

① **Main Operations Menu**

- Start new case
- Retrieve old case
- **Provide Example(s)**
- Combining Format
- Print
- Save
- Save As

(Level 2 menu includes new option)

(Selected examples are shown in same format as old cases.)

② **EXAMPLES**
- Product naming
- Advertising media plan
- Committee formation
- System design
- Worker-Job Allocation

③ *(user has now selected old case of Example 9.1)*

COMBINING STRATEGY
- ☐ Randomly browse
- ☒ Fix "nucleus"
- ☐ Alphabetize first
- ☐ Preference order/ and-or label

④ *(User selects elements to be fixed.)*

DIMENSIONS of Transportation System and their elements (alternatives)

A. POWER SOURCE
1. electric
2. **gasoline engine**
3. nuclear engine
4. steam
5. solar
6. |

B. CONTAINER/VEHICLE
1. conveyor belt
2. wheeled vehicle
3. **suspended basket**
4. wheel-less container
5. |

- ☐ Change strategy
- ☒ Start combine
- ☐ Quit

⑤ **COMBINE**

```
A B   C D.....
      1 1
 2    2  2
 3    3 3
      4  4
      5
```

A2 and B3 have been fixed in the previous step.)

(user selects C4 and D2)

COMBINED ELEMENTS
- ☒ SHOW IT
- ☐ CANCEL
- ☐ QUIT

Gasoline engine/suspended basket/ (C4)semiautomated/ (D2) airways

3. *Alphabetically ordered scanning*
   In this approach the user can opt for the entries within each categorical dimension to be placed in alphabetical order as a means of facilitating an orderly search and synthesis strategy. The system should also facilitate keeping track of which alphabetical groupings have been scanned and allow the user to refer to alphabetical designations in selecting groups of entries to scan within each categorical dimension.
4. *Arbitrary preference ordered scanning*
   In this approach the user can place the entries in each categorical dimension list in any order desired before combinations are formed. The criterion for ordering need not have any relation to observable physical attributes of the entries themselves (such as in alphabetic first letter sequencing), but can refer to any subjective criteria of preference or other means of categorization in the mind of the user. The system should also enable the user to tag groups of entries in such a subjectively ordered sequence with group numbers and/or descriptive group phrases that can serve as reference labels in order to subsequently facilitate the search-synthesis process. Furthermore, ordering need not be complete with respect to an entire list, and it should be possible to intersperse one or more miscellaneous groupings with meaningfully grouped and labelled entries. In a manner similar to that described for alphabetically ordered scanning, the labels should be available to help the user keep track of which groupings have been scanned and to allow the user to refer to them in selecting groups of entries to scan within each categorical dimension.

Divergent Search Support Level 3—The Generative Level

At level 3 for divergent search support, the system can add to the functions at the two lower levels by automatically generating and displaying new combinations at the user's initiative. The alternative synthesis-search strategies discussed above for level 2 module 1–2–2 can be specified by the user in conjunction with the use of generative support. Example 9.3 illustrates the use of level 3 divergent search support modules identified below.

Level 3 Modules

Module 1–3–1 Combination Generator

This module automatically generates complete combinations of idea elements. The orderly iterative generation of combinations should be controllable by the user selected optional search-synthesis strategy. This enables combinations to be automatically generated by the computer through a randomized selection process, or through a process which adds to a prescribed nucleus combination, or through alphabetically or otherwise ordered lists of dimensional category entries.

EXAMPLE 9.3

DIVERGENT SEARCH—LEVEL 3 SUPPORT

① **Main Operations Menu**

Start new case

Retrieve old case

Provide example(s)

Generate Combinations

Combining format (for manual combine)

Print

Save

Save As

(Level 3 menu includes new option.)

② **Combining Strategy**

Before generating: *(none of these options need be selected.)*

☐ Fix nucleus

☐ Alphabetize

☐ Preference order/ add labels, comments

☒ Generate in order. *(Selected unless changed by the user.)*

☐ Generate randomly.

③ **Display Strategy**

(Indicates 5 at a time unless changed by the user.)

Show | 4 | at a time.

Continuously scroll?

☒ No

☐ Yes

Show labels/comments?

☒ No

☐ Yes

④ **GENERATED COMBINATIONS**

    A1   B1   C1   D1

1. electric/conveyor belt/user driven/paved road

label:

comments:
                              D2

2. electric/conveyor belt/user driven/airways
                              D3

3. electric/conveyor belt/user driven/waterways
                              D4

4. electric/conveyor belt/user driven/space trajectory

☐ Quit

☐ Go on

Module 1–3–2 Combination Display Strategy Manager

This module should enable the user to control the number of combinations to be shown in any given display grouping, to choose between a static one frame at a time display or an automatically continuously scrolled display, and to opt for displays with or without various optional labels and associated headings or user comments.

Redefinition / Generalization Support Modules (Method Type 2)

As described in chapter 8, the method of successive generalization has been used in order to remove boundaries and constraints associated with specific entities or means of implementation in order to arrive at more generic underlying purposes or principles. Successive generalization requires the construction of a hierarchy of entities, with each higher level entity representing a more general form of the essential nature, purpose, or some salient characteristic of the next lower level entity. The successively generalized hierarchy of entities thus comprise a series of logical sets, with each set representing a subset of the next larger set in the series. When attempting to remove boundaries and thereby arrive at a less constrained heart of the matter understanding of purposes or utility, the direction of building the hierarchy is usually to work from the particular toward the more general. This is illustrated in exhibit 9.2.

Redefinition/Generalization Support Level 1—The Secretarial Level

Level 1 support for redefinition/generalization can be generally described in a similar manner to that of level 1 support for divergent search with respect to its essentially secretarial nature. However, the particular functions of some support modules will differ because the logical function of generalizing in a hierarchical series differs from that of specifying categorical dimensions, identifying, and combining their elements. Thus the method 2–level 1 modules identified below will be referred to by the same or similar names as method 1–level 1 modules, although specifics of their functions will clearly differ. In addition to the modules identified below as specifically designed to support method 2, the *save/retrieve manager (module 1–1–5)* and the *print manager (module 1–1–6)* previously listed for method 1 should be sufficiently general to apply to method 2 and to the subsequently discussed other methods as well. An example dialogue for level 1 support of method 2 is given in example 9.4.

Level 1 Modules

Module 2–1–1 Input/Display Interface Manager

This module manages the system-user dialogue, solicits entry by the user of an initial idea element or entity as well as subsequent higher level entities, and displays the successive entries in a logical hierarchy.

Exhibit 9.2

Problem Redefinition Using Successive Generalization

PROBLEM: Redefine/generalize our paper selling business.

The hierarchy

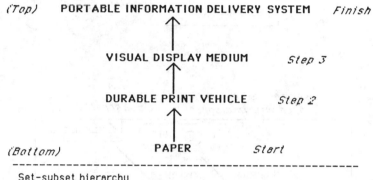

(Top)   **PORTABLE INFORMATION DELIVERY SYSTEM**   *Finish*

↑

VISUAL DISPLAY MEDIUM   *Step 3*

↑

DURABLE PRINT VEHICLE   *Step 2*

↑

(Bottom)   **PAPER**   *Start*

Set-subset hierarchy

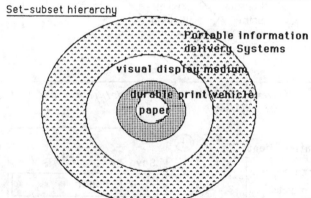

EXAMPLE 9.4

GENERALIZATION—LEVEL 1 SUPPORT

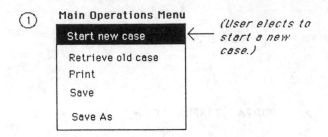

① **Main Operations Menu**

> **Start new case**
>
> Retrieve old case
> Print
> Save
>
> Save As

(User elects to start a new case.)

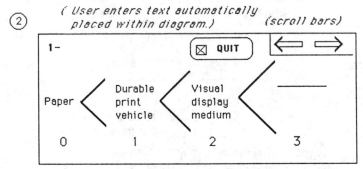

② *(User enters text automatically placed within diagram.)*

(scroll bars)

1–   ⊠ QUIT   ⇐ ⇒

Paper < Durable print vehicle < Visual display medium < _____

0   1   2   3

(User may add, modify or delete any entry at any level.)

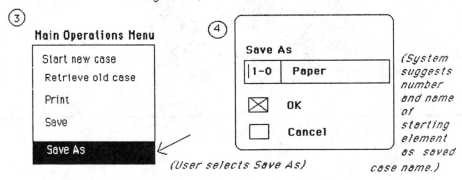

③ **Main Operations Menu**

> Start new case
> Retrieve old case
> Print
> Save
> **Save As**

(User selects Save As)

④ **Save As**

| 1-0 | Paper |

⊠ OK

☐ Cancel

(System suggests number and name of starting element as saved case name.)

Module 2-1-2 Edit/Modify Manager

This module enables the user to change, delete, or add elements within a previously created hierarchy.

Redefinition/Generalization Support Level 2—
The Framework-Paradigm Level

At this level the system provides the user with examples of hierarchical generalizations for certain frequently encountered or generally useful problem paradigms. Alternative ways of generalizing from the same starting entity are also illustrated by annotating the alternative examples presented with explanations of the salient characteristics of the entity chosen as referents in the process of generalization. The use of level 2 redefinition/generalization support is illustrated in example 9.5. Again, it should be noted that at this level both the uniquely level 2 functional modules described below are used in combination with level 1 modules previously identified.

Level 2 Modules

Module 2-2-1 Reference Generalization Hierarchy Provider

This module displays user selected reference hierarchies and their rationales for commonly encountered business and organizational problems. As stated with respect to the corresponding method 1 module, the limits of the problem area and extent of the references provided should be determined by the data base associated with this module. The examples provided should be transferrable to working storage and accessible for modification and further processing by the user.

Module 2-2-2 Generalization Strategy Guide

This module can support the user in identifying and selecting among alternative salient dimensions or features of the entity being considered as the key referents in formulating successive generalization hierarchies. Alternative criteria are presented and the alternative hierarchies formed with respect to each criterion are shown for selected examples previously stored in a data base. For example, reference to the following alternative considerations, as well as combinations of them, would usually lead to respectively different generalization hierarchies:

1. Main functional use of the entity
2. Main convenience or ease-of-use features of the entity
3. Method of gaining access to or delivery of the entity
4. Size or scale of the entity
5. Locale or environmental characteristics associated with use
6. Psychological meaning or valence associated with ownership or use

EXAMPLE 9.5

GENERALIZATION—LEVEL 2 SUPPORT

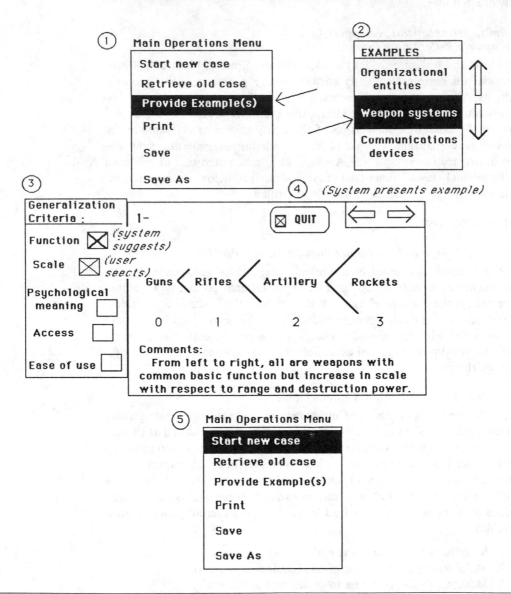

① **Main Operations Menu**
- Start new case
- Retrieve old case
- **Provide Example(s)**
- Print
- Save
- Save As

② **EXAMPLES**
- Organizational entities
- **Weapon systems**
- Communications devices

③ **Generalization Criteria :**
1-
- Function ☒ *(system suggests)*
- Scale ☒ *(user seects)*
- Psychological meaning ☐
- Access ☐
- Ease of use ☐

④ *(System presents example)*

☒ QUIT ⇐ ⇒

Guns ‹ Rifles ‹ Artillery ‹ Rockets

0   1   2   3

Comments:
From left to right, all are weapons with common basic function but increase in scale with respect to range and destruction power.

⑤ **Main Operations Menu**
- **Start new case**
- Retrieve old case
- Provide Example(s)
- Print
- Save
- Save As

EXAMPLE 9.6

GENERALIZATION—LEVEL 3 SUPPORT

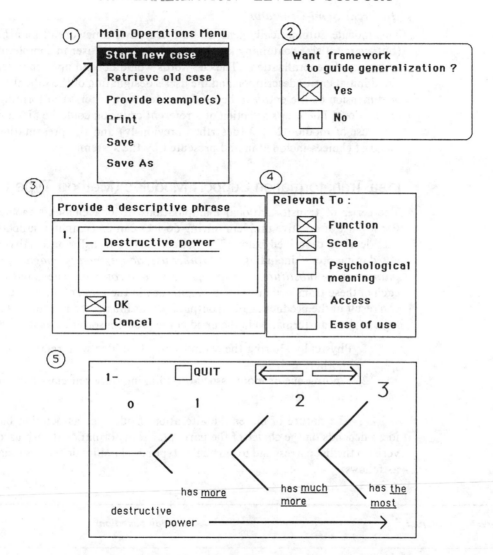

① **Main Operations Menu**

> **Start new case**
> Retrieve old case
> Provide example(s)
> Print
> Save
> Save As

② Want framework
to guide generalization ?

☒ Yes

☐ No

③ **Provide a descriptive phrase**

1. — Destructive power

☒ OK
☐ Cancel

④ **Relevant To :**

☒ Function
☒ Scale
☐ Psychological meaning
☐ Access
☐ Ease of use

⑤

1-   ☐ QUIT   ⇐ ⇒

0   1   2   3

has more   has much more   has the most

destructive power ⟶

Redefinition/Generalization Support Level 3—The Generative Level

The opportunity for this level of support would appear to be quite limited without formulating new advanced artificial intelligence approaches capable of automatically generating hierarchical generalizations. A limited form of generative support capability not requiring AI techniques might be provided by the generation of a partially filled-in template to be used merely as a basis for user modification and completion. Example 9.6 illustrates the use of this kind of limited level 3 support module (which is further described below).

Level 3 Module

Module 2–3–1
Hierarchy Semi-Generator

This module automatically generates a hierarchy framework of an arbitrary (but average) size containing key cue words to aid the user in completing the hierarchy of generalizations. The cue words would depend upon the user provided initial entity description and the user's designation of the salient feature or dimension of the entity to be used as a referent criterion in forming generalizations. The user's selection of a referent criterion could be aided by the prior use of module 2–2–2 (described previously) and the presentation of a menu of choices included in and presented by the system.

Idea Transformation Support Modules (Method Type 3)

The series of transformational manipulations of idea elements included in Parnes' list of creative problem solving devices can be computer supported at each level as described below. The list consists of transformational verbs as noted in chapter 8, including: *put to other use, adapt, modify, magnify, minify (miniaturize), substitute, rearrange, reverse, and combine*. The application of each of these transformations to an input idea in the mind of a problem solver can result in the production of an output idea, as illustrated in exhibit 9.3. The logic of the transformation in the mind of the problem solver depends on either:

1. Physically altering the components of an idea with relation to one another; and/or
2. Finding one or more associations linking different classifications or sets of ideas.

The nature of either the alteration of ideas or association between ideas depends on the choice of the particular transformational verb used. The verbs in the list correspond to particular types or classifications of associations, as follows:

Category:	Verbs:	Association based on:
I	put to other use, substitute, adapt	function
II	modify, magnify, minify (miniaturize)	physical dimensions
III	rearrange, reverse	location
IV	combine	general association
	(can refer to one or more of the above types)	

Exhibit 9.3
The Idea Transformation Process

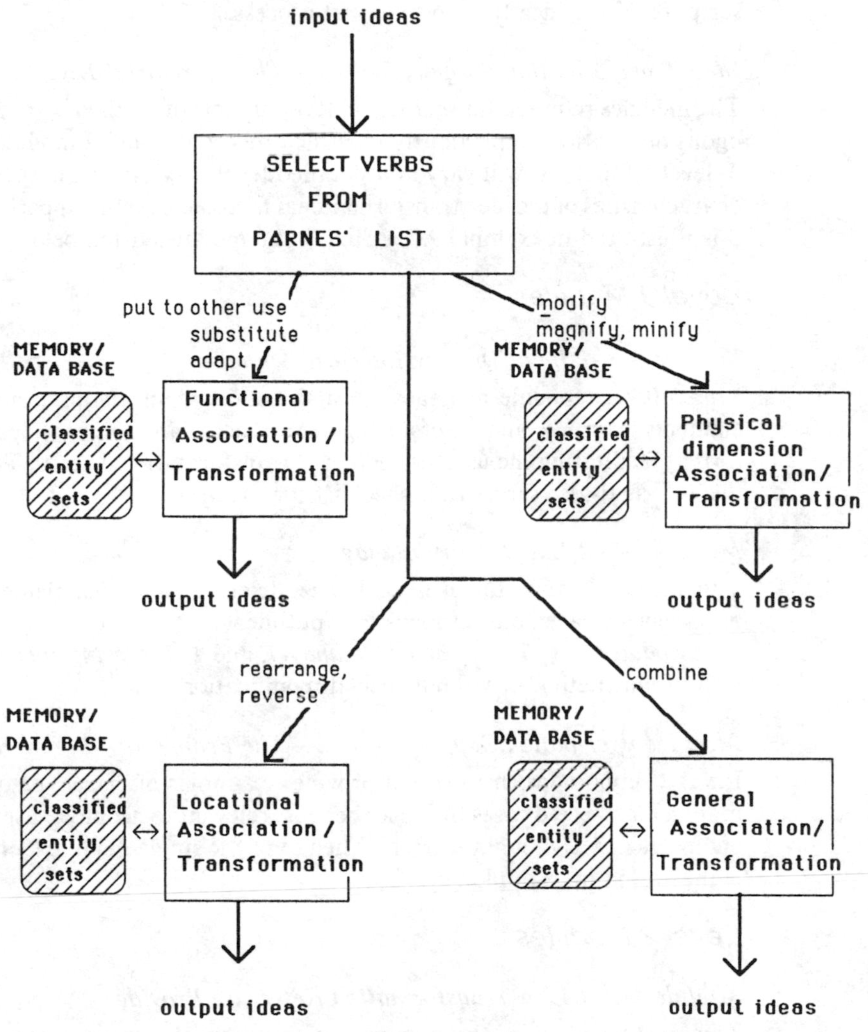

input ideas

↓

**SELECT VERBS
FROM
PARNES' LIST**

put to other use
substitute
adapt

modify
magnify, minify

MEMORY/
DATA BASE

classified
entity
sets

↔ **Functional
Association /
Transformation**

MEMORY/
DATA BASE

classified
entity
sets

↔ **Physical
dimension
Association/
Transformation**

output ideas

output ideas

rearrange,
reverse

combine

MEMORY/
DATA BASE

classified
entity
sets

↔ **Locational
Association /
Transformation**

MEMORY/
DATA BASE

classified
entity
sets

↔ **General
Association/
Transformation**

output ideas

output ideas

Each of these types of characteristic associations leads to different paths of linkage between different object sets, or to different ways of creating a physical rearrangement of idea components, thereby resulting in different output ideas.

The support modules described below are derived from this general description of the idea transformational process.

Idea Transformation Support Level 1—The Secretarial Level

The modules required for secretarial level support of method 3 are either analogous or identical to previously identified methods 1 and 2 modules. Method 3–level 1 functions will vary at a detailed level because of the special logical characteristics of the idea transformational method. Level 1 support for method 3 is illustrated in example 9.7, utilizing the modules listed below.

Level 1 Modules

Module 3–1–1 Input/Display Interface Manager

This software module manages the dialogue in which the user supplies idea elements as inputs and enters categorically associated output ideas within a format facilitating the user's selection of transformational verbs. The verb list menu format also serves as a checklist for the user.

Module 3–1–2 Edit/Modify Manager

This module enables the user to change, delete, or add idea elements as part of previously saved output ideas or input ideas.

Modules 1–1–5 save/retrieve manager, and *1–1–6 print manager,* can be utilized for method 3 without special modification.

Idea Transformation Support Level 2—The Framework-Paradigm Level

Level 2 support for this method provides examples of each type of transformation for selected cases that may be most relevant to neophyte users as either end results or as thought starters. The use of the single module identified here is illustrated in example 9.8.

Level 2 Modules

Module 3–2–1 Idea Transformation Reference Provider

This module provides the user with a selection of representative cases. For each case, when selected by the user, a relevant input idea element is displayed followed by output ideas categorically associated with each type of verb transformation. These cases can subsequently be modified by the user and saved in

EXAMPLE 9.7

IDEA TRANSFORMATION LEVEL 1 SUPPORT

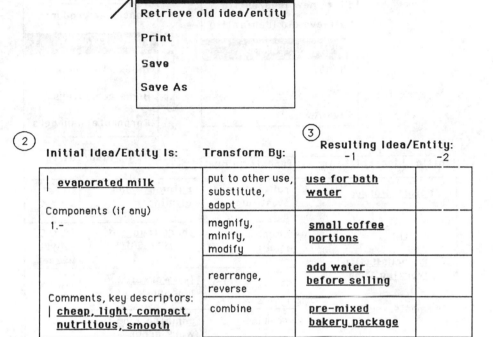

① Main Operations Menu

Start new idea/entity
Retrieve old idea/entity
Print
Save
Save As

② Initial Idea/Entity Is:

Initial Idea/Entity Is:	Transform By:	Resulting Idea/Entity: ③	
		−1	−2
evaporated milk	put to other use, substitute, adapt	_use for bath water_	
Components (if any) 1.-	magnify, minify, modify	_small coffee portions_	
	rearrange, reverse	_add water before selling_	
Comments, key descriptors: _cheap, light, compact, nutritious, smooth_	combine	_pre-mixed bakery package_	

☐ QUIT   ⟸ ⟹

the user's working files. This module leads the user toward consideration of alternative strategies for association and idea transformation by means of presenting the checklist menu that is inherent to the verb list method. For this reason, it would appear that no special additional module (similar in purpose to that of method 2's *module 2–2–2 generalization strategy guide*) to guide the user toward the selection of an idea transformation strategy is needed for method 3–level 2 support.

EXAMPLE 9.8

IDEA TRANSFORMATION—LEVEL 2 SUPPORT

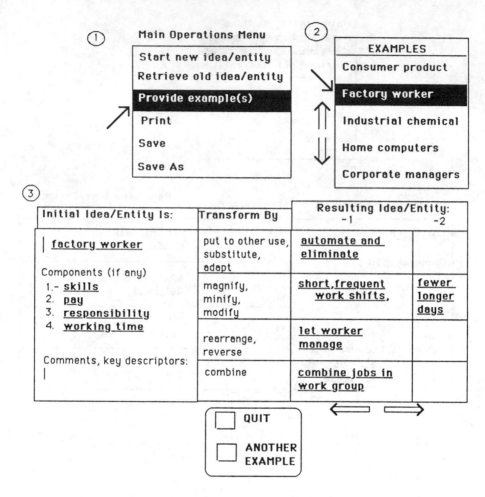

Idea Transformation Support Level 3—The Generative Level

Automatic generative level support for the rearrange and reverse forms of transformation (category III) use processing logic that produces a physical rearrangement of input idea components. The other methods depend on using the categorical basis of the association (categories I, II and IV) or the particular verb within that category as pointers to link input ideas with previously stored associated output ideas or mentally associated variations of them. The use of the modules identified below at this level are illustrated in example 9.9.

EXAMPLE 9.9

IDEA TRANSFORMATION —LEVEL 3 SUPPORT

① **Main Operations Menu**

Start new idea/entity
Retrieve old idea/entity
Provide example(s)
Print
Save
Save As

②

Initial Idea/Entity Is:	Transform By:	Resulting Idea/Entity
		-1 -2
sandwich filling	put to other use, substitute, adapt	
Components (if any) **A. meat** **B. cheese** **C. sauce covering** **D. garnish sprinkle**	magnify, minify, modify	
	rearrange, reverse	☒ AUTOMATIC ☒ GO ON A.meat ☐ MANUAL ☐ CANCEL D.garnish C.sauce
Comments, key descriptors: **above order is bottom to top**	combine	B.cheese

⟷

④

(System generated rearrangements are shown here)

☒ **REARRANGE**   **BETWEEN**   **AND**

| A B C | D E F |
| B | D |

Between A and C

| B C A | D E F |

☒ **RANDOMLY**   show
☐ **ORDERLY**   [2] at a time

☐ OK
☐ Cancel

☐ **REVERSE**   **FROM_____AND BEFORE**

| A B C | D E F |

Level 3 Modules

Module 3–3–1 Rearranger (Permutation Generator)

This module automatically generates permutations of idea components in cases for which an idea consists of more than one element; in other words it assigns idea elements (components) to different places within a sequence. Similar to the operation of the *combination generator (module 1–3–1),* the user controls the strategy of formulating and presenting the permutations to the user (see module 3–3–2 below).

Module 3–3–2 Permutation Strategy Manager

This module is used in connection with the *rearranger* described above. It enables the user to select various alternatives for the generation and display of permuted ideas, including:

1. An orderly exhaustive generation of all possible permutations, displayed in blocks of a user determined size, continuing until stopped by the user or until the last permutation has been displayed;
2. A random generation of permutations, displayed in user-determined block sizes;
3. A user-defined constrained generation (either random or orderly) of permutations, in which one or more idea components is restricted in advance to particular nth relative position assignments.

Module 3–3–3 Reverser

For ideas consisting of m elements ($m \geq 2$), this module takes the first (left-most) n idea elements ($n \geq 1$; $n < m$) and places them to the right of the remaining (m-n) idea elements. The user can select n, the size of the left-most block, or a system default will set $n = 1$.

Module 3–3–4 Transformational Associator

In a manner similar to that of *module 2–3–2 (generalizer),* this module finds associated ideas in data base storage that are linked to an input idea through a particular transformation verb. These associated ideas are then displayed to the user. The nature of the logical linkage is illustrated in exhibit 9.4. (As is true of *module 2–3–2,* if this module is to operate on a nontrivial scale, it could be said to apply an AI function analogous to mental association and to utilize a data base structure that represents a semantic network.)

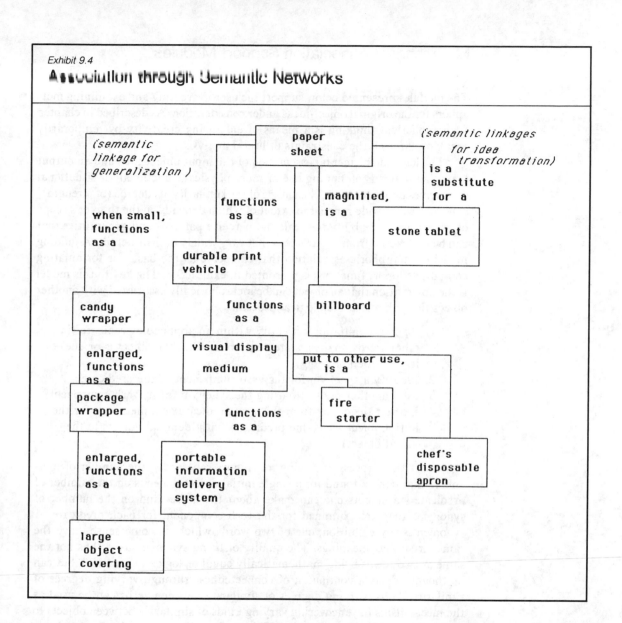

Exhibit 9.4

Association through Semantic Networks

(semantic linkage for generalization)

(semantic linkages for idea transformation)

paper sheet

is a substitute for a

when small, functions as a

functions as a

magnified, is a

stone tablet

candy wrapper

durable print vehicle

enlarged, functions as a

functions as a

billboard

package wrapper

visual display medium

put to other use, is a

enlarged, functions as a

functions as a

fire starter

large object covering

portable information delivery system

chef's disposable apron

Metaphorical Association Support Modules
(Method Type 4)

The modules presented below support the user in creating and examining metaphors for the original object-ideas under consideration. As described in chapter 8, metaphorical thinking is a means of enhancing creativity by temporarily breaking through the constraints of literal analysis.

The logic of the mental association of the input object-idea and an output metaphor depends on finding one or more physical, functional, or situational similarities between them. The nature of the similarity, its degree (or strength), can vary over a wide range, the extent of which depends on the thinker's scope of experience and ability to recall and perceive patterns and generalities that can be abstracted from object-ideas that vary widely in their details. A guiding model of metaphoric association that can serve as the basis for formulating computer support functions is presented in exhibit 9.5. The key to this model is the observation that an object can be metaphorically associated with another object through a four step logical process:

1. Place the initial object entity within an applicable predicate (in other words, make a statement about what the object is or does or its condition of being);
2. Identify a synonym for the verb component of the predicate;
3. Find another predicate using the synonym for its verb component;
4. Extract the object from this new predicate as a metaphor for the initial object (rejecting predicates with identical objects to the initial object).

Using this process of finding metaphors repeatedly, the number of metaphors that can be found for a single initial object depends on the number of predicate statements one can make about the object and on the number of synonyms that are examined for the verb component for each predicate. A synonym is, by definition, one of two words which, in some sense, have the same, or similar meanings. The quality of being synonymous is thus not the same as two terms being mathematically equal or logically identical, but can be thought of as a continuum of connectedness through varying degrees of similarity. Thus, varying degrees of similarity between verbs can be used as the mechanisms for uncovering varying kinds of similarity between objects to which those verbs can be applied. This method, like any mode of metaphoric thinking, is not a content-free logical algorithm but requires one to have some prior knowledge about the initial object and about other objects before one is capable of identifying a metaphor.

Exhibit 9.5

A Model of Metaphoric Association

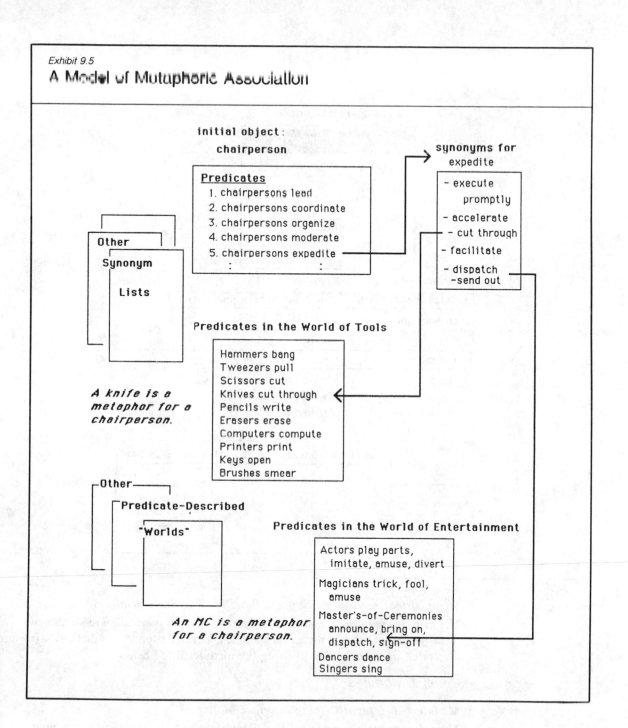

initial object:
chairperson

synonyms for
expedite

Predicates
1. chairpersons lead
2. chairpersons coordinate
3. chairpersons organize
4. chairpersons moderate
5. chairpersons expedite
   ⋮   ⋮

- execute
  promptly
- accelerate
- cut through
- facilitate
- dispatch
- send out

Other
Synonym
Lists

Predicates in the World of Tools

Hammers bang
Tweezers pull
Scissors cut
Knives cut through
Pencils write
Erasers erase
Computers compute
Printers print
Keys open
Brushes smear

A knife is a metaphor for a chairperson.

Other
Predicate-Described
"Worlds"

Predicates in the World of Entertainment

Actors play parts, imitate, amuse, divert

Magicians trick, fool, amuse

Master's-of-Ceremonies announce, bring on, dispatch, sign-off

Dancers dance
Singers sing

An MC is a metaphor for a chairperson.

EXAMPLE 9.10

METAPHORICAL ASSOCIATION—LEVEL 1 SUPPORT

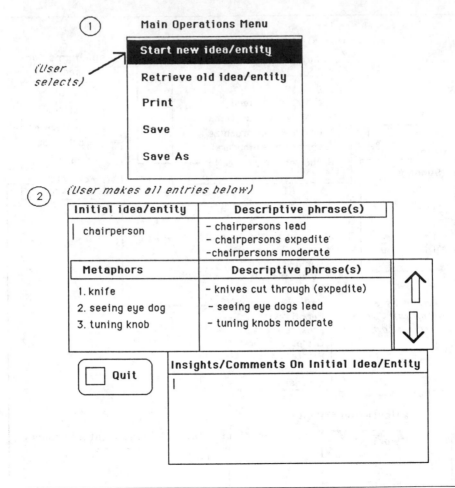

Metaphorical Association Support Level 1—The Secretarial Level

The modules required for secretarial level support of method 3 are similar to those for the previously discussed methods. Level 1 support for method 4 is illustrated in example 9.10 utilizing the modules listed below.

Level 1 Modules

Module 4–1–1 Input/Display Interface Manager

This software module manages the dialogue in which the user supplies an input entity and is prompted to then list as many other entities that are in some sense similar. The user is also prompted to enter a predicate phrase next to each entry that expresses the sense in which they are similar.

Module 4–1–2 Edit/Modify Manager

This module enables the user to change, delete, or add entities or associated predicate phrases.

Modules 1–1–5 save/retrieve manager, and *1–1–6 print manager*, can be utilized for method 4 without special modification.

Metaphorical Association Support Level 2—
The Framework-Paradigm Level

Level 2 support for this method provides examples of metaphors for selected objects that may be relevant in organizational and business situations. Both object entity couples that are metaphors for each other are displayed as well as an accompanying pair of predicates in which each entity is included. Metaphor examples are also categorized by the respective "worlds" from which they come. These categorized examples and the choices of worlds offered to the user comprise a framework upon which the user may expand by adding further entries and/or adding new worlds. The support modules identified here are illustrated in example 9.11.

Level 2 Modules

Module 4–2–1 Metaphor Example Provider

This module provides the user with a selection of representative cases. For each case, when selected by the user, a relevant input entity is displayed followed by output entities that are metaphors for the input entity. For each metaphor pair, a pair of predicates is also displayed which illustrates the sense of the metaphor. These cases can subsequently be modified by the user and saved in the user's working files.

Module 4–2–2 World Organizer

This module takes the system-provided examples accessible through *module 4–2–1* above and displays them within a grouped display format that labels each group with a heading descriptive of its world. The user can also take retrieved prior metaphor entries of his own and place them within the world categories provided. The user can also add new worlds within this module and place entities provided by the system or by the user into these worlds. Such new world definitions, when saved, become available as part of information associated with retrieved user cases, as part of the world menus provided for displaying examples, and for expanding the data base available for use in level 3 support (described below).

Module 4–2–3 Predicate-Synonym Organizer

This module lists all verb components of predicates previously stored in the system as examples and displays them within groups of synonyms. The module also facilitates the user's addition of synonyms and creation of new synonym lists to accommodate user supplied predicate entries. The use of this module

EXAMPLE 9.11

METAPHORICAL ASSOCIATION—LEVEL 2 SUPPORT

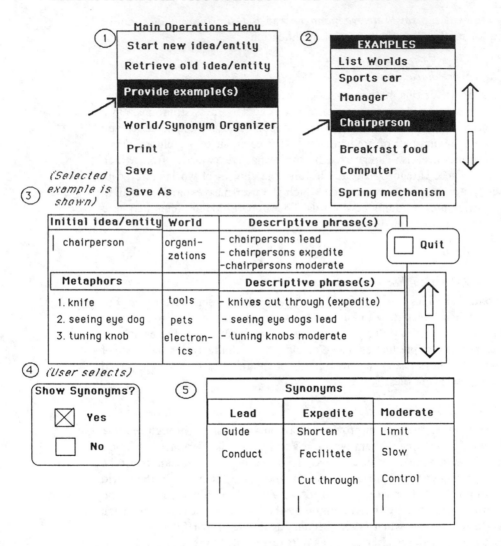

① Main Operations Menu

Start new idea/entity

Retrieve old idea/entity

Provide example(s)

World/Synonym Organizer

Print

Save

Save As

(Selected example is shown)

② EXAMPLES

List Worlds

Sports car

Manager

Chairperson

Breakfast food

Computer

Spring mechanism

③

Initial idea/entity	World	Descriptive phrase(s)
chairperson	organi-zations	– chairpersons lead – chairpersons expedite –chairpersons moderate

Metaphors		Descriptive phrase(s)
1. knife	tools	– knives cut through (expedite)
2. seeing eye dog	pets	– seeing eye dogs lead
3. tuning knob	electron-ics	– tuning knobs moderate

Quit

④ *(User selects)*

Show Synonyms?

☒ Yes

☐ No

⑤

Synonyms		
Lead	**Expedite**	**Moderate**
Guide	Shorten	Limit
Conduct	Facilitate	Slow
	Cut through	Control

may stimulate the user in perceiving new ways in which entities may be similar by means of thinking of new dimensions that can be applied to synonym development. This module also serves to build the synonym-linked data organization required for expanding level 3 support.

Metaphorical Association Support Level 3—The Generative Level

Support at the generative level for metaphorical association requires an AI type of support approach using a form of knowledge organization based on the model illustrated in exhibit 9.5. Example 9.12 illustrates the use of the module described below for the automatic user-controlled generation of metaphors.

Level 3 Module

Module 4–3–1 Metaphor Generator

This module finds metaphoric entities already in data base storage that are linked to an input entity through synonym verb components of predicates, as indicated in exhibit 9.5. The user may request that the system display one or more metaphors from particular worlds designated by the user. If the system already knows something about the input entity (that is, one or more predicate statements referring to this entity have already been stored within the system's knowledge base), the system can then seek a metaphor through the linkage of applicable verb synonyms. If the system does not already know anything about the input entity, or, at the user's option, the system will accept the user's statement(s) about the input entity as the basis for seeking verb synonym linkages (actions or states of being that apply to the input entity as well as to its metaphor entity). Any metaphors thus found are then displayed to the user. The ability of the system to generate any metaphors at all, metaphors from particular worlds, and interesting or stimulating metaphors, depends on the extent of the predicate and synonym entries stored in the knowledge base. However, it is difficult to know in advance of experimental usage what the critical minimum size might be for a nontrivial useful knowledge base for this function. It should also be noted, that the knowledge base should be expandable by the user (through the use of level 1 and 2 modules) as a by-product of usage experience.

A complete description of a data base method for generating metaphors automatically can be found in Young [1987].

EXAMPLE 9.12

METAPHORICAL ASSOCIATION—LEVEL 3 SUPPORT

Main Operations Menu

① **Start new idea/entity**

Retrieve old idea/entity

Provide example(s)

World/Synonym Organizer

Print

Save

Save As

② *(User entries)*

③ *(User selects)*

Initial idea/entity	World	Descriptive phrase(s)
chairperson	organi-zations	- chairpersons lead - chairpersons expedite -chairpersons moderate

☒ **Generate metaphors**

☐ **Manual**

☐ **Quit**

④

World ?

Any ☒

Pets ☐

Tools ☐

↑ ↓

(User can select world)

(System automatically generates metaphors)

⑤

Metaphors		Descriptive phrase(s)
1. knife	tools	-knives cut through (expedite)
2. seeing eye dog	pets	- seeing eye dogs lead
3. tuning knob	electron-ics	- tuning knobs moderate

↑ ↓

☐ **Quit**

Scenario Building and Analysis Support Modules (Method 5)

The scenario building method can also be supported at least by relieving the user of much data processing work associated with constructing and analyzing these event sequences. This kind of support can be tailored to the particular structure and general features of scenarios. Whether or not useful AI methods for the automatic generation of qualitatively described scenarios can be developed is an open question for further AI research. System functions at each of the support levels are described below.

Scenario Support Level 1—The Secretarial Level

The modules required for secretarial level support of method 5 are similar to those for other methods but are designed to fit the particular features of scenarios. Level 1 support for method 5 is illustrated in example 9.13 utilizing the modules listed below.

Level 1 Modules

Module 5-1-1 Input/Display Interface Manager

This software module manages the dialogue in which the user supplies scenario components within a standard format supplied by the system.

Module 5-1-2 Edit/Modify Manager

This module enables the user to change, delete, or add any portion of previously entered scenarios.

Modules 1-1-5 save/retrieve manager, and *1-1-6 print manager,* can be utilized for method 5 without special modification.

Scenario Support Level 2—The Framework-Paradigm Level

Level 2 support provides the user with sample scenarios and facilitates the analysis of these or user constructed scenarios. This is illustrated in example 9.14

Level 2 Modules

Module 5-2-1 Scenario Sampler

This module provides a menu of example scenarios related to business situations. For each example case, three different scenario variations can be selected and displayed : an "optimistic" scenario; a "pessimistic" scenario; and a "most likely" scenario. These displayed examples are modifiable by the user and the modified versions can be saved for future reference by the user.

EXAMPLE 9.13

SCENARIO BUILDING/ANALYSIS—LEVEL 1 SUPPORT

① Main Operations Menu

(User selects)

Start new scenario
Retrieve old scenario
Print
Save
Save As

② *(User makes entries and selections)*

Scenario Name	Version designation
Product XT Introduction	☒ Optimistic ☐ Pessimistic ☐ Most Likely ☐ Other |

③

Scenario: Product XT Introduction	Optimistic Version		
Time period	**Environment/Conditions**	**"Actor"**	**Action**
01/89	Low inflation–high employment. Moderate to good growth and income.	Our company.	Set unit price at $ 15,990. Use own sales force.
Outcomes: 1. First month sales lower than target at 10 units in test market. 2. | ⇧ ⇩		Aim at high income single men.	⇧ ⇩

(User makes entries within above suggested format.)

☐ Quit

EXAMPLE 9.14

SCENARIO BUILDING/ANALYSIS—LEVEL 2 SUPPORT

① **Main Operations Menu**

Start new scenario
Retrieve old scenario
Provide example(s)
Print
Save
Save As

(User selects) →

(Example menu shown if user chooses " Provide example(s).)

② *(User selects.)*   ③ *(User selects)*

Scenario Name	Versions
Product XT Intr	**Optimist**
	Pessimist
	Likely
↓	↓

Options	Time Periods	Actors
Group by:	⊠	☐
REMINDER DISPLAY Show Only Selections	☐	☐
Show All ⊠	☐	☐

④

Scenario: Product XT Introduction	Optimistic Version		
Time period	**Environment/Conditions**	**"Actor"**	**Action**
01/89	Low inflation-high employment. Moderate to good growth and income.	Our company.	Set unit price at $ 15,990. Use own sales force.
Outcomes: 1. First month sales lower than target at 10 units in test market. 2.	↑ ↓	Aim at high income single men.	↑ ↓

(System displays retrieved scenario according to user's choices.)

☐ Quit

Module 5-2-2 Scenario Extracter/Analysis Aid

This module enables a user to extract and display only certain aspects of a scenario that are specified by the user (eg; select all events within a particular time period, select only actions taken by "others" such as a competitor) or to reformat and display the contents of the entire scenario in other than entry sequence order (eg; in groups according to the "actor," such as our company versus a competitor; grouping all events by season rather than sequential months or days).

Scenario Support Level 3—The Generative Level

AI methods for the automatic generation in whole or in part may be developed but will not be included here. The module included below could be implemented using relatively straight forward methods to find existing scenarios according to attributes of their contents rather than by explicit reference to a particular scenario.

Level 3 Module

Module 5-3-1 Scenario Finder

This module allows the user to specify particular types of occurrences or sequences of occurrences as qualifiers for the selection of scenario cases. Example scenarios that have been previously stored and that contain within them events or event sequences entered as qualifiers by the user in the form of key words or phrases, will be found by the system and displayed to the user.

Additional Methods:
Idea Organization/Extended Memory Support

The previously discussed support functions were derived from specific methods or creativity enhancing heuristics that have already been in use for many years as interactive human processes, but which have been operating without computer support. They are not meant to be an exhaustive inventory of potential idea processing support functions. It is likely that other ways to organize, develop, and analyze ideas will be identified as computer-supportable methods. Some of these potentially supportable methods may not be immediately apparent because they represent modes of thinking that have become so commonplace that they have blended into the background of our awareness. Other methods may represent variations or evolved forms of the methods already discussed.

Two general areas that hold promise for the identification of additional support functions are:

1. General approaches to support the human process of idea or knowledge organization;

2. General approaches to extend human memory through new ways of organizing and communicating the thinking of others in both the past and the present through the medium of the computer.

With respect to the first area, particular structures for the organization and association of ideas have already been described within the context of several idea processing methods. The method of morphological analysis addresses the organization of ideas by means of defining major dimensions (or components) and identifying particular alternatives within these dimensions. The method of successive generalization uses a hierarchical form of organization but does so along a single dimension at a time, in a manner that places an idea or entity inside a larger or more general entity, and so on, like a set of conceptual Chinese boxes, one inside another. A generalized combination of these modes of idea organization is the development of a *hierarchy of ideas* along many, or all, identified dimensions of an entity simultaneously. This could be approached in a bottom-up manner, going from the more specific toward the more general, or in the reverse top-down (general toward more detailed) direction. Indeed, the latter approach is the essence of all forms of analysis, which, in a variety of forms, attempts to take a complex entity and better understand it by a process of successive decomposition into its parts. This is the process of chemical analysis, it is used in documenting a complex physical assembly through an "explosion diagram," it is used in the systems analysis documentation tool of hierarchy diagrams (part of the HIPO method), and it is represented by the outlining approach to planning large writing projects.

In contrast, moving from detailed pieces and generalizing from bottom to top involves identifying the attributes of the pieces and successively classifying or grouping them according to these attributes. This is the process of synthesis required to build anything new or to formulate taxonomies according to underlying similarities. *Hierarchical idea organization* is thus basic to both understanding things that exist and creating new things and has already been supported by a variety of representational methods. These, and other methods based on attribute listing, categorization, and hierarchical organization, could be (and have been, as described in chapter 10) supported by interactive computer systems, at least at support levels 1 and 2.

With respect to the second aspect of idea development mentioned above, that of networking human memory in the present and between past and present, several modes of computer support are possible. In a limited manner, the level 2 modes of support previously discussed are instances of extending the memory and experience of an individual by making the past experience of others available through selected case examples. Extensions of the support offered by these method-dependent examples may be found in three additional forms of memory extension support:

1. Case history analysis support;
2. Wisdom-base support ; and
3. Recent communications extract support.

Case history analysis support would be similar to aspects of scenario-related support. But while scenarios are created future "histories," cases are actual histories. Unlike scenarios, which help to illuminate what might happen given certain actions, case histories record what actually did happen when certain actions were taken. Computer support for recording, retrieving, and analyzing full context case histories can provide the user with an extended base of experience to guide present and future decision making. Case history support should facilitate comparative analysis (identifying what is similar and what is different between past and present situations) and the derivation of general policy guidelines as well as particular decisions for the current situation.

Wisdom-base support would provide the user with access to the generic kinds of principles and guidelines for action provided by recognized superior thinkers of the past and present. These prescriptions for behavior known as wisdom apply to generic categories of situations rather than to highly specific case details. They are thus not meant to provide users with an automatic specific decision or recommendation, but with a general guide to help users in coming to their own conclusions. A wisdom-base support system could operate in an analogous (but more comprehensive) manner to the type of exhibit found in the Benjamin Franklin Museum in Philadelphia, which enables the user to selectively display particular wise sayings of Franklin on a wide variety of subjects, such as lending money, marriage, war, or friendship. Organized wisdom bases should consist of categorized judgments about useful courses of action. Wisdom, when it can be found, is the highly generalized derivative of extensive experience in case analysis. If the user provides as input the salient features which categorize a situation, the wisdom-based support system shoud be able to find and retrieve general prescriptions that have been deemed successful in the past. A wisdom-base, containing such categorized and accessible generalized judgments, differs from a knowledge base associated with expert systems, the latter being:

1. More specific in the type and scope of expertise it represents;
2. More detailed in its representation of logical associations between particular aspects of a situation and its conclusions;
3. More specific in its conclusions or action recommendations for the particular case at hand.

The third type of support, recent communications extract support, would be concerned with enhancing access to the recorded relevent recent statements reflecting the ideas and conclusions of others in formulating ones own ideas and actions. Such a support system could be provided as an extension to a computer-based electronic mail message communications network, or to a computer word processing system. This type of support would enable a user to request and obtain (within established rules for safeguarding confidentiality and security) any text document or message stored in the system that would relate to the subject of current interest to the user. A means of abstracting and key word or category coding all text messages in the communications system would have to be provided as the means of linking user requests in the support system to text captured in the communications or word processing system.

Data Base Concepts and Idea Processing Support

In all of the forms of idea processing support discussed, it is necessary for users, in one way or another, to relate ideas to one another in organizing, building, analyzing, assessing and retrieving those ideas. The division of labor between the support system and the user is mainly along the lines of the system providing the kind of logical processing that is usually associated with data base systems and the user performing the final assessment of computer outputs and control functions needed to arrive at a useful final result. The computer system does the functions necessary to store, organize, categorically relate, retrieve according to user supplied attributes, format, arrange, rearrange, and display, while the user does the inferential mental processing needed to assess what the system displays and to decide on the next step in processing. The system designer for IP support systems needs a logical framework for organizing the words, phrases, and text segments representing the conceptual entities, cases, scenarios, wisdom, messages, and other forms which embody the expression of ideas. The various forms of logical data organization that can serve as referents for this purpose are the same as the basic modes of logical data base organization:

1. Hierarchical organization;
2. Network organization; or
3. Two-dimensional tables, or relational organization.

Standard data base systems can generate and display new information for a user by *projecting* selected data meeting certain attribute requirements and *joining* other data elements that have some common linkage. Idea processing support requires analogous general functions for the selection and association of idea representations (words).

While standard data bases generally may consist of numerical data elements as well as alphabetic or mixed data, idea bases usually consist of alphabetic string representations. Thus idea processing support does not include certain arithmetic types of functions (such as computing totals, subtotals, ranges, averages, percentaging, and generating new data elements by arithmetically combining existing data elements) usually included in query support functions associated with data base systems. Another difference is that the equivalent of a data element or field in an IP support system often will be much longer (in number of characters in the text string representing the idea component) than the usual length of a standard data element.

Exhibit 9.6

Relational Data Base Organization for Standard and Idea Processing Applications

A. A Standard Type: A Marketing Data Base Example

Customer

NAME	ADDRESS	INDUSTRY CODE	ANNUAL $ PURCHASES	CREDIT CODE
Acme Inc	2 Main NY	1001C	2,550,000.	AA
Metro Co.	1 Wall NY	1230A	30,000,000	A

B. Idea Processing: Metaphoric Association Example

Sports World Activities (Predicates)

ID NO.	OBJECT	VERB (ACTION OR STATE OF BEING)
0001	Teams	Play
0002	Teams	Win
0003	Teams	Lose
0004	Players	Play
0005	Players	Practice
0006	Balls	Are Thrown
0007	Scores	Are Tied

C. Idea Processing: A Case History Example

New Product Cases

PRODUCT TYPE	NAME	PRIMARY MARKET	INTRO. PRICE	INTRO. AD BUDGET	TIME TO COMPETITIVE ENTRY	SALES ($000) 1st Quarter $	Units	1st Year $	Units	Market Share (%) Yr1	Yr2
industrial cleaner	Kludge	U.S. Chemical plants	$5/gal.	$250,000.	16 months	500	100,000 gals.	1600	320,000 gals.	100.	80.
consumer food											
financial service											

Exhibit 9.6 illustrates logical relational schemas for a standard data base system and for idea bases related to several of the IP support methods previously discussed.

While it may be useful for designers to be aware of the applicability of some data base concepts to IP support, it would seem that existing data base or query software packages would be limited in their ability to provide support for many IP functions without significant modification and extension.

Review Questions, Exercises, and Discussion Topics

Review Questions

1. *a)* Are the types of computer operations known as data processing applicable to supporting idea processing?
   b) What is analogous about using data processing operations to convert *data* into *information* and the need to process raw ideas into a more useful form?
2. What noncomputerized methods of idea processing can provide a basis for studying how idea processing computer support functions can be identified?
3. Why can't the methods of idea processing be easily automated rather than supported?
4. What kinds of standard data processing operations are relevant to the support of:
   a) Divergent search?
   b) Problem redefinition and generalization?
   c) Idea manipulation (transformation)?
5. To what extent has level 3 (generative) support been described for each of the methods discussed in this chapter?
6. *a)* Has it been proven that support of the five idea processing methods described in this chapter are the only forms of feasible support?
   b) What other general areas of idea processing support, if any, have been suggested to hold promise for support?
7. What similarities and differences are their between scenarios and case histories?
8. How might the generalized judgments that could comprise a wisdom base differ from a knowledge base appropriate for an expert system?
9. How might a hierarchical form of data base organization apply to the method of successive generalization?
10. How might relational data base organization be applied to the method of metaphorical association?
11. What is the similarity, if any, between a *join* operation that is needed to pull information together from two different relational data base records and the need to link associated idea elements? Give examples to illustrate any similarity.

Exercises

1. The examples given in this chapter assume that a "mouse-based" interface is available (for use in selecting main operations in "pull-down" menus, for pointing to a "boxed" action in order to select it, etc.).

    Redesign the examples of one of the methods, illustrating the main features of a command language type of interface that does not utilize a "mouse" or a similar selection tool.

2. Compare the relative ease of use and generally critique each of the two types of interfaces (mouse-type given in the chapter example versus your own non-mouse example) for the method you illustrated in the prior exercise.

3. Describe an application situation and develop examples that illustrate the use of level 1 and level 2 support for any one or more of the methods discussed in the chapter that might be appropriate in this case.

4. Support for each of the methods discussed in this chapter was described separately. Design and illustrate an interface example that would serve to provide an integrated framework that would include all five methods. Show how the user might choose which method was to be used. Assess whether or not it would be useful to transfer results between methods and show how the user could accomplish this.

5. Illustrate and describe an interface for support functions for a system providing access to a wide-ranging business wisdom-base.

Discussion Topics

1. Discuss the likelihood that managers and staff specialists will or will not be receptive to support software based on the use of some or all of the methods described in this chapter. Which kinds of people are more likely to be more receptive, which are less likely? How might a software vendor explain what these tools are good for in an introductory marketing campaign?

2. Discuss the forms more advanced kinds of level 3 support might take for each of the five methods for which support functions were described in this chapter.

3. Discuss how much more useful a system might be that included each of the kinds of level 3 support you identified in the previous discussion topic item 2.

4. Discuss the likely utility of the kinds of support functions discussed in this chapter for nonbusiness application areas (such as scientific work, historical analysis, fiction writing, educational methods design, invention, or public policy development).

References

Allen, M. 1952. *Morphological Creativity.* Englewood Cliffs, N.J.: Prentice-Hall.

Anderson, J., Bower, G. 1973. *Human Associative Memory.* Washington, DC: Winston.

Burch, J. G. Jr., Strater, F. R., Grudnitski, G. 1983. *Information Systems: Theory and Practice.* (3rd ed.) New York: John Wiley & Sons.

Simmons, R. F. 1973. Semantic Networks: Their computation and use for understanding English sentences. In *Computer Models of Thought and Language.* Edited by R. C. Schank, and K. M. Colby. San Francisco: Freeman.

Young, L. F. 1983. Computer Support for Creative Decision-Making: Right-Brained DSS. In *Processes and Tools for Decision Support.* Edited by H. G. Sol. Amsterdam, New York: North-Holland Publishing Company.

Young, L. F. 1987. The Metaphor Machine: A Database Method for Creativity Support. *Decision Support Systems,* 3:309–17.

Idea Processing Software and Development Guidelines

10

In this chapter, two of the first idea processing support software packages to appear commercially are described and assessed, and other early software development and experimental efforts are discussed. These early experiences and assessments of idea processing support software are examined in the light of research on human decision-making behavior. Based on this examination, guidelines for further software development are presented.

It is assumed that additional commercial software for idea processing support of various kinds will continue to become available. While it is not possible to provide extensive and timely coverage of this dynamically changing situation through the textbook medium, the material of this chapter may aid prospective users in evaluating and selecting new offerings as they become available.

"ThinkTank": The Tip of the Iceberg Emerges

The first commercial product to use the designation "idea processor" was *ThinkTank®*. The marketers of ThinkTank (Living Videotext, Inc. Mountain View, California) claim that it opens up "the creative synergy between you and your computer" by helping users put initial ideas into an organized outline form.

When first introduced, the package's vendor reportedly had difficulty gaining the acceptance of retail computer stores because of the problem of explaining the precise function and utility of this nontraditional application. Since then, thanks largely to early triers and word of mouth, ThinkTank has gained wide acceptance. As a reliable indicator of market acceptance, ThinkTank gained the competition of other packages such as Ashton Tate's *Framework®*, which supports outlining as well as other functions, including spreadsheets, graphs, and word processing (Brevdy 1984), and Select Information Systems' *Freestyle®*, an outline processor linked to word processing software (O'Connor 1984). As a further mark of success, new versions of ThinkTank have been issued by Living Videotext. These include a RAM-resident outline processor called *Ready!* and a multifunctional package called *MORE,* which adds the ability to create presentations and hierarchical diagrams from outlined material. Another recent competitive outline processor package is called *MaxThink* (MaxThink, Inc.), which includes an expanded command repertoire (Spezzano 1986).

Applications of this kind of idea organization support tool are unlimited as to their subject, with some of the most common applications being the planning of proposals, reports, or other written documents. Outlining has been recommended to generations of high school English students as the first step in writing a composition. But outlining a subject on paper has a more generic function as a kind of visible working storage for aiding the organization of ideas into a hierarchical logical framework. Idea organization in general, and hierarchical idea structuring in particular, was identified in chapter 9 as one of the areas of computer support that holds potential for development in a variety of forms. The ThinkTank package belongs within this general functional category of hierarchical idea organization support. Hierarchical idea organization, and thus the use of ThinkTank, can apply not only to planning the structure of a piece of writing, but to the development of one's mental model of any complex entity, including the design of a system, the formulation of a competitive strategy, a philosophy, or a corporate or national policy. Whether or not a complete written document is to be prepared following the development of a hierarchical outline, the outline serves the purpose of recording and reflecting back the user's view of the content and structure of the conceptual entity being considered. Information systems designers are familiar with other hierarchical documentation techniques such as Warnier-Orr diagrams or HIPO hierarchy diagrams, in which the system-subsystem-subprocess-substep structure of an information processing system (or data set-data element organization) is represented in the form of annotated diagrammatic symbols* that are logically equivalent to hierarchical outlines.

---

*An extension of hierarchical outlining support could draw HIPO and Warnier-Orr diagrams as a component of a systems designer's "tool kit." I have designed such an interface for a Macintosh called DISH (Documenting Integrated Systems Hierarchies).

EXAMPLE 10.1

A THINKTANK APPLICATION EXAMPLE.

Defining A Marketing Plan

File   Edit   Extra   Fontsize

+ Market plan for our new software package
    + Define the market
        | Primary users
            − College students
            − Systems analysts
            + Applications
            + Value of application to users
            + Size of user group
        + Secondary users
            − Trade school students
            − Miscellaneous business users
    + Pricing and sales estimates
    + Promotion-advertising
        + Premiums
        + Press releases
        + Media advertising
    + Cash flow and profit estimates

A support system that is well designed to aid the user in outlining and performing related ancillary functions must be more than just a specially formatted word processor or automatic diagram generator; its true function is to serve as a kind of lever for the mind in thinking through the structure of hierarchically related concepts. Its leverage derives from type 1 and type 2 support levels (as defined in chapter 9) in helping to:

1. Release the user from the many manual tasks involved so that effort can be extended in more comprehensive cognitive analysis; and

2. Provide a visual and highly dynamic "scratchpad" extension to the user's working memory (a function that is only partially performed by static and unwieldy written, paper scratchpads).

Example 10.1 shows a ThinkTank application of defining a marketing plan. A user could develop such an outline by initially making entries as they come to mind, without regard to any logical hierarchical relationships between individual ideas or topics. Later, the user can rearrange the individual entries into related groups or topics, providing each topic with a separate heading or subheading entry, as required. Alternatively, one could first define major and minor topics, and then partially or completely group detail entries under these topics as they are entered. Thus users can follow their own thought process and style, working out a hierarchical structure from the bottom up, from the top down, or in any mixed mode that ultimately leads to a consistent logical hierarchy that is satisfactory to the user. The system makes it easy to collect topics at any level, rearrange entire sections or selected items with a few keystrokes or "mousestrokes," or to add or delete entire classes or items.

ThinkTank automatically provides and updates the "+" sign or the dash "−" preceding each text string entry. The "+" indicates that associated subentries have been previously entered and stored (whether or not they are currently displayed) for this line at a lower level in the hierarchy. The "−" preceding a line indicates that no lower level entries have yet been subsumed under this entry. The Macintosh version of ThinkTank makes use of the Macintosh interface features of "pull down" menus and the mouse-controlled pointer to select and operate on specific lines. Selecting any line preceded by a "+" sign and double-clicking the mouse causes lower level entries to appear in the display. The lower level lines are as easily made to disappear by again double-clicking on a selected higher level entry.

The "extra" pull down menu includes two functions the user can select: "search" and "sort." When "search" is selected the user is asked to enter key words which the system subsequently searches for in the full outline. If the key words are found, the system highlights them by "inverting" them, showing white letters on a black background. (The search seems overly literal, however, in that upper case letters and lower case letters are not considered by the program's logic to be equivalent.) The "sort" function places entries at the same level in the hierarchy in alphabetical order according to the text itself.

Example 10.2 (parts a through c) shows a developing sequence of major to minor topics in another ThinkTank application, that of an early version of outlining the contents of chapter 9 of this book. By using the mouse to select and move a heading by "dragging" it from its current location to a new one, all subtopics and text under it are automatically moved along with it. For example, in examples 10.2b and 10.2c the boxed-in lines have been selected. If either of these lines were moved to a different location in the hierarchy, all lower level entries would remain attached to it and would move along with it to their new relative positions in the same order. This order could, of course, also be modified by selecting and moving individual lower level lines. Lower level entries also can be moved to the left and thus automatically made into higher level entries. Similarly, a shifting towards the right of an entry places it at a lower level in relationship to the entry above it.

Text editing capabilities are also provided, making it easy for the user to modify previous entries. An option is provided so that displayed outlines can be printed with or without the leading "+" and "−" symbols.

EXAMPLE 10.2a

THINKTANK OUTLINE FOR CHAPTER 9 MAIN TOPICS

```
 ⌐                                                            ¬
    ⌕  File  Edit  Extra  FontSize

   ┌──────────────────────────────────────────────────────────┐
   │ + │Chapter 9— Toward Functional Specs for Idea Processing Support│
   │    +  Purpose, scope of this chapter                       │
   │    +  Potentially supportable IP functions from models, methods of ch 8│
   │    +  For each, specify computer-human functional allocation│
   │    +  Beyond Heuristics: Integrative-Extended Memory Forms of Support│
   │    +  Applicability of Data Base Concepts to IP functions  │
   │                                                            │
   └──────────────────────────────────────────────────────────┘
 └                                                            ┘
```

EXAMPLE 10.2b

THINKTANK OUTLINE FOR CHAPTER 9
MAIN TOPICS PLUS SOME SUBTOPICS

```
 ⌐                                                            ¬
    ⌕  File  Edit  Extra  FontSize

   ┌──────────────────────────────────────────────────────────┐
   │  +  Chapter 9— Toward Functional Specs for Idea Processing Support│
   │      +  Purpose, scope of this chapter                     │
   │        -  Extract potentially supportable noncomputer IP functions│
   │        -  Identify computer-human tasks at IP support levels 1, 2, 3│
   │        -  Relate these computer support tasks to data base concepts│
   │      + │Potentially supportable IP functions from models, methods of ch 8│
   │        +  IP as capturing, relating, synthesizing ideas into problems,│
   │        +  Methods of above that are supportable          │
   │      +  For each, specify computer-human functional allocation│
   │      +  Beyond Heuristics: Integrative-Extended Memory Forms of Support│
   │      +  Applicability of Data Base Concepts to IP functions│
   │                                                            │
   └──────────────────────────────────────────────────────────┘
 └                                                            ┘
```

EXAMPLE 10.2c

THINKTANK OUTLINE FOR CHAPTER 9 MAIN TOPICS PLUS SUBTOPICS PLUS SOME SUB-SUBTOPICS

```
  File  Edit  Extra  FontSize

 Chapter 9— Toward Functional Specs for Idea Processing Support
 +  Purpose, scope of this chapter
     -  Extract potentially supportable noncomputer IP functions
     -  Identify computer-human tasks at IP support levels 1, 2, 3
     -  Relate these computer support tasks to data base concepts
 +  Potentially supportable IP functions from models, methods of ch 8
     +  IP as capturing, relating, synthesizing ideas into problems, c
         -  Manipulate, synthesize, associate—within IP phases
     +  Methods of above that are supportable
         +  Divergent searches for alternatives
             -  combination of elements
             -  convergent methods for subproblems within divergent sea
         +  Problem redefinition and generalization
         +  Idea Manipulation (transformation) Aids (Parnes' list)
         +  Metaphorical association
         +  Scenarios
 +  For each, specify computer-human functional allocation
 +  Beyond Heuristics: Integrative-Extended Memory Forms of Support
```

The strength of a package such as ThinkTank is that it implicitly (and unobtrusively) supports the function of idea organizing independently of the process of filling in content. The explicit representation of idea organization in the form of a hierarchical outline and the ability to perform rearranging operations upon it provides the user with an accessible structured model (or schema) of an idea "information set." Similar to the role of a data base schema for an information system, such a schema focuses attention on logical structure and enables organization and reorganization to be dealt with more thoroughly, resulting in a more cohesive and complete idea information set. In principle, on-paper outlining could accomplish the same result. But the significantly lesser convenience of the manual process can be expected to decrease a user's time investment and thus decrease the likelihood of a result of comparable quality. Thus, like the benefits of other kinds of DSS software, increased convenience is used not to merely save time, but to convert efficiency improvements into effectiveness improvements.

The hierarchical outline schema also provides a compact representation of organization that can potentially be used to subsequently gain access to selected portions of a full set of text information. Large collections of full text information such as those created using word processing systems generally lack any special coded format and structure for units or sections of text. The user's problem of remembering or easily becoming informed about detailed content, structure, and means of access, is no less important than supporting the process of creating an initial organization of the ideas elaborated upon by the full text. The power of access afforded by a skeletal model of organization enhances the utility of any large complex information set. The augmented power to comprehend and access information set contents facilitates the functions of reorganization and the ability to select, join, and display subsets of information. These facilitating functions increase a user's capability of applying portions of text to new situations and needs. If, for example, it is made easy enough for a user (or for the system itself) to understand contents and gain access to a hierarchical idea structure for topic A (say, a marketing plan), it may become apparent that some portion of that structure also applies to topic B (say, the formulation of a new business plan). The applicable portion of text described by structure A can then be extracted and used for developing the structure and text of B. This kind of capability would enable a related network of idea structures to be built upon one another rather than requiring the user to treat each idea organization task as an independent problem. The current method of finding particular subject references within a larger text depends on key word searches. This approach does not utilize a model-directed access to content, but depends largely on the user's inspection and efforts to carry out a step by step search before completing any extraction or rearrangement of larger chunks of text information.

The initial version of ThinkTank does not facilitate this kind of text accessing capability or cross-referencing, or joining between separate outlines. This seems to be a useful direction for further development that has already being pursued by software developers such as the vendors of Framework and Freestyle.

Framework and Freestyle not only provide for retrieval of full text through reference to an outline, but also support the rearrangement of text segments by merely changing the outline which refers to the text. Framework also uses the outline as a basic organizing principle for its integrated package so that outline entries can refer to graphs, spreadsheets, or even other outlines. This approach may enable hierarchical outline processors to ultimately become the nucleus of an idea processing management system (IPMS), in which an IPMS performs an analogous role for managing idea-related text and numerical information to the function of mainframe data base management systems (DBMS).

While the initial ThinkTank offering may appear modest in its functional power as compared with later packages such as Framework and Freestyle, it represents an important conceptual breakthrough as a first instance of using computer support solely for the purpose of facilitating idea organization. For many users, Think Tank has become a valued and often-used tool that enhances their ability to plan and organize complex idea structures.

"Consultant": Idea Generation Aids

Consultant® was released by ODS, Inc., (Palatine, Illinois, 60067) in 1985. Using the Macintosh interface and icon logos (see below) consisting of a sketch of a human skull divided down the middle into black and white halves (presumably representing the right and left brain hemispheres), the package's title display carries the phrase "Helps you use your whole brain to think and work more productively."

CONSULTANT Icons

The package's functions are described as of three types:

1. Procedures,
2. Aids, and
3. Helps.

The procedures are mouse-accessed through pull-down menus as shown across the top of exhibit 10.1. The **File** and **Edit** menu headings are for standard Macintosh functions such as naming and saving files, printing out displays, or cutting and pasting, with the seven other menu headings—**Begin, Detect, Discover, Create, Plan, Sell,** and **Work**—representing Consultant's own special Procedures menus, the functions of which are briefly described in exhibit 10.2.

Each procedure menu consists of a list of prescribed steps, presented in their logically sequential order of execution (although the user can usually start, procede and stop anywhere) as a framework for the user to follow in completing the particular procedure selected. In following the procedure, the user merely responds to each menu item by typing in relevant entries. Nothing else automatically happens or need happen within the context of using a procedure; the user just responds to the system's lead. However, the user can follow up by making use of one or more of the aids functions with respect to developing any of these entries. (The aids functions are described later.) Used by themselves, the procedures functions focus on the level 2 framework-paradigm type of support as defined in chapter 8. They seem likely to be useful mainly

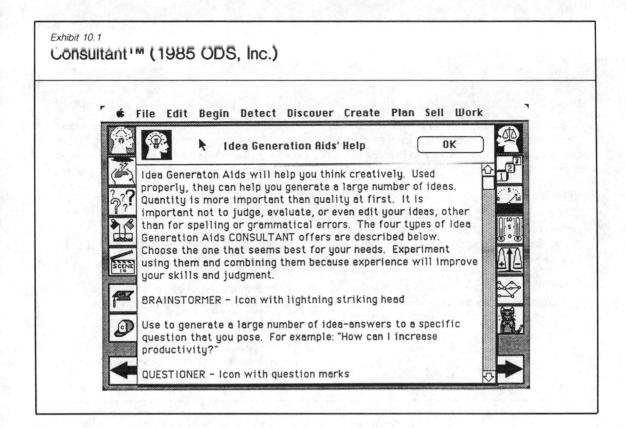

Exhibit 10.1
Consultant™ (1985 ODS, Inc.)

File   Edit   Begin   Detect   Discover   Create   Plan   Sell   Work

Idea Generation Aids' Help   OK

Idea Generaton Aids will help you think creatively. Used properly, they can help you generate a large number of ideas. Quantity is more important than quality at first. It is important not to judge, evaluate, or even edit your ideas, other than for spelling or grammatical errors. The four types of Idea Generation Aids CONSULTANT offers are described below. Choose the one that seems best for your needs. Experiment using them and combining them because experience will improve your skills and judgment.

BRAINSTORMER - Icon with lightning striking head

Use to generate a large number of idea-answers to a specific question that you pose. For example: "How can I increase productivity?"

QUESTIONER - Icon with question marks

for students or those with little experience in the normally prescribed steps of planning projects, problem-solving, or selling procedures. But for this type of user, the frameworks are very useful until they become so familiar and internalized that the user can create personal variations or skip them entirely.

The plan menu, for example, consists of three groups of action items that represent a useful framework for a neophyte planner, as follows:

1. First group—Identify goals, establish objectives, determine units, quantify objectives, assign time limits.
2. Second group—Identify tasks, identify interdependencies, assign people, identify milestones.
3. Third Group—List resources, quantify resources, determine costs, determine benefits, test plan.

Exhibit 10.2
Consultant's procedures menus

Begin

Solicits identifying names from the user to be used in subsequent headings and asks for identification and description of what is to be done that is of concern to the user.

Detect

A somewhat nondescriptive name for a set of general problem-solving steps in stages of problem description, fact-gathering, explanation, and identifying solutions.

Discover

Essentially covers the scientific method of hypothesis formulation, experimentation, and testing

Create

A somewhat misleading title for a general qualitative mode of problem-solving approach that includes gathering facts, determining objectives, identifying obstacles, and other steps; with the main creative focus on the single step in the list of "generate ideas."

Plan

Consists of the steps previously listed above.

Sell

A prescribed set of steps for identifying sales prospects and making sales presentations.

Work

Essentially a list of steps related to monitoring and managerially controlling operations after they are initiated.

Example 10.3 illustrates Consultant's help function called "coach" as it applies to the *establish objectives* item in the first group of the *Plan* procedure entries. A "coach" selection is accomplished by the user mouse-pointing to and clicking on the coach's cap icon shown at the bottom left margin of the Consultant display window (see exhibit 10.1). A coach-provided example is provided for all of Consultant's procedures and aids functions. The other help function provided (by selecting the academic cap icon just above the coaches cap) is called "tutor," and it offers the user a brief explanation of the purpose and description of each procedure and aid function.

The two sets of aids functions associated respectively with each half-brain are labeled "Idea Generation Aids" and "Decision-Making Aids." The decision-making aids generally include quantitative methods and are represented by the icons shown vertically (again, see exhibit 10.1) along the right-hand margin.* The idea generation aids' icons are on the left-hand side of the

EXAMPLE 10.3

THE "COACH" HELP FUNCTION FOR A CONSULTANT "PROCEDURE": "PLAN: STEP 2. ESTABLISH OBJECTIVES"

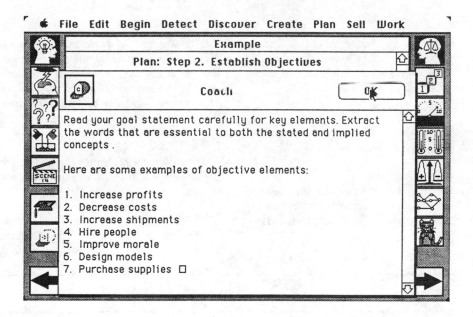

display window. The decision-making aids, briefly described in exhibit 10.3, are useful analytical tools but of less interest in the present context of discussing idea processing. The idea generation aids, however, are directly relevant to idea processing and include some of the functions discussed in chapter 9. These are inventoried in summary form in exhibit 10.4 and discussed further below.

*Note the weighing scales inscribed in the head profile at the top of the right column. The profiled head is facing leftward and thus we are looking at the left side of the skull containing the left brain hemisphere, which is associated with quantitative thinking. The profiled skull on the top left side of the display contains the light bulb and is facing rightward, so we are looking at right brain hemisphere which is associated with qualitative, creative thinking. We may assume this layout was intentional, although it's significance in this regard may be lost on casual user-viewers. It perhaps would be a more appropriate positioning and a more obvious association if the positions of these margins were reversed so that the left hemisphere related functions were shown in the left-hand margin and the right hemisphere functions were shown on the right margin. Of course the two profiles would then be looking outward, away from the center, whatever that might imply.

Exhibit 10.3
Consultant's Decision-Making Aids

Prioritizer

(The top icon right-hand in exhibit 10.1 containing three numbered cubes.) Supports prioritizing or preference ranking of items by means of soliciting a series of paired comparisons.

Grader

(The numbered dial icon.) Facilitates assignment of 0–10 scale values to items.

Rater

(The icon with two thermometer-type bulbs.) Creates a score for items consisting of the product of user-supplied values on two equally weighted 0–10 scales.

Evaluator

(The weighing balance icon.) Enables a user to evaluate one or more alternatives on a variety of factors representing either advantages or disadvantages on user-weighted and user-assessed 0–10 scales (in a manner sometimes referred to as the Kepner-Trego decision-making method).

Relator

(The flow network icon.) Facilitates assigning and considering task precedences and interdependencies (as in the PERT method).

Categorizer

(The cat icon.) Facilitates the identification of categories and the assignment of items to them.

Exhibit 10.4
Consultant's Idea Generation Aids

Brainstormer

(The lightning striking the brain icon.) Solicits a large number of user idea responses to a previously supplied stimulus-question. (See example 10.4.)

Questioner

(The icon with several question marks.) Utilizes a user-supplied "question stem" (eg., "How can I make our product . . .") in combination with the user's list of relevant qualifiers or attributes (eg., "more attractive, cheaper, better, . . .") in order to generate a series of questions to which the user supplies as many potential answers as possible.

Combiner

(The icon with two buckets spilling their contents into a common vat.) Solicits user entry of items in each of as many categories as the user specifies and subsequently generates a list of all combinations of items taking one item from each category at a time. (See example 10.5a,b,c.)

Scenario

(The cinema clapboard icon.) Leads the user through defining the elements of a scenario before finally entering the sequential event scenario one event at a time. (See example 10.6a,b,c.)

EXAMPLE 10.4

A CONSULTANT "BRAINSTORMER" EXAMPLE

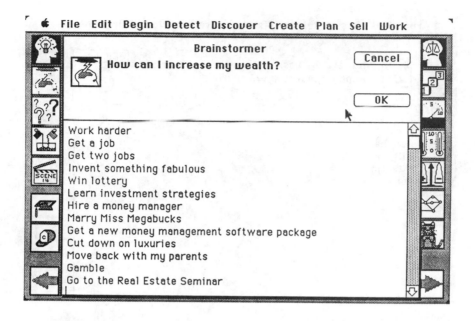

The first two idea generation aids, brainstormer (see example 10.4) and questioner are essentially aimed at the same function of stimulating the user to generate many ideas in response to a stimulus question (following the general prescription of the brainstorming method as described in chapter 8). By combining a "question stem" with a series of qualifiers or attributes (as described in exhibit 10.4), the questioner function adds support of a basic level 3 type (generative) to the generation of relevant questions, as well as levels 1 and 2 support to facilitate capturing the user's responses. As the brainstorming method requires, simultaneous or immediate assessment of new ideas is not encouraged or supported as part of these aids, but the user's responses can be saved and subsequently assessed with some of the quantitative decision-making aids (such as prioritizer, grader, rater, or evaluator).

The frameworks presented by brainstormer and questioner for the stimulus and capture of user-generated ideas are support tools for divergent thinking. But they deal with support at a more general level than do the functions described in chapter 9, which are directed more specifically to component functions of divergent thinking, such as the several idea transforming functions in Parnes' method, and support for metaphorical thinking relevant to

EXAMPLE 10.5a

A CONSULTANT "COMBINER" EXAMPLE: STEP 1

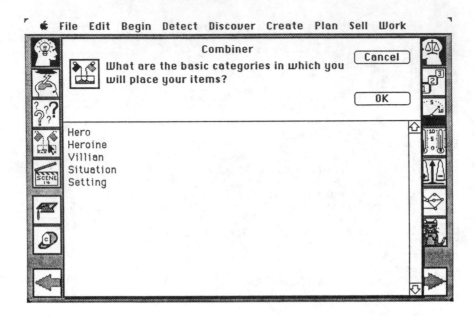

brainstorming, synectics, and other creative processes. Both these more specific support functions and the general type of support offered by Consultant may be useful as part of a repertoire of support functions that can be selected at the user's option. However, as mentioned earlier with respect to some of the procedures, it seems likely that the more generalized and basic the level of framework support tools, the more rapidly users will outgrow them as they gain experience. If the same support system also offers more focused tools, users can continue to use the system, merely bypassing the beginner's level of general framework support when it is not needed.

The combiner function (illustrated in examples 10.5a, b, and c) differs from the previous two idea generation aids in that its payoff to users does not depend mainly on leading the user to respond.

Combiner automatically generates combinations, as described in chapter 9 under level 3—generative support for divergent search (method 1). However, Consultant's combiner function is considerably more basic and provides none of the user options discussed in chapter 9 for different search and display strategies. This is perhaps appropriate for an introductory and broadly-functioned package such as Consultant. However, when the number of combinations becomes large (as they easily can, faster than the user may expect)

EXAMPLE 10.5b

"COMBINER" EXAMPLE: STEP 2

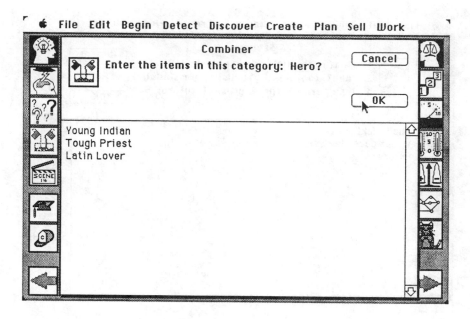

EXAMPLE 10.5c

"COMBINER" EXAMPLE: LAST STEP

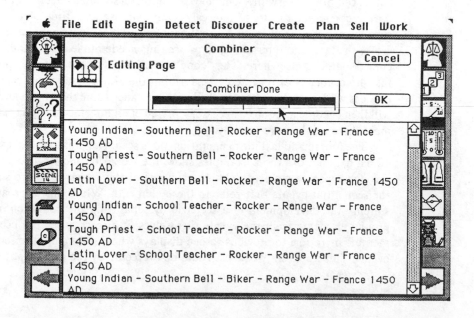

EXAMPLE 10.6a
A CONSULTANT "SCENARIO" EXAMPLE: FIRST STEP

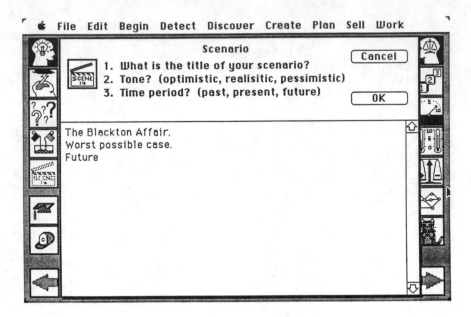

a combiner user may be inconvenienced by the need to scroll through a long list of combinations while somehow retaining, assessing, selecting, and comparing particular results of interest. (Only one use at a time of the "copy" function under the **Edit** menu can mitigate this problem, but each use of "copy" erases the last, and intervening steps are thus needed to leave off and save the copied material elsewhere. The "copy" function therefore does not provide a fast direct means of repeatedly performing the above assessment-related operations while scrolling through the list.) One can assume that a pad and pencil will then become a required accessory, in lieu of an interface design that would meet these needs more directly.

The fourth and last idea generation aid is scenario, illustrated in examples 10.6a, b, and c. As these examples show, the scenario function takes the user through separate steps of defining elements of the scenario before soliciting the sequential events that refer to these elements. While this approach may simplify the development of a scenario by separating the definition of background elements from the events themselves, it also requires the user to remember or return to previous screen displays when developing the sequential events. This apparent weakness could be overcome by the use of split screens,

EXAMPLE 10.6b

"SCENARIO" EXAMPLE: NEXT STEPS

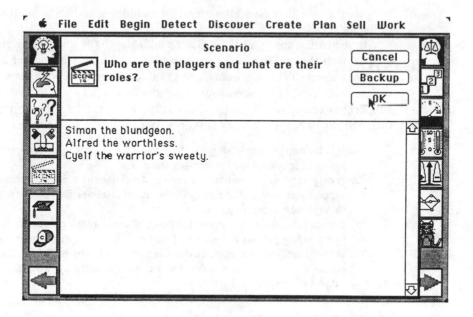

EXAMPLE 10.6c

"SCENARIO" EXAMPLE: FINAL STEP

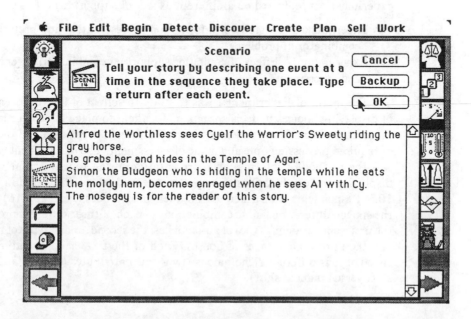

the ability of scrolling through the previously defined elements as needed, or some other redesign of the standard display used for entering scenario events. In addition, no special scenario analysis aids are presented. This is unfortunate because they could be especially useful for examining and assessing the results of longer scenarios.

In general, Consultant is a welcome addition to the growing inventory of support tools that go beyond the initial standard DSS microcomputer software for spreadsheets, data base query, and graphics. It covers a wide scope of procedures and aids, but it seems fair to characterize it as sacrificing depth of support power in favor of scope of coverage. This may be appropriate for an introductory package breaking new ground. Consultant is important because:

1. It is innovative in providing the first commercial package offering explicit support for several idea processing functions;
2. It may serve as a stimulant for further development of idea processing support software, either through subsequent later versions of Consultant or through new competing offerings;
3. It goes beyond the independent support of certain idea processing functions by providing at least a basic interface between some quantitative decision-analysis methods and some qualitative idea processing methods. (The potential for further development of this type of integrative support is the subject of chapter 13.)

Some Relevant Research

Two experiments related to formulating and assessing combinations (a key function in divergent thinking processes) were run by Young in 1983. Each experiment concentrated on a different aspect of support, as follows:

Experiment 1—A study of information representation and preference in combinatorial problems.

Experiment 2—Effect of computer support on combinatorial generation and assessment.

The intent of Experiment 1 was to study the effect of four different ways of displaying choices to decision makers for them to place in rank order as to preference. The effects (dependent variables) that were considered were that of required processing time and mode of assessment. The independent variable was the method of information representation, using four different ways of displaying the combinations to be preference ranked, as illustrated in exhibit 10.5. Respondents were asked to rank their preferences (from 1 to 16) among the sixteen different possible combinations in each of three different problems, the first a choice among types of automobiles, the second among types of movies, and the third among types of houses. Each of the sixteen combinations consisted of four different dichotomous (two-state) attributes (such as automatic shift versus manual shift).

Exhibit 10.5

Four Modes of Representation Used in Experiment I

Mode A: Boxed words in sorted order
(Example—Descriptors of movies)

1.
Musical	Current
American	G -rated

2.
Musical	Current
American	R -rated

3.
Musical	History
American	G-rated

etc.)
....

Mode B: Boxed words in random order

Musical	History
American	R -rated

Drama	History
Foreign	R -rated

Drama	Current
American	R -rated

....

Mode C: Boxed letter-coded in sorted order

M	C
A	G

M	C
A	R

M	H
A	G

....

Mode D: Symbol and letter-coded in sorted order

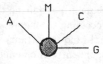
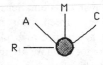
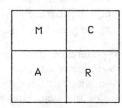
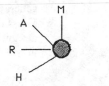
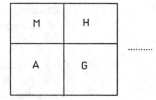

....

The main results of this experiment were as follows:

1. The average processing time for the first of the three problems was least for sorted words representation (mode A), with randomly ordered words (mode B) taking the next least amount of time, followed by letter-coded sorted order (mode C), and the letter and symbol-encoded display (mode D) taking the most time.

2. For all four modes of representation, the time required consistently decreased from the first problem to the second and to the third problems, indicating respondent learning. By the third problem, the average time to process the initially unfamiliar symbol-encoded choices presented in mode D was equal to the time to process the mode B random word representation. For the third problem, mode A sorted words still took the least amount of time, but the sorted letters of mode C now moved into second place, followed by the tied modes B and D.

3. Analysis of the preference orders in all three problems indicated that an underlying general preference processing algorithm could explain most of the results (with little deviation). The underlying preference processing algorithm was Tversky's theory of choice known as "elimination by aspects" (Tversky 1972). In brief, this decision algorithm procedes by the subject first considering the one most dominantly important attribute and considering only those choices which have this most desired attribute. Among those choices, the decision maker then considers the second most important attribute, and follows the same procedure until all choices have been exhausted.

Although an exploratory and limited experiment of this kind can not produce conclusive results, lacking further evidence some potential guidelines for software development can be posed as follows:

1. At least for those preference situations for which "elimination by aspects" is appropriate, an efficient mode of computer representation would be to first solicit from the user which attribute or dimension is most important (such as method of shift for an automobile) and then solicit the preferred form of that attribute (such as automatic shift), before going on to inquire about next most important attribute. This would be more efficient than first generating all or many combinations and subsequently requiring the user to assess them. However, forcing this mode of processing through a strong design, may have a serious drawback in unusual (and important) situations in which users cannot evaluate attributes independently of one another but must look at a combination as a complete entity before assessing it. The failure to "browse" through or systematically examine many combinations before making final assessments is a violation of the brainstorming dictum to seek a creative solution by separating the idea generation stage from the judgmental stage. A support system should cover both contingencies through user-controlled options in combinatorial choice situations, that of assessing familiar situations for which "elimination by aspects" may be the user's natural mode, and less familiar situations where divergent thinking is most appropriate.

2. Words and phrases usually require more space and thus present design problems when many qualitative situations must be represented via a computer display, but they are the most familiar symbols for conveying ideas and therefore the easiest and fastest symbols for human processing. Words should be the preferred design choice for idea representation. But when space is a critical need, the association of simple special symbols with abbreviations may be acceptable when sufficiently frequent or lengthy usage enables initial learning to pay off during subsequent usage.
3. A logically sorted order of presentation is an important way to facilitate the user's ability to scan and assess many choices.

Experiment 2 studied the effect of computer generation support on the assessed quality of combinations in a somewhat different problem situation than that of the previously described experiment. Two groups of matched subjects were each given two different tasks to perform:

Task 1: Create and assess a name for a new analgesic product by building 1, 2, or 3 syllable combinations out of prefixes, stems, and suffixes.

Task 2: Form a strategic task group for developing a marketing plan for an old declining product by choosing members described by their departmental affiliation, professional training, and personality type.

The first experimental group was supported by a microcomputer software system programmed with a support system to automatically generate and facilitate display and assessment of combinations (with features similar to those described for this type of support in chapter 9, as opposed to the Consultant "combine" aid). The second group relied on paper and pencil manual methods. Neither group was told of the existence of the other group. Users in each group were given a fixed period of time for each task and asked to assess their best combinations on a five-point scale of very good to very poor. The subjects were also asked to fill out a questionnaire immediately after completing the tasks in order to learn users' reactions to aspects of the tasks and their approaches to carrying them out.

In summary, the results were that the distributions of the users self-evaluations on both tasks were significantly more positive for the computer-supported group. However, the advantage for the computer-supported group was of a different nature for each of the tasks. In the product naming task (task 1), the computer users assessed more of their results at the highly rated end of the scale than did the manual subjects. For the planning group formulation task (task 2), the advantage of the computer users was that they had significantly fewer low rated results. This difference was probably due to the different natures of the tasks, with the key to the naming task depending more on finding an unusually striking name, while the team formation problem was more likely to have as its salient features both finding a reasonable balance and avoiding negative forms of imbalance and potential clashes or biases due to the makeup of a group.

The questionnaire responses helped to interpret the sources of the better results for the computer-supported group. The main themes in these responses were:

1. The computer-supported group took their tasks somewhat more seriously than did the manual group, apparently their perception of the seriousness of the exercise being influenced by the fact of the computer system being made available. (This attitude may also have affected their satisfaction with their own results and hence their higher ratings.)
2. Most of the manual group said they really needed more time to perform both tasks, while most of the computer users did not feel that more time would have changed their results. The time-saving efficiency provided by computer support was apparently a major source of increased effectiveness in producing better results.
3. The manual group found both tasks to be "tedious" and "taxing." However, the computer users had a clear consensus that the computer support system was a clear asset to performance only for task 1 (product naming). Several subjects provided clues as to why this was not as clearly the feeling about supporting Task 2 (team formation). They indicated that they had particular criteria and selection rules that they wanted to apply in Task 2, but that the system did not facilitate these particular approaches. (Many of these comments indicated that either an "elimination by aspects" approach was being followed or that particular combinations of people were either sought as a nucleus for a team or being avoided.)

These results indicate that the capabilities of a system to support combinatorial synthesis and assessment should be sufficiently robust to be applicable to different modes of processing, each appropriate for different situations. The user may not perceive in advance which mode is most appropriate, and therefore the system should facilitate the user's ability to try out and switch between varying approaches.

Based on both these experiments and on experience with the relevant functions of Consultant, more specific features that appear to be desirable follow the lines indicated in chapter 9, and include the following:

1. Allow the user to make entries of attributes in any order on each of a number of lists (typically up to ten lists seems manageable and sufficient).
2. Provide the user with the option to sort the lists, either
   a) automatically, in alphabetical order, or
   b) in order of subjective preference, supported by the system in either a direct rank number assignment mode or a paired comparison mode that subsequently generates a rank preference order.
3. Provide the user with the option to specify a rank order of importance among (between) the lists themselves. Lists represent different dimensions of the problem realm. The user may or may not possess subjective assessments of the relative importance of the dimensions as well as the attributes within each dimension list.

4. Enable the user to choose between alternative ways for the system to generate combinations in n-member display groupings. The user can also control the setting of n (n is the display group size, typically five to ten). Options for selecting combinations should include:

a) In *regular* order; that is, in the order in which attributes appear in their respective lists within the order of the list dimensions themselves (with the last attributes changing most rapidly as the inner loop). If the entries are in alphabetical order, this will result in alphabetically ordered combinations. If the initial ordering of attributes and lists is according to preference or importance ranking, the generated combinations will generally follow the user's preference. The user's assessment of the full combinations, however, should be able to alter these derived preferences.

b) In regular order, as above, but selecting for display only every mth combination (where m is set by the user from two up to a suitable limit, such as twenty). This enables the user to browse through combinations within some convenient ordering without looking at every adjacent (and therefore similar) combination.

c) In randomly selected order, thereby enabling the user to browse through combinations unlike one another and in no preconceived order.

5. Enable the user to save and recall any combination or displayed group of combinations for subsequent consideration.

6. Allow the user to alter (edit) any saved combination and/or to attach comments to it which are saved and displayed along with the combination itself.

7. Allow the user to alter the mode of combination generation at any point, or to discontinue combination generation entirely.

8. Allow the user to modify or add to the attribute list entries and to change the order of the attributes or the lists.

9. Allow the user to produce a hard copy printout of any saved combinations (with or without associated comments).

Further Research and Development

There is need for building a larger base of research and development for idea processing support before more comprehensive design guidelines can be postulated and accepted as being reliable. As it has been with the quantitative types of DSS software, it seems likely that much of what will be learned will stem from trial and error experience in using new software as it emerges. Few software development efforts along these lines have been openly discussed or published, either at universities or by commercial vendors. One such developmental software system intended to encompass multiple creativity-supporting functions was described as being under development by Manheim at Northwestern University (Manheim 1985).

The research and development efforts that have been presented, however, have generally been greeted with a great deal of interest. Further research is being conducted. (A doctoral research project to assess the performance contribution of using Consultant has reportedly been conducted at the University of Texas by one of Joyce Elam's students.) The commercial offerings such as ThinkTank and its followers, and Consultant, that have appeared have been well received. It is the thesis of this book that idea processing support is a natural twin to DSS for general managerial decision making. If this assertion is correct, new forms of idea processing support will continually emerge. Managers should be prepared to seize the opportunity to use the potential of this new kind of mind-lever. Researchers and software developers can be expected to be more actively involved in this avenue for extending the frontier of computer support.

Review Questions, Exercises, and Discussion Topics

Review Questions

1. What does outlining a large writing project have in common with some computer systems design documentation techniques? With systems design techniques?
2. What purposes does outlining serve for a writer?—for a planner?—for a project manager?—for a system designer?
3. What is the nature of the structure of logical associations between ideas that serves as the basis for outlining?
4. What benefits can be derived from a software tool such as ThinkTank that are not as readily obtainable through the use of paper and pencil manual aids?
5. What level of support is the main focus of Consultant's procedures? Explain your answer.
6. What are the specific items listed in the Consultant procedure called **Plan?** How might these items relate to an outline to be used as a guide for completing a large planning project?
7. What are the important differences between the two types of "aids" Consultant calls decision-making aids versus those called idea generation aids?
8. What does Consultant's combiner function do and how does it differ from similar functions described in chapter 9?
9. Describe the manner in which Consultant's scenario aid works and how this differs from similar functions described in chapter 9?
10. *a*) Describe the decision process known as elimination by aspects?
    b) Give an example of the type of problem situation to which this process might apply.
11. *a*) Describe the likely effects of representing a large number of choices for a user to assess in the form of words versus special symbols?
    b) What are the likely effects of presenting these choices in random versus sorted order?

Exercises

1. a) Develop an outline for a fairly lengthy written completed document or report that does not contain a table of contents (on any subject with which you are familiar). The outline should represent the present structure of the document. Either prepare the outline manually or if the ThinkTank package or another outline processor is available to you, use it.

   b) Now examine the outline that represents the present structure of the document and revise it (add, delete, edit, reorganize) as thoroughly as you can in any manner you feel will cover the topic best. Keep track of each individual change made. Assess the degree and kind of improvements provided by the second outline. (If some students used an outline processor and others used manual methods, compare the number and type of changes made between the two groups.)

2. Identify one or more current users of an outline package (such as ThinkTank) and interview them to obtain their assessments of any benefits of usage, frequency of use, types of applications, desired changes in the software, how they heard about it and obtained it, and any other relevant opinions and attitudes they may have.

3. Use the Consultant **Plan** procedure menu items as the initial basis for completing an outline for a plan for a business purpose or any large project. How useful was the **Plan** menu for you? In what ways, if any, did you need to modify the items presented?

4. Based on the description of Consultant presented in this chapter, discuss your initial reactions to its likely attraction and potential relevance to you, and also to an average manager involved in planning and innovation? (Would you be interested in trying out a package like this? What kinds of needs might you apply it to?) If the package itself is available to you, prepare a critique based on its actual use.

5. Find an application that you might apply the method of generation of combinations to in searching for a useful solution. How many attribute types or dimensions can you define as being relevant and important? How many alternative items can you list under each of these attribute dimensions? How many total combinations can be generated out of these items, selecting one from each attribute dimension? In a set limited period of time (such as fifteen minutes) generate and examine different combinations and select the one you prefer most. Discuss the approach you took to this task and how a computer support system might have helped.

6. Follow Consultant's framework and sequence of steps to manually prepare a scenario on a subject which is familiar and relevant to you. Use separate pieces of paper for each step in defining the elements of the scenario and finally, the sequence of events of the scenario itself. Use this exercise to assess how a support system might have made this task easier or in other ways provided any benefits in creating the scenario and in assessing the results of the scenario.

Discussion Topics

1. Assess and compare the amount of training a noncomputer specialist manager would be likely to require to use an outline processor such as ThinkTank versus a typical microcomputer spreadsheet package or query package. Do you feel that managers who have a need to prepare many lengthy plans, make speeches, prepare large reports, would find such a package useful? To what extent do you think they would repeatedly use it (or not use it) after being introduced to it? (See exercise 2 above and relate your answer to it, if possible.)
2. What do you think the value is, if any, in putting the quantitative methods of Consultant's decision-making aids in the same package as its idea generation aids? Do you feel it might be better to package these separately? Would your answer depend on the type of user and the application? Specify.
3. If you were the vendor of Consultant, discuss changes you would be inclined to make in a "version 2" release of this package from the point of view of both resales to present users and sales to new users.
4. Assuming you were able to obtain reliable guidance from research experiments in answering the prior question, what would be the list of questions you might submit to researchers. Discuss how these questions are relevant to your design decisions.

References

Bonner, P. 1984. "Enter, The Powerful New Idea Tools." *Personal Computing,* 70–79, January.

Brevdy, June. 1984. "Reviews: Framework." *Infoworld* 6(October 29)44:53–58.

Manheim, M. L. 1985. "Theories of Decision-Making and Their Implications for Development of Creativity-Supporting DSS." *Transactions, Fifth International Conference on Decision Support Systems, DSS–85* 113–14, IADSS, April.

O'Connor, R. J. 1984. "Outline Processors Catch On." *Infoworld* 6(July 2)27:30–31.

Spezzano, C. 1986. "Unconventional Outliners." *PC World* 168–75, March.

Tversky, A. 1972. "Elimination by Aspects: A Theory of Choice." *Psychological Review* 79(July)4:281–99.

Young, L. F. 1983. "Information Representation and Assessment in Right-Brained (Qualitative) Decision Support Systems." *WPS 83–3,* Working Paper Series, College of Business and Administration, Drexel University, Philadelphia, PA 19104, July.

Young, L. F. 1983. "An Experiment With a Computer-Based Idea Support System." TIMS/ORSA International Conference, Copenhagen, Denmark, June, 1984 ,(retitled from *WPS 83–7,* Working Paper Series, College of Business and Administration, Drexel University, Philadelphia, PA 19104) August.

Common Issues in DSS and Idea Processing

Part 3

—Knowledge-based Systems
—Economics of Support Systems
—Potential Misuse
—Integrated "Whole-brained" Support

Knowledge-based Systems and Expert Systems: Their Relation to Both DSS and Idea Processing

11

Socrates: . . . Tell us once more what knowledge is.
Theaetetus: I cannot say it is judgment as a whole, because there is false judgement; but perhaps true judgement is knowledge. You may take that as my answer. If, as we go further, it turns out to be less convincing than it seems now, I will try to find another.
From "Theaetitus" in Plato's *Theory of Knowledge* by F. M. Cornford, London: Routledge and Kegan Paul Ltd. 1935.

The use of a computer-based system as an interactive consulting expert was briefly described in chapter 1. Expert systems were again mentioned in chapter 5 in terms of their potential as a means of aiding DSS modeling by nonexpert modelers. Chapter 8 also contains a discussion with regard to using future expert systems in supporting human thinking processes and their limitations in explicitly modeling deep managerial expertise. This chapter brings these threads together and presents a more complete picture of expert systems and the more comprehensive category of knowledge-based systems to which they belong.

The objectives of this chapter will be to:

1. Define and describe the nature of expert and knowledge-based systems;
2. Describe basic methods of their development and use;
3. Clarify their differences and relationships to decision support and idea processing systems;
4. Put into perspective their accomplishments, potential, and limitations as adjuncts to DSS and IP support systems or as stand-alone forms of support.

Definitions and Distinctions Between Knowledge-Based Systems and Expert Systems

The term expert systems has attained wide usage but is often misused. Strictly speaking, an expert system should be capable of providing counsel in its realm that equals or exceeds the proficiency of true human experts. In this definition, true human expertise is taken to mean more than merely acceptable skill and knowledge of an average practitioner, but represents the scope and depth of professional knowledge and abilities to apply that knowledge that are possessed by only the few most proficient practitioners. Typically, these practitioners are recognized by their peers as being outstanding experts and rarely do they include more than 1 percent of the people in any given field.

In contrast, knowledge-based systems are computer systems that are capable of counseling their users at various levels of competence that may range from mere intelligent assistance in limited problem domains, through peer-level types of assistance of about the average practitioner's competence, up to the extreme high profiency of true experts. According to this definition, expert systems are only a subcategory of the wider class of knowledge-based systems.

Artificial Intelligence and Knowledge-Based Systems

Artificial intelligence (AI) is the field of computer science that is concerned with developing computer systems that exhibit the general characteristics of human intelligence associated with such tasks as understanding language, reasoning, learning, solving problems, understanding and interpreting perceptions and observed patterns. Particular areas of AI include robotics, computerized visual recognition, automatic theorem proving and general problem solving, voice recognition and natural language interpretation, as well as the field of knowledge engineering.

Knowledge engineering is the area of AI that is concerned with the design and development of knowledge-based systems, including expert systems. It includes the problems of how to elicit knowledge from its human possessors, how to represent and store knowledge in a computer usable form, how to make inferences from knowledge that are relevant to problems at hand, and how to enable knowledge-based systems to learn and revise their own knowledge representations and inference capabilities. The problems of knowledge engineering are related to other areas of AI concern such as general problem solving, computer learning, reasoning, and natural language understanding, but knowledge engineering is a rapidly growing area of AI in its own right.

Types of Knowledge Included
in Knowledge Based Systems

While philosophers continue to struggle with the question of what knowledge really is and is not, for purposes of knowledge-based systems two general types of knowledge are generally recognized. These are:

1. Declarative knowledge, which consists of factual statements and relationships between factual statements that are declared to be true or assumed to be true for the immediate purposes at hand;
2. Procedural knowledge, which consists of an internally consistent set of steps to be followed in operating with and upon factual knowledge.

Examples of declarative or factual knowledge are:

1. John is a young man.
2. Sally is a young woman.
3. John and Sally have a lot of free time.
4. Men and women are persons.
5. Young persons with a lot of free time sometimes get into trouble.

An example of procedural knowledge is the following set of steps:

a) Find common descriptive elements or terms among all pairs of the above five statements.

    eg. 1. John is a *young* man—2. Sally is a *young* woman

      1. John is a young *man.*—4. *Men* and women are persons

      2. Sally is a young *woman.*—4. Men and *women* are persons

      4. Men and women are *persons*—5. Young *persons* with lot of free time sometimes get into trouble

      3. John and Sally have a *lot of free time*—5. Young persons with a *lot of free time.*

b) Combine all paired statements with common descriptive elements or subjects into new single statements.

    e.g. 1. and 2. John is a young man and Sally is a young woman.

      1. and 4. John is a person and women are persons.

      2. and 4. Sally is a person and men are persons.

      etc.

c) Repeat operations a) and b) on the new set of statements obtained from b) until the number of statements cannot be reduced further.

Final result: John and Sally are young persons with a lot of free time who will sometimes get into trouble.

A special characteristic of knowledge-based systems that distinguish them from other computer applications is that knowledge-based systems explicitly separate declarative knowledge from procedural knowledge. Ordinary programming languages often intermix declarative statements and procedural knowledge and both may be implicitly defined by the processing logic of program algorithms. This characteristic of ordinary programming languages makes the knowledge they represent less immediately understandable and amenable to change compared to that of knowledge-based systems. This feature of knowledge-based systems may make them valuable as a better means of expression or control language for certain computer applications, completely independent from any value they may have in providing knowledge-based counsel to users.

Realms and Managerial Purposes of Knowledge-based Systems

While all knowledge-based systems have the common general purpose of counseling their users at various levels of competence, they can be further categorized by their subject area or realm and by the manner with which they provide counsel to users. It should first be noted that while knowledge-based systems can be applied to important nonmanagement areas such as medical diagnosis, engineering design, and others, our concern here is limited to their application as means of augmenting managerial tasks.

A standard frame of reference for management information systems in general is also a useful application-oriented scheme for categorizing the realms of knowledge-based systems for supporting organizational management. That is, the following three dimensions are combined to form application realms:

1. Business functions (marketing, production, finance, personnel, logistics, etc.)
2. Managerial activities (eg. planning, analysis and diagnosis, control)
3. Managerial levels (strategic, tactical, operational)

From an applications planning viewpoint, as it is with other types of systems, it is useful to examine every function-activity-level combination in a given organization to identify potential uses for knowledge-based systems. However, from a technical point of view, the key dimension that determines system architecture (complexity and form) more than any other is likely to be that of level. The reason is the same as that which applies to DSS, the question of the degree of problem structure and complexity. As noted with respect to DSS, less structure and higher complexity is usually found in management concerns at higher organizational levels than at lower levels. Therefore knowledge-based systems intended to serve higher levels can be expected to require larger, more complex knowledge bases containing declarative knowledge and possibly also more complex forms of procedural knowledge.

Within any given realm of application, knowledge-based systems' primary role is to provide direct support to users through the knowledge-transfer functions of interactive guidance and tutelage. In respect of their supporting rather than supplanting role, they are similar to both decision support and idea processing systems. However, knowledge-based systems can vary in their degree of emphasis on the following additional kinds of purposes:

1. *To automate rule-driven tasks, rather than merely counsel users.*
   This emphasis is more likely to apply to low-level operations, such as those requiring clerical decisions or standard rule application. Such systems may also provide a degree of human interaction to monitor and override the system, especially in exceptional cases. Thus they can still be classified as interactive advisory systems even though their required level of knowledge is relatively low (certainly below that required to be designated as expert systems) and they may seldom require human intervention. Such systems can be characterized as capturing the kind of knowledge usually found in operating manuals and standard procedure manuals.

2. *To provide an accessible form of organizational memory.*
   The declarative and procedural knowledge in systems that emphasize this purpose would make statements about the content and manner of handling past cases rather then necessarily limiting themselves to general prescriptions for the present. In this manner, even if the system does not have the built-in ability to automatically learn from an analysis of the past and modify its own knowledge, users can recapture the past and perform their own assessments as guides to apply in present situations. Such systems could also be structured to represent the manner in which particular individuals handled things, thus retaining their knowledge for the organization even when they themselves are gone. The levels of knowledge required for useful purposes of this kind are likely to vary from moderate to expert.

Another special purpose knowledge-based system that seems likely to be required as such applications grow might be deemed a knowledge-base management system (KBMS). Analogous in purpose to a data base management system (DBMS) or a model base management system (MBMS), a KBMS would assist users in finding which knowledge-based system or set of systems may exist that apply to the problem at hand, in gaining access to the systems through a common interface, and in organizing, integrating, and maintaining the full repository of knowledge-based systems as an organizational resource rather than as isolated and independently controlled applications.

Exhibit 11.1
Architecture of a Knowledge-Based System

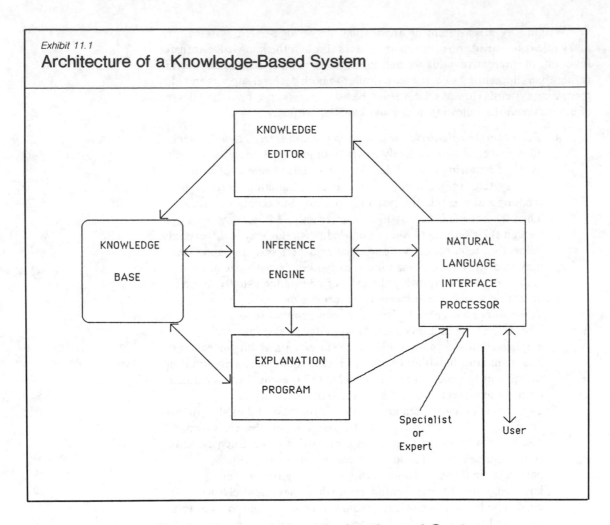

Technology of Knowledge-based Systems

General System Architecture

The main software and data storage components of a knowledge-based system are shown in exhibit 11.1. The realm of knowledge contained in such a system is represented in the storage component called a knowledge base. A software component called an inference engine provides a means of using the knowledge base in order to deduce new facts or conclusions. A user-system interface component is needed, as is required for other interactive support systems, in order to provide a natural and easy to use means of general user control over the system. A knowledge refining component enters new knowledge, modifies existing knowledge, and reorganizes the knowledge base as needed. Finally, an explanation software component can refer to both the inference engine and the knowledge base in responding to user requests for explanations of conclusions provided by the inference engine through the user-system interface.

Knowledge Representation

Knowledge engineering has developed several modes of knowledge representation that can be adapted to computer storage schemes for the knowledge base. The main methods in use include semantic networks, frames and scripts, and production systems (rules).

A semantic network is essentially a graphic charting method of showing objects, ideas or other elemental entities as encircled or boxed nodes which are connected to one another by lines that represent some functional relation or logical association. The connecting lines are labelled with a word or phrase that expresses the nature of the connection. An example of the graphic semantic network representation can be found in exhibit 9.4 in chapter 9. Such a graphic representation can be converted into a standard data base schema such as network representation through the use of pointers, so that data base management and processing methods can be applied.

Frames or scripts are similar to semantic networks with regard to the use of relational linkages connecting nodes. But the nature of the informational content of each node is very much richer and is no longer merely an atomic label of an entity or idea. The nodal information is now a complete frame or script containing slots of information related to the entity represented by the frame. A frame is similar to a data record in a traditional computer file or entry in a relational data base scheme in that the slots in the frame are filled with values of particular characteristics of the entity. However, some of the slots may contain attached procedures that can be used to determine the value of the slot if it is not expressly provided. Slots, whether directly valued or indirectly valued by the use of procedures, can contain subslots, which in turn can contain further subslots. Thus frames can themselves comprise networks or hierarchies of associated knowledge. A frame representation is shown in exhibit 11.2.

The majority of existing software packages for knowledge-based systems currently use the production system or rule method of knowledge representation. The rules of a production system are expressed in the form of a set of *if* (*a*) *then* (*b*) statements. The method is illustrated in exhibit 11.3. The *if* (*a*) entry in a rule expresses an existing condition or situation or a premise and the *then* (*b*) entry states a prescribed action or conclusion. The popular use of rules in knowledge-based systems is probably due to the relative ease

Exhibit 11.2
Frame and Script Representation

Frame Organization

Each frame is named with a capitalized label and is linked with other frames through a hierarchy denoted by the "slot" "Specialization__of." The slots provide expected places for knowledge to be filled in from experience. Slots can also identify procedures which when executed will fill in slot values.

Example

BUSINESS__STUDENT frame

Specialization__of: COLLEGE__STUDENT

Gender: male, female

Year_of_study: integer less than 6

Major: marketing, finance, operations management, MIS, accounting, quantitative methods, general management, organizational behavior

Grade_point_average: range: 0 to 4.0

Address: Campus dorm address or street address

Event_sequence: default: STUDENT__LIFE

BUSINESS_STUDENT_Joseph_Brown frame

Specialization_of: Business_Student

Gender: male

Year_of_study: 2

Major : MIS

Grade _point_average: range: 0 to 4.0

if_needed: Get JOSEPH_BROWN_GRADES, compute weighted average

Address: Campus dorm Mulberry House

Script Organization

Similar to frames, scripts contain slots describing their characteristics, but these slot entries represent typical expected event sequences and the surrounding conditions for the particular script. Note that the frame BUSINESS_STUDENT above refers to an event sequence provided in the script below. A script can describe what occurs in a place frame or other type of frame entity related expected action sequence.

Example

STUDENT_LIFE Script

Props: Dorms, computers, books, cars, beer joints

Roles: Student, friend, date, clubmember, freshman, upper classman, graduate, co-op worker

Place_of_occurrence: On campus

Event_sequence : first : student becomes freshman then : if survives, becomes upper classman then : sometimes studies, becomes a clubmember or goes on co-op, either way goes to beer joints, buys a car then : if survives and completes courses, becomes a graduate

The Use of Production System Rules

A rule is an *if-then* statement which is operated upon in a production system by comparing the left hand side (the entry denoted by the *if* condition) against "factual" data listed in a data buffer. (The entries in a data buffer are typically user-provided input in a knowledge-based system.) If the left hand side of a rule matches an element in the data buffer, the right hand side action entry (the part after the *then*) is placed in the data buffer. The equivalence of a left hand side to an element in the data buffer causes the rule to be "fired" or considered to be "true." Any production rule that would add a duplicate entry to the data buffer is deactivated. This operation is carried out repeatedly for all rules according to a prescribed strategy defined in an interpreter or inference engine. A stopping test is applied to end the process such as the inability of the system to find any more rules that are "true."

Example

Rule 1 IF smith or jones or brown or hawkins THEN subscriber

Rule 2 IF subscriber THEN admit

Rule 3 IF admit and product a or b or c THEN fill order

Rule 4 IF fill order THEN send bill

Rule 5 IF send bill and product a THEN bill $10

Rule 6 IF send bill and product b THEN bill $15

Rule 7 IF send bill and product c THEN bill $20

Initial Data Buffer Contents

brown   product b

Final Data Buffer Contents

brown product b subscriber admit   fill order send bill bill $15

Processing:

Rule 1 is true so *subscriber* is added and rule 1 deactivated. Rule 2 then becomes true and *admit* is added to buffer. Rule 3 is then true so *fill order* is added to the buffer. Rule 4 then becomes true so send *bill* is added. Rules 5 and 7 are false and cause no action. Rule 6 is true so *bill $15* is added to the buffer.

with which such *if-then* statements are translated into programming code and also because such rules are a natural and easy to use means of human communication of knowledge. However, straight-forward rule representation can become extremely cumbersome for complex structural relations, and may need to be modified in order to handle the use of quantification in logical expressions. Logical quantification includes two kinds of logical expressions:

1. Universal quantification—*For all X*
2. Existential quantification—*There exists at least one X*

These types of quantifications could individually or in combination be included in either or both the (*a*) condition and the (*b*) conclusion of an *if* (*a*) *then* (*b*) rule statement. The formulation of such rules, as well as the inference engine logic needed to process them, can become complex. The use of rules often has to be further modified in order to represent uncertainty. Especially in complex semistructured situations, uncertain knowledge and information must be used in order to produce an actionable but uncertain conclusion rather than merely a formally true statement.

Those who are familiar with traditional data processing methods may recognize that there is nothing entirely new about the use of basic if-then statements to represent rules. A method dating back over twenty-five years is the use of decision tables (see exhibit 11.4). Each column in a decision table expresses a rule, with the row entries in the upper portion of the table representing the presence or absence of various conditions and the row entries in the lower portion representing prescribed actions. Such tables were mainly recommended as documentation techniques for clerical transaction processing systems (which are largely structured rule-driven processes). Several software packages also existed (but were not widely used) for processing without programming by the direct interpretation of an analyst's decision table applied to transaction data files. More recently, many early microcomputer spreadsheet packages have included the use of if-then logical statements to control their processing. These earlier approaches can be said to have provided means of representing and applying knowledge, and thus they were knowledge-based systems to some extent. But the extent of what we now refer to as knowledge-based systems far exceeds these earlier approaches in terms of the potential size and complexity of their knowledge bases, as well as in their ability to provide more powerful inference engines, a natural user interface, and an explanation capability.

Methods of Knowledge Elicitation

A key aspect of knowledge engineering is the methods and means by which the knowledge that resides in the minds of skilled specialist practitioners is elicited and made manifest in a form that can be translated into one of the knowledge representation schemes. Essentially two strategies have been proposed for the elicitation of knowledge:

1. *Direct self-elicitation.*
   This approach argues that the possessors of specialized or expert knowledge should be provided with software and systems to enable them to directly communicate what they know without the need to go through an additional communications link that increases the possibility of miscommunication as well as adds to the cost of the process. This would be analogous to the process of end-user modeling that might be done using spreadsheet software or other modeling languages by the decision maker without first describing the problem domain to a management scientist modeling specialist.

Exhibit 11.4
Use of Decision Tables

Use of decision table format for same rule content as exhibit 11.3

CONDITIONS	rule a	rule b	rule c	rule d
1. Smith or Jones or Brown or Hawkins	No	Yes	Yes	Yes
2. product a	–	Yes	No	No
3. product b	–	No	Yes	No
4. product c	–	No	No	Yes
ACTIONS				
admit		X	X	X
fill order		X	X	X
send bill		X	X	X
bill $10		X		
bill $15			X	
bill $20				X
do not process order	X			

2. *Elicitation by a knowledge engineering analyst.*

   This approach argues that the possessors of specialized knowledge are often unable to articulate it in the complete and internally consistent form required. Part of this problem is attributed to the need to translate human knowledge into the limited language of a knowledge representation scheme. The argument is that knowledge elicitation and translation itself requires special expertise. Just as systems analysts and mathematical model builders are often needed to elicit information from users in order to specify system requirements, knowledge engineers can serve as useful intermediaries to elicit knowledge and build knowledge bases.

There are unresolved problems with both of these approaches when they are applied to less structured realms requiring highly expert levels of knowledge. For these kinds of knowledge realms the knowledge base becomes complex and extensive, thereby making it more difficult, if not impossible, for experts to self-organize and express what they know in the required limited form of any of the knowledge representation schemes. Moreover, it is difficult, and some would argue that it is impossible, for experts to reduce everything they know to the language of production system if-then rules, for example. Software to elicit highly expert knowledge that is both easy to use and that provides sufficient guidance and internal controls for consistency and completeness is not yet generally available on a commercial basis.

The use of knowledge engineering analysts for the task of eliciting complex expert knowledge is the more usual approach. But this approach also has its limitations for some of the same reasons, as well as others. The use of a skilled knowledge engineer does not eliminate the possibility that significant aspects of expert knowledge may inherently not be translatable into production system rules or other formal modes of knowledge representation. Also, the communication skills and knowledge required by knowledge engineers are rare and the methodology of knowledge elicitation has not been sufficiently well developed and formalized so as to be less dependent on individual talents. The methods of knowledge elicitation depend largely on interviewing the specialist and asking the right questions to uncover how they think and approach their tasks, identifying and analyzing key cases that illustrate the knowledge content and approach of the expert, and using an incremental or prototyping approach to building the knowledge base in stages so that the system can be tested against the expert's own judgment at increasing levels of scope.

Inference Engine Methods

In designing the software component called an inference engine, a method must be adopted that is appropriate to the form of knowledge representation employed in the knowledge base. As noted earlier, the inference engine provides a means of using the knowledge base in order to deduce new facts or conclusions. Two approaches to designing the processing logic of an inference engine are particularly suitable in conjunction with the use of production rules. These are known as forward chaining and backward chaining.

Forward chaining, also known as a data driven approach, begins by examining the current data conditions describing a situation and all of the production rules with *if-then* conditions and conclusions that are consistent with these starting data. These rules are then considered to be true and their *then* conclusions (the right hand or "*b*" part of *if (a)-then (b)* rules) are taken as new conditions for a next step search of production rules that have equivalent *if* (left-hand) conditions. The process proceeds in this manner, chaining *then* conclusions with equivalent new *if* conditions until a final conclusion or set of conclusions has been reached. These final conclusions then are conveyed to the system user as a situation diagnosis or a recommendation. If the user so requests, the system can reproduce the chained steps of its inference process and report them to the user. The user may then supply new data so that the reasoning process can be repeated and revised as may be appropriate.

Backward chaining is referred to as a goal driven or expectation driven approach. It begins with a goal or hypothesis and looks for equivalent actions or conclusions in the right hand part of *if (a) then (b)* rules. When these are found, the left hand side conditions of those rules are examined in order to see what other rules would make them "trigger" (be considered true). These new rules are then used in turn to extract their left hand side conditions to see what other rules would trigger them. This backward chaining of rules continues until it can or cannot be concluded that the starting goal is consistent with the known data or conditions supplied by the user. This process also can be retrieved for purposes of explaining the system's reasoning at the user's request, as well as revised and redone according to a modified initial goal or modified conditions.

Knowledge Engineering Languages and Software Tools

There are three categories of software available for the implementation of knowledge-based systems:

1. *Programming languages*

    The main programming languages specially designed for artificial intelligence applications and knowledge engineering are LISP and PROLOG. Exhibit 11.5 illustrates these languages with simple short examples of their use. LISP is an acronym for list processing and has been the most popular choice for AI work in the United States. The LISP language contains few primitive operators that can be used in a very flexible manner to define entities and logical conditions in stages of increasing complexity. PROLOG, an acronym for programming language for logic, has been used more extensively in Europe. It consists of declaring collections of facts and relationships that comprise rules, and the execution of inquiries that test the truth of new propositions.

Exhibit 11.5
Illustration of LISP and PROLOG

LISP

(define **MEMBER** (**HENRY** LIST)

(cond((null LIST) false

((equal **HENRY** (first-member LIST)) true

(member **HENRY** (list-less-first LIST))

[The above function **MEMBER** determines whether or not HENRY is a member of a list. If the list is null (empty), then HENRY is not a member and the proposition is false. Next the program determines if HENRY is the first member of the list. If so, the proposition is true. Finally, the last statement checks all list entries after the first to see if the proposition is true (that is, that HENRY is a member of the list.) The use of uppercase denotes a new function and its arguments. Lowercase is used for built-in or predefined functions.]

PROLOG

/*program*/

person (ANY):—woman (ANY)

woman (Sally).

/*execution:*/

?—person (Sally).

yes.

[The first line after the program declaration is a rule that states that if anything is a woman, then it is a person. The next line declares the fact that Sally is a woman. Then a query is executed asking if Sally is a person, to which the response is "yes". (":—" in PROLOG stands for "if")]

2. *Packaged software tools*

This category consists of knowledge-based system development tools or "shells" that provide the framework for entering the knowledge base and the inference engine for applying it. These tools are far simpler and faster to use than LISP or PROLOG and open up the building of knowledge-based systems to less specialized programmers (possibly to the specialists or experts themselves). Their use is analogous to the use of spreadsheet packages or modeling languages for creating mathematical models rather than writing such models in a programming language such as FORTRAN. Two early knowledge engineering software tools are Teknowledge Inc.'s S.1 and M.1 systems and Intellicorp's KEE system. The Teknowledge packages are rule-based systems with backchaining controls and the Intellicorp system is described as a frame-based system. Early versions of these packages cost about $60,000 but new software, including microcomputer packages, is continually becoming commercially available at generally lower prices.

3. *Software tool and knowledge modules within DSS packages*

This category includes knowledge engineering shells as described above as well as built-in knowledge content modules, both as integrated parts of decision support software such as spreadsheet or modeling languages or data base query systems. They represent significant extensions of the if-then functions present in many earlier versions of DSS packages, thus providing the marriage of knowledge-based systems with more traditional decision support tools. The "shell" modules typically utilize production rules as the means of knowledge representation. Continuing development work by many of the vendors of DSS software aims at incorporating knowledge content rather than mere shells for users to fill in themselves. These content-oriented efforts would provide modeling support systems with the capability to explain model analysis results to users in an easily understandable manner upon request and also would include automatic modeling features to guide the user in selecting or formulating models. Such features often are geared to particular application realms such as financial modeling.

It should be noted that often these knowledge engineering packages are themselves written in FORTRAN or the C language rather than in LISP or PROLOG.

A general trend in the development of software tools of both the stand-alone and DSS-integrated varieties is the enlargement of their rule capacities. Most earlier systems and applications consisted of a few hundred rules, more recent systems are capable of including over a thousand rules, and the advanced knowledge-based systems proposed in the Japanese Fifth Generation project would contain over 20,000 rules. Over and above technical feasibility, whether or not the development and application of very large knowledge bases for management support will prove to be operationally feasible remains to be seen.

Hardware Tools

One development stream in knowledge engineering has contended that special computers must be designed in order to efficiently run knowledge-based and other AI applications. Some so-called "LISP machines" have been developed by companies such as Lisp Machine Inc., Symbolics, Tektronix Inc., Texas Instruments, and Xerox Corp. The Japanese Fifth Generation project aims at development of a new computer architecture that will incorporate parallel processing abilities particularly suitable to knowledge-based applications. However, IBM, Digital Equipment Corp., and Data General have all supported the running of LISP on some of their standard larger mainframes and minicomputers. In addition, LISP processing software is available for ordinary microcomputers, as are DSS packages which integrate the knowledge-based system features previously described.

Applications of Knowledge-based Systems and Management

Since AI researchers began to work on knowledge-based systems in the late 1960s, several applications have emerged. One of the first was the MYCIN system in the mid–1970s, which utilized about 400 rules for the medical diagnosis of bacterial blood infections. This was followed by a more recent system called EMYCIN, which provided a shell for creating rules rather than a specific knowledge base enmeshed within a program to draw inferences from the rules. By separating the knowledge base itself from the software editor used to create it and from the inference engine used to operate on it, EMYCIN is credited with being the first example of a knowledge engineering software tool.

Other applications have arisen in engineering design and the maintenance of technical equipment from Boeing's early work with Stanford and Carnegie Mellon universities. In 1983, Boeing instituted its own artificial intelligence center, which has worked on developing applications such as the design of space stations, helicopter repair, and the diagnosis of airplane engine problems.

In the early 1970s, a system called TAXMAN attempted to evaluate the tax consequences of certain kinds of corporate reorganizations. In 1982 TAX-ADVISOR was developed in order to interact with a human tax consultant in developing the estate planning strategy that would minimize death and income taxes while providing adequate insurance and without sacrificing sound investments. Other applications have aimed at supporting geologists in evaluating sites for potential mineral deposits (Prospector), the diagnosis of faults in hardware and systems software (Raffles and Crib), the selection of suitable auditing procedures (Auditor), the configuring of VAX–11/780 computer systems (R1), the formulation of mathematical concepts (AM), and several medical diagnosis systems in addition to Stanford's MYCIN system (PIP, MIT; Internist/Caduceus, University of Pittsburgh; Casnet, Rutgers; Puff, Stanford; and MDX, Ohio State University).

Missing from lists of early developments are applications in general management activities of planning, control, and decision making, or functional management oriented applications in areas such as production management and marketing. However, these applications are beginning to emerge and expand. Promoter (MDS) is a system to help assess the effects promotions have on the sales of consumer packed products. However, it must use MDS's human consultants to help tailor the system to a company's specific situation and it must be used in conjunction with MDS's Express DSS package, which costs about $100,000 for a license to use the system (Promoter use has associated add-on costs). Various applications in other areas of management, especially in production management and in financial planning and analysis, are also being developed.

Many of these newer management applications are less visible for several reasons. These include:

1. The use of generally available packaged general software tools rather than tailored systems with unique names;
2. The experimental nature and thus uncertain outcomes of much of this work;
3. The proprietary and competitive nature of many of these applications, which leads to secrecy rather than open promotion;
4. The incorporation of knowledge-based components as ancillary functions within some DSS applications, thus merging their identity and making these applications less identifiable as specifically knowledge-based systems.

While it appears likely that knowledge-based management applications will continue to grow, it is highly questionable whether these will include true expert systems, that is, systems representing the deep expertise possessed by outstanding star-level managers. As has been noted previously in chapter 8, the knowledge possessed by these expert performers, whether it is of an analytical or intuitive and creative variety, may be so complex and of such a holistic pattern-associated nature, that it is inherently not amenable to explicit rule-based knowledge representation methods and linear forms of inferencing that are characteristic of knowledge-based systems. Thus, the greatest direct impact of knowledge-based systems in the field of management may be at lower levels of expertise that are less complex and more structured. While the impact in this arena may be significant with regard to operational efficiency and organizational control, this level of management skill, almost by definition, seldom initiates strategic organizational objectives. Thus knowledge-based systems would appear to have greater potential for assisting in running an organization along prescribed paths than in directly helping to steer it in strategic new directions.

However, knowledge-based systems with less than expert direct management knowledge could be used in another capacity that could have greater strategic impacts on management. This potential lies in the use of knowledge-based systems modules as particular kinds of enhancements for both decision support and idea processing systems. This, and other aspects of the relationship between knowledge-based systems and decision support and idea processing systems, is discussed in the next section.

Relationships Between Knowledge-based Systems and Decision Support and Idea Processing Systems

Certain kinds of uses of knowledge-based systems, and the particular subcategory of expert systems, have become an identifiable trend in decision support systems research and in the development of DSS software packages. These uses generally include adapting knowledge engineering tools or knowledge base content to facilitate the use of support systems. The potential of embedding intelligent aids to modeling within model-based DSS software, for example, has already been mentioned earlier in this text. Carrying this notion further, both traditional DSS and idea processing support systems can be enhanced by the integration of knowledge-based modules within them to advise the user on methodological matters as well as on substantive issues of content. Methodological advisory functions can include choice of methods, effective ways of using these methods, and the assessment or interpretation of results. Advisory content functions can include generating and suggesting material for inclusion in DSS models or for divergent idea processing explorations. Expert system modules can potentially play additional roles in the tying together of DSS and idea processing within a single extended support system (or super-DSS). This latter potential is discussed further in chapter 13.

However, the limitations of the role of knowledge-based systems as part of broader support systems and the essential differences between the two independent approaches of support systems and knowledge-based advisory systems needs to be clarified. Basic differences between the two approaches include the following:

1. Knowledge-based systems are, both by intent and within the limitations of current technology, relatively closed systems, whereas support systems are essentially intended to be open and adaptive.
2. The degree of user control over knowledge-based systems is relatively limited to supplying certain inputs and requesting explanations of results as opposed to the wider potential range of user control in well-designed support systems.
3. The flexibility of use of knowledge-based systems is much more circumscribed than that of support systems.

The relatively closed, inflexible, and internally controlled nature of knowledge-based systems stems from their inherent definition as repositories of prescribed knowledge and the means of drawing inferences from that knowledge. The knowledge contained within the system is generally someone else's knowledge (it is knowledge and expertise transfer that is the *raison d'etre* for the system). The means of drawing new knowledge out of the system or applying existing knowledge to new situations is a fixed function of the built-in inference engine.

In contrast, support systems are primarily intended to enable users to apply their own knowledge, create their own mode of analysis, and draw their own conclusions. Even when support systems utilize a fixed data base supplied by someone other than its user or by some independent process, the data base is just that—a base of raw data which only becomes information relevant to the user when the user causes self-defined processing functions to be implemented to convert the raw data into situationally relevant information.

Thus, when used as stand-alone approaches, the knowledge-based system approach is fundamentally different from that of support systems. Nevertheless, there is no more contradiction between using knowledge-based functions in a subordinate and circumscribed manner within the broader framework of a support system than there is in similarly using an optimization technique or other fixed algorithms as limited functions within a support system. The analogy of knowledge-based systems to optimization techniques is useful in clarifying their differences and relationship to support systems. The model which expresses relations between variables is analogous to the knowledge base, while the optimization algorithm that derives a solution from the model is analogous to the inference engine. Optimization, like knowledge-based systems, should be used as an alternative approach to that of support systems under certain circumstances. For optimization techniques to be applicable, a structured problem and a structured solution processing method are needed. For a knowledge-based system to be applicable, a reliable, recognized, manifest, structured body of problem-relevant realm knowledge is required, along with a structured process of using that realm knowledge for the pragmatic purposes at hand. However, the relatively unstructured situations that call for the support systems approach can contain within them some subproblems that are suitable for optimization techniques and some that are suitable for knowledge-based system functions.

Organizational Aspects

The development, maintenance and support of knowledge-based systems applications requires a new organizational effort just as did the new needs brought to the fore by support systems. A new set of staff capabilities relevant to knowledge engineering is needed. Few colleges and universities provide extensive training in knowledge engineering, although this situation is changing. The relevant skills and knowledge are not automatically found among those specializing as applications programmers for administrative data processing applications or among those who are familiar with mathematical modeling or decision support systems. As a result, knowledge engineers currently are in short supply and those who are available are often self-taught, building upon an educational and experiential base that may range among computer science, operations research, various branches of engineering, systems analysis, linguistics, and cognitive science.

Knowledge engineers must have an overall knowledge of the technology, must be familiar with one or more languages or software tools for building knowledge-based systems, must have good analytical and logical abilities, and possess good communications skills in order to facilitate the elicitation of knowledge from specialists as well as to participate in proposing, planning, and documenting new applications, and in counseling users.

Organizations should generally begin with relatively small but useful applications that do not require extensive or complex knowledge bases. Given a good foundation of personal intellectual capacity, initial staff training needed to develop these applications can be acquired in a few weeks. After initial training, continuing access to an external support network, attendance at periodic seminars and professional meetings, and a flow of literature about developments in the field should be provided. Initial applications should be developed, given the availability of appropriate software tools, in a few months. Subsequently, as experience is gained, the internal staff, supplemented by outside consultants where needed, can be used to develop more ambitious applications.

As was stated in regard to the planning and organization of support systems, after a few early applications have been completed it will become important to integrate organizational plans for knowledge-based systems within the overall MIS plan. Because some knowledge-based systems may have strategic importance to an organization and all planned systems should be relevant to expected future business situations, planning for these as well as other MIS applications must also be integrated with and flow from general organizational strategic plans.

Organizationally, knowledge engineering specialists should be placed within the MIS organization with close ties to support systems staff specialists. It seems likely that knowledge engineering staffs will develop along further specialized lines, with some staff members serving as specialized programmers, others as knowledge elicitation analysts and systems designers, and still others as internal consultants on such matters as software acquisition, management planning, and user and staff education and training. The mix of staff specialities and skills needed will partially depend on the strategy of user-developed versus specialist-developed systems, which in turn will depend on further developments in the available software tools.

As organizational experience with knowledge-based systems becomes more mature, new problems associated with their design and management are likely to emerge, some of which are analogous to experience with support systems. These will include problems of:

1. Making initially separate and independent knowledge bases compatible and more amenable to integration with one another;
2. Finding better means of managing, maintaining and updating knowledge bases as new knowledge becomes available through both organizational experience and external developments;
3. Quality control management procedures over the choice of expertise to include in knowledge bases, verification of its proper representation, and the maintenance of its integrity;
4. Developing new interfaces between knowledge bases and other components of information systems such as data bases and the telecommunications electronic mail system;
5. Creating a knowledge base system as a corporate resource and a corporate knowledge management function as part of information technology management.

Conclusion

Knowledge-based systems have important potential to management in their own right when used as independent systems, but they are different and not co-equal approaches to the same ends aimed at by support systems. Because the technology as well as goals of knowledge-based systems differ in significant ways from those of support systems, these two approaches require different background and educational materials, and are likely to require separate and distinct, although coordinated, staff functions. They are not going to supplant the need for support systems any more than support systems have supplanted or will supplant the need for structured analytical applications or needs for basic information reporting systems and administrative data processing systems. Furthermore, knowledge-based systems are unlikely to ever supplant the need for all forms of human expertise in organizations or, for the foreseeable future, to be capable of representing and applying all of the many varieties of human knowledge. The approach may be limited not merely by the current state of the art, but by the inherent inability to render deep human expertise and thinking processes as manifest machine simulations.

Aside from their limited but important role as stand-alone applications, knowledge-based systems can also play an important subordinate role in enhancing support systems as embedded modules within those systems. For this reason, they are an important contributing technology to support systems and support systems workers must become knowledgeable in the basics of this technology.

In addition, aside from any function they may have as knowledge repositories and knowledge transfer mechanisms, knowledge engineering technology is likely to provide us with useful new languages and software tools for instructing computers in carrying out processes that are characterized largely by qualitative logical relationships rather than by computational or data manipulation functions. This linguistic facilitation of our ability to communicate effectively and efficiently with computers may open up further new applications aside from those we now recognize as knowledge-based systems. Just as we cannot and should not always limit the tools of support systems to support applications, the tools of knowledge engineering may find other uses in the hands of imaginative users.

Review Questions, Exercises, and Discussion Topics

Review Questions

1. What is the strict definition of an expert system?
2. What is the definition of a knowledge-based system? How do you distinguish between an expert system and a knowledge-based system, according to the definitions you have given?
3. What is the relationship between artificial intelligence and knowledge-based systems?
4. What are the two basic types of knowledge? Give a brief example of each.
5. How do ordinary computer programming languages deal with the two types of knowledge and how does this approach differ from that of knowledge-based systems?
6. What three dimensions can be used to categorize management application realms of knowledge-based systems?
7. What relation is there between managerial level and the size and complexity of a managerial knowledge-based system application?
8. In addition to providing knowledge counseling to managers, could a knowledge-based system emphasize alternative purposes? Describe them.
9. Name and describe the functions of each major component of the architecture of a knowledge-based system.
10. Name and describe three major modes of knowledge representation.
11. Which of these modes of knowledge representation is generally the most frequently applied method in knowledge-based systems?
12. What two alternative basic strategies can be followed in knowledge elicitation?
13. What advantages and limitations are associated with each of the two basic strategies for knowledge elicitation?
14. Describe the generally recommended approach to eliciting expertise and building an extensive knowledge base for an expert system.
15. What two general design approaches have been taken to the processing logic of an inference engine? Describe each of them.

16. What three general categories of software were identified for the implementation of knowledge-based systems?
17. Which two programming languages have been most often associated with AI applications and the programming of knowledge-based systems?
18. Why are packaged software tools for the development of knowledge-based systems often described as shells?
19. Could a knowledge-based system be developed using FORTRAN or C or even BASIC? Explain.
20. Can the LISP language be run on an ordinary mainframe or minicomputer? On a microcomputer? What is needed beside the computer in order to run a LISP application program?
21. Name two or three early nonmanagerial applications of knowledge-based systems.
22. Identify actual or likely potential managerial application areas for knowledge-based systems.
23. What general factors may have inhibited the visibility of managerial applications of knowledge-based systems?
24. What main characteristics differentiate the knowledge-based systems approach and the support systems approach?
25. What similarity is there between a knowledge-based system and an optimization system using mathematical modeling?
26. What role can knowledge-based systems play to enhance support systems?
27. What capabilities should be possessed by knowledge engineering specialists?
28. What existing formal educational disciplines are most relevant to knowledge engineering?
29. Where in an organization should the knowledge engineering function be placed?
30. What special issues and problems are likely to arise in an organization after the early stages of knowledge-based systems applications?

Exercises

1. Take the statements given as examples of declarative knowledge in the early part of this chapter under the section headed **Types of Knowledge Included in Knowledge-Based Systems** (e.g. 1. John is a young man. 2. Sally is a young woman.). Convert these into the format of if-then production system rules. (You may want to refer to exhibit 11.3 for examples of production system rules.)
2. Identify some realm of special knowledge that you yourself are familiar with. Create a set of initial basic production rules (at least fifteen) representing the most basic aspects of this realm knowledge. Describe areas of additional knowledge that would be relevant to this realm but were not covered by your initial set of rules.
3. Generally describe either a model-based or a data-based DSS application you have some knowledge about. (a) Identify realm knowledge that might be useful to incorporate in the system to advise neophyte practitioners of

that realm who might use this DSS. (*b*) Identify and describe guides to formulating a strategy for using this DSS that might be useful to incorporate as a knowledge-based module. (*c*) Describe the functions of knowledge-based modules that might be included to help the user to properly interpret results and avoid certain pitfalls of misuse.

4. Take any example of idea processing functions or applications based on part 2 of this text (chapters 8, 9, and 10) and describe how knowledge-based modules might be usefully embedded within an idea processing support system.

5. Assess an actual software package with DSS or idea processing capabilities for (*a*) its actual inclusion of knowledge-based systems capabilities, and (*b*) potentially useful knowledge-based systems enhancements not presently found in the package.

6. Survey an actual organization and identify the extent, if any, to which they have used knowledge-based systems. Have there been any actual managerial applications? Are any such applications in development or planned? Can you identify potentially useful new managerial applications in the organization? Report the results of your survey.

Discussion Topics

1. Take the side in a debate that argues that deep managerial expertise can never be properly represented in a knowledge-based system. Outline your arguments and be prepared to take part in a debate.

2. Take the opposite side of the argument defined in item 1 above. Prepare to support your side of this question in a debate.

3. Discuss the screening criteria and methods you would recommend that an organization actually employ to start a new knowledge engineering group by selecting people from within the company.

4. Discuss the prospects for mitigating the lack of availability of sufficient numbers of competent specialists of a particular type through the use of knowledge-based systems. Pick a particular specialty that is relevant to management such as operations research modeling experts, MIS computer systems analyst designers, marketing planners, or financial analysts.

References

Barr, A., Feigenbaum, E. A. 1982. (Editors) *The Handbook of Artificial Intelligence*. Volumes I and II. Los Altos, Calif.: William Kaufmann, Inc.

Blanning, R. W. 1984. "Management Applications of Expert Systems." *Information and Management* 7(December):311–16.

Bonczek, R. H., Holsapple, C. W., Whinston, A. B. 1981. *Foundations of Decision Support Systems*. Orlando: Academic Press.

Briggs, W. 1985. "Software Tools for Planning: DSS and AI/Expert Systems." *Planning Review* 13(September):36–43.

Davis, R. 1979. "Interactive Transfer of Expertise: Acquisition of New Inference Rules." *Artificial Intelligence* 12(August):121–57.

Davis, R., King, J. 1977. "An Overview of Production Systems." *Machine Intelligence* 8:300–322.

Elam, J. J., Henderson, J. C. 1983. "Knowledge Engineering Concepts for Decision Support System Design and Implementation." *Information and Management* 6(April):109–14.

Ford, F. N. 1985. "Decision Support Systems and Expert Systems: A Comparison." *Information and Management* 8(January):21–26.

Gevarter, W. B. 1983. "Expert Systems: Limited But Powerful." *IEEE Spectrum* 20(August)8:39–45.

Harmon, P. H., King, D. R. 1985. *Expert Systems: Artificial Intelligence in Business.* New York: John Wiley and Sons.

Hayes-Roth, F. 1984. The Knowledge-Based Expert System: A Tutorial." *IEEE Spectrum* 21(September).

Horwit, E. 1985. "Exploring Expert Systems." *Business Computer Systems* 48–57, March.

King, D., Morgan, R. 1986. *Knowledge-Based Systems: An Overview.* 35–01–40, Management Series, Systems Development Management portfolio. Pennsauken, N.J.: Auerbach Publishers, Inc.

Konopasek, M., Sundaresan, J. 1984. "Expert Systems for Personal Computers." *Byte,* May.

Lee, R. M. 1983. "Epistemological Aspects of Knowledge-Based Decision Support Systems." *Processes and Tools for Decision Support,* Proceedings of IFIP WG8.3/IASSA Working Conference, Schloss Laxenburg, Austria, Amsterdam: North-Holland. 25–36.

Michaelson, R., Michie, D. 1983. "Expert Systems in Business." *Datamation* November.

Minsky, M. 1975. "A Framework for Representing Knowledge." in *The Psychology of Computer Vision,* Computer Science Series, Advanced Book Program, Edited by P. H. Winston. New York: McGraw-Hill.

Sen, A., Biswas, G. 1985. "Decision Support Systems: An Expert Systems Approach." *Decision Support Systems,* 1(September):197–204.

Thinking Machines." *The Economist,* 92–93, May 11, 1985.

Vassiliou, Y., Clifford, J., Jarke, M. 1985. "Access to Specific Declarative Knowledge by Expert Systems; The Impact of Logic Programming." *Decision Support Systems* 1(September):123–41.

Warren, D. H. D., et al. 1977. *Prolog—The Language and Its Implementation Compared with LISP.* LNEC, 1977, and SIGART/SIGPLAN Symposium.

Waterman, D. A. 1986. "A Guide To Expert Systems." *Teknowledge Series on Knowledge Engineering* 2. Reading, Mass.: Addison-Wesley.

"What's Happening With Expert Systems." 1985. *EDP Analyzer* 23(December):1–16.

Caveats and Dissenting Voices: 12
Economic Justification and Potential Misuse of Support Systems

---

. . . my way is to divide half a sheet of paper by a line into two columns; writing over the one "pro "and other "con." Then during three or four days consideration I put down under the different heads short hints of the different motives that at different times occur to me for and against the measure. When I have thus got them all together in one view I endeavor to estimate their respective weights; and where I find two, one on each side, that seem equal I strike them both out. If I find a reason pro equal to some two reasons con, I strike out the three. If I judge some two reasons con equal to some three reasons pro I strike out the five; and thus proceeding I find at length where the balances lie. And, though the weight of reasons cannot be taken with the precision of algebraic quantities, . . . I have found great advantage from this kind of equation in what may be called moral or prudential algebra."
From *Benjamin Franklin*, Carl van Doren, Garden City: Anchor Books. 1941

The need for economic justification and concern for avoiding potential misapplication apply to both quantitatively oriented DSS and qualitatively oriented idea processing support systems. This chapter will discuss these issues and suggest approaches toward economic justification and avoiding the pitfalls of misuse. The differences in the nature of DSS versus idea processing applications will be considered in discussing the kinds of costs and risks associated with their respective misuse.

Economic Justification of Support Systems

Several aspects of economic justification will be discussed in this section. These include:

1. The essential character and suitability of value analysis for support systems as opposed to traditional cost-benefit analysis;
2. The difference between economic justification and optimization with respect to cost-effectiveness;

3. The kinds of alternatives to be weighed against support system approaches for both quantitative DSS and qualitative idea processing;
4. The differing roles of prior justification versus post-usage value assessment;
5. Paradigms (reference models) for prior justification.

Value Assessment Versus Cost-Benefit Analysis

As discussed in chapter 6, the economic justification of a DSS approach should utilize the broader concepts of *value* and *value analysis* or *value assessment* rather than the typically narrower focus of cost-benefit analysis on measurable or estimable cost-avoidance and cost reduction outcomes of computerization. The value analysis approach applies equally to idea processing support, although the underlying sources of values involved are likely to differ significantly from those related to more quantitatively oriented DSS applications.

Value is essentially subjective, and (as pointed out in chapter 6) should be seen as determined by what a rational, responsible, and knowledgeable user would be willing to expend both directly and indirectly to acquire and use the system. In contrast, the measurement of traditional systems' cost reduction derived benefits is seen as resting primarily on an objective third party staff analysis of historical and projectable facts. This kind of cost benefit analysis can be characterized as taking a production-oriented viewpoint while the value analysis approach takes a marketing or consumer oriented viewpoint.

The production-oriented viewpoint focuses on the *producer's* relative costs of alternative ways of delivering the same standard product. The marketing-consumer viewpoint associated with value assessment rests upon an economic-marketing principle of what *users* perceive as value for their particular purposes and circumstances and are thus willing to spend to acquire that value-providing resource. Because automation systems are usually intended to produce standard products and services, the production-oriented viewpoint is an appropriate approach for their economic justification. Support systems are not intended to produce standardized products but are instead flexible, user-controlled, general tools. Therefore, their economic justification should stem primarily from the reponsible users' perceptions of value. Because of its subjective nature, value assessment cannot be an abstract and purely logical exercise devoid of real flesh and blood people, but depends on the characteristics, attitudes, and working style of the users involved. This does not mean that individuals in an organization should be encouraged to indulge their private whims, but that complex semistructured skills involve the whole professional person and are not robot-like cooky-cutter procedures. Therefore, different individuals can be expected to assess the value of support system features differently.

Some support capabilities will contribute more directly toward the likelihood of better performance and others may have an effect mainly on hygiene factors, whose presence is unlikely to directly cause better than average performance but whose absence might lead to lower than average performance. Convenience of usage, for example, cannot be directly linked with effective use of a system's capability, but the absence of convenience may inhibit usage, thereby leading to less thorough efforts, which in turn decreases the likelihood of a higher quality (more effective) outcome. If hygiene factors are highly valued to the individuals involved and their cost is a relatively low percentage of these employees' direct compensation, this may be sufficient justification. In this respect, hygiene factors embodied in support systems may require no more justification than that of providing (within reason) more pleasant office furniture and carpeting to important and well-paid staff members (or, for that matter, more pleasant workplaces for factory workers). Personnel costs, especially for professionals and managers, are continually rising while the unit costs of basic computer support (for the use of microcomputers, software, and secondary storage) are generally decreasing. These trends, as illustrated in exhibit 12.1, can provide the basis for justifying at least a minimum form of support.

However, as has been indicated in chapter 7, a complete organizational strategy for support systems ultimately requires more facilities than those included in estimating initial costs for microcomputer-based individual support. Value assessment for more comprehensive support capabilities thus cannot be so easily dismissed as this limited view might indicate.

While value analysis should rest on users' *subjective* assessments, that should not reduce it to an *arbitrary* assessment. The assessment can be rendered more comprehensive and reliable through the assistance of a staff analyst who is knowledgeable about usage patterns and trends, the nature of the tasks being performed, and in attitudinal measurement methods and scaling techniques. Accountability must also be established by recording the assessment, monitoring actual future satisfaction with usage, and tracking overall support costs against overall performance. These control mechanisms should not be used to attempt tight third party control over actual usage, but to provide users themselves with feedback that enhances their future ability to assess value and to establish accountability for aggregate expenditures.

Value assessment and justification should not only consider the budget dollars the user is willing to allocate to support systems acquisition, but also should include consideration of the willingness to voluntarily expend personal effort for learning and improving systems usage skills. Because support system usage is essentially optional and not a required means of carrying out one's assigned tasks, the personal investment of time and effort a user is willing to make can be a key indicator in assessing whether or not a system will be used and in estimating its perceived value.

Exhibit 12.1

Basic Microcomputer Support Facility Costs Relative to Professional-middle Manager Costs

---

(Note: All costs are approximated for illustration purposes.)

Basic Annual Unit Costs for Volume Purchased Micro plus Extra Storage

Purchase = $ 5000.
Annual cost assuming above costs are amortized over a two-year period = $2500.

Basic Annual Personnel-Related Costs

Annual Salary = $45,000
+ 10 % Benefits of $4,500

$49,500
Plus secretarial support $18,000

$67,500

Basic Support To Personnel Cost Ratio = 2500/67500 = 3.7%

Assuming Annual Cost Changes of
7% increase in Personnel Costs and 5 % decrease in computer costs

Next Year's Ratio = 3.3%
2-Years hence Ratio = 2.9%

Justification Versus Optimization

Economic justification does not always require the determination of which alternative (one form of new system or another or retaining current methods) is optimal. Neither conventional cost-benefit analysis nor value analysis typically uncovers the best of all feasible alternatives, that is, literally the optimal alternative. *Economic justification requires only that there be an acceptable expectation that a new expenditure for attaining new resources will produce a net economic gain.* After justifying a particular alternative, an exhaustive analysis of all alternatives could be carried out that might identify an even better alternative. When two alternatives are both feasible and economically justified, but alternative *a* produces either more benefits or requires less costs than alternative *b,* then alternative *a* is said to be more *cost-effective* than alternative *b.* It is usually not possible or not worthwhile to carry out so exhaustive a study as would be required to identify and assess all possible alternatives so that the most cost-effective system can be found. For that reason it is rarely appropriate to claim that a new system would be an "optimal" choice. It is often sufficiently difficult to establish that a particular system would provide enough of a payoff to be economically justified, let alone optimal.

Alternatives to DSS and IP Support

In establishing the economic justification of a support system, at a minimum a comparison must be made to the present method, if any present method exists, or to doing nothing. If it is feasible, however, more than one new alternative should also be assessed in order to uncover a possibly more cost-effective (although not necessarily optimal) alternative. Alternatives to any given form of computer support can be classified into several categories. For either DSS or IP support, initially the present method alternative usually provides no computer-based support system at all. But for quantitative problems, an alternative to DSS forms of support that should be considered is that of developing or installing a more structured traditional computer-based system such as an operations research model-based system that provides a more direct solution to a more highly structured problem definition. A second computer-based alternative might be the development of a new regular reporting system that provides managers with information needed on a fixed-cycle basis rather than in the ad hoc mode of DSS data base query support. The appropriateness of such non-DSS computer-based alternatives should ideally be discovered in the feasibility assessment step of the situation analysis phase of development, as pointed out in chapter 6. Failure to do so can result in economic penalties that are not usually obvious in advance. This is a major potential pitfall and will be discussed further later in this chapter. Because of its importance, it is useful to include a second consideration of non-DSS computer alternatives in the value assessment cost justification phase.

Idea processing support differs in regard to what type of alternative can be considered. There is typically no *structured* computer-based system alternative that presents itself. The alternative to a particular form of IP support is usually either another form of IP support or no computer-based system at all. If advances in artificial intelligence and expert systems were ever to reach a point where turning over a complex qualitative reasoning process to a computer becomes a feasible alternative, then we would confront a new issue of whether we can justify using an automation system versus a support system. This issue (not presently in sight) would be likely to involve more than just economic justification, but would also have to consider social policy and other values.

Pre-justification Versus Post-assessment

The best approach for carrying out a value analysis for support systems depends, among other factors, on whether development of an individual application (such as the development of a specific DSS for marketing planning) is under consideration or whether the acquisition of generic tools (such as a DSS generator or a general IP software package such as ThinkTank or Consultant) is being assessed. Procedures for economic justification during an earlier era when no generalized software packages were available had to consider some costs of initial programming and subsequent additional programming as an application evolved. Under these conditions, it was appropriate to limit the initial version of a support system in both scope and cost so that the first round of actual usage could be post-assessed in order to justify the next round of development. Later, as generalized software became available for mainframe computers at a substantial cost of acquisition, it became necessary to prejustify the larger initial cost, usually by assessing in advance the aggregate value of a number of future applications. Even if a single important application was earmarked to bear the entire burden of justification for acquiring an expensive package, it was now more urgent to assess value prior to actual usage. Thus earlier approaches to an incremental strategy of incurring costs for software development and assessing value in successive stages, such as that suggested by Keen (1979), became less appropriate for many situations after generalized software was more widely available. Post-usage assessment, or a successive series of incremental post-assessments, is less applicable as the sole approach to justification in an era that relies on setting up facilities such as packaged software, microcomputers, and communications facilities that are expensive in the aggregate. Incremental development which uses already existing facilities can rely less on prior justification and more on step by step post-assessment, but "big bang" (large set-up) requirements call for more comprehensive prejustification.

However, post-assessment still has a role to play, used in ways that complement rather than replace prior assessment. Post-assessment of the value of support systems is an ingredient of the broader purpose management practices of performance measurement and accountability. In instances where centralized management allows considerable local autonomy in allocating overall budgets, it is not necessary to carry out a formal detailed prejustification for each expenditure and submit it to higher authority for approval. However, if it is known by managers that a post-assessment of the overall performance of their organizational units will hold them accountable for final results, they are more likely to exercise prudence in prior self-assessment of the manner in which they allocate their limited resources. This type of accountability usually requires only a post-examination of aggregate performance with respect to general objectives and need not necessarily examine whether or not particular resources such as support systems individually contributed positively or negatively to bottom-line results. However, post-assessments for internal use rather than for external accountability should examine support system applications in order to provide the feedback necessary for managerial learning and improvement. This, in turn, can improve the judgment and knowledge applied to subsequent efforts to justify new applications and resource acquisitions in advance of their usage. These different but complementary roles for prior and post usage assessment are illustrated in exhibit 12.2.

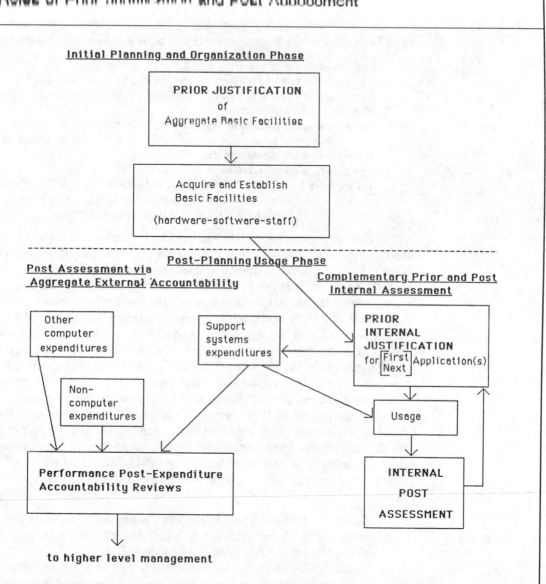

Exhibit 12.2

Roles of Prior Justification and Post Assessment

Initial Planning and Organization Phase

PRIOR JUSTIFICATION
of
Aggregate Basic Facilities

Acquire and Establish
Basic Facilities

(hardware-software-staff)

Post-Planning Usage Phase

**Post Assessment via
Aggregate External Accountability**

**Complementary Prior and Post
Internal Assessment**

Other
computer
expenditures

Support
systems
expenditures

PRIOR
INTERNAL
JUSTIFICATION
for First Next Application(s)

Non-
computer
expenditures

Usage

Performance Post-Expenditure
Accountability Reviews

INTERNAL
POST
ASSESSMENT

to higher level management

Paradigms for Prior Justification

Approaches to prior justification based on value analysis are similar whether applied to an individual specific application, a group of specific applications, or to the acquisition of general resources for the support of general functional areas. Three general paradigms can serve as a basis for prior value assessment:

1. *Outcome-based assessment*
   The generally preferable approach, that focuses upon the potential for increasing the value of outcomes related to the supported processes.
2. *Resource-based assessment*
   An approach that focuses on the current value of the resources already allocated to the affected processes and the justification of augmenting these resources with computer support.
3. *Function time-based assessment*
   An approach that focuses on managerial and staff time currently spent on the general functions involved in the process to be supported, and the potential for increasing the yield of that time through computer support.

All three approaches are related and similar but differ with respect to how directly they assess the final payoff of support through increasing outcome values. The outcome-based approach does this directly and therefore, other things being equal, it is the preferred approach. To illustrate the outcome-based assessment approach one can consider the problem of investment in the development of a truly new product or service offering. In the case of an entirely new offering, no historical data is available on sales, profits, or costs. Costs are not so difficult to estimate, given at least a general plan for how the new offering is to be implemented. The activities and resources involved, such as people, materials, distribution channels, or advertising, may be directed toward new ends, but are not themselves unique, nor are the costs associated with varying amounts of these resources and activities unknown or without precedent. Demand and the potential users' perceptions of the value of the new offering, however, are much more difficult to estimate in the absence of actual market tests or limited trial offerings. An initial on-paper subjective assessment of these factors can be based on the combined use of two guidelines:

1. A backwards assessment (Young 1984[b]), which is essentially the same as a break-even analysis or a goal seeking type of analysis often provided in DSS modeling systems;
2. Subjective likelihood estimates applied to results of the backwards assessments, aided by referent analogies to other new offerings in situations with at least some important relevant parallels.

In a highly simplified aggregate form, a backwards assessment for an initial assessment of a concept for a new offering could be carried out by first estimating costs, then calculating how much would have to be sold at a given price in order to just break-even, and finally assessing the likelihood that at least that amount of sales would be attainable. If this likelihood is thought to be too low to be acceptable, then the new offering concept may be rejected at that point, or a few other price-demand combinations may be examined to determine whether break-even or better is likely to be attainable for any combination. If attaining the break-even point appears to be very likely, the analysis may procede to examine higher feasible levels of attainable profitability and to then adjust and elaborate on the specifics of a strategy to attain them. The logic of the backwards assessment is that it is easier and more efficient to first assess the likelihood of the mathematically determined break-even point than it is to start out by attempting a more comprehensive estimate of demand and profitability. A similar approach can be applied in an outcome-based prior assessment of a support system as follows:

Let C = estimated total costs of acquiring and maintaining the support system in operation over some defined period of time taken as the planning horizon.
Let M = the current magnitude of the outcomes that might be affected by the support system, measured in monetary units.
Let e = a factor representing the proportion (or percentage) of increased outcome value that would be attainable through implementing the support system.

Given the above definitions, at break-even between the costs of support and the outcome value of support, $C = e * M$.

Suppose one is considering implementing a system that would cost approximately $200,000 to acquire and maintain over a two year period (assuming that two years is the planning horizon which was set by a policy decision which took into account the degree of stability in the company's competitive strategic situation, changes in computer technology and pricing, and other factors). Further suppose that this system is intended to support top executives in their consideration of mergers and acquisitions according to a growth strategy that is expected to result in one or more acquisitions costing approximately $200 million. A break-even value of increased effectiveness attributable to the system's usage can be directly obtained as follows:

$$e = C/M = 200,000/200,000,000 = 0.001 \text{ or } 0.1\%$$

This value means that the usage of the system would have to result in obtaining an increase in the value of the outcome of an acquisition by 0.1 percent in order to just repay the costs of the system. The use of the system may affect the value of the outcome in several ways. The main categories of contribution to increased value could stem from using the system to conduct a more extensive search and analysis that can result in discovering (or increasing the chances of discovering) a better company acquisition candidate without increasing the cost of acquisition, avoiding a poorer acquisition, gaining an advantage over competitors in being able to react more quickly to an acquisition opportunity, and, of lesser but not negligible value, possibly expending less expensive executive time and analysis time in the acquisition process. Of greater importance than saving the direct cost of executive time may be avoiding negative impacts on other areas of the business that might be neglected if the acquisition process was not supported. Given a broad area of opportunity for higher value outcomes, a small increased effectiveness factor such as 0.1 percent (the break-even value of **e** in the example given previously) may be assessed as having a very high likelihood of attainability. Also, any risk of loss associated with the support expenditure not being fully effective or even being entirely wasted is relatively small in the context of the magnitude of the decision impact. The acceptance of the possibility that the support system will not return any value at all is similar to the willingness to pay an insurance premium, which most usually returns no value but may avoid a large loss if the unusual occurs. The cost of a support system can be viewed as a positive insurance premium, that is, it may avoid an *opportunity loss* associated with not using the system.

Assuming the support system is judged to be relevant and appropriate to the users and to their approach to the task, the subjective value of the system in the previous example may be assessed as being highly likely to be *significantly in excess of its cost*. In terms of the simple relationship being considered, it is sufficient that $e * M \gg C$ (the double greater than sign $\gg$ should be read as "much greater than"). This determination suffices to justify the system without attempting further analysis to more precisely estimate the most likely value of the support system, that is, the expected value of $e * M$. The process of economic justification itself incurs costs and should be limited to addressing the question of whether or not the system is likely to be a prudent investment, without dealing with unnecessary detail.

It should be emphasized that the increased effectiveness value of a support system should not be thought of as something attributed to the computer (or to the computer department or even to the support staff). The value of a support system is only attained through leveraging the capabilities of the users themselves. The interaction between system and user makes it inappropriate to attempt to partial out some amount of credit to the system, leaving the remainder to the user. The system-user *combination* may result in increased value over an unsupported process. This concept will be undermined if an interdepartmental competition for credit sharing is allowed to take place. In general, if it is necessary to assign economically measured credit for increased effectiveness, it is better to let full direct credit for increased effectiveness resulting from systems acquisition and usage go entirely to users. The computer staff and department can be adjudged to be successful and recognized to the degree that their users are successful in their tasks and are satisfied clients eager to continue being clients. They can and should be recognized by their users, but should not be in competition with them for credit.

In the example given previously only a single general application area, that of mergers and acquisitions, was considered. When general support facilities are being considered for a wide area of future applications, not all of which may be currently identifiable, the process of prior justification may be somewhat more extensive but would follow essentially the same logic. Total support system costs would still be represented by C, while the total magnitude of the identifiable affected outcomes would be arrived at by summing the outcome values for each of the affected areas. This total outcome value can then be represented by ΣM, so that the break-even equation becomes $C = e * \Sigma M$. A conservative approach may reduce the value of ΣM by some factor based on the assumption that not all of the potentially affected areas of application will actually be implemented during the planning horizon. On the other hand, new unforeseen application areas may arise later during the period being considered and this may be adjusted for by adding some adjustment proportion to ΣM. An illustrative example is given in example 12.1.

As stated previously, resource-based assessment focuses on the current value of the resources already allocated to the processes involved, and, in a manner similar to that of exhibit 12.1, considers the proportional increase in those costs incurred by implementing a support system. The relevant equation to be considered changes from $C = e * M$ to $C = f * R$, where f is the proportional increase in resources allocated to the process as a result of the support system's costs, and R is the current costs of resources used (without the support system). R can generally be arrived at by adding up the personnel-related costs (salaries + benefits + direct staff and other directly supporting equipment, service, space, and supply costs) for the people performing the affected tasks (which may be only one person or many people). The magnitude of R is an indicator of the implicit value to the organization of the tasks being performed. Suppose the implementation of a support system would increase these resource costs by, say, 4 percent ($f = 0.04$). The assumption can be made that if it were found to be worthwhile and feasible to add 4 percent to the conventional resources (such as adding more people or supporting staff) the

EXAMPLE 12.1

AN OUTCOME-BASED ASSESSMENT OF MULTIPLE SUPPORT FACILITIES FOR MULTIPLE APPLICATIONS

C = $440,000

(Costs for software, 25 microcomputer-terminals, 2 support staff personnel, mainframe usage, miscellaneous, for two year planning period.)

Application Areas	*2-Year Magnitude of Value Affected*
1. Marketing Planning (DSS)	M_1 = **$5,000,000**
2. New Product Development (IP and DSS)	M_2 = **$3,000,000**
3. Financial Budgeting (DSS)	M_3 = **$80,000,000**
4. Human Resource Planning and Management Development (IP and DSS)	M_4 = **$10,000,000**
ALL AREAS	ΣM = **$98,000,000**

Estimated reduction for unrealized application coverage in first two years = **.5**

ΣM^1 = .5 ΣM = $49,000,000

Estimated increase in coverage for unforeseen applications = **1.2**

ΣM^2 = 1.2 ΣM^1 = 1.2 × $49,000,000 = $58,800,000

Break-even Value:

C = e * ΣM^2
e = C / ΣM^2 = $440,000/$58,800,000 = .007 or .7%

Decision Question:

In the judgment of the managers responsible for the areas affected, how likely is it that the value of outcomes will be increased by significantly more than 0.7 percent through the use of the support systems?

organization would have already done so. By this consideration alone one might conclude that added costs for a proposed support system (or an additional staff person) should be rejected, unless the business activities have themselves been expanded. But suppose the organization had the opportunity to buy an additional resource with a value much higher than that of the average existing resources, say a super-performing manager. Should the company pay a premium salary for such a potential star performer? Many rational executives would approve both the hiring and paying of an above average salary in such a circumstance. The value assessment of the support system in question then can be reduced to the question of whether the additional 4 percent cost would buy considerably more value, on average, than a similar expenditure for conventional resources. *A computer-based support system largely represents a substitution for conventional staff support.* If its cost/yield ratio is expected to be considerably more favorable than that of an incremental expenditure for conventional staff support, than it may be economically justified. It should be emphasized again that it is not the reduction of cost but the disproportionately high increase in yield (effectiveness) that is the main concern. While it is difficult to estimate how much more a support system might yield compared to an additional average conventional staff person, the computer support system would seem to have certain inherent advantages. Unlike human staff, it is tireless, more rapid, more controllable, more even, predictable, specifiable, and testable in its scope, power, and responsiveness. It can generally be spread across a wider user base than can a human staff person, and for that reason alone can provide a larger multiplier on the effectiveness of users. In any case, the resource-based assessment must still rely on managerial judgment and assumptions in deciding on the relative value of a proposed support system. However, this approach can provide a useful framework to put the decision into perspective.

A function time-based assessment can be used alone, or in conjunction with either of the previously discussed approaches. It requires that an estimate first be made of the amount of staff time currently used to carry out the tasks to be supported (such as an analysis of a plan) and an estimate of how much time would be required for completing the same tasks to the same extent using the proposed support system. If, for example, a support system cuts the time required in half, it can be assumed that twice as many alternatives can be examined without any increase in staff time expended. This assumption is consistent with the notion that support systems are not intended to reduce processing costs as an end in itself, but that potential efficiencies are to be converted into increased effectiveness through the means of more thorough effort leading to attaining higher valued final outcomes. In a function time-based assessment, the costs of support, **C,** are balanced against the value of **g * T,** where **g** is the ratio of unsupported time required to supported time required (for example, **g = 2** if the time required can be halved for the same completed work), and **T** is the current amount of time expended on the task. The assessment of value then can be expressed as a question in the following form:

What is the likelihood that completing twice (**g** times, in this case) as much work in decision problem processing (such as analyzing twice as many alternatives using a planning model, or searching through and assessing twice as many combinations in a divergent idea processing problem) will yield a final outcome value in excess of **C,** the cost of the support system?

The assumption is that as **g** increases, the likelihood of attaining value in excess of **C** increases. In other words, a function time-based assessment focuses explicitly on the yield of time alone. In contrast, a resource-based assessment explicitly considers the cost of the expended resources, while only implicitly considering how the increased yield of those resources is to be achieved (whether through increasing the thoroughness of processing via increased speed or increasing the quality of processing through facilitating a broader skills repertoire or a more effective processing strategy). An outcome-based assessment is most explicit about the value of the final outcomes that may be affected, and not at all explicit about how the support system may lead to attaining added value. All of these approaches provide a somewhat different way of framing the question for the decision maker's judgment about value. None of them provide an objective or precise measure of economic value, but used in conjunction with a post-usage assessment they can provide benchmarks for learning and continually sharpening judgment. They may be used individually or in combination, according to the preferred managerial orientation and available information in a given situation.

Potential Misuses of Support Systems

The use of support systems may represent a mixed blessing. With the best of intentions and the highest quality software, there may be situations in which the organization's best interests might be better served by either no computer-based system at all or by a different kind of computer-based system. The potential pitfalls are different for DSS and IP, and these will be discussed separately below.

Penalties of DSS Amateurism

The use of DSS cannot and should not be tightly controlled. DSS usage should be allowed to evolve and flourish according to the aided learning process of users. The nature of the semistructured processes and problems DSS is intended to serve requires *user* control over the manner of usage. Users can, and should, be trained and advised by a supporting staff (as discussed in chapter 7). However, the availability, freedom to use, and ease of use of DSS tools, unavoidably carries with it a degree of risk of misuse stemming from lack of specialized expertise. This risk is greater to the extent that support systems are designed to be weaker rather than stronger (do less to force the user along a particular processing path, as described in chapter 6) and softer rather than harder (provide more generic capabilities enabling the user to tailor them in a wide variety of ways).

The DSS movement, in effect, increased the risks associated with user amateurism in reaction to the already apparent penalties and risks of traditional management science approaches. If the downside risk of DSS can be attributed to increased *amateurism,* then it must be balanced against the penalties of management science *utopianism* (Young 1984[a]). It has been argued that a utopian credo and outlook underlies (often at a consciously unaware level) the approaches of all modern systems professions. Boguslaw (1965) described that credo as follows:

"All component functions will be manifest: intended and recognized by the designer. None will be latent (that is, neither intended nor recognized)."

Boguslaw points out that such a credo is common to all forms of classical utopias and is applicable to socio-political notions of ideal systems as well as to technocratic beliefs that specialists possess a superior wisdom to managers and other generalists.

By the 1970s, at least a significant number of practicing management scientists disabused themselves of such earlier utopian attitudes. Experience indicated that they were both unrealistic and counter-productive. The accumulated evidence had shown that:

1. Overly complex and structured systems approaches to many processes simply would not be used by managers (who tenaciously refused to abdicate their own judgment and responsibility to that of a mathematical model or to that of the model builder).
2. There were not, and it seemed unlikely that there ever would be, enough highly skilled and knowledgeable management science specialists to ensure that inferior systems would not be created under the guise of superior expertise.

The utopian approach too often resulted in a great deal of time and effort expended to build large computer-based systems that either never worked, were not accepted by their intended clients, or were abandoned after a brief trial usage period. The DSS approach arose to avoid these pitfalls of management science utopianism. Many early experiences of DSS could point to systems that were accepted, used, and appeared to satisfy managers, where prior attempts to develop more traditional systems had failed. But after some time, DSS in turn, has been subjected to new criticisms, such as those expressed by Sutherland (1983) that:

1. DSS takes a too accommodating posture toward clients rather than applying more stringent criteria derived from more scientific methods.

2. DSS emphasizes local rather than more universal requirements, and thus fosters suboptimization.
3. DSS uses casual rather than structured design procedures that lead to poorly designed and more expensive to operate systems.

More specifically, the DSS brand of computer-supported amateurism can result in penalties incurred both by what might be termed "sins of commission" as well as "sins of omission." These include the following:

Sins of Commission

• Incorrect and misleading models.

Inexpert modelers may use inappropriate or inconsistent mathematical relationships that in turn lead to "learning" or concluding things about the real world phenomenon that are grossly untrue. If no outside model audit takes place and no feedback of real world information is provided to enable such errors to be detected, decision makers may persist in building their world-views and decisions upon this faulty foundation.

• Use of inappropriate data.

Without sufficient control or counseling as to the meaning and sources of data, data used may be assumed to measure something it actually does not, or an indirect measure may be used when a more direct one is available. The associated penalty for this may vary from arriving at entirely unfounded conclusions to biased or less accurate views leading to less effective decisions.

• Wheel-spinning analysis efforts.

Data based query capabilities, "what if" and other analysis features, may be used in undisciplined, wasteful, and ineffectual round-about ways that may not lead to reaching any logically founded conclusions, may take inordinate amounts of time and computing resources, or in the worst case may be inordinately costly ways to reach the wrong conclusions.

• Misinterpretation of results.

Results of using systems that foster ad hoc analyses may be misinterpreted by users who are not trained in analytical methods and not prone to spend sufficient time to critically question the implications of results on each ad hoc usage occasion. The very strengths of fast reaction to variable or one-time needs may give rise to unfamiliarity with the meaning and proper interpretation of results.

• Advocacy and personal bias masquerading as analysis.

Personal control over support systems may be used to produce a larger amount of impressive back-up data in presenting a position for higher-level approval that consciously or unconsciously misrepresents reality. More thorough analysis may in actuality merely be more thorough argumentation of a weak but computer-obfuscated case. (While traditional management science systems usage is not immune from this pitfall, the increased individual control of DSS makes it easier to accomplish or fall prey to disguised advocacy without the compliance of others.)

Sins of Omission

- Underdeveloped regular reporting information systems.

    The DSS approach may be used as a stratagem for MIS managers to avoid carrying out thorough systems analysis and development of regular reporting systems for many functions and levels of the organization. Under the guise of providing flexibility and local user control, the organization is denied the stable, consistent, and common view that can be provided by well-designed summary reporting systems for the purpose of process-level control.

- Failure to develop more structured and standard model-based systems.

    The emphasis on supporting local or individual end-user systems may lead to failure to perceive the need for access to specialized management science consultants and development efforts directed toward more standard, formal, structured model-based systems where they are appropriate.

Mitigating DSS Pitfalls of Misuse

The chance of any misuse of DSS cannot be entirely eliminated without a stifling degree of control that would strangle the very benefits it seeks to preserve. But many of the above pitfalls can be mitigated by a few important management practices. These include:

1. Maintaining an appropriate supporting staff mix.
2. An effective continuing program of user and staff education.
3. Establishing application development and software selection process guidelines and standard practices.
4. Establishing appropriate organizational structures, auditing and accountability practices.

Most of these points have been discussed previously, particularly in chapters 6 and 7. However, it seems appropriate to emphasize here the critical importance of having the right staff mix, without which it is not possible to be entirely effective with regard to any of the other aspects of good management. Understanding of the variety of staff roles is prerequisite to recruiting and organizing the right people. Effective DSS implementation, as well as many other aspects of managing computer-based systems, are contributed to by the difficulty general managers often have in distinguishing between various kinds of specialists that have some computer-related knowledge. It is not always as clear as it could be that the following occupational categories (with their boundaries further blurred by variable nonstandard job titles) have little or nothing in their skills and knowledge repertoires that overlaps, other than that all of them have something to do with computer applications:

—A DSS information center facilitator/consultant
   One who understands and aids users mainly in the mechanical aspects of using DSS software.

—An MIS information systems analyst/designer

One who understands how to extract and specify user needs for regular information and can design standard systems to provide it.

—A data processing systems (methods) analyst

One who can document the operations of a current system for processing transaction-level data and specify the logic of an automated replacement system.

—A management science (operations research) consultant

One who is educated in analytical methods, model building, statistical methods, has consulting skills, and can differentiate between various computer-based approaches such as DSS and traditional MS/OR.

Once roles and responsibilities have been clarified, an effective team of these and other specialists can be established through a mix of regular staff employees, use of outside consultants, and outside service vendors for such functions as training and education, software selection and applications development, value assessment and systems auditing.

Penalties of Idea Processing Misuse

The penalties of misapplying idea processing support are less clear than are those for DSS misuse. The reasons are: (1) there is no obvious alternative category consisting of thought-optimization computer methods for divergent qualitative IP problem applications, and (2) available software and usage experience with IP support is still quite limited compared with traditional DSS. However, certain potential pitfalls have been speculatively identified and these may merit the consideration of users and the attention of researchers. These suspected pitfalls are related to inadvertently fettering creativity through negatively influencing natural thinking and social interaction processes. Concerns along these lines are not based on actual observation or research but on a cautious attitude toward tampering with ill-defined human processes that currently, at least for outstanding performers, seem to work very well. It has been seen that with many other complex systems (such as ecological systems), a delicate balance can be upset with consequent negative outcomes by an attempt to adjust some local problem aspect of the system.

It may be countered that users are not systems of nature without any self-awareness and can be trusted to decide for themselves. Since support systems are used or not used according to the discretion of users, the naturally gifted and already highly creative thinker who will not benefit can be expected either to never use such systems or to try them and discontinue usage if no benefits are perceived. Maintaining the free option to use or not use does seem to be the main line of defense in preventing the worst potential abuses of psychological straight-jacketing or thought pollution, but it still may be possible that users perceive benefits while not perceiving some negative influences.

Another aspect of suspected potential misuse is related to influences on the social process of human interaction with other humans. The availability of computer support may decrease exchanges between people and substitute more solitary and intellectually incestuous individual-computer interaction. The neophyte may have less opportunity to interact with a star performer and to learn from the star in ways that cannot be supplied through present-day support systems. Stars may have less interaction with other stars who can balance their own thinking and provide competitive stimulus. This factor may merit some attention from researchers, but it has already been observed that end-user computing (and other forms of technology) often results in opening new paths for human interchange even as it may decrease other kinds of human contacts. User groups, user telecommunications networking, informal contacts in information centers, and user workshops, all increase professional peer contacts. Reliance on human secretarial and staff support of some kinds may decrease as computer support is added.

An entirely different pitfall may be the reinforcement of existing tendencies to miscategorize the nature of some problems. It is possible that users who are not familiar with quantitative analysis methods may see a problem as being divergent and qualitative in nature when, in fact, it would be appropriate to define the problem differently and apply a convergent analytical approach. This pitfall always exists, of course, with or without computer support systems. The availability if IP support, however, may tend to reinforce and legitimize the user's tendency to define problems in ways that best fit their own methods repertoire instead of seeking expert guidance and assistance.

The remedies for these potential pitfalls are essentially the same as for DSS misuse; relying mainly on broader educational programs, a more complete mix of readily accesssible staff expertise, selecting highly robust software that is designed to increase the level of user guidance (with more built-in help and expert consulting modules) while retaining the user's control over the process. For IP support applications, the mix of supporting staff expertise should be broadened even further than the disciplines previously discussed, to include staff members with knowledge of creativity-enhancing processes.

Review Questions, Exercises, and Discussion Topics

Review Questions

1. How does value analysis differ from cost-benefit analysis? Which approach is more subjective? Which approach tends to focus more on cost avoidance or cost reduction as the primary source of benefits?
2. How does the production oriented viewpoint differ from the marketing-consumer viewpoint and what do these viewpoints have to do with value assessment?

3. What are the prevailing cost trends that tend to make it easier to justify at least a minimal level of individual computer support for managers?
4. Does economic justification require that one identify the optimal cost-effective system alternative? Explain.
5. What computer systems might be more suitable alternatives to DSS in some situations? How do the alternatives to IP support differ from the alternatives to DSS?
6. What reasons make post-implementation economic assessment worthwhile?
7. What aspects and trends of DSS package usage and telecommunications needs have made an incremental staged post-assessment approach to DSS economic justification less sufficient as an effective policy?
8. What are the main differences between the approaches to justification referred to as:
   a) Outcome-based;
   b) Resource-based; and
   c) Function-time based?
9. What is meant by a backwards assessment?
10. What are the main potential sins of omission with regard to DSS usage?
11. What are the main potential sins of commission with regard to DSS usage?
12. What measures can be taken to mitigate the potential pitfalls of DSS misapplication?
13. What are the possible penalties that have been speculated about with regard to idea processing support systems?
14. How might these potential misuses of IP support be avoided or mitigated?

Exercises

1. In a particular situation for which support systems are used or would be appropriate to use, carry out a general prior economic justification analysis using each of the approaches of an outcome-based assessment, a resource-based assessment; and a function-time based assessment.
2. Survey some large organizations in order to identify their policies and actual practices with respect to cost justification for support systems. Assess the effectiveness of these practices.
3. Document and report on an actual case of post-usage assessment for a support system.
4. Assume your company comptroller wants to institute a lowest cost policy of purchasing microcomputer support software; that is, the comptroller wants users to prepare functional specifications so that vendors bids can be obtained as to meeting these written requirements and stating their prices, after which the purchasing department will automatically buy the lowest price offering that meets the stated requirements. Write the comptroller a memo explaining why this policy should not be instituted and suggesting a more effective approach.

5. Find a case or describe a realistic situation in which you can identify a need for a regular report-producing information system to aid managerial control that was not met because it was thought that managers could meet these needs through the use of a query-type data base system. Discuss what organizational penalties such a misuse could or did cause.

Discussion Topics

1. Discuss the nature of any relationships that may exist between efficiency and effectiveness that could be gained through the use of support systems.
2. What arguments would you personally make for or against the utopian view of how to provide an organization with more effective decision-related processes?
3. Under what circumstances, if any, would you argue that formal methods of economic justification and administrative control and approval for support systems are not needed or might even be counterproductive?
4. Discuss the likelihood that creativity-supporting IP systems may significantly increase or decrease the effectiveness of:
    a) Highly successful intuitive but nonanalytical managers,
    b) Successful analytical but nonintuitive managers,
    c) Neophyte managers who have not yet become expert in learning analytical methods or in developing their creative intuition.

References

Boguslaw, R. 1965. *The New Utopians*. Englewood Cliffs, NJ: Prentice-Hall.
Keen, P. G. W. 1979. "Decision Support Systems and the Marginal Economics of Effort." *paper No. 48, Center for Information Systems Research;* No. 1089–80 Sloan School of Management, MIT.
Sutherland, J. W. 1983. in *IEEE Transactions on Systems, Man, and Cybernetics*. SMC-13 (May–June)3.
Young, L. F. 1984. "Control: Wielding the Double-Edged Sword." *Journal of Information Systems Management* 1(Spring)2:93–96.
Young, L. F. 1984. "Justifying Information Systems." *Journal of Information Systems Management* 1(Summer)3:93–95.

Toward Integrated Whole-Brained Support Systems

13

> *When the Illustrious Buddha taught about the world, he had to divide it into Samsara and Nirvana, into illusion and truth. . . . One cannot do otherwise, there is no other method for those who teach. But the world itself, being in and around us, is never one-sided.*
>
> "Siddhartha", by Herman Hesse, p 115, New York: New Directions Publishing Corp. 1951

In this final chapter, the essential unity of ultimate concerns for idea processing support and the more traditional forms of DSS is emphasized. The need for support systems that integrate the qualitative idea processing (or more right brain oriented creativity support) and the quantitative, analytical decision aids (traditional left brain oriented DSS) will be explored. The forms such integration may take will be presented. These will include two different types of integration:

1. Internal or intrasystem integration
   A system that includes support for both quantitative analysis and qualitative idea development and enables the user to select either type of support function without leaving the system.
2. External or intersystems integration
   A system that supports both idea development and analytical forms of DSS, but also provide a direct support capability for redefining and "migrating" an application from one mode of problem-solving into the other.

Extended DSS: The Unity of "Left-Analytical" and "Right-Creative" Support Systems

It is a central premise of this book that, despite their obvious functional differences, the types of support systems that have come to be identified as DSS and the emerging newer forms of support for the development of qualitative thinking are two sides of the same coin of support systems. First, the two categories are intended to serve common ends. Their common objective is the improvement of decision processes relevant to organizations. In chapter 8, the concept of idea processing support was defined as those aspects of idea development that were goal-directed toward organizational concerns that required decision making. The objectives of IP (as defined here) include the recognition and formulation of decision problems and approaches toward identifying strategies for coping with organizational situations. While the means of supporting divergent thinking styles, idea formulation, and idea organization, clearly differ from the means of supporting convergent analytical approaches, both approaches involve decision making as part of the processes used in carrying them out and they both aim to serve the ultimate objective of more effective organizational decision making.

In addition to their commonality of ends, the two approaches are linked because they both have the essential characteristics of support systems. As support systems (in contrast to systems intended for automation), both are interactive, user-controlled, flexible and evolutionary means to enhance user learning and effectiveness in dealing with semistructured problem situations. With the common objective of ultimately improving decision making and the characteristic earmarks of support systems, it would not be inappropriate to think of idea processing support as an *extension* to DSS rather than as comprising a different genus of computer applications requiring a separate identity. However, the addition of idea processing to the DSS repertoire represents more than just a technical extension of computer software tools. Recognition of idea processing modes of support and their place alongside older support methods also represents a conceptual break-out. Much as an earlier confrontation between the marketplace's needs and the operations research orientation provided the seed-bed for the birth of the conceptual break-out that led to DSS, current forces are pushing DSS in new directions. In the 1960s and 1970s, many practicing operations researchers discovered that the structured modeling methods in which they had been trained often failed to be used by their clients, practicing managers. Some OR practitioners were of a sufficiently flexible turn of mind to assume that the explanation might lie in the incompleteness of the OR bag of tricks rather than in the inadequacy of managers. These practitioners evolved the new approach later recognized by academics and called DSS.

Similarly, idea processing extensions to DSS can be seen as arising from the parentage of early DSS experience and a renewed recognition of certain rich and unsupported management decision styles. As mentioned in chapter

8, the intuitive styles of many top managers and the style of coping with messy networks of concerns rather than with insular problems has yet to be adequately supported by any form of computer-based approach. Zmud (1986) has discussed possible approaches to better serve top-level management styles and suggested that, among other things, "thought support" (Zmud's term for what we have defined as idea processing support) may serve this end. Young (1987) has suggested an approach to extending forms of idea processing within a future interface for supporting messy dynamic networks of managerial concerns. Increasingly, one can hear leading figures at DSS conferences talking about, if not giving formal papers about, the need to consider how creativity and intuition can be more directly supported.*

The most obvious avenue for seeking such new forms of support were the behavioral creativity enhancement processes already identifiable as human group support processes. These interactive human protocols have only recently been recognized (Taggart and Robey 1982; Young 1982, 1983, 1985; Manheim 1985) as a potential basis for using the computer as the interactive supporting mechanism. This new recognition is concurrently being spurred by the appearance of software such as ThinkTank and Consultant, discussed in chapter 10, and other commercial packages that seem sure to follow. Further recognition among scholars is likely to follow the future publication of currently ongoing doctoral research on the effect of using this type of software on performance.

As it becomes more accepted that early DSS leaves many of the support needs of managers entirely unanswered, it also seems clear that the kinds of idea processing support discussed in this book must continue to evolve and have not yet begun to address all of the potentially supportable styles of managerial decision making. As part of this evolutionary growth, themes such as telecommunications technology and expert systems techniques can be expected to help to complete the blending of a new form of extensive, robust, and powerful DSS. This chapter speculates on how the major themes of idea processing and early DSS may be brought together within an integrated common support environment—a support environment usable by different individuals independently employing different approaches, or by the same individual using each kind of approach in different problem situations, or by one or more individuals blending both approaches within the same situation.

Because of its relative newness, it has been necessary to treat idea processing as a separate kind of support system in much of the discussion in this book. But the underlying unity of support systems is both recognized and espoused. It is not intended that the term idea processing become a new buzzword, nor that it (or other terms such as extended DSS or neo-DSS) supplant

---

* At the International Federation for Information Processing (IFIP) WG8.3 Working Conference on Decision Support Systems, (Noordwijkerhout, Netherlands, June 15–18, 1986) Peter Keen ventured in his closing remarks that DSS practitioners must not be afraid of addressing that sometimes unutterable notion—creativity—in developing new forms of support. A task group (dubbed "'COGMOD'") of WG8.3 members was also formed to work on "Cognitive Modeling and DSS Specification," a subject seen as including "thinking support."

Exhibit 13.1

An Extended Framework for DSS

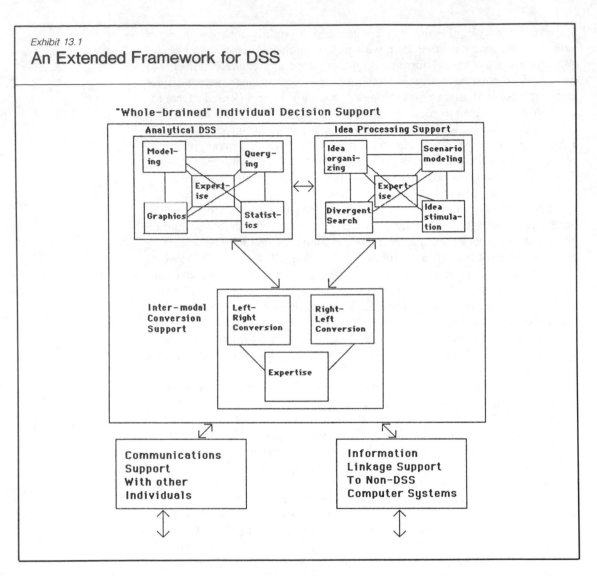

"Whole-brained" Individual Decision Support

Analytical DSS
- Modeling
- Querying
- Expertise
- Graphics
- Statistics

Idea Processing Support
- Idea organizing
- Scenario modeling
- Expertise
- Divergent Search
- Idea stimulation

Inter-modal Conversion Support
- Left-Right Conversion
- Right-Left Conversion
- Expertise

Communications Support With other Individuals

Information Linkage Support To Non-DSS Computer Systems

the term DSS, which has now received respectability, acceptance, and general understanding from both scholars and practitioners. As long as such acceptance does not lead to a rigid orthodoxy of thinking, the DSS concept remains a meaningful and useful common label. Once the identity and utility of newer forms of decision support become clearly established, it would seem desirable to think of DSS in the more comprehensive way we have described here or that may evolve in the future.

A general framework for such an extended form of integrated DSS is shown in exhibit 13.1 and will be referred to in the discussion which follows. Also, the two types of integration discussed below and the role of the expertise modules are illustrated in example 13.1.

EXAMPLE 13.1
USE OF A "WHOLE BRAINED" DSS
A New Product Screening Case

First Problem Phase: Explore for unsatisfied consumer needs in order to identify potential new product concepts appropriate to our business.

General Approach: A single analyst is to consider general consumer needs, our own products and capabilities, look for suitable match. Delay assessing potential.

First Steps

Support Subsystem Used: Idea processing support

Functions Used:

a) Divergent search to identify dimensions and categories of needs, possible combinations of needs.

b) Use successive generalization to identify alternative ways to define our business according to our basic capabilities.

c) Examine combinations of business capability definitions and consumer needs.

Results: Select as business generalization definition—"The marketing of portable electronic tools for personal growth"; Identify such needs/capabilities combinations as Entertainment-games, Learning-instruments, Travel-information-planning kits, Work-career planning aids, etc.

Next Step Digression

Support Subsystem Used: Analytical DSS

Function Used: Data base query to retrieve lists of consumer product categories from Commerce Department and Industry Association data bases

Results: Identify additional categories to consider under headings of personal beauty care, personal hygiene, etc. Save selected categories for idea processing module use in divergent search and combination.

Next Step

Support Subsystem Used: Idea processing support

Function Used: Divergent search to identify additional needs/capabilities combinations.

Results: Identify additional combinations to consider.

Next Step

Support Subsystem Used: Idea processing support

Function Used: Idea transformation using Parnes' list to seek redefinition or modification of some of our existing products to better meet selected needs combinations identified in the previous steps.

Results: Identify potential new product concepts to consider.

Next Problem Phase: Perform first analytical screening assessment of potential new product concepts.

General Approach: A group of mutually responsible managers will join the initial analyst in screening possible products through a rough judgmental rating assessment to select several of the best for further examination. A single analyst will then develop a general logical-mathematical model to assess the selected best alternatives for the magnitude of major factors such as manufacturing, distribution, and product promotion costs, revenues, profit, market share.

First Steps

Support Subsystems Used: Intermodal conversion support and analytical DSS.

Functions Used: Expertise to guide in identifying an appropriate method for the judgmental rating of alternatives and aid in accessing the combinations saved by idea processing for use by the

EXAMPLE 13.1 continued

appropriate analytical DSS. Then a subjective rating and evaluation module (such as that of the **Evaluator** decision-making aid of the Consultant package) is used by each of the group of managers in contact with each other through communications support in order to separately rate the same factors and to pool the ratings in a common average rating. (Alternatively, the Expertise module of the analytical DSS subsystem could guide users in tailoring a spreadsheet modeling function for this specific rating mode of analysis.)

Results: Users take system suggestion to follow a judgmental weighting and rating scheme, select and enter combinations and assessment criteria under the system's guidance to complete a scoring, ranking, and selection of the best alternatives for further assessment.

Next Steps

Support Subsystems Used: Intermodal conversion support and analytical DSS.

Functions Used: Expertise in both the intermodal conversion support and analytical DSS subsystems is used to guide the single appointed analyst user in identifying and naming the relevant variables, in estimating parameters and the nature of modeled relationships. (The system presents a series of questions and answers, elicits user estimates, presents its assumed mathematical relationships to the user in graphic and tabular numeric form for the user's approval, and thereby builds a basic model with the guidance and approval of the user. The user can skip over or modify any of these model-generation functions, in keeping with the user's level of personal expertise and knowledge.)

The resulting model is then used in a series of "what if" analyses using the modeling component of the analytical DSS subsystem.

Results: The user reduces the product alternatives to two that seem most promising and has identified for each of these the general relationships and trade-offs that seem to exist between general pricing, distribution, and promotion policies for the relevant product-market segments.

Next Problem Phase: Presentation of results and group agreement on a strategy for further product development and testing.

General Approach: The principle analyst is to prepare a presentation to clearly communicate the results of the prior analysis and to provide the basis for a discussion and group consensus decision on developing a prototype product and proceeding with market testing.

First Steps

Support Subsystems Used: Intermodal conversion support and analytical DSS

Functions Used: Analytical DSS graphics features, expertise and other features of left-right intermodal conversion support to (*a*) aid the user in identifying key sensitive associations and comparative results, (*b*) convert key results of mathematical analysis into keywords in a presentation chart mode, (*c*) choosing appropriate graphic presentation modes, (*d*) producing graphic displays, (*e*) facilitating consistency of terminology and style between tables, key word displays, and graphics, and (*f*) following rules for good presentation, visibility of visual aids, limitation of text material per visual, color coding, estimating length, organization, and timing of presentation, etc.

Results: Preparation of a relevant and effective presentation based on the key analytical results cast in a language to facilitate general understanding.

Next Steps

Support Subsystems Used: Communications support and analytical DSS subsystems.

Functions Used: GDSS features for presentation display, polling and voting supplied through the communications support subsystem, and the use of querying and graphics components of analytical DSS to retrieve information requested by group members to facilitate their understanding of issues discussed prior to polling and voting.

Results: An efficient and effective meeting addressing relevant issues and reaching a consensus on a plan of action.

Intra-system (Internal) Integration

In this form of integration, a common interface is provided to the user through which either or both the analytical DSS component functions and the idea processing support functions can be accessed. This is represented by including both of these subsystems within the same whole-brained individual decision support system shown in exhibit 13.1. The connecting two-directional arrow between these two subsystems is intended to indicate that the user can move from one form of support to the other within a common context without leaving the system and having to reenter through an entirely separate set of procedures (typically entailing loading a different software package with its own style of interface language). This kind of direct and easy movement from function to function, however, is still not transparent to the user, who must remain conscious of moving from one kind of processing to another by at least selecting a particular function (through a mouse selection or the entry of a specific command or menu selection). This is what was described in chapter 2 as quasi-integration. It has been the general level of integration provided by such multifunction DSS packages as Lotus 1-2-3. Within this form of integration, a limited capability may also exist for copying data or text from a "left-analytical" function to a "right-qualitative idea" function or vice versa. For example, portions of text comprising a sequential scenario, lists of items and their combinations, or pairs of words linked with each other through some metaphoric connection, may be created and modified within the idea processing support subsystem and subsequently copied into a data base format that could be accessed via a data base query function. Similarly, text elements could be selected from a data base via a query function and subsequently manipulated via one or more idea processing functions. However, the direct application of standard graphics, spreadsheet modeling, and other analytical functions would not usually be directly applicable to the textual elements of idea processing nor would idea processing functions directly apply to numerical inputs or outputs of analytical DSS.

One may ask how much the extension of a common interface framework to include both analytical and idea support subsystems would actually be used. In most cases it would seem likely that users would be able to meet their needs by using multiple functions within only one subsystem. It may also be the case that users often can meet their needs during any one processing session by using only one DSS function (such as a spreadsheet function). However, on those occasions when a user may want to graph the results of modeling, for example, the convenience of being able to do so directly has already proven to be quite valuable to users. Similarly, users may not often need to extract items generated through idea processing and use them either as data base entries or as variable names or descriptions in a subsequent model. But when they do want to do so, the convenience of being able to accomplish this directly may be considered to be valuable by users. Research and usage experience is not yet available to assess the utility of this kind of integration. Lacking definitive evidence to the contrary, it would seem most in keeping with the principles of flexible user control, varying personal styles, and broad applicability to varying decision problems and situations, to provide this kind of integration rather than to omit it.

Furthermore, DSS designers should not rely solely on system requirements based on present (noncomputer supported) methods and practices. The bottom-up orientation of present method analysis is the automation approach to specifying requirements and is not sufficient for the evolutionary nature of DSS development. As a learning tool, DSS not only enables users to learn about the problems to which it is applied, but also can facilitate learning and developing new problem analysis strategies and personal processing styles. Thus the availability of greater flexibility in using DSS tools and gradual user experimentation may lead to new usage paths and new requirements users could not specify in advance.

A final argument for including this type of integration does not depend upon the application of different subsystem functions on the same problem, or on passing data or text between functions in different subsystems. An advantage is provided if the same user only uses both types of subsystem functions for different problems on different usage occasions. That advantage is derived from the familiarity the user gains with a common interface style and context and the subsequent ease of use that is transferable across different system functions. This ease of use benefit is referred to by Bennett (1983) as arising from a "framework that gives a uniformity of structure." Such a framework facilitates the users ability to structure and restructure and evolve a process that utilizes multiple system functions, but it also simplifies the independent use and access of single functions in ways that are already familiar from experience with using other functions. This kind of framework is provided in the Consultant package described in chapter 10, in which similar procedures are used to select procedure icons, obtain aids and helps, for both of the package's sets of decision-making aids and idea generation aids.

Inter-system (External) Integration

The external type of integration would be provided through a separate and additional type of support subsystem—shown in exhibit 13.1 as inter-modal conversion support. The function of this new subsystem would support the user in making transitions between casting a problem situation in qualitative terms for idea processing and more quantitative terms for the use of analytical methods. The relevance of this type of support is twofold:

1. Mathematizing qualitative thinking when appropriate. (Right-Left Conversion)
   The process of model development (as pointed out in chapter 3) generally begins with a phase that identifies the initial content of a model without necessarily specifying units of measurement or mathematical relationships.

In addition, general qualitative idea processing that initially does not aim at the development of a mathematical model may result in reaching a stage in which judgment free, eruptive, divergent thinking has served its purpose of disclosing new possibilities (e.g., new strategies, new products, or new services), and further development requires more analytical assessment. In these instances, the user must apply a translation process to migrate and harden the problem situation from a relatively ambiguous qualitative form into a more precise analytical quantitative form. This translation process is not completely structured, although certain rules may apply. It thus appears to be a useful application of the DSS approach, assisted by an expert system module to embody the rules (or guidelines) that are part of the knowledge base of skilled model builders.

2. Humanizing mathematical meaning when appropriate. (Left-Right Conversion)

The meaning of the results of mathematical analysis are often more understandable to the user and to others with whom the user must communicate when they are expressed in ordinary language. While the power of mathematics is based on its precision of meaning and the explicit operations that can be performed on mathematical statements, the power of ordinary language is based on its power to evoke relationships and associations based on human experience. Such associations may, on occasion, be very direct and sometimes they are more diffuse and indirect, but their impact and richness of meaning cannot typically be conveyed in the limited language of mathematics or symbolic logic. It thus appears useful to support the user in recasting quantitative problem formulations into a form more amenable to idea processing, whether that processing is to be computer supported or not. This translation process would also be supported by the guidance embedded in the expertise module for this specific purpose, which is illustrated in example 13.1 and discussed further in the following section.

Expert System Modules within the Extended DSS

Expert system modules (labeled expertise) are shown in each of the subsystems shown in exhibit 13.1. The knowledge base in each of these modules would consist primarily of methods and processing knowledge that would be possessed respectively by operations researchers in the case of the analytical DSS subsystem, by cognitive psychologists and others with creativity-enhancing protocol knowledge in the case of the idea processing support subsystem, and with selected knowledge overlapping both of these areas of expertise in the case of the inter-modal conversion support subsystem. This use of expert system modules is an extension of notions expressed by Reitman (1982), Elam and Henderson (1983), and Turban and Watkins (1985) that the integration of artificial intelligence and knowledge through using expert systems in a supporting role to DSS will create a new breed of "super-DSS" (to use Turban and Watkins' term). Hwang (1985) has surveyed the use of such systems for automating many aspects of model building and uses the term "intelligent decision support systems" (IDSS) for the substitution of user interaction with an expert system in place of user interaction with a human staff specialist (a scarce, expensive, and often inaccessible resource) such as a model builder. The general manner in which any of the generalized supporting expertise modules in an extended DSS would interact with the user is outlined as follows:

1. The system asks the user questions in order to generally diagnose the nature of the problem so that guidance can be provided by the system as to the choice of a method to be applied.
2. The system elicits from the user more detailed descriptions of the problem situation so that problem size and other parameters can be identified or estimated, terms of reference, variable, or dimension names can be captured for further use in system-user dialogues and displays, and so that more specific guidance on methods can be provided by the system on a continuing basis as a process evolves.
3. The system suggests methods to the user, describing them and providing help in their use, as needed.
4. The system monitors the user's implementation of methods, diagnoses the correct application of methods, and intervenes with questions, warnings, and guidance to the user as the diagnosis of usage may indicate.
5. The system aids the user in interpreting the results of processing and in understanding limitations on their significance, as well as in conveying this understanding to others.
6. The system can aid the user in translating the interpretation of results into a focused presentation for communication to others, including providing guidance derived from expertise on advocacy, communications, negotiation and selling principles, as may be appropriate.

In addition to the above generic functions, an expert system module could also have access to a knowledge base or several different knowledge bases with more problem domain specific expertise derived from experience in a wide variety of particular situations, so that the system could provide more specific guidance or even provide an option to perform an automatic analysis for the user. However, it should be pointed out that this latter function of expert systems, that of automatic decision making with reference to a closed world of experientially-derived stored knowledge, is not entirely consistent with the DSS approach of user controlled, flexible and evolutionary decision processing.

Communications Between Individuals
and Specific Support of Group Processes

The extended DSS is shown in exhibit 13.1 as being linked via a communications support module with other individuals. This type of linkage can be comprised of two different levels or modes of group support:

1. Group communications support for independent individual processing
   This type of support provides only communications between individuals through which each user can selectively transmit the results of their own processing to others, with or without accompanying messages, and also can receive selectively transmitted results and accompanying messages from others. For this kind of support individuals carry out whatever processing they themselves deem appropriate for their own independent decision processes and merely determine what transmitted results of others they wish to consider and what results of their own they may wish to transmit at any point in their processing.
2. Interactive support of group procedures
   This type of support includes special modifications of the actual support functions used and the addition of other functions so that unique interdependent group decision processes are supported rather than merely providing communications among a configuration of individuals engaged in independent processes.

According to Huber (1984) and DeSanctis and Gallupe (1985), a true group decision support system (GDSS) is one that provides the second type of support for interdependent group decision processes such as those made jointly by committees, project teams, or executive boards. Gray (1986) points out that although the evolution of GDSS concepts, research agendas, and initial experimentation has been rapid, GDSS is still mainly in a laboratory stage. Its relationship to the support of qualitative forms of idea processing, however, is apparent, and they may be expected to develop together. Among the kinds of joint decision processes mentioned by DeSanctis and Gallupe (1985) to be supported by GDSS are brainstorming (a group creativity support procedure discussed in chapter 9), delphi (a process involving a sequence of usually qualitative assessments by experts), and nominal group technique (a method in which individuals work independently in the presence of others to prepare their own ideas before subsequently pooling these ideas for general discussion). Synectics, like brainstorming, was initially conceived of as a group procedure to support creativity, and would similarly be a candidate application for GDSS. Synectics use of metaphoric thinking, for example, could make use of a metaphor generator module within an idea processing support system as an adjunct to the collection and use of metaphors generated by team members.

While the restricted definition of GDSS covers only joint decision processes that have their own rules and procedures, such processes can often be expected to make use of some of the same functions as either idea processing support or analytical DSS. A communications support subsystem could be defined as providing more than just a communications link between individuals and could call into operation both individual support modules for repetitive group use as well as new modules unique to some aspects of group processes (such as polling users and combining numerical individual judgments and pooling idea lists).

It also seems appropriate to note that regardless of how GDSS has been defined, the mere provision of a direct communications link between the independent processes of individuals may by itself be expected to change and enhance the nature of a decision and thinking process. The convenience and shorter interval exchanges provided by such a link can result in an added frequency and amount of human interaction which affects the quality of each individual process as well as the aggregate results of the group. In a wider sense, all decision making in organizations can be thought of as being embedded in group processes. Individuals are aware they are part of a larger social system in which the support, cooperation, and approval of others is needed to varying degrees even when one may complete large units of work independently. Added convenience in exchanging results may lead to shorter intervals in which each individual receives reactions from others. This may affect both productivity and shorten the "time span of discretion" of individuals. It may also facilitate learning and the mutual stimulation of ideas.

Final Notes on the Art of Thinking, Intuition, and DSS

Theodore Roszak, a professor of history, points out in *The Cult of Information* (1986) that—

> If there are any rules we can follow for the generation of ideas, it may simply be to keep the mind open and receptive on all sides, to remain hospitable to the strange, the peripheral, the blurred and fleeting that might otherwise pass unnoticed.

The computer and any manner of extended DSS cannot be a substitute for human experience, human thinking, and human creativity. No support system can be expected to change a dullard into a genius. A more serious question may be whether the use of such systems may inhibit or enhance the development of the ability to think creatively, to develop ideas, and to manifest that illusive quality we call intuition. There is, as yet, no conclusive evidence on this question. Decisions seem unlikely to benefit much from such systems. But what about the rest of us?

It is true that ideas are unlike data or discrete packets of information and perhaps it is misleading to even speak of idea processing if that implies to some that human thinking is similar to computer processing. In his book *The Intuitive Manager,* Roy Rowan (1986) states: "Logic and analysis can lead a person only part way to a profitable decision." After that, Rowan claims, the "eureka factor," that intuitive flash of recognition based on knowledge and insight gained without conscious thought, can come in the middle of the night during sleep or in the middle of play. He bases these assertions on interviews with business leaders over several years, including one with Trammel Crow, the country's biggest real estate developer, who states:

> Anyone who tries to make site determinations mathematically, by charts, or by other scientific methods is wrong. . . . It's that vast body of experience that you retain in your brain and pull out as you need it that's important in picking winners.

But it is not the intention of this book to urge the substitution of any form of computer-based analysis for experience, thought, and intuition. If there is a basic assumption behind efforts to develop a more extended form of DSS embracing qualitative thinking processes, it is precisely the notion that the mind should be kept open and receptive on all sides, hospitable to the strange, and that the computer may provide a way to *support* us in pulling out some of the experience and knowledge residing in our own brains.

Idea processing support systems and other extensions of the DSS concept have begun to appear and their development is likely to continue. It seems no more reasonable to blindly resist such innovations as to lead a crusade to push them into every conceivable area of human endeavor. We should critically examine any proposition that smacks of the "technological imperative" to do whatever it seems can be done with technology. But exploring many paths to reshaping the computer as a potential lever for the human mind, used or not used, according to the free choice of individuals, is worthy of continuing research, experimental development, and trial application and assessment in the real laboratory of our dynamic organizational systems.

Review Questions, Exercises, and Discussion Topics

Review Questions

1. What commonality exists, if any, with respect to the objectives of idea processing support and more traditional analytical DSS?
2. Recognizing the basic differences in the methods of analytical DSS and idea processing support, what underlying commonality exists with respect to the manner in which these systems are used?
3. What is meant, according to this chapter, by intra-system or internal integration within an extended DSS?
4. What is meant, according to this chapter, by inter-system or external integration within an extended DSS?
5. What benefits to the user might be provided by intra-system (internal) integration?
6. What function(s) might be provided by an inter-modal conversion support subsystem to provide inter-system (external) integration.
7. What type of knowledge and expertise would be provided by an expertise module within each of the following subsystems:
   a) Analytical DSS subsystem.
   b) Idea processing support subsystem.
   c) Inter-modal conversion support subsystem.
8. Describe how the system would interact with the user in providing expert support within an extended DSS.
9. Distinguish between the linking of individual support systems through communications and the specific support of group decision processes in an extended DSS.

Exercises

1. Develop a realistic example of a decision process that might, in various phases, profit from the use of each subsystem in an extended DSS. Use a format similar to that of example 13.1 for describing the example. Discuss the differences in the process that would be used in the same situation, but—
   a) Without the application of any computer-based support system;
   b) With only the use of an analytical DSS.
2. Describe an instance in which you yourself developed an idea that proved to be useful. Describe what related events, processes, actions took place prior to, during, and after the occurrence of the idea. Assess what might have been the effect in that situation if you had available and applied an extended DSS with a full range of functional, expertise, and communications capabilities.
3. Design an experiment or a fact-finding and analysis project that might assess the effectiveness of using an extended DSS in various problem situations.

Discussion Topics

1. Discuss the following position taken by a particular computer scientist and state your own reasons for agreeing or disagreeing:

   DSS has nothing whatever to do with the fuzzy ways of thinking that some people call "creativity." DSS is already well defined and "creative idea processing" has nothing to do with it. If you ask me, the whole idea of idea processing support is a little peculiar. Not that computers are incapable of being used to analyze fuzzy problems. As a matter of fact, I am convinced that artificial intelligence will ultimately advance to the point where computers can exhibit greater creativity, more effective judgment, and can innovate new ideas better than any human alive. But that is AI, not DSS.

2. Discuss the issue of "what's in a name?"—whether the term DSS should be limited to what this chapter refers to as analytical DSS functions and a new term, such as idea processing, should be used for qualitative thinking support without trying to extend the definition of DSS to include the latter approach.

3. Discuss the concern that the use of a computer-based support system can never compete with, and might well inhibit, the true art of thinking.

References

Bennett, J. L. 1983. "Analysis and Design of the User Interface for Decision Support Systems." Chapter 3 in *Building Decision Support Systems* edited by J. L. Bennett, Reading, Massachusetts: Addison-Wesley.

DeSanctis, G., Gallupe, B. 1985. Group Decision Support Systems: A New Frontier." *DATA BASE* 16(Winter)2:3–10.

Elam, J. J., Henderson, J. C. 1983. "Knowledge Engineering Concepts for Decision Support System Design and Implementation." *Information and Management* 6(April).

Gray, P. 1986. "Group Decision Support Systems." in *Decision Support Systems: A Decade in Perspective* (Proceedings of IFIP WG8.3, June 15–18, Noordwijkerhout, The Netherlands, Edited by E. R. Mclean and H. G. Sol) Amsterdam: North-Holland. 157–71.

Huber, G. 1984. "Issues in the Design of Group Decision Support Systems." *MIS Quarterly* 8:3:195–204.

Hwang, S. 1985. Automatic Model Building Systems: A Survey." *Transactions of the Fifth International Conference on Decision Support Systems—DSS–85* Edited by Joyce Elam, San Francisco, California, April. 22–32.

Manheim, M. L. 1985. "Theories of Decision Making and Their Implications for Development of Creativity-Supporting DSS." *Transactions of the Fifth International Conference on Decision Support Systems—DSS–85* Edited by Joyce Elam, San Francisco, California, April. 113–14.

Reitman, W. 1982. "Applying Artificial Intelligence To Decision Support." in *Decision Support Systems* Ginzberg, M. J. et al. Amsterdam: North Holland.

Robey, D., Taggart, W. 1982. "Human Information Processing in Information and Decision Support Systems." *MIS Quarterly* 6(June)2:61–73.

Roszak, T. 1986. *The Cult of Information—The Folklore of Computers and the True Art of Thinking.* New York: Pantheon Books.

Rowan, R. 1986. *The Intuitive Manager.* Boston: Little, Brown & Co.

Turban, E., Watkins, P. R. 1985. "Integrating Expert Systems and Decision Support Systems." *Transactions of the Fifth International Conference on Decision Support Systems—DSS–85* Edited by Joyce Elam, San Francisco, California, April. 52–63.

Young, L. F. 1982. "Computer Support for Creative Decision-Making: Right-Brained DSS." *Processes and Tools for Decision Support* (Proceedings of IFIP WG8.3, July 19–21, Schloss Laxenburg, Austria, Edited by H. G. Sol), Amsterdam: North-Holland. 47–64.

Young, L. F. 1983. "Right-Brained Decision Support Systems." *Data Base* 14:4:28–36.

Young, L. F. 1985. "Idea Processing Systems: Definitions, Concepts, and Initial Applications." *Transactions of the Fifth International Conference on Decision Support Systems—DSS–85,* Edited by Joyce Elam, San Francisco, California, April. 125–34.

Young, L. F. 1987. "A System's Architecture for Supporting Senior Managers' Messy Tasks." *Information and Management* 13:85–94.

Zmud, R. W. 1986. "Supporting Senior Executives Through Decision Support Technologies: A Review and Directions for Future Research." *Decision Support Systems: A Decade in Perspective* (Proceedings of IFIP WG8.3, June 15–18, Noordwijkerhout, The Netherlands, Edited by E. R. Mclean and H. G. Sol) Amsterdam: North-Holland. 87–101.

Index